The Struggle Between the Robe and the Woman

The Struggle Between the Robe and the Woman

FORTY ONE YEARS OF CELIBACY, FIRE SHUT UP IN MY BONES

Leticia Rouser

Library of Congress Control Number: 2015921031
ISBN: Hardcover   978-1-5144-3677-6
               Softcover   978-1-5144-3678-3
               eBook   978-1-5144-3679-0

Scripture quotations marked NLT are taken from the Holy Bible, New Living Translation, copyright © 1996, 2004, 2007. Used by permission of Tyndale House Publishers Inc. Carol Stream, Illinois 60188. All rights reserved. Website

Any people depicted in stock imagery provided by Thinkstock are models, and such images are being used for illustrative purposes only.
Certain stock imagery © Thinkstock.

Print information available on the last page.

Rev. date: 01/28/2016

To order additional copies of this book, contact:
Xlibris
1-888-795-4274
www.Xlibris.com
Orders@Xlibris.com
726836

How It Started

This book it dedicated to my sister Gwendolyn Rouser Jones Smith. She inspired me to pray the prayer, "Lord, help me to hold out until my name is change."

My sister was my mentor, my example, my image of Christ on earth. I wanted to do everything she did. One day, she came into the house frustrated from the pressing questions about boys her age; she ran into the bathroom and fell upon her knees. I peeped through the keyhole of the bathroom and heard her cry out to God, "Lord, help me to hold out until my name is changed!" She stayed there for about an hour, crying before the Lord. I could not wait until she came out so that I could run into the bathroom and pray the same prayer. I did not realize what I was asking God for, but as I became older, I understood the journey to live holy before God.

My sister was eighteen years old, and I was fourteen. I asked God to move in my life so that I could live before his presence in a special way. This prayer took me through forty-one years of battles with the fire shut up in my bones. I prayed this prayer in 1973, and in 1977, I met Kelvin Ambrose Thigpen. We both were students at Xavier University. We started dating around 1977; he gave his life to Christ and was baptized. He laid the foundation for my life of celibacy; he was a saved man and treated me with the utmost respect. Because he taught me how a man should treat me, I was able to ward off those men who wanted me to put out before marriage. He was a perfect gentleman, sometimes too good to be true. In 1987, we went our separate ways and started life with other people.

I was married in 2000. At this point in my life, I really wanted to experience sex before going to heaven. I met a tall, dark, and handsome guy that seemed to be the perfect candidate for a husband and intimate partner. Despite all the warning signs, we entered into covenant with each other, and I thought it would last forever. Our forever came to an end three years later. I found myself back in the same shape I was in before, living without a man to love me. This time, living without sex was more difficult, because I had experienced what it meant to be in a man's arms and held all night.

The Struggle between the Robe and the Woman is about a female preacher who elevated the gift of preaching and submerged the fact that she was a woman who wanted to be loved by a man. The Word of God and the word of the body are expressed in this book.

The following pages are filled with body talk—what the woman was saying behind the robe. Enjoy!

Acknowledgments

Thanks to the Ancheta family who shared their home with me while I wrote this.

To my mother, who planted me in her garden.

To my seven brothers, who protected me from the Big Bad Wolf.

To the eighth brother and my pastor, who guided and counseled me through my teenage years to adulthood.

To the Reed, Mathew, Wills, and Rankin Family for supporting me during my Military Career, special thanks to Alvin, Alycia and Alijah who showed me nothing but love.

To Arlene, Michelle, Felice, and all of the California cousins who share in the holiday fellowship. Niki, Natasha, and Trevor this is for you.

To the members of my churches who supported my dream to be a writer.

To my new addition through marriage Adam and Valencia Thigpen, thanks for all your support, your mother Regina is smiling on you each day.

To my Prayer Ministry Four Corners: Belinda, Pastor Gwen Smith, Dr. Pullen, Mary, Rhonda, Frandrea, Natasha, Laticia, and SSGT Jackson for praying me through this book.

Last but not least, to my two sons David and Zaye—who have walked and traveled the journey with me through thick and thin.

My journey through celibacy started at fourteen years old. I was determined to get married before I had sex. I did not know that the journey would last for another twenty-seven years. I dreamed of having ten children—I never gave birth to one. I have six children through adoption and foster care. By the time I was thirty-nine, I had a surgery that cancelled any possibility of me ever giving birth to a child. I was very angry with God because I saved myself, while the other was given up. But God blessed me with daughters and sons that I love dearly. I am proud to be their mom.

The struggle between the woman and the robe began the day I put the robe on. I had lived twenty-five years of my life and never felt but one fire—that was the Holy Ghost. But as soon as I answered my call to the ministry, I felt another fire burning in my loins. The battle between the preacher and the woman began. I had never noticed men in the church before. Now, I am sitting in the pulpit, and I am seeing men I never noticed before. I had to rebuke my own thoughts as I prepare for worship. Now I understand what Pastor Brandon was talking about when he said, "Pastor, you have never preached until you preach with two fires burning." I was wondering how it was possible to have two fires burning at the same time until I experienced it. I was in the dark, but I understood it clearly when it happened to me. The war began with the woman and the robe.

It was hard to accept the fact that I was anointed by God to preach, yet the attack on my body could happen in the same arena. How is that possible? Paul said it like this, "For we are not fighting against flesh-and-blood enemies, but against evil rulers and authorities of the unseen world, against mighty powers in this dark world, and against evil spirits in the heavenly places" (Eph. 6:12). Journey with me through the struggle as I try to live in God's holy presence.

JANUARY 29, 1988 (12:01 A.M.)

A Letter to Him

As I reminisce over the past few weeks, I can find many moments filled with joy. I have enjoyed especially the moments I've spent with you. I really don't know what brought this change over our relationship, but maybe "it's for the good of those who love the Lord." My heart hurts because a lot of my dreams and visions have been shattered. My hope was that we would learn how to love and support one another for a season. I did not think our relationship would ever become so confusing. It was like we were intentionally sending each other through changes. I don't want to grow any farther apart from you. I want us to at least be friends. To be the man in my life is very difficult, and the shoes are extra, extra large. He must be self-confident, self-assured, and able to stand his ground without intimidation. I love you and miss you too.

Dear Lord, please help me to do what is right. I need your support in this situation. Please show me the way, Lord. Help me to hold out until my name is changed.

Amen.

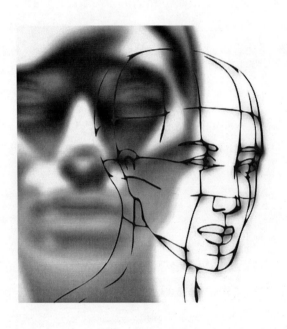

December 3, 1989 (1:00 a.m.)

A man's spirit sustains him in sickness but

a crushed spirit who can bear?

—Proverbs 18:14

Dedicated to the man that taught me how to live on the edge.

I'm Living on the Edge

He taught me to live on the edge. He gave me sugar so sweet; he made me feel loved and wanted. He told me he wanted to spend the rest of his life with me. I'm living on the edge.

He led me to deepest depths of love and disappeared. I thought he was walking with me, but he turned around; he left me at the edge of a cliff called love. I'm living on the edge.

When I arrived at the edge of love, I woke up, and I was all alone. All the sweet sugar that led me there had turned sour. Now I no longer feel wanted and needed. I feel useless in his life. I'm living on the edge.

All the love he once showed me had been burned in a fire of disagreement. He no longer needed to wake up to my voice in the early morning or lie down at the close of day to my sounds. I'm living on the edge.

Our plans are like sounding brass. I no longer hear the wedding march, and I only hear that old familiar tune: "It's a thin line between love and hate." I'm living on the edge.

At one time, I wanted to jump over the edge and fall into an endless pit of despair; but at the edge of the cliff, I turned to my strength, and it told me it was just a test. I'm living on the edge.

After weeks of struggles and battles, I found something positive. I realized that my very foundation was shaken. Yet through it all, I was still on the edge. I'm living on the edge.

This man taught me how to live through the impossible and continue to see life. He taught me how to live on the edge. I'm living on the edge.

Dear God, I thought I had lost my life in him, but you pulled me back to reality. Thank you for letting me know your love and your peace that passes all understanding. I need you every hour of the day; continue to keep me saved.

Amen.

DECEMBER 9, 1989 (2:30 A.M.)

A Letter to Him

I have tried to explain to you in words what my heart is feeling. For the last three weeks, I've called you more than you expected. The reason is because I was trying to see if the man that loved me was still alive. It is crazy, but I talk to you, and I feel like I am talking to a stranger. The person that loved me was so kind and gentle. Lately, the person I talk to is cold and distant. I'm not trying to hurt you, nor am I bitter. I felt good about myself for the first time in a long time. Through the process of writing, my heart is being revealed to me. The love I have will keep on growing. The man I love will live in the time zone of my heart. I hope this is a time for a new start and not an old one. Ending, I will face and live with a new understanding of love; it blows me into a new world. How deep your love tapped me. I'll never ever forget the powerful lessons I've learned about love, patience, joy, sadness, endurance, and hope. You gave me a new attitude. Thank you so much. I shall be forever grateful.

December 11, 1989 (1:30 p.m.)

Jesus said to her, "I am the resurrection and the life. He
who believes in me will live, even though he dies."

—John 11:25

He Died

The man I loved died. I can't tell you when, but I know he died. He
died and I wasn't invited to the funeral or wake, but I know he died.

I was only allowed to spend a few months with him. I had no
idea that the time we had together was so short, but I know he died.

Maybe he died from the shock of love or a reality attack, but I
know he died. He never once told me he was dying or going away,
but I know he died.

Maybe he only lived in my heart and eyes, and no one else have
ever met him. Maybe I dreamed about him, and when I woke up, I
had to face reality. He died.

I thought about him last night and said to myself, your imagination
made him exist, but now your eyes are opened. He is dead; he died.

Dear God, lead me through the shadow of death so that I may fear
no evil. I am going through something I don't understand, but, God,
you know just what I need before I ask. Guide me, oh Great One.

Amen.

December 11, 1989 (8:00 p.m.)

A Letter to Him

I would like to share some information with you, I really thank for God for you. You and I are uniquely different, and this will be a challenge for the both of us. Well, I just wanted you to know that God is not finished with me yet. I will work very hard to both honor and respect you as a part of me. Please remember that I am a committed servant of God with a special anointing in my life.

I feel happy and sad, I feel up and down, I feel strong and weak, I am faithful and afraid, and I feel together and alone. I know that I must leave you, yet my heart wants to remain with you until we meet again. My desire is to be in God's perfect will; it does not permit me to act crazy. Please keep me in your heart.

My prayer for you is to be happy in everything you do. I've already decided that I have no place in your life, I hope you notice also. We both thought something wonderful could happen, but it's not possible. Please take care of yourself, and I will keep you in my heart.

December 12, 1989 (2:00 a.m.)

I press toward the goal for the prize of the
upward call of God in Christ Jesus.

—Philippians 3:14

I Can't Go Back to Yesterday

Yesterday I had the blues. Yesterday everything I tried, I would lose. Yesterday I had no tools. I can't go back to yesterday.

Yesterday I wanted to give up; yesterday I didn't want to choose. But today I can't lose. I can't go back to yesterday.

Yesterday was cold and dreary; yesterday I was freezing and weary. Today I'm warm and tender. I can't go back to yesterday.

Dear God, thank you for your keeping power. I feel new mercy every day. I am glad you make house calls. Thanks for dropping by here.

Amen.

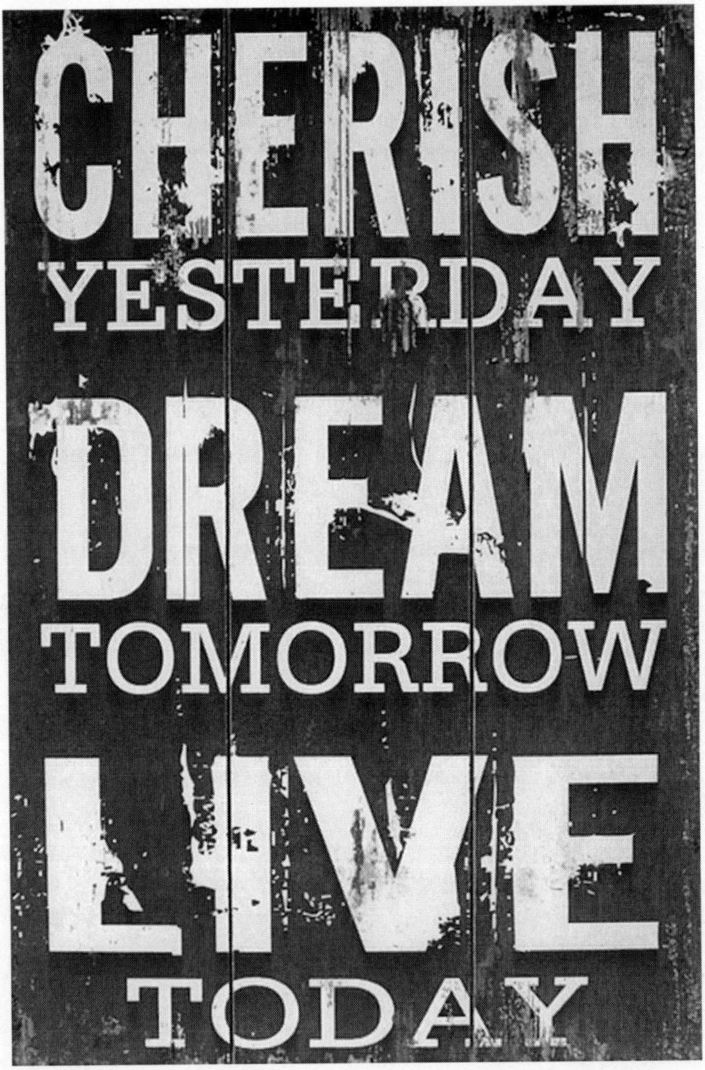
CHERISH
YESTERDAY
DREAM
TOMORROW
LIVE
TODAY

DECEMBER 12, 1989 (7:30 A.M.)

Let us not become weary in doing good, for at the proper
time we will reap a harvest if we do not give up.

—Galatians 6:9

I Thought

I thought I could talk to you and tell you my deepest thoughts. I thought I could never tell you anything that would cause you to stop loving me. I thought I could be honest with you and share my whole heart. I thought.

I thought loving you would be a mountain top experience. I thought I could never go through the valley as long as you were by my side. I never thought I would live in the valley of dry bones of love. I thought.

I thought you were the one that would make my dreams come true. I thought I could make all your dreams come true too. I thought when you looked in my eyes that day and said, "Where have you been all my life?" I thought I was what you were looking for. I thought no one else could take my place. I thought I was waiting for you to find me? I thought.

I thought we make beautiful music together. I thought no one else could write a tune that we could dance to without each other. I thought I had you and you had me. I thought.

I thought we connected in a way that no one else could reach us. I thought the blues were over and happy days were here again. I thought you loved me. I thought.

Dear God, help me to understand that love is patient, kind, and true love never fails.

Amen.

A Letter to Him

While sitting between these four walls of concentration, I decide to go into deep meditation concerning you. It seems like just yesterday you were holding me tight. Now my heart is wondering: why not tonight? I miss your sweet lips against mine. It's 2:01 a.m., and I am very tired, but you are on my mind.

December 14, 1989 (4:30 p.m.)

I will lie down and sleep in peace, for you
alone, of Lord, make me dwell in safety.

—Psalm 4:8

My Love Is Asleep

The man I love is in a deep sleep. I don't understand it. I thought he was dead, but I heard his voice the other day. He is sleeping in a living body, not buried in a grave. My love is asleep.

I thought he was gone to the place of no return, but my love is buried beneath the load of trouble. He has been smothered by every day cares, but he is not dead. My love is asleep.

I wonder what it will take to wake him up. Sleeping beauty woke up from a kiss from her chosen one. How can I wake up my love? He was tied of the burden of this life. My love is not dead. My love is asleep.

What can call him back to me? I really have no idea. I have heard of resurrections, calling people back to life. I wonder if this could help me at all. My love is not dead. My love is asleep.

Dear God, please heal my imagination. I have great expectation, but only you are perfect.

Amen.

December 17, 1989 (2:30 a.m.)

The Lord himself goes before you and will be
with you, he will never leave you nor forsake you.
Do not be afraid; do not be discouraged.

—Deuteronomy 31:8

No One Can Love Me Long

I have never been loved a long period of time. Every relationship starts and has an ending. I was thinking the other day, why is that I've never been loved a long time: because no one can love me long.

I can't see why. I seem to be a lovable person. I know I need love, but a love that's free. I guess everyone that ever loved me, loved me for a little time. They wanted to can my sugar and that was impossible. No one can love me long.

Every man I ever loved and loved me back wanted to stack me away and keep me all to themselves. I've never met a man yet that did not try to limit my movement. No one can love me long.

I guess I'm strange to most men, and they are unable to deal with the freedom I want in a relationship. I don't want supervised love. I want a love with trust and freedom. No one can love me long.

Dear God, because of my commitment to you, no one wants to be with me. Once they find out I'm not giving up my body, they soon leave. God give me peace, and let my spirit rest in you.

Amen.

Have I not commanded you? Be strong and courageous;
do not be terrified; do not be discouraged, for the
Lord your God will be with you wherever you go.

—Joshua 1:9

He's a Part of Me

As I sat in anticipation, waiting for the time that we will be together again. I looked around at all the people in the airport, and I felt a touch of loneliness. On the inside, I felt a deep sensation. He's a part of me.

I realized I wasn't alone anymore, but he was with me. No, he wasn't with me physically, but I felt him on the inside. I don't want to expect. I feel him. He is a part of me.

How did we ever make it the last six months? I wonder. I feel we are one, but we have been divided. I lost myself and gained him. He's a part of me.

Dear God, it feels good to be a part of another person life. I pray that you send me someone who will stay and wait until marriage.

Amen.

JANUARY 29, 1990 (8:00 A.M.)

Create in me a clean heart, oh God,

and renew in me a right spirit.

—Psalm 51:10

Be Still, My Broken Heart

A heart that is tensed and sad with lots of cracks may be bad. But beneath that all is flesh because your heart does blush. Be still my broken heart.

A smile so deep I see even though you reserve the right to keep. No one can take your heart away. You must be ready for a new day. Be still my broken heart.

In the stillness of your night, beat hidden in the deep chest of experience is your heart disclosed. Yet overheated lions dream and has a tendency to creep into the fantasies you leap. Broken heart, be still. Be still my broken heart, be still. Heart is not free, it yours taken, woken, yet broken. Be still my heart broken, be still.

Dear God, thank you for the ability to go through the storm of a broken heart, and still stand. You are the love of my life, my constant friend.

Amen.

SEPTEMBER 30, 1990 (3:30 A.M.)

A Letter to Him

How are you? I hope all is well and this letter finds you in the best of health. I just wanted a minute of your time to express myself to you. On Saturday—September 29, 1990—I met a very special man. He was so kind and gentle. Little did I know he was a superstar. His stardom was not important to me. I saw a very special proud black man.

I did not come to steal your spotlight or to share your fame. I came to spend privileged time alone. I wanted to get to know you better as a friend. I didn't come to get a husband or be seduced. I came to find out what it meant to share time with you. I cried the whole time I wrote this letter because when I look back on the events of the day, men in your place are looking for meat parties. I always say "treat a woman like you want your daughter and mother to be treated." Out of respect, I am writing this letter. I've always been a private person. I apologize if I invaded your space. Please forgive me for being out of date with what happens at parties today. I hope that we can be friends, even if it means we will never see each other again. Slow down and take care of yourself.

No all these things we are more than
conquerors through him who love us.

—Romans 8:37

He Is High on a Star

The next time I saw him, I knew who he was. It did not change the way I felt about him. But the fans were cheering—what could I do? He was high on a star.

I looked on in amazement as the fans reached out to him. "It's his day, it's his day," they all screamed out to say. It was a moment I never would forget. He was high on a star.

The more they came toward him, the higher he got. They lifted him from mortality and to a much higher height. He seemed to be floating so high I could not see. What I can say? He is high on a star.

Dear God, teach me to honor you in everything that I do. May my heart, mind, and soul belong to you only.

Amen.

OCTOBER 1, 1990 (4:00 P.M.)

Trust in the Lord with all your heart and lean not
on your own understanding; in all your ways submit
to him, and he will make your paths straight.

—Proverbs 3:5–6

Superstar Blues

What kind of troubles can a superstar have? He's on top right now, and he doesn't know how? I walk in his shadow softly and sweet. I didn't want the world to see him with me. I walk behind him most of the time, for he was the star, and I was not one of his kind.

Dear God, life in the spotlight is too much for me. To walk next to a superstar is like walking on a tightrope. I need clarity for my journey. I can't see the forest for the trees. Help me to see you in the middle of all the bright lights. I love you more than I did yesterday. Keep me safe.

Amen.

OCTOBER 9, 1990 (4:00 A.M.)

My heart goes out to you, and all the prayers that are in me tonight. I'm thinking of you and hoping you are feeling wonderful. I can't express to you what it means to have a friend like you. Moreover, I am impressed with the fact that God can do anything but fail. The day before I met you, I told God I was going out and to find me a husband. It was quite amusing and funny to God. The next day, I met you and saw a sign from God. Don't get me wrong, I'm not thinking of you as my husband. I am thinking of you as a sign that God can do anything but fail. The day before I met you, I told God I was going to get me a husband. It was quite funny—a real joke unto the Lord. The very next day, I met you and remembered what I had told God. Don't get me wrong. I'm not saying that you are my husband, but I am acknowledging that God has the power to bring a star in your life in a desert place. It was a revelation to me that God has me in his view and understands what I am going through. In other words, if God allows me the privilege to be in your company in the wilderness, then God can place my husband in my path whenever he is ready.

There are many women who would jump at the opportunity to sleep with you or make passionate love with you. I, unable to do any of the above, am saving myself for my husband. You are very sexy and fine, but I can wait. I respect the fact that you are honest and open with me concerning the things that are important to you. Someday

24

you will meet Mrs. Right, and you will know that playtime is over. You will be singing, "Let's get serious and fall in love."

I wish you the best and the greatest happiness in your life. In many ways, I wonder what your role was in my life. I understand that your ways are not like my ways, and your god is not my God. Have a great life. I'll see you on TV.

November 21, 1990 (10:30 a.m.)

A Letter to Him

Eyes are better pupils and more willing than ears. Good teaching can be misunderstood, but good living never would. Because you lived by creeds, it's an example that every kid can heed. No smoking, no dope, nothing but hope, that's a fact. You are the payback.

Hands learn to do because you have done. They have watched you in action and learned faster than with your tongue. Your lectures may be wise and true, but children watch and observe the good you do. Visiting drug centers, sponsoring football clinics, and sharing your dreams on a larger scope, allowing young people to cope, and that's a fact. You are the payback.

You've paid the world back with a life lived in glass. They can't complain because you have reached the highest goals that has been told. Children are able to see your walk and know it's not talk. You are a perfect role model for all to follow, that's a fact. You are the payback.

"In the last days," God says, "I will pour out my spirit on all people. Your sons and daughters will prophesy, your young men will see visions, your old men will dream dreams."

—Acts 2:17

Delusion

I was driving in my car, and all of a sudden, you were there—in the front seat. You reached over to kiss me, and I moved toward you to receive it. I wanted one of those big juicy kisses; but before I could touch your sweet gentle lips, you disappeared. What a deception: I was kissing air. It was only a delusion.

When I arrived home, I opened the door, and you were standing there. You asked me how my day was. I began to tell you about all the difficulties I had experienced. You extended your arms and said, "Come here, baby, I'll make it better." I ran into your arms, but you disappeared. What an illusion. I was holding on to my coatrack. It was just a delusion.

I got into the shower to wash off the dirt of the day, when you touched me. You stroked me straight down the middle of my back. Chills ran up and down my spine. You said, "Baby, let me massage your back." I turned toward you to caress you, but you were gone in an instant. It was only a delusion.

I climbed into bed in my red teddy and turned off the lights; and out of nowhere you came, my shining knight. You climbed into bed and slid up and down my body. I became your prisoner of love. You moved over me with soft, long strokes. It drove me crazy. I began to climb the walls. All of a sudden, I hit the light shade. You took me to the ceiling and disappeared. It was only a delusion.

I went to sleep and dreamed that I turned into a chocolate chip cookie. I was lying on your table, and you picked me up. The moment you touched me, I began to break. I could hear you say as you dropped me into your mouth, "Chocolate melts in your mouth and not in your hands." It disappeared. It was just a delusion.

It was so confusing when the mind began to play games—so many allusions from the heart. I wonder what it would be like to experience it all. Maybe I have in my mind's eye; but in reality, it is just a delusion.

Dear God, I am in a constant battle with my ministry and the woman. Somehow, some way, take control of her—because she is out of control. I pray before I go to sleep for rest, but she wakes me up in the middle of the night, pouring out her desires. I plead the blood of Jesus over her. Please help us!

Amen.

For God so loved the world that he gave his
only begotten son, that whoever believes in him
should not perish, but have everlasting life.

—John 3:16

Love Is Crazy

So many people try to define what love is, but for many, love has different meanings. I tried so many times to explain this love I have for him, but love is crazy.

Love has no rules. I've often tried to limit it and put restrictions on it, but love breaks all boundaries. Love has no end; it just flows from eternity until eternity. Love is crazy.

I am convinced that all I can do is sit back, relax, and be cool and let it flow smooth—because love will have its own way in the end. A songwriter said, "If it doesn't fit, don't force it." I say "If it fits, don't fight it. Because love is crazy."

Dear God, thank you for crazy love. For loving me when I was yet a sinner. You are my greatest inspiration. Don't leave me alone.

Amen.

JANUARY 2, 1992 (2:00 A.M.)

You will keep in perfect peace him whose mind
is steadfast, because he trusts in you.

—Isaiah 26:3

You're on My Mind

I find that you're on my mind more often than any other thoughts. Sometimes I bring you there purposely to console me, or to warm me, or just to make my day a little brighter. But so often you surprise me and find your own way into my thoughts. You're on my mind.

There are times when I awaken and realize what a tender part of my dreams you have been. And on into the day, whenever a peaceful moment seems to come my way. My imagination is free to run, but it takes me running into your arms. Thinking about you allows me to linger there. Knowing that I want to be with you and no place else, my thoughts and reflections of the loving hopes of my heart are forever wandering to you. They always take me to you. You're always on my mind.

Dear God, keep my mind stayed on Jesus so that I can have perfect peace.

Amen.

JANUARY 6, 1992 (11:30 A.M.)

I therefore, the prisoner of the Lord, beseech to walk
worthy of the call with which you were called.

—Ephesians 4:1

Prisoner of Love

I want to be your prisoner of love. Shackle me with you vivacious presence. Incarcerate me with your luring lips. Cause my mind to lose all thought but you. I want to be your prisoner of love.

Let your thighs of romance surround me with the passion of ecstasy. Let my heartbeat tick to the muscle of your body. Lock me with the chains of your arms. Leave me nowhere to run; let me stay with you. I want to be your prisoner of love.

Give me a cause to think about you day and night. Send my body temperature soaring to an all-time high. Rapture me with your brown hands, moving across me so sensuous elevating me through the stars. Let me fly as your pilot of love. I want to be your prisoner of love.

Wrap your legs around me like Fort Knox, I want to feel your 14-karat gold. I want my veins flowing with hot bubbling love. Arrest me for I am guilty of loving you. I have broken all your laws. I have invaded your privacy; I desire to be punished. I want to be your prisoner of love.

Sentence me for I've committed the highest crime. I've exposed you in my mind and should pay the penalty. Give me life without probation. I deserve to be electrocuted by your love. I plead the mercy of the court; allow me to be your prisoner of love.

Dear God, I feel locked up inside myself. I feel like all the doors are shut in my life but there's one door that seeks to be loved by a man. I am somehow thinking about this in the middle of the night because the thoughts that come to mind are not of the woman who wants to be single. God, direct my path and order my thoughts in your word. I want to live so that you can use me every day. I have no idea what happens in the middle of the night, but I am ashamed of the thoughts I write down. Why is she hunting me? Why won't she be quiet and wait until her change comes? What is her hurry? Why can't she be like me—holding on to you? Why am I constantly fighting with her? Sometimes I think I am losing control of me. She only comes out in the middle of the night, when I'm too tired to fight. I give all this to you, God. In Jesus's name I pray.

Amen.

JANUARY 6, 1992 (11:50 P.M.)

And God said to Moses, "I am who I am. Thus you shall
say to the children of Israel, 'I am have sent me.'"

—Exodus 3:14

Who Are You?

A heart so new, yet broken from the past. A face so blue, yet laughter
in the midst of dew. Why, behind that smile is a caution sign. Who
are you?

Such a friendly person, an air of happiness. Yet behind that
personality is a glare of sadness. Look into your eyes, there is a story
to be told. Some good, some bad, and some bold and beautiful. Who
are you?

What is your favorite color? What is your favorite food? Who
do you dream about each day and night? I wonder in my deepest
thoughts: *who are you?*

Are you the sweetest hangover, or are you a nightmare come true?
Are you the invisible man, or are you true red, white, and blue? In
my mind, I know time will tell and reveal who you are.

Dear God, show me who you are. Fight my battle for me, and
please stand by my side.

Amen.

JANUARY 10, 1992 (5:00 P.M.)

Thou preparest a table before me in the
presence of my enemies; thou anointest my
head with oil; my cup runneth over.

—Psalm 23:5

You're Not a Drive-Thru Window

The other night, you talked to me, saying, "I am here for you, and I'll service you for your benefit."

Mainly, you need someone to be there for you. You're not a drive-thru window.

I thought about what you said and knew that it could not be read. How could I come to you with all my needs, fill myself up, and leave without a please? You're not a drive-thru window.

How can you be my friend, and I never do anything but take and never give? That kind of relationship only drains and never fills up. You're not a drive-thru window.

Somewhere in you is a restaurant. A place to sit and eat. A place to get comfortable and rest your feet. Just remember all I have to say, "I would never eat and not pay." You're not a drive-thru window. You are a plush dining room.

Dear God, thank you for giving me the courage to say no. You have allowed me to see myself as worthy of a lifetime commitment, rather than a Happy Meal. Thanks for your guidance and your strength to stand firm on your word.

Amen.

A Letter to Him

Many people tried to ignore the fact that your color does not make you great or small. You are playing the highest position in the game. They cannot take away the fact that you are the greatest at this time in your field. The world had to stop revolving for at least three hours to take notice of you. You are the great contender.

Heisman Trophy would have been nice, but the Hall of Fame is an excellent choice. God has elevated you among the stars. There must be a planet named after you in the depths of the galaxy. You are counted with the great liberators. You are listed with mighty men like Moses, Daniel, Martin, a cloud of fame. Somewhere in the universe, there is a cloud in your honor. You are the great contender.

I do not care what men may say about you or what the media has released. The world must always note in the history of the twentieth century, one man's life that changed the cycle of superstars. Everyone must stop and pause for a moment and focus on you because you opened a door in sports that can never be closed. You are the great contender!

Jesus answered and said to her, "Whosoever drinks
of this water will thirst again, but whoever drinks
of the water I shall give them will never thirst. But
the water that I shall give him will become in him a
fountain of water springing up into everlasting life."

—John 4:13–14

Empty

To be lost in nowhere and find no hope. To be missing something and unable to cope. He told me just a minute ago that he was empty, and I did not understand. A tall black man with a light brown tan and a heavy African stand. How could this be when he brings magic to my heartbeat? Empty.

He is divided and separated between two opinions. Happy and glad one minute, and later, miserable and sad. He was bold, but now he is cold. How can this be when he brings magic to my heartbeat? Empty.

He is like a puzzle with the centerpiece missing. He is incompetent and standing flat on his feet. How can this be when his smile brings sunshine into my darkness? Empty.

He has canned up his sugar and decided not to love. He has stopped his heartbeat and delayed his hugs. He is really not empty; he is quite complete. Empty.

His heart is on hold, his thoughts are untold, and his emotions are ice-cold. He is not willing to unfold. He has decided to be empty and alone on the road of life. Empty.

Dear God, I feel empty and depleted of all your presence. I need a fresh touch from you; I need you to fill my cup and let it overflow with your love. I am a blank page; I need you to write your Word all over me. Seal me with your Spirit; I am thirsty for you. My water is dried up, and my well is empty. Let the water of your Word fill me until I can take no more. I need you now, God. I need you now in Jesus's name.

Amen.

JUNE 1, 1992 (2:30 A.M.)

Then God said, "Let us make man in our image, according
to our likeness, and let them rule over the fish of the sea
and the birds of the air, over the livestock, over all the
earth, and over all creatures that move along the ground."
So God created man in his image, in the image of God
he created him; male and female he created them.

—Genesis 1:26–27

Ditto

Deep, you are the River Nile. High, you are the Allegheny Mountains.
Incomparable, you are the mighty Earth. You are a far journey, and
I've been traveling on it. My destination is total ecstasy. Ditto.

You shine, you 14-karat gold. Who am I to melt you and mold
you, yet you are able to discover the world when I am walking with
you. Oh mighty conqueror! Ditto.

Continue to speak with heart and not mind, and your shadow
shall be one with our shadows, and we shall blend into the darkness
finding light easy like Sunday morning. Ditto.

You, great African King, sit on your throne and receive honor
where honor is due. You great black-brown-chocolate strong man,
you are more than enough to reckon with. You are atmosphere! Ditto.

Dear God, please continue to remind me that I am in your image,
and you are the greatest King ever. You are Lord of lords and King
of kings. I love you.

Amen.

Therefore I will give him a portion among the great,

and he will divide the spoils with the strong, because

he poured out his life unto death, and was numbered

with the transgressors. For he bore the sin of many,

and made intercession for the transgressors.

—Isaiah 53:12

Part of You

I wish your love would flow through my body from my head to my toes. I wish I felt the warmth and power rushing through my veins like the blood that runs from my heart to my soul. I wish I had all of you, but the question is will I settle for part of you?

I wish that you wanted to give me all of you, but I know that's not true. You want to fill my loins with fire. You want to overload me with desire and teach me love in fifty flavors. I know you want to cream me with your sugar. I wish I was your Sweet'N Low, but I'm just NutraSweet. I know I can only have a part of you.

When the night comes and the passion spills over into my bedroom, thoughts of you come to mind. I want to be tied up in your arms, tangled up in your legs, and wrapped up in your love. I want to be where you are when my urge boils to the top of my emotions. I want you even though I can only have a part of you. Be still, my heart!

Dear God, cover me with your grace and mercy. Make my heart still so you can use me. I am depending on you to see me through stormy weather. I ask this in the mighty name of Jesus.

Amen.

How sweet are your words to my taste,

sweeter than honey to my mouth!

—Psalm 119:103

Sweet Lips

A drip of your lips is like a chocolate chip. You are so sweet that Hershey's asked to copy them because you melt in my mouth and not in my hands. Sweet lips.

Your lips are better than Lay's—you can't just have one. I gotta have both of them in my mouth. If sweetness was a crime, you would be serving life in prison. When I taste your lips, I know I've got the right one, baby. Baby, you are the real thing. Sweet lips.

There are many sugar substitutes—but, baby, I want you to know that NutraSweet or Sweet'N Low can never take your place, because your lips are Sugar Twin. Sweet lips.

MARCH 7, 1993

Therefore submit to God, resist the devil
and he will flee from you.

—James 4:7

Let It Be

I long for you like I've never longed before. I tried to resist you and run away. I tell myself I am crazy to stay. Allowing myself to anticipate you each day. No matter what my mind says to my heart, from the depths of my hearing voice I say, "Let it be."

There are times I want to pick up the phone and call you and say I never want to see you again. Please wipe me out of your destiny date; but the spirit moves me to you, won't let me make that call. Sometimes I feel like a lion, no longer able to roam free in the jungle because you have coded me for a season. No matter how hard I pull at the bars around me, the sound of the forest says, "Let it be."

I would really like to know what it is you have that I can't find in another man. What's so special about you that I couldn't find anywhere else. My mind goes on the warpath with you. I try my best to get you out of my system. I don't want to love you. I don't want to love you. I don't have a choice; destiny is changing my life as I write the words on this paper. Let it be.

Dear God, the heart is a funny thing, and my heart is all over the place. In my mind, I wake up writing to a stranger I don't even know. My life must be really lonely in writing a letter to an imaginary man.

God, hear my prayers and what my body is crying out for. You are no shorter than your Word. Supply what I need even before I ask. In your name, I pray.

Amen.

MARCH 9, 1993 (7:30 P.M.)

Come to me, all you who labor and are
heavy laden, and I will give you rest.

—Matthew 11:28

I Move Toward You

My fight is not with you, it's with myself. My concern is not about you, it's about me. I struggle about the relationship between us two. I move toward you.

My mind has been confused and troubled as I add you in my life. I know not the road I travel, because I never did it before. It's all about the time you take from me. I move toward you.

My heart is beating on full speed; it's not because of your good deed. I cover my feelings for protection, knowing I have great affection for you. It's all based on the feeling that grows from me to you. I move toward you.

My body is ready to be caressed by you. I know that most of the time that is true. My touch of fantasy love is all about a sensation from my body to you. I move toward you.

Dear God, I am fighting within myself. I am warring between my spirit and my flesh. Please help me to know when I am asleep and awake in you. I need power to war against my number 1 enemy: ME. Thank you for your ability to look beyond my faults and see my needs. I also thank you for grace and mercy. It is in your son Jesus's name I pray.

Amen.

JUNE 1, 1993 (11:25 P.M.)

A Letter to Him

How are you, sweet lips? You taste delicious. While locked between these four walls, I decided to write you a letter from the heart. Though we are hundreds of miles separate physically, I spiritually place you with me. I'm unable to rationalize between what is real and fantasy. When I bring your vision to my person, it seems so real. I hear your laughter in the air, I see your face at picture show, and I hear your sweet music on the radio. Come, time; come, place, yea! This exclamation is to the one I love. Maybe it's just my imagination running away with me.

You, baby, are time; and you are space occupied. Deep, you are the river Nile; and high, you are the great mountains. Incomparable, you are the mighty earth. You are a far journey I have been traveling to my destination. Shine, shine, you 18K gold. Who am I to melt you? Yet you discovered all of me when I was not looking. You are a mighty conqueror.

Continue to speak with heart and mind, and your shadow shall be one with my shadow. We shall blend into the darkness, easy like Sunday morning. You great African King, sit on your throne and receive honor where honor is due. You great black-brown-chocolate sweet man, you are more than enough to reckon with. You are atmosphere!

JULY 12, 1993 (12:30 P.M.)

You shall have no other gods before me. You shall not make
for yourself an idol in the form of anything in heaven above or
the earth beneath or on the waters below. You shall not bow
down to them or worship them; for I, the Lord your God, am
a jealous god, punishing the children for the sin of the fathers
to the third and fourth generation of those who hate me.

—Exodus 20:3–5

Reserved Only for You

There are places in my heart that only you have traveled—no one has
touched, and no one has felt. The skin virgin until you came into my
life . . . reserved only for you.

My mind was free and happy-go-lucky until you pierced it with your
essence. I began to rave about your being. My mind flowed to places I
had never ventured in body. There are memories reserved only for you.

I am ashamed of what you do to my temperature. How you make
my body tremble. I move at the sound of your voice, and I am delirious
in your presence. No one can make me feel like you do. This human has
beeped into the depths of my agenda to a place reserved only for you.

Dear God, in my spirit, I know that my whole life is yours. I
cannot give you a piece of me. I reserve every area of my life for you.
Please fill my agenda with worship and praise for you. I pray this
prayer in Jesus's name.

Amen.

As long as it is day, we must do the work of him who sent me.
Night is coming, when no one can work.

—John 9:4

Inspired By My Thoughts of You in the Middle of the Night

Wouldn't it be something if, in the middle of the night, my thoughts met up with your thoughts and had dinner? I said "in the middle of the night." By then, judges have ceased to render decisions, and bailers have gone home. The only sound you hear is the sound within.

Wouldn't it be something if, in the middle of the night, my face met your face in the middle of our flight? I said "in the middle of the night"—when fax machines stop ticking and clients are not clicking. No more conversations waiting and you are no longer taken. Your space is now empty.

Wouldn't it be something if, in the middle of the night, we could share a dream? We would not have to leave our houses or places. We only have to reach and find each other's mental taste. I said "in the middle of the night"—not when you are busy working long hours, not when you are off to see your family or friends with flowers. Only when you are too tired to think or move. When your mind is on cruise, I want to meet you in the middle of the night when the real you comes out. Wouldn't it be something?

Dear Jesus, my nights are very complicated. I dream and have visions of your love and mercy for me. But I also have dreams and visions of being loved by the man you are going to send me. Please know that I love you, and I am doing everything possible to be true to you. Sometimes, in the middle of the night, I have to write down what I am thinking. Bless my thoughts in the middle of the night. Keep them in line with your Word.

Amen.

The righteous cry out, and the Lord hears them;
he delivers them from all their troubles.

—Psalm 34:17

Then you will call, and the Lord will answer.
You will cry for help, and he will say: "Here am I."

—Isaiah 58:9

Call to me and I will answer you and tell you great
and unsearchable things you do not know.

—Jeremiah 33:3

My Body Cries Out in the Middle of the Night

Darkness all around and you can't be found. I think of you, and I don't know what to do. The heat, sweat—it makes me wet. My flesh says I'm in a desert place. Maybe because no one is carrying my case. My physical body calls out for libation. It's dry, untouched, and isolated from human hands. Tell me, tell me what's your plan? My body is untouched and isolated from human hands. Tell me, tell me what's your plan? My body cries out in the middle of the night.

You are on my mind all the time. What shall I do? It's not my time to be true. Interrupted in the midst of my thoughts, my unborn child calls out from my womb, "Mommy, Mommy, when will I come? How will this be done? Can you carry a son?" My body cries out in the middle of the night.

Sometimes I believe it is not human to live like I do. Maybe the divine has taken rapture of me. In the stillness of the midnight, my natural inclination fuels up. The maintenance lights are flashing— caress me, rock me, and conquer me now! My tank is empty. I'm hungry and malnourished. Milk me easy like Sunday morning. My body cries out in the middle of the night.

Don't deny me. Don't you feel me rising up in you? I'm your physical woman. You put me on hold too long! I've never been rolled in jelly and laid in affection. I suffered. I'm in drought! I'm thirty, and I thirst for something! My body cries out in the middle of the night.

Unbelievable and hard to understand, your imagination has taken control. No, these works come from the deep well of a woman who has forgotten she is a woman. I am bolding, unfolding right before my eyes. In the middle of the night, my body cries out.

Dear God, the night is getting harder to endure. I watch the right things on TV. I don't read rated material. I don't go to the movies at all. Why am I having a problem? What is going on? Where are you when I wake up in the night? Control my thoughts and my body because they are out of control. Please fix me, Lord Jesus. Just fix me.

Amen.

APRIL 2, 1996 (2:00 A.M.)

A Letter to Him

I write from the depths of my soul, and where I hunger for love that is faithful, free, and secure. I search with thirst for a fountain that will fill my deepest desires and imaginations. I reach for a bright light to shine inside out to expose my dry and desperate places. My heart is a desert land, no gardener to water it, no caretaker to pick the weeds, my well has never been explored. All my gold is beneath it. I have wants, I have needs, I have dreams, and I have visions. I seek a love that is unending; I promote a love that is without fault. I am woman, I am girl, I am child, and I am baby. I am here, I am there. I am sad, I am glad. I am complex with a capital *C*.

Run away now, my dearest, for to stay is to encounter troubled love. Run far away, my love, for to be near is to experience struggle. Your face is tender and smooth, your eyes wait, do not hinder. Your lips are like candy dripping off a stick; disappear before you are captured. You, my dearest, should run far away, from all of it. Take your thick hands away, and let them rub the midnight sky. Hurry, my dearest, for you have a chance to escape the fury.

Then Jesus said to his disciples, "If anyone desires to come
after me, let them deny himself, and take up his cross, and
follow me. For whoever desires to save his life will lose it,
but whosoever loses his life for my sake will find it. For what
does it profit a man to gain the world and lose his soul?"

—Matthew 16:24–26

I Asked for Intimacy

I asked for intimacy, and God gave me you. Young, gifted, and
black—it's just a fact. You strutted into my life, innocent and without
guilt. You got power over me. I asked God for intimacy, and God
gave me you.

I searched for love and fulfillment, joy unspeakable, grace
unrelenting, a man of mercy with forgiveness that ever flows. You
bubble up in me, you make my cup overflow. You, man, are an
instructor of pure ecstasy. I asked for intimacy, and God gave me you.

I was pugged up, caught up, and stuffed up—but you released
my hot air and left my raw essence. You, man, exposed my soul and
my starving heart. Captured by a shock that unhoused the W-O-M-
A-N in me; it's trouble with a capital *T*. I asked for intimacy, and God
gave me you.

Depths and heights cannot reveal to me the magnitude and
places you send my mind. The great valleys of the world cannot
compass the space you take me to. You bring song in the morning

and thrills in the night. You bring shills in the noonday light. You are awesome. You are divine. You are hope shut up in my bones. You are me. You are God's man. I asked for intimacy, and God gave me you.

Dear God, I am holding on to your grace and mercy. I am waiting for the one you have planned for me. Keep me strong and wise that I might make the right choices. The enemy is forever in my face; I know you are able to keep me safe. I pray for love to come in my life. I pray for a strong man that can stand by my side. You are the wise one. Thanks for your love.

Amen.

OCTOBER 25, 1999 (7:24 A.M.)

The Lord is my shepherd, I lack nothing. He makes me lie
down in green pastures, he leads me beside quiet waters.
He refreshes my soul. He guides me along the right paths
for his name's sake. Even though I walk through the
darkest valley,[a] I will fear no evil, for you are with me;
your rod and your staff, they comfort me. You prepare
a table before me in the presence of my enemies. You
anoint my head with oil; my cup overflows. Surely your
goodness and love will follow me all the days of my life,
and I will dwell in the house of the Lord forever.

—Psalm 23

I Can Feel You

In the middle of the night when all is calm, I feel your troubled
soul leaping into a storm. I know there is hope, but sometimes it's
hard to cope. I can feel you.

Young and restless, searching for the peace of tomorrow, yet
haunted by past sorrows. Understanding that you can do all things
through Christ, you struggle for your rights. I can feel you.

Why is it so easy to believe disaster instead of laughter? Why is it
so easy to become heavy laden instead of light and soft like a sunrise
in the morning? I can feel you.

Yesterday you had to carry this pain alone. Today you have a friend, a confidant, a helpmate, and a soul mate that will share your heavy load. I can feel you.

Life is funny and sometimes incumbent by many disappointments and letdowns. The glue that will help you in the midst of your storm is love that is not prejudiced, a love that is not jealous, a love that can feel you in the middle of the night. I can feel you.

Dear God, I know that there is a struggle going on in this relationship. I don't know what it is, but I know you have the answer. I am praying for a move of God in his situation, move by your power and might. Please fix this distance that I feel because of worry and pain. You said in your Word that even when I walk through the darkest valleys, I will fear no evil. I am counting on you to see me through stormy weather. Love you, Lord. I ask everything in Jesus's holy name.

Amen.

OCTOBER 29, 1999 (4:42 A.M.)

Behold, I give unto you power to tread on serpents

and scorpions, and over all the power of the enemy:

and nothing shall by any means hurt you.

—Luke 10:19

Have You Ever Held Power Before?

Feels like steel wrapped up in a bronze brown laid in the form of God. Shape and fashioned in God's will. Steadfast and unmovable, lying in my arms. Have you held power before?

The strength of the navy and the might of all black men. The tenacity of the eagle, the bodacious attitude of the lion. Encouraged by the word that will not fail, I've wrapped my legs around him. Have you ever held power before?

Protective and secure like Fort Knots, caring like Jesus. Submissive like the earth to the Spirit of God. Designed like a great king, he laid in my chest daily. Have you ever held power before?

Sometimes solid as rock, and other times easy like Sunday morning. Sometimes filled with the sunshine of a new day, and other times bearing the cloud of a rainy day. Born and shaped in iniquity, nestle and caressed in me. Have you ever held power before?

Dear God, I have felt your power; I know you are the greatest force in the whole world. Continue to shape me in the manner that you want me to grow, my heart is yours. I am fighting a war daily, but you already know. I know that the punches are harder than before, but let me be faithful to you, oh great redeemer.

Amen.

OCTOBER 29, 1999 (8:33 A.M.)

No greater love has no one than this, to
lay down one's life for his friend.

—John 15:13

I've Lain in the Arms of Love

The ability to stretch from the Kentucky River to the Atlantic Ocean, running over with hot bubbling brown sugar, holding life in the middle of his hand, I've lain in the arms of love.

Thick like a mountain, warm and toasty like the sun beaming down on a chilly afternoon, arresting trouble, I've lain in the arms of love.

Charity deeper than an endless pit, dripping from shoulder to shoulder, chest painted with the hope of tomorrow, muscles pumped up like soft pillows, hands moving away fear like a milky way, I've lain in the arms of love.

Blessed with strong coffee colored African American potential, covered with the scent of pleasure, wrapped in the wisdom of God, I've lain in the arms of love.

Life does not promise us the road will be easy. There are many trials and tribulations to come. But life for me is much easier because I've lain in the arms of love.

Dear God, I dream of the perfect man for me, yet not my will but yours be done. The race is not given to the fast, nor the battle to the strong one, but to the one that endures. Help me to endure the fight with myself, help me to do what your word says, and help me to hold out until my name is changed.

Amen.

October 31, 1999 (8:30 a.m.)

A Letter to Him

I love you. I resolve that whatever it takes to please you, I am willing to do. I want to love you from the toe up. You are my inspiration, and that is why I am dedicated to making you happy too. I am so new at love and making love, but I promise I will learn to please you in every way that makes you feel good. This morning, when I woke up, I was concerned about your satisfaction. I want you to be filled and not hungry. I prayed to God to keep you still until his will is fulfilled in our lives. I know as I prepare to leave you, I will hunger for your touch early in the morning, and I will thirst for your hands at night. Words can never tell you what you mean to me, but I pray that someday soon, I can show you what I really feel.

I want to share with you something I have not shared with anyone else. I want to love you in fifty flavors. I want to find a hundred ways to make you love me. I want to caress you and touch you in the places that send you off into ecstasy. I want to be your Bionic Woman and your million-dollar lover. I want to draw you to me and be drawn to you. I want to touch your soul. I want us to experience total satisfaction. I want to be loved only by you.

My celibacy ended when I met my first husband. We were married and lived together for three years. The irony of it all was I never changed my name. I prayed for God to help me to hold out until my name was changed, and I did not change my name.

Remember the guy I met in college? Yes, Kelvin. Well, we went our separate ways in 1987, but we met again in 2013 at my mom's ninetieth birthday party. He had just lost his wife. I was sad when I heard the news about his wife. She was a very sweet lady. Throughout the years, we would accidentally run into him and his wife. I had a lot respect for her, and she was always very pleasant.

I was divorced and living in California, serving as a chaplain in the navy. Kelvin and I talked on the phone for the next year. I was clear we should not date until after a year had passed. I had an opportunity to see him a few times before the year was up, but we never even held each other's hands. Not that he would ever forget his wife or stop loving her—I want him to be ready for a relationship. I did not want him to rush into something because he was grieving and was looking for a replacement for his wife.

After a year, we started dating. Now, because we had dated for almost ten years, we had been to many family gatherings on both sides of the family. He met my great-grandmother and father on my daddy's side, all my grandparents. I met his father's mother, his aunts and uncles on both sides of the family. We pretty much knew neither of us were connected to a dark past. We felt safe enough to begin planning our forever. On August 8, 2015, we held our wedding on the beach in Maui, Hawaii, at sunset. Today, we are happily married and are enjoying all the thrills that we never experienced with each other before. By the way, I still have not changed my name.

Galatians 6:9 states, "Let us not become weary in doing good, for at the proper time we will reap a harvest if we do not give up."

PS. Ladies and gentlemen, if you have pledged your life to God and taken a vow of celibacy and a made a mistake, ask God for forgiveness. Please don't give up; start all over again. There is an old saying: "If you slip, don't slide." You get me drip?

Edwards Brothers Malloy
Thorofare, NJ USA
October 14, 2016

Keynesian Reflections

Effective Demand, Money, Finance,
and Policies in the Crisis

edited by

Toshiaki Hirai

Maria Cristina Marcuzzo

Perry Mehrling

OXFORD
UNIVERSITY PRESS

OXFORD
UNIVERSITY PRESS

Oxford University Press is a department of the University of Oxford.
It furthers the University's objective of excellence in research, scholarship,
and education by publishing worldwide. Oxford is a registered trademark of
Oxford University Press in the UK and in certain other countries

Published in India by
Oxford University Press
YMCA Library Building, 1 Jai Singh Road, New Delhi 110001, India

ISBN-13: 978-0-19-809211-7
ISBN-10: 0-19-809211-3

Typeset in Minion Pro 10.5/12.7
by alphæta Solutions, Puducherry, India 605 009
Printed in India at Rakmo Press, New Delhi 110 020

Contents

Tables

Figures

Keynesian Reflections

An Introduction

TOSHIAKI HIRAI, MARIA CRISTINA MARCUZZO,
AND PERRY MEHRLING*

The global financial crisis, which began in August 2007 and continues with no end in sight as we write these lines, has thrown macroeconomics into turmoil.

The New Classical idea that economies can be understood as if they were in full intertemporal general equilibrium at all times, shifting about in response to external shocks, was never taken very seriously by the majority of economists, neither as an empirically relevant description of reality nor as a normatively compelling guide to economic policy. Rather, the challenge of the New Classicals was always mainly to the theoretical structure and underpinnings of Old Keynesian orthodoxy circa 1970. The response to that challenge was the construction of a New Keynesian orthodoxy that achieved professional dominance with the publication of Michael Woodford's *Interest and Prices: Foundations of a Theory of Monetary Policy* (2003). Synthesizing decades of academic research, Woodford replaced the static monetary Walrasianism of the Hicks-Samuelson IS-LM

* We are grateful to an anonymous referee for helpful suggestions and criticisms, and to Oxford University Press, India, for supporting the idea of the book as well as seeing the manuscript through the various stages. We are indebted to Iolanda Sanfilippo in Italy for her excellent editorial assistance, and to Sophia University, Tokyo, for generous financial support towards the project.

(Investment-Saving/Liquidity preference-Money supply) model with the full Dynamic Stochastic General Equilibrium (DSGE) model preferred by the New Classicals, but with sufficient rigidities and imperfections added to create room for active policy intervention. This is the macroeconomic lens through which the majority of economists viewed the global financial crisis as it hit.

Unfortunately, that lens was ground with a particular set of economic problems in mind, the problems of the 1970s and 1980s, and so provided little insight into what was happening during the financial crisis, much less helpful policy advice concerning what to do about it. A model without banks is not going to help you very much when the problem you face is located in the banking system. Policymakers had to act, and they did act, but mainly by drawing on a hotchpotch of insights from outside modern mainstream economics, including some from the very practitioners who had built the financial house of cards that was collapsing around them, and also from older economics such as the rejected IS-LM. In response, economists had to act, and they did act, but mainly by adding financial frictions of various kinds to the pre-crisis DSGE orthodoxy.

The central purpose of the present volume is to suggest another possible road for the future of macroeconomics, a road that would confront economic reality without the comforting illusion of automatic (albeit imperfect) adjustment towards an intertemporal general equilibrium with rational expectations. If the world was really like that, we would know how to fix it, but the evidence of our senses tells us that it is not much like that. To paraphrase Keynes, the social object of economic policy should be to defeat the dark forces of time and ignorance which envelop our future, not to build models that take for granted the defeat of those forces. Keynes was, throughout his life, engaged with the concrete problems of his time, always starting from the economics that he knew, but never afraid to invent new economics as the situation might require. It is this Keynesian spirit, above all, that provides the linking theme for the chapters in this volume, chapters written originally for conferences held in Tokyo (2010, 2011) and in Florence (2012).

The present volume was initially conceived as a follow-on companion to The Return to Keynes (Bateman et al. 2010), a volume inspired by the aggressive worldwide policy response, both fiscal and monetary, to the global financial crisis that started in 2007. The more sober tone

of the present volume reflects the mood of the present moment, when retrenchment and austerity are the themes of policy in most of the Western economies. Instead of celebrating the return to Keynesian policy, we find ourselves engaging with the more structural problems of our own time, starting from the economics that Keynes invented but then adapting and going beyond Keynes himself, as modern conditions require.

But what exactly is 'the economics of Keynes' and how, if at all, does it differ from the Keynesian economics presented in macroeconomic textbooks and described in the media? There is no easy answer to this question since many varieties of Keynesianism have made their way into the profession, competing for the 'best' interpretation of Keynes. Similarly, opposition to Keynesian policies has also been argued on multiple grounds, ranging from the purported superiority of market mechanisms to fear of government deficits and the ensuing size of the public debt. This book situates itself in the very middle of this maze of argument, and seeks to provide a modern key for those seeking to engage the modern debate over whether to support or to oppose Keynes and Keynesian theories and policy.

In all of its varieties, Keynesian economics is usually associated with an emphasis on changes in the level of income (rather than the interest rate) as the central mechanism that brings saving and investment into line with one another. A further idea is that it is mainly saving that adjusts to investment, rather than the other way around, since investment is determined by the independent fluctuation of the marginal efficiency of capital. A central question is *why* the adjustment mechanism does not guarantee that the level of income/output comes to rest in a position corresponding to full employment/capacity.

There are two views on the matter: one explanation is rigidity in prices, wages, and the interest rate (via a 'liquidity trap'); the other explanation is found in the role of money and expectations. The price rigidity view, which goes back to the formulation of the 'old' neoclassical synthesis developed between the 1950s and the 1970s (Arena 2010), has always been rejected by those who claim to be closer to the spirit of Keynes himself. Price flexibility, far from facilitating adjustment to full employment, may actually aggravate the downward trend in output and employment. Lower prices and nominal wages increase the interest payment burden of debtors, causing them to cut back on spending so that effective demand is likely to fall rather than to rise.

Rather than engaging in argument with fellow Keynesians, the New Keynesians in the 1980s preferred to focus their efforts on justifying the assumption of rigid prices or wages by the use of optimizing models—such as the efficiency-wage hypothesis, insider-outsider bargaining theory, and menu costs. Thus was the IS-LM model transformed into the DSGE model. In effect, the New Keynesians preferred to respond to the anti-Keynesian critics, who urged the superiority of optimizing models, and the necessity of building a bridge between microeconomics and macroeconomics, even if doing so took them farther away from the real world and its problems, where they had found their initial inspiration.

Another dividing line among the varieties of Keynesianism is whether Keynesian economics applies only to macroeconomic questions, such as deviation from full employment, or whether microeconomics is also at stake. For those who argue the latter, the emphasis is on deficiency of the standard model of the rational economic agent who makes choices under constraint in an environment in which radical uncertainty does not exist and risk is calculable. As against this caricature of human behaviour, Keynes himself presented a theory of individual decision-making which rejected the use of mathematical expectation as a criterion for making decisions, and instead built on his own theory of probability. Keynes's interpretation of probability, different from chance or frequency, treats it as a property of the way individuals think about the world. This way of thinking then leads to an explanation of human conduct whereby decision rules under uncertainty incorporate a measure of the degree of confidence in probability assessment. Since for Keynes the degree of confidence in the available evidence is as important as the amount of information, the weight of argument has a central role (Basili and Zappia 2010).

This way of thinking about human behaviour under uncertainty has far-reaching implications for how we think about markets and the economy as a whole. If risk cannot always be effectively tamed and priced, it follows that markets cannot always properly assess risk and shift it to those best able to bear it. Even more, the demand for liquidity as a kind of haven in a world of incalculable risk means that money and expectations are inextricably involved in determining macroeconomic outcomes. Until recently, this 'fundamental Keynesian' critique of standard finance and macroeconomics was a

distinctly minority view. But the events which started in 2007 have made manifest that financial and macroeconomic instabilities cannot be explained with the standard macro models, and the profession is beginning to shift.

De Grauwe provides a compelling description of the status quo ante:

> A graduate student in a typical American or European university studying the subject of macroeconomics would be taught that the macroeconomy can be represented by representative consumers and firms who continuously optimize a multi-period plan, and in order to do so, use all available information including the one embedded in the model. These consumers and firms not only perfectly understand the complex intricacies of the workings of the economy, they also know the statistical distributions of all the shocks that can hit the economy. As a result, they can make scientifically founded probabilistic statements about all future shocks. In this world of God-like creatures, there is no uncertainty, there is only risk. Coordination failures do not occur because representative agents internalize all possible externalities. Bankruptcies of firms and consumers are impossible. Bubbles and crashes cannot occur because rational agents using all available information would never allow these to happen. Prolonged unemployment is impossible except when consumers choose to take more leisure.

Having mastered the intricacies of DSGE models, our brilliant new PhD graduate would then start a career teaching this model to the next cohort of PhD students (De Grauwe 2010: 157–8).

This book challenges the current mainstream macroeconomic tradition known as New Keynesian economics in so far as it shares common ground with the New Classical models. Specifically, this book rejects the view that some form of nominal rigidities in the goods market and/or in the labour market makes the indispensable core of an economics based on Keynes. And it further rejects the view that whatever shock hits the economy, the response is an automatic and rapid move towards market equilibrium that pulls the economy out of any kind of difficult situation.

In the world of Keynes himself, price rigidity is not at the source of economic fluctuations; economies could enter into depressions even with perfectly flexible prices and perfect competition. Further, policy intervention is needed not as short-run medicine, while waiting for the economy to return to the 'true' equilibrium values, but because shocks tend to amplify their consequences. Indeed, there

is plenty of scientific evidence to the effect that there exists no *permanent* trend towards market automatic adjustment, in the sense of market clearing with full employment. As such, this book explicitly aligns with one of the most strenuous contemporary defenders of the distinction between Keynesian economics and the economics of Keynes:

> The Old Neoclassical Synthesis, which reduced Keynesian theory to a general equilibrium model with 'rigid' wages, was an intellectual fraud the widespread acceptance of which inhibited research on systemic instabilities for decades. Insofar as the New Synthesis[a convergence of DSGE modelling technology with imperfections of capital markets and price inflexibility] represents a return to this way of thinking about macroproblems it risks the same verdict. The obvious objection to this line of theorizing is that the major problems which have had to be confronted in the last twenty or so years have originated in the financial markets—and prices in those markets are anything but 'inflexible'. But there is also a general theoretical problem that has been festering for decades with very little in the way of attempts to tackle it. Economists talk freely about 'inflexible' or 'rigid' prices all the time, despite the fact that we do not have a shred of theory that could provide criteria for judging whether a particular price is more or less flexible than appropriate to the proper functioning of the larger system. More than seventy years ago, Keynes already knew that a high degree of downward price flexibility in a recession could entirely wreck the financial system and make the situation infinitely worse. But the point of his argument has never come fully to inform the way economists think about price inflexibilities. (Leijonhufvud 2009: 12)

Old and New Keynesian models both built on the neoclassical model of individual behaviour to provide an underpinning for their aggregative models. The neoclassical canon is based on the rational optimizing assumption; economic agents are depicted as making optimizing choices under constraints. Keynes agreed that economic theory is about human choice, but always insisted that it is also about institutions (money, markets, and organization), which are not the outcome of individual choice but have evolved as social activities. He agreed that agents make constrained choices, but the constraints are mainly 'the dark forces of time and ignorance'. In such a world, optimizing behaviour is best approximated by groping and the trial and error method. Non-chosen results are precisely

what macroeconomics is about: composition effects and unintended consequences are all examples of non-chosen results which are part and parcel of aggregate behaviour.

The essays in this volume represent explorations towards a new more satisfactory macroeconomics, on both analytical and empirical grounds, building on Keynes's legacy but also reaching out in new directions.

EFFECTIVE DEMAND IN THE CRISIS

In Part I, three chapters consider the present crisis and policy response from the perspective of Keynes's own teaching rather than textbook Keynesianism or stereotyped Keynes. All three share a common concern that Keynes's arguments have not been fully engaged in the 'Return to Keynes' euphoria. As a consequence, there is real danger that the return may be short-lived, and that many other promising future developments will be halted prematurely. Keynes's vision of economics as a realm of possibility to promote social values should inform our research agenda; behind the current crisis lies a 'failure of ideas' (De Grauwe 2010: 159) quite as much as a failure of markets.

The Keynesian resurgence has so far largely been a change in the political mood and the attention of the media, rather than a change in academia; no academic breakthroughs appear yet associated with the resurgence. The boost to aggregate demand through government expenditure and the injection of liquidity into the system to fight depressions and offset credit crunches are merely policy recipes, invoked often by people of non-Keynesian persuasion whose search for alternatives to mainstream economics looks in different directions. The fear expressed in the first chapter is that 'Scholars and admirers of Keynes may fail to persuade sceptics and opponents, and there is no telling whether a new generation of economists will take today's lesson to heart' (Marcuzzo).

Let it not be misunderstood. The lesson of today is all about the issue of aggregate demand, *not* the issue of debt and deficits that occupies so much of current policy debate. As Keynes taught in his 1936 *General Theory of Employment, Interest and Money*, the economy fluctuates mainly because of variations in the marginal efficiency of capital, which cause fluctuations in investment spending. Fluctuations can

therefore be damped if the level of investment is sustained directly by public intervention, or indirectly by structural reforms that reduce uncertainty and improve profitability.

In a crisis, the primary concern must be to forestall the vicious circle whereby an initial decrease in income is followed by a fall in demand which then induces a further fall in income. The aim of policy should be to raise the level of effective demand closer to full employment. Ideally this is done not by stimulating consumption (private or public), but rather by targeting investment. Against the argument that we cannot afford to undertake stabilization policy because government deficits are creating a burden that will rest on future generations, Keynes's original insights still hold, as neatly summarized in the second chapter of the collection: 'investment creates assets that can compensate for, if not outweigh, the costs of any debt created in the process of building it up' (Backhouse and Bateman).

Granted the role of aggregate demand in generating income and employment, there are two issues still debated between the pro- and anti-Keynesian camps, namely the effects of changes in income distribution on the level of output and employment, and the ability of economic policies to exert a lasting influence on those variables. These issues are addressed by the third chapter of the section. In all the countries under his investigation (US, Japan, France, Germany, Spain, UK), López-Gallardo concludes that the evidence is on the Keynesian side:

> First, we find that a higher share of wages encourages demand and output in the short and in the long run.
>
> Second, higher government expenditure also stimulates demand and output. Let us note here that this positive effect takes place even when such expenditure is financed with higher taxes. ...
>
> Third, monetary conditions also influence demand and output, not only in the short but also in the long run. When credit conditions are relaxed and broad money grows, or when the interest rate declines, growth is stimulated (López-Gallardo).

In conclusion, the principle of effective demand remains the defining feature of a type of macroeconomics that does not rely on price and wage flexibility to bring about full employment. Since aggregate demand is likely to remain insufficient for significant periods, public intervention to sustain it is the only way to prevent serious recessions.

ECONOMIC THEORY AND THE WORLD RECESSION

Noguchi argues that Keynes went too far, as also do those who would start from Keynes today. But his real target is not Keynes, rather the Old Keynesian orthodoxy, IS-LM circa 1970, compared to which he asserts the superiority of New Keynesian orthodoxy. We include his essay in this collection partly as balance and contrast—all other chapters criticize the New Keynesian orthodoxy along one dimension or another—but more importantly as the strongest possible signal against a possible misinterpretation of the overall message of this book. Let it be clear that, like Noguchi, this book rejects Old Keynesian orthodoxy. Our call for a genuine return to Keynes is just as much a call for rejection of the Old as of the New; like Noguchi, we urge a new road for the macroeconomics of the future, not a return to the failed macroeconomics of the past.

In Noguchi's view, the macroeconomics which has evolved since the 1970s—that is, monetarism, rational expectations, and the real business cycle approaches—provides better policy guidance than the previous so-called Keynesian models. He writes:

> Most economists, if they are sincere, would agree with Krugman's contention that recent events have been forcing economists to shift the focus of their research, and that they should pay more attention to the actuality of an economic model than to its mathematical rigor. However, they would not agree with the statement that rather than subsequent macroeconomic theories including the new Keynesian economics, the old Keynesian economics, dominating the field until the 1970s, could better serve as a tool to analyse the recent crisis and to provide a policy prescription.

It should be noted that Noguchi's criticism is directed not so much against Keynes himself, but rather against the naive 'hydraulic Keynesianism' that Joan Robinson famously dismissed as an illegitimate American interpretation of Keynes. His criticism therefore opens the door to other potentially more productive ways of building on Keynes, which is the theme of the last section of the book.

The continued relevance of the classic Keynesian point of view is demonstrated in practice by two chapters that use it as a frame to understand Japan's bubble performance and the European crisis, respectively.

Rogers argues that Japan, which has suffered from a long period (18 years) of below par growth, finds itself in a predicament not unlike that of post–First World War Britain after its loss of export markets and return to gold at an overvalued parity which depressed the marginal efficiency of capital. There is, however, an important difference between the two, he argues:

> …Japan finds itself 'trapped' on the US dollar standard in much the same way that Britain was trapped on the gold standard in the 1920s and 1930s—committed by the power of convention to stay on the US dollar standard even though that commitment puts it at a strategic disadvantage because it depresses the structural marginal efficiency of capital and the domestic point of effective demand. In Japan's case, not because it forces domestic interest rates up as was the case with Britain on the gold standard, but because the post–Bretton Woods non-system has allowed the US to induce an ever appreciating yen, and also allowed some countries to hold exchange rates for sustained periods of time at undervalued rates. (Rogers)

While the case of Japan represents a cautionary tale of the difficulties of emerging from a prolonged recession, the situation in Europe can be seen as a premonition of a similar scenario looming in the near future. The Euro crisis started with the fiscal crisis in Greece in the Fall of 2009—one year after the collapse in the US banking system following the subprime crisis and the Lehman shock. The policy response was a massive bailout implemented by the European Commission, the European Central Bank, and the International Monetary Fund, but accompanied by the condition that the countries concerned should pledge to carry out austerity measures. The point made in Hirai's essay, drawing on Keynes's analysis of similar circumstances occurring after the First and the Second World Wars, is that these austerity measures are sharply deflationary and far from offering a fundamental solution to the crisis.

In both cases, we are faced with a situation in which a recession has turned out to be broader and deeper than ordinary downturns, and in which standard policies that may have worked in ordinary downturns prove inadequate to the larger task. A combination of monetary and fiscal expansionary measures, combined with a new set of rules (structural reforms) for the international financial market and monetary system, are seen as the only adequate response to the present recession. Some in the economics profession have warned of

'need for considerable caution regarding the pace of fiscal consolidation in depressed economies where interest rates are constrained by a zero lower bound' (DeLong and Summers 2012: 1). We feel that more should be conceded to Keynes's argument that concern about long-term debt levels should never be a priority over the level of unemployment and income.

MONEY AND INTERNATIONAL LIQUIDITY

In Part III, four chapters focus attention on what is perhaps the most distinctive feature of Keynes's vision of the working of capitalist economy, that is, its monetary nature. For Keynes, the role of money, both in private hands (household and banks) and in the public sector (central banks and supranational monetary institutions) is not in any sense 'neutral' with respect to the 'real' variables in the economy and the working of the market mechanism. Kregel sets the scene by showing how present ideas and prescriptions are in fact recycling ideas already present in Keynes's 1930 A Treatise on Money, where recipes such as zero interest rate policy (ZIRP) and quantitative easing (QE) were spelt out with Keynes's typical clarity of language and thought, explaining why central banks might be forced to step 'into shoes which the feet of the entrepreneurs are too cold to occupy' (Keynes 1930: 335). Today, the same desperate measures are being adopted as central banks substitute for the cold feet of fiscal authorities and political leaders.

Keynes's attempt to understand how these monetary interventions worked, and why ultimately they did not work well enough, led him to invent new economics, in particular his conception of liquidity preference. Unfortunately, however, this key invention has survived in the economics literature only in a simplified and therefore distorted version. Cardim de Carvalho argues convincingly that liquidity preference is more than Keynes's preferred word for the demand for money; it is the central core of his distinctive theory of asset pricing. Asset markets have of course changed much since Keynes's day, but if we extend the application of Keynes's theory to banks, we find a clue to much of what we have observed in the financial markets during the current crisis, in which commercial banks borrowed from central banks but then refused to roll over brokers' debts or to extend them new loans.

This issue of liquidity preference is further elaborated in the next chapter (Fantacci) which argues that what has occurred, since the summer of 2007, is not so much a cancellation or restructuring of non-performing loans, but rather a substitution of one kind of non-payable debt for another kind of non-payable debt: from private debts, to public debts, to foreign debts. In current policy discussion, the emphasis is on what to do about the sovereign debts of potentially insolvent states, but Fantacci maintains that the problem is not solvency but sustainability, which requires the possibility of selling domestic debts on liquid international markets. From this point of view, the focus of policy discussion should be on the sources of international liquidity, including the state of the international reserve currency, the strength of issuing institutions, and the size of global imbalances. For developing this alternative frame, Keynes's intuitions and proposals, such as 'Bancor' and the Clearing Union, provide a fruitful place to start.

For modern conditions, however, Keynes's vision of a world central bank empowered to impose ceilings for account balances, and to distribute reserves according to political priorities, is arguably impossibly utopian (Spahn). What seems to be emerging instead is a system with two or even three key currencies, accompanied by regulations on the scope and structure of reserve holding. Our challenge today is to imagine how this emerging new system will work, and how it can be made to work better.

FINANCE AND INTERNATIONAL ECONOMIC DISORDER

In the final Part IV, four chapters engage with what is arguably the central issue of the present moment: speculation, finance, and global markets. The opening piece (Sen) offers an explanation of the recent pattern of rising commodity prices in the global economy, viewed through Keynes's writings on uncertainty and risk, and revolving around his notion of probability. This Keynesian perspective is contrasted with explanations based on conventional economic thinking, in which price volatility and trends are attributed mainly to fundamental supply and demand factors. Building on the foundations laid by Keynes, the author emphasizes the dominance of speculation which is made possible by the increased 'financialization' of commodity markets. Unlike the mainstream literature on derivative trading, speculation is viewed here as a de-stabilizing factor.

Next, and more generally, Wray focuses attention on the 'financial instability hypothesis' put forward by Hyman Minsky as an alternative way of developing the ideas of Keynes for the modern world. Wray's focus is on the emergence of money market capitalism, and the role of pension funds and money managers in fuelling the asset price boom and subsequent bust. The point made here is that the financial superstructure of managed money has become too large to be supported by the nation's ability to produce output and income. In the absence of growth (and of policies for it), the 'financialization' of the economy—layering and leveraging existing levels of production and income—poses a continuing structural challenge, quite apart from the immediate problem of crisis.

The next piece is an excursion into the intricacies of the sophisticated money market as it has developed in the recent years, and into the changed role of the Fed, from lender of last resort to dealer of last resort (Mehrling). To appreciate fully why this has happened, the author brings us back to the beginning of the subprime mortgage story, showing us how the assets were funded in global money markets through cross-border banking and explaining in detail how this worked. This new capital market–based credit system—sometimes called the 'shadow banking system'—is seen as nothing less than the latest institutional form taken by financial globalization, as it has grown up in the last 30 years. Bringing together the discussions on the international dollar funding system, the emerging institutions of the derivative clearing system, and the Fed's role during the crisis, Mehrling suggests a new line of departure for thinking about how to regulate the emerging new system.

In the closing piece of this collection, Carabelli and Cedrini make a plea that the global order should be reformed so as to use international discipline as a tool to enhance, rather than repress, national policy space. By contrast, the evolution of the international economic system since the 1980s has been in exactly the opposite direction. The Washington Consensus paradigm as applied by the international financial institutions in the 1990s was an attempt to construct a global order based on a highly unbalanced relationship between international discipline and national policy space. 'Private licence' has been mistaken for 'public liberty', and shared responsibility has been cast aside. As a consequence, international economic *disorder* has emerged. The road forward, following Keynes, is to recognize the

complexity of international economic relations, a sphere involving analyses of the fallacy of composition between particular and general interests, and of the policy dilemmas which face both debtor and creditor countries.

Keynesian Reflections has been chosen as the title of this collection of essays to indicate the connecting theme that Keynes remains a relevant and vital starting point for understanding modern problems, as well as inspiration for the hard work of inventing the new economics that modern problems demand. The word 'reflections' has been chosen to denote both Keynes's original insights which we are now seeing more clearly, and also the process of deliberately and reflectively building something new on those foundations. We have been witness to Keynes's ideas being reflected in varieties of Keynesianism and distorted in the stereotyped image of a defender of 'big government' and 'less market'; several essays in this volume bring back to life those aspects of Keynes's thinking which have been neglected in the recent revival of interest in his work.

The distinguishing feature of the Keynesian approach is a conception of economics as extension of human possibilities, proposing remedies to safeguard the general interest as condition for prosperity and social harmony. The concept of reasonableness, as opposed to rationality, captures what in general separates the economics of Keynes from the conventional approach. The tenets of economic rationality lie behind current demands to bring debtors to book, imposing indiscriminate sacrifices, ignoring the pleas of the weakest, invoking rigorous laws, and threatening social protection and security. In the name of rationality, we are urged to implement policies which may threaten confidence in democracy, fuelling various forms of political radicalism as a response to social disruption and distress. By contrast, Keynes's reasonableness urges judgement on the basis of specific circumstances, and exercise of the imagination and creativity in seeking solutions characterized by analysis of the consequences from the overall point of view. His approach appeals to the principles of shared responsibility between debtors and creditors, collective action in place of individual self-interest, and the pursuit of individual liberties within a context of norms and rules. Keynes's middle way between extreme liberalism on the one hand and pervasive government intervention on the other still seems to us a viable path towards equitable growth.

Just so, for Keynes and for economists of Keynesian persuasion today, the question of income distribution revolves crucially around institutional factors and arrangements, such as the existence of trade unions, laws governing minimum wages, employee rights at work, and systems of social protection such as unemployment insurance. The dismantling of these institutions in pursuit of higher flexibility and efficiency of free markets has proven to favour rather than to prevent the onset of the crisis. Increased vulnerability on the real side of the economy has exacerbated fragility on the financial side of the economy, since the loss of safeguards against low wages and unemployment made private debts the only viable option for sustaining consumption during downturns.

Conflicts of economic interest are not the only obstacle to the acceptance of the philosophy of shared responsibility. The inability to foresee all the consequences of a given policy and lack of openness to consider unconventional thinking also stand in the way of reforms and change. The challenge of applying Keynes's approach thus requires us to enlarge the basis of consensus to include the general public and the media, as well as academia. Each of these has its own source of knowledge about the questions involved, which leads each to respond differently to different issues.

In his activities as policy adviser, Keynes was in constant contact with ministers, civil servants, officers, politicians, bankers, and opinion makers. The extraordinary number of his correspondents testifies to the compelling need he felt to keep in touch with opinions and points of view coming from different quarters. In this respect, *The General Theory* is better portrayed as a study in *persuasion* rather than in *policy making*. It offers not a set of recipes or rules to be followed in all circumstances, but rather a brilliant example of the power of argument for guiding human decision-making in a time of grave uncertainty. Similarly, though more modestly, the present book should be understood primarily as a study in persuasion for our own time of grave uncertainty. We offer the reflections in this book not as the end of the matter, but rather as the beginning of a new discussion. Our aim is to provoke and inspire others to do better in developing the new economic thinking that is needed for the world of today.

December 2012

REFERENCES

Arena, R. 2010. 'From the "Old" to the "New" Keynesian–Neoclassical Synthesis: An Interpretation', in B.W. Bateman, T. Hirai, and M.C. Marcuzzo (eds), *The Return to Keynes*. Cambridge: Harvard University Press, pp. 77–93.

Basili, M. and C. Zappia. 2010. 'Keynes and the Financial Crisis', mimeo, paper presented at the Annual Conference of the European Society for the History of Economic Thought (ESHET), Amsterdam, 25–27 March.

Bateman, B.W., T. Hirai, and M.C. Marcuzzo (eds). 2010. *The Return to Keynes*. Cambridge: Harvard University Press.

De Grauwe, P. 2010. 'The Return of Keynes', *International Finance*, 13(1): 157–63.

DeLong, B. and L. Summers. 2012. 'Fiscal Policy in a Depressed Economy', Spring 2012 Brookings Panel on Economic Activity, Brookings Institution, Washington, DC, 22–23 March, available online: http://www.brookings.edu/about/projects/bpea/editions/~/media/projects/bpea/spring%202012/2012_spring_bpea_delongsummers.pdf (accessed 7 May 2012).

Keynes, J.M. 1930. *A Treatise on Money. Vol. II: The Applied Theory of Money*. London: Macmillan.

Leijonhufvud, A. 2009. 'Out of the Corridor: Keynes and the Crisis', mimeo.

Woodford, M. 2003. *Interest and Prices: Foundations of a Theory of Monetary Policy*. Princeton, NJ: Princeton University Press.

I
Effective Demand in the Crisis

1

Re-embracing Keynes

Scholars, Admirers, and Sceptics in the Aftermath of the Crisis

MARIA CRISTINA MARCUZZO

Today we have involved ourselves in a colossal muddle, having blundered in the control of a delicate machine, the working of which we do not understand. The result is that our possibilities of wealth may run to waste for a time perhaps for a long time.

—Keynes, *The Great Slump of 1930* (CWK IX: 126)

We cannot, as a community, provide for future consumption by financial expedients but only by current physical output.

—Keynes, *The General Theory* (CWK VII: 104)

PREMISE

While there has never been a real halt in the flow of scholarly literature, undoubtedly the 2008–9 crisis has seen an upsurge in the wave of references to Keynes, in the media, the economic press, and political discourse.

The number of admirers has gone up and for the first time in a very long time those who look back to Keynes have outnumbered the sceptics. On the other hand, the Keynes revival has brought back to

the fore doubts aṅd objections to the relevance of Keynes's arguments to contemporary problems and issues.

In this chapter I investigate which aspects of Keynes's analysis and recommendations economists wish once again to see accepted and implemented and which are still rejected and misunderstood. I am also concerned to find out whether the 'return to Keynes' plea is matched by original research into his work and how much is sheer rhetoric or relies on second-hand knowledge.

In this chapter I will not attempt a systematic review of material published on this matter in the last couple of years; my more modest purpose is to illustrate a few cases and some issues. My point is that in the face of unqualified admirers and sceptics alike, scholarly investigation into Keynes's writings more than ever is called for in order to take stock of his work and teaching.

GOVERNMENT DEFICIT

The standard 'return to Keynes' argument is the need for fiscal stimulus to boost the economy from the depths of recession. The burden of the deficit is not seen as the main drawback of government intervention, but a necessary measure to address a failure in aggregate demand.

There are still many economists who oppose this view, as witnessed by the manifesto sponsored by the Cato Institute and signed by 237 American economists (the most renowned among them being M. Bordo, J. Buchanan, J. Cochrane, E. Fama, S. Horwitz, D. McCloskey, A. Meltzer, E. Prescott, V. Smith, R. Whaples, and L. White) who refused to endorse the statement made by President Obama in January 2009 that 'we need action by our government, a recovery plan that will help to jumpstart the economy'.

The signatories declared:

Notwithstanding reports that all economists are now Keynesians and that we all support a big increase in the burden of government, we the undersigned do not believe that more government spending is a way to improve economic performance. More government spending by Hoover and Roosevelt did not pull the United States economy out of the Great Depression in the 1930s. More government spending did not solve Japan's 'lost decade' in the 1990s. As such, it is a triumph of hope over experience to believe that more government spending will help the US today. To improve the economy, policymakers should focus

on reforms that remove impediments to work, saving, investment and production. Lower tax rates and a reduction in the burden of government are the best ways of using fiscal policy to boost growth.[1]

Similarly, in the UK, an open letter, signed by 20 economists,[2] was sent to the *Sunday Times* (14 February 2010) advocating a more rapid reduction of Britain's budget deficit than currently planned, 'to support a sustainable recovery'.[3]

This pronouncement provoked a reaction in the form of two letters sent to the *Financial Times* (18 February), signed by R. Skidelsky and others 57 economists,[4] and by R. Layard and eight more economists.[5]

In the first it is argued that the signatories of the *Sunday Times* letter 'seek to frighten us with the present level of the deficit' but 'they omit to say that the contraction in UK output since September 2008 has been more than 6 per cent, that unemployment has risen by almost 2 percentage points'.[6]

The second letter points out that 'it would be dangerous to reduce the government's contribution to aggregate demand' since it 'would not produce an offsetting increase in private sector aggregate demand, and could easily reduce it'.[7]

Concern about the size of the government deficit is not in itself a sign of opposition to the Keynesian argument;[8] it is, rather, acceptance of the classical presupposition that supply creates its own demand, or of the 'Treasury view' according to which public expenditure 'crowds out' a corresponding amount of private expenditure.

Samuel Brittan (2010) has pointed out that the fiscal debate recently has been impoverished by lack of understanding that logically there are in fact not two (pro or against the reduction of public deficit through curbing public expenditure) but four positions: there are also the options of reducing the level of public expenditure, matched by lower takes, or leaving it at the same level, but in any case not urging the cuts in the deficit.

The dividing issue between Keynesian and anti-Keynesian positions is in fact the relationship which is established between the size of the deficit and the level of income and unemployment.[9] (For comparison of world unemployment in October 2009, see Figure 1.1). Since there is no theory to justify the 'right' size of deficit nor the amount of government spending, the issue at stake is the scale of priorities: in times of recession and high unemployment—so the Keynesian

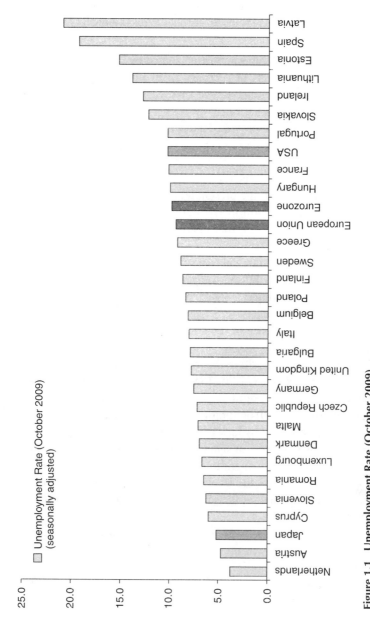

Figure 1.1 Unemployment Rate (October 2009)

Source: Eurostat. Available at http://www.banknoise.com/wp-content/uploads/2009/12/unempl_20091220intl.png.

argument goes—the priority is to sustain the level of aggregate demand, to increase the level of income and employment; this is the only way to reduce the size of the deficit and to prevent the vicious circle of lower income–lower government revenue.

Economists of Keynesian orientation have argued that the Stability and Growth Pact[10] is at the root of the problem in Europe, since the European monetary system imposes a deflationary bias by restricting fiscal space. Others have argued that in the US the crisis originated from a distribution of income problem, that is, a private debt which has increased to offset the fall in wages and salaries. So the remedy is to substitute public for private debt, increasing expenditure on health, education, and housing, so as to restore an adequate and sustainable level of aggregate demand (Barba and Pivetti 2009).

Moreover, Krugman has argued that, contrary to the widespread view that Germany which chose austerity did better than the US which went for Keynesian policy, as far as real gross domestic product (GDP) is concerned, data for 2008–10 show quite the opposite: during the last two years, actual government purchases of goods and services (excluding transfer payments from the federal government to states) have been higher in Germany than in the US (Krugman 2010; see Figures 1.2a and 1.2b).

So the effectiveness of fiscal policies is back at the core of the disagreement between economists who favour or do not favour a 'return to Keynes', as it was in the 1970s between Keynesians and Monetarists.[11] I rather doubt whether econometric exercises designed to measure the impact of the current fiscal stimulus engineered by the countries of the Organisation for Economic Co-operation and Development (OECD) in recent months (see Table 1.1) will prove conclusive and persuasive.[12] As in the 1970s testing the values of the elasticity of the LM-IS curves helped neither contending party to win its case, estimates of the value of the multiplier associated with each fiscal measure are not going to regroup economists between the two camps.

However, since Keynes's original argument has seldom been reappraised, it is worth considering it more carefully.

Commenting on the Report of Steering Committee on Employment (1944), Keynes objected that 'it would be a *failure* to adopt a remedy for severe cyclical unemployment which may have [the] effect' to destabilize the national budget since 'measures to stabilise the national

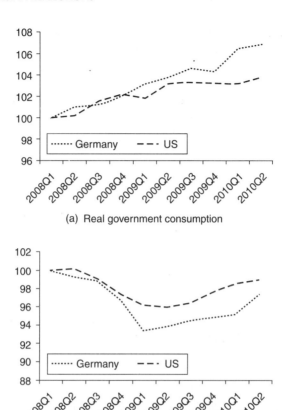

(a) Real government consumption

(b) Real GDP

Figure 1.2   Real Government Consumption and Real GDP
Source: Krugman (2010).

income are *ipso facto* measures to stabilize the national budget' (CWK XXVII: 366). And he continued:

> The Committee give the impression that, whilst the measures they propose to avoid unemployment are admittedly necessary and advisable, a price has to be paid for them in the shape of budgetary deficits and perhaps a consequent weakening in international confidence in our position. Exactly the opposite is the truth. It would be a failure to take such measures which would inevitably unstabilise the budget and weaken confidence. Is it supposed that slumps increase the national wealth? (Ibid.)

Table 1.1 Employment and Output Effects of Fiscal Stimulus Packages

	Total Fiscal Package (% of GDP)	Employment Elasticity of Growth	Income Multiplier Effect (Multiplier of 0.5)	Employment Effect with Income Multiplier 0.5 (% Age Change)	Income Multiplier Effect (Multiplier of 1)	Employment Effect with Income Multiplier 1 (% Age Change)
Argentina	3.9	0.01	1.95	0.02	3.9	0.04
Australia	2.5	0.56	1.25	0.70	2.5	1.4
Belgium	0.5	0.57	0.25	0.14	0.5	0.29
Brazil	0.2	0.68	0.1	0.07	0.2	0.14
Canada	2	0.44	1	0.44	2	0.88
Chile	2.3	0.28	1.15	0.32	2.3	0.64
China	13	0.17	6.5	1.11	13	2.21
France	1.1	0.57	0.55	0.31	1.1	0.63
Germany	2.8	0.05	1.4	0.07	2.8	0.14
Hungary	3.8	0.03	1.9	0.06	3.8	0.11
India	0.3	0.36	0.15	0.05	0.3	0.11
Indonesia	1.2	0.43	0.6	0.26	1.2	0.52
Italy	0.3	0.74	0.15	0.11	0.3	0.22
Japan	2.3	-0.24	1.15	-0.28	2.3	-0.55
Korea	2.7	0.38	1.35	0.51	2.7	1.03
Malaysia	7.9	0.67	3.95	2.65	7.9	5.29

(contd.)

Table 1.1 (contd.)

	Total Fiscal Package (% of GDP)	Employment Elasticity of Growth	Income Multiplier Effect (Multiplier of 0.5)	Employment Effect with Income Multiplier 0.5 (% Age Change)	Income Multiplier Effect (Multiplier of 1)	Employment Effect with Income Multiplier 1 (% Age Change)
Mexico	4.7	0.67	2.35	1.57	4.7	3.15
Netherlands	0.8	0.7	0.4	0.28	0.8	0.56
New Zealand	0.8	0.6	1.9	1.14	3.8	2.28
Norway	0.6	0.26	0.3	0.08	0.6	0.16
Philippines	3.7	0.76	1.85	1.41	3.7	2.81
Portugal	1.1	0.4	0.55	0.22	1.1	0.44
Russia	1.1	0.13	0.55	0.07	1.1	0.14
Saudi Arabia	11.3	1.11	5.65	6.27	11.3	12.54
South Africa	1.2	-0.23	0.6	-0.14	1.2	-0.28
Spain	0.8	0.72	0.4	0.29	0.8	0.58
Switzerland	0.3	0.1	0.15	0.02	0.3	0.03
Thailand	2.8	0.38	1.4	0.53	2.8	1.06
United Kingdom	1.3	0.37	0.65	0.24	1.3	0.48
United States	5.6	0.2	2.8	0.56	5.6	1.12
Vietnam	0.9	0.35	0.45	0.16	0.9	0.32

Source: Jha (2009).

Thus, Keynes's first tenet against traditional thinking is based on reversal of the causality relation between deficit budgeting, level of income, and international confidence in a country.

The second tenet is that public expenditure as a means to reduce unemployment should be interpreted as a means to increase aggregate demand rather than to adjust supply to the *existing* level of demand. In the so-called 'pro free market' literature, Keynes's position is ridiculed as being based on the 'digging holes in the ground' argument: it does not matter how public money is spent, as long as it is spent, since it will generate income and through the multiplier the savings necessary to finance the initial expenditure.

Keynes's 'digging holes' suggestion is meant to illustrate the principle, not to provide a blueprint of 'useful' public work schemes. He illustrates the point with reference to expenditures on goods which have no useful purposes from the point of view of consumption, but which nevertheless produce the desired effects.

Gold mining, which is just another form of unearthing bottles dug in the ground, or pyramid building had positive effects on income and employment because they yielded fruits that 'could not serve the needs of man by being consumed' and therefore do not 'stale with abundance' (CWK VII: 131). Keynes then writes:

> Just as wars have been the only form of large-scale loan expenditure which statesmen have thought justifiable, so gold mining is the only pretext for digging holes in the ground which has recommended itself to bankers as sound finance; and each of these activities has played its part in progress—*failing something better*. (Ibid.: 130) [emphasis added]

There are two points here. The first is that 'it would, indeed, be more sensible to build houses and the like; but if there are political and practical difficulties in the way of this, the above would be better that nothing' (Ibid.: 129). The political difficulties arise mainly from 'the education of our statesman on the principles of the classical economics' (Ibid.). The second point is that expenditure on 'useful things' may not be as effective: 'Two pyramids, two masses for the dead, are twice as good as one; but not two railways from London to York' (Ibid.). The argument is that the decreasing marginal efficiency of investment, 'unless the rate of interest is falling *pari passu*', sets a limit to the possibility of increasing the stock of wealth by means of 'useful'

forms of loan expenditure.[13] Waste results not when expenditure is directed to objects which are not 'useful', but when they are not 'economically' viable.

The purpose of increasing aggregate expenditure is to generate income and employment, and this may not be sufficient to increase the stock of useful wealth. In Keynes's argument, financial availability is not the constraining factor in the augmentation of objects which 'could serve the needs of man', as are the constraints of their diminishing of marginal utility and the provisions for user and supplementary costs to maintain them.

UNCERTAINTY AND PROBABILITY

Many have argued that among the failures that contributed to the financial crisis it is pre-eminently the failure of ideas as originating in the new macroeconomic paradigm that developed during the 1970s and 1980s, where 'consumers and firms … know the statistical distributions of all the shocks that can hit the economy. As a result, they can make scientifically founded probabilistic statements about all future shocks. In this world of God-like creatures, there is no uncertainty, there is only risk' (De Grauwe 2010: 157).

This is the main point in Skidelsky's latest book: 'underlying the escalating succession of financial crises we have recently experienced is the failure of economics to take uncertainty seriously' (Skidelsky 2009: 188).

The 'return to Keynes' is interpreted here as the need to take on board his division of economics (CWK VII: 293–4) between 'the study of those economic activities in which "our views of the future are… reliable in all respects" and the study of those in which "our previous expectations are liable to disappointment and expectations concerning the future affect what we do today"' (Ibid.). The former allows for probability calculation, while the latter is dominated by the notion of uncertainty.

Keynes reached this conclusion on the basis of his theory of probability. While it cannot be fully analysed here, the main point can be outlined following Lawson (1985) and Roncaglia (2009).

Keynes's definition of probability (P) is that of a logical relationship between a proposition h (premise) and a proposition a (conclusion). If knowledge of h (premise) allows for a rational belief in a

(conclusion), there is a probability relation of degree a (CWK VIII: 4). This description is supplemented by another concept, the 'weight of the argument', which is positively correlated with the 'magnitude' of the evidence of h. It is an indicator of confidence, providing a broader base for the rational belief. So, while probability establishes the degree of rational belief in the conclusion, the weight expresses the confidence in that probability.

How does uncertainty get into the story? To answer the question, we need to distinguish between two types of knowledge, that is, 'that part of our rational belief which we know directly and that part we know by argument' (Ibid.: 2). Knowledge is thus obtained either 'as the result of contemplating the objects of acquaintance' (Ibid.: 18) or through the probability relation.

If, in the probability relation:

$$a \mid h = \mathrm{P} \qquad\qquad (A)$$

we define a as the primary proposition and the probability relation (A) as the secondary proposition, uncertainty can be defined as the absence of a secondary proposition, or the lack of a probability relationship. It refers to an immeasurable relationship between premise and conclusion *in the absence* of a secondary proposition. In the absence of a secondary proposition, no comparison between magnitudes of probabilities of different contingent outcomes is possible, and uncertainty prevails.

'Thus uncertainty, is not merely a situation in which the probability relation is known and the primary proposition, a say, relative to the evidence, gives rise to a numerical probability that is less than unity' (Lawson 1985: 914).

It refers to all those cases, Keynes writes, 'in which no rational basis has been discovered for numerical comparison. It is not the case here that the method of calculation, prescribed by theory, is beyond our powers or too laborious for actual application' (CWK VIII: 30).

It follows that we cannot hope to remove uncertainty by becoming more skilful in calculation or by collecting more information. It is uncertainty which we cannot cope with by means of probability (Svetlova and Fiedler 2011).

Why does Keynes's distinction matter? First, it rejects the presupposition that risk can be measured and allocated in such a way as to

prevent uncertainty of the outcomes. This is at the root of the current crisis and financial instability, as pointed out by Minsky (1982)[14] long ago and recently repeated by several commentators of Keynesian orientation.

'Not distinguishing *uncertainty*, which is not calculable, from *risk*, which is, banks, embracing the assumptions of neoclassical or efficient markets finance with mathematical algorithms, believed that they were able to calculate risk with a "high probability of being right"' (Bresser-Pereira 2009: 12).[15]

The consequence of embracing the assumption that all risks can be calculated, following the 'efficient market economics' rather than a type of economics inspired by Keynes, has been to increase rather than reduce the frequency of financial crisis, as many studies have demonstrated.[16]

A number of studies comparing the 1930 crisis with the present meltdown have almost unanimously shown how in the recent crisis the behaviour of the monetary authorities that adopted Keynesian policies of reducing interest rates and increasing liquidity, rather than relying on the allegedly self-adjusting market forces, has drastically curbed the fall in income and employment.

Second, reliance on the risk calculation of financial assets has loosened the connection between the monetary and real sides of the economy. 'The increasing instability of the financial system is a consequence of a process of the increasing autonomy of credit and of financial instruments from the real side of the economy: from production and trade' (Bresser-Pereira 2009: 19).

THE STATE OF ECONOMICS

The remark made in Blanchard (2008) that 'the state of macro is good' is often quoted in a derogatory sense. What is the good of an approach that failed to accommodate the *facts* of the current crisis?

Blanchard (2008: 13) openly admits that in the basic New Keynesian[17] model there is no unemployment, but he believes that the problem can be 'fixed' by introducing a more sophisticated explanation of the *real* and *nominal* wage rigidity assumption as prevailing in the labour markets.

Blanchard is also adamant that the model 'falls short of the mark' in assuming an 'arbitrage approach' to the determination of the

term structure of interest rates and asset prices, leaving no room to the role that financial institutions play in the economy. However, his optimism—'one can be confident that progress will happen rapidly'—is simply anchored to the '*urgency* of understanding the current financial crisis' (Blanchard 2008: 18; emphasis added).

On the other hand, Colander et al.'s (2009) the Dahlem Report, 2008,[18] while denouncing the '*systemic failure of the economics profession*', before in predicting and now in understanding the crisis, invoke the legacy of economists of alternative traditions,[19] failing to mention Keynes as a source of inspiration. In their critique of the prevailing approach, they focus, rather, on the study of interactions and connections between actors as the missing feature of current macro analysis.

Their research agenda includes items such as study of the interconnectivity of the economic system (mainly through network analysis), the informational role of financial prices and financial contracts, and the construction of indicators 'warning' of bubble formation.

Likewise, the pitiless *j'accuse* of the 'complete markets macroeconomics'[20] by W. Buiter is accompanied by the belief that the future 'belongs to behavioural approaches relying on empirical studies on how market participants learn, form views about the future and change these views in response to changes in their environment, peer group effects etc.' (Buiter 2009).

The profession and many of its leading journals still remain in the thrall of free-market thinking while other economists get very little hearing, their work largely ignored and marginalized. Very few cases of recantation are on record. A notable case is Richard Posner, who in September 2009 made a public endorsement of Keynes:

> Until last September, when the banking industry came crashing down and depression loomed for the first time in my lifetime, I had never thought to read *The General Theory*. ... Baffled by the profession's disarray, I decided I had better read [it]. Having done so, I have concluded that, despite its antiquity, it is the best guide we have to the crisis.[21]

Another case is Gregory Mankiw, who in November 2008 repudiated the judgement he had made in 1992 that *The General Theory* was an 'out dated book', saying: 'If you were going to turn to only one economist to understand the problems facing the economy, there is little doubt that the economist would be John Maynard Keynes.'[22]

Thus, while welcoming the wind of 'return to Keynes', we must not be oblivious to the fact that there has been very little change in the positions held in the professions. For instance, in response to Posner, Gary Becker reiterates the usual 'sticky wage' fallacy in interpreting Keynes:

> Keynes and many earlier economists emphasized that unemployment arises during recessions because nominal wage rates tend to be inflexible in the downward direction. The natural way that markets usually eliminate insufficient demand for a good or service, such as labor, is for the price of this good or service to fall. A fall in price stimulates demand and reduces supply until they are brought back to rough equality. Downward inflexible wages prevents that from happening quickly when there is insufficient demand for workers.[23]

Moreover, the 'return to Keynes' in many cases turns out to be lip service with very little original work done on those aspects of Keynes which are relevant to the present recession and crisis of economics. P. Krugman and J. Stiglitz have been very vociferous in the media in propounding and defending Keynesian ideas. While Stiglitz has built his academic reputation by introducing rigidities, market imperfections, and asymmetrical information into the 'classical synthesis' model, Krugman has remained critical of the New Keynesian approach and seems, therefore, closer to Keynes's main message in *The General Theory*.[24]

The strand of literature which has remained faithful to Keynes and is accused of 'preaching to the converted' relies, with few exceptions, on scholarly work done in the 1980s and 1990s. I believe that there are areas in which we can expand the scope of the 'return to Keynes' agenda and which should be taken up in the current debate.

A RESEARCH AGENDA

The economics of Keynes is not just about government spending and injection of liquidity in times of crisis, but also about international cooperation on matters of finance, primary commodities, and international payments to provide the appropriate framework to a market economy. It is the conviction that markets and economic behaviour are to be guided by a logic of coordination and rules, rather than left to the pursuit of individual interests and to the freedom resulting from the lack of public intervention and regulation by the institutions.

It incorporates a view of rational behaviour under uncertainty, where reasonableness as opposed to rationality is praised (see Marcuzzo 2011). While irrationality ('animal spirits' and 'herd behaviour') may at times dominate investment decisions or financial markets, ample room is left to rationality bounded by knowledge, judgement, and experience.

In their recent book, Akerlof and Shiller (2009) explicitly draw from Keynes the notion of 'animal spirits' as opposed to 'rationality' to explain behaviour in the economy. Driving human actions are confidence, fairness, corruption, money illusion, and stories, which are the 'real motivations for real people' (Ibid.: 174). While I have some doubts that their 'animal spirits' are what Keynes meant by them, I agree that they capture the distrust in the Benthamite calculus which underlies the economic theorizing that Keynes was firmly opposed to.

A distinguishing feature of Keynes's approach is also to be seen in a conception of economics as extension of possibilities, as opposed to the logic of scarcity; it is an appeal to judgement on the basis of the circumstances and a plea to the exercise of the imagination and creativity in seeking solutions, rather an appeal to the timeless 'iron laws' of a physical science. Keynes's economics is a 'moral' science which 'deals with introspection and with values … it deals with motives, expectations, psychological uncertainties' (CWK XIV: 300).

I would like to give a couple of examples of the directions in which today's favourable wind of 'return to Keynes' could drive the research agenda.

The first is appraisal of Keynes's contribution to finance theory, which has been overshadowed by almost exclusive attention to the effects on economic aggregates expressed in real terms of expenditure policy measures.

Keynes was led from his early belief that rational agents stabilized financial markets through arbitrage and speculation to the realization that markets can remain unsettled, which explains why he claimed that *institutions* are needed to maintain order in those markets.

De Cecco (2010) and Kregel (2010) have made important contributions towards an understanding of the development of Keynes's thoughts on finance from the *Tract* to *The General Theory*, providing further theoretical grounds to explain why he mistrusted markets. The basic ideas are: unarbitraged margins preventing the law of one price from prevailing in financial markets may be widespread occurrence;

the 'beauty contest'—picking what one thinks others are most likely to think that others think are the best choices—is the framework within which decisions are made and actions carried out in stock markets;[25] 'noise trading'—when uninformed agents derail the operations of rational agents—sends the market in unstable directions. In conclusion, much of what is 'new' in contemporary behavioural finance can be found in Keynes's 'old' bottles.

The second line of research is in the area of reform of the institutions in charge of overseeing the international system of payments and taking action to smooth prices and output of those commodities which play a crucial role in international trade.

Two issues preoccupied Keynes throughout the whole of his theoretical and practical activity: monetary reform and the stabilization of commodity prices. This can be appreciated if we take into account the unpublished material, at the level not only of theoretical reflection but also of Keynes's concrete experience as a speculator, mainly on the futures markets for raw materials and money.[26]

Keynes's conviction was that there are strong links between fluctuations in prices of primary commodities and agricultural products on the one hand, and financial crisis and structural trade imbalances on the other. He held that in the absence of buffer stocks for commodities, and with insurance against price volatility based only on market mechanisms, the system is doomed to instability and any policies aiming at stabilizing commodity and currency prices must go hand in hand with reform of the international monetary system.

While it appears that some of the ideas prevailing before the crisis, namely that financial markets should be deregulated, that private ownership yields more efficient results, that governments should balance their budgets, and that central banks should only aim at price stability, are losing ground, the demand for a new set of rules to govern international trade, currency, and financial markets is not satisfactorily catered for. The suggestion here is to take a fresh look at Keynes's wide range of proposals (searching through his less known writings) and not to make do with simple-minded so-called Keynesian policy. The risk is that 'hydraulic' Keynesianism—'stop and go' policies—may again take the lead, losing track of the theoretical basis that supports them, and again squandering the opportunity to exploit to the full the richness of Keynes's thought.

* * *

According to Wolf (2008), there are 'three broad' lessons to be derived from Keynes's teaching. The first is to discard the notion of 'efficient markets' and to endorse the notion of uncertainty; the second is to accept that the economy cannot be analysed or managed in the same way as an individual business; the third is to disown the belief that individual self-seeking behaviour guarantees a stable economic order.

Will these lessons find their way back into the corpus of economic teaching and research agenda?

The boost to aggregate demand through government expenditure and injection of liquidity into the system to fight depressions and off-set credit crunches are policy recipes also invoked by people of non-Keynesian persuasion, whose searches for alternatives to mainstream economics look in different directions. Thus, a new research agenda is needed to provide food for thought to those sceptics who doubt the utility of Keynes's ideas in rebuilding an alternative paradigm, and also to admirers who have little and narrow acquaintance with Keynes's writings.

While 'the return to Keynes' wind is certainly to be welcomed, it may not outlive the present crisis. Scholars and admirers of Keynes may fail to persuade sceptics and opponents, and there is no telling whether a new generation of economists will take today's lesson to heart. The hope is that Max Planck's *dictum* (1950: 33) quoted in Kirman (2009) applies not only to a 'new' but also to an 'old' theory: 'a new scientific truth does not triumph by convincing its opponents and making them see the light, but rather because its opponents eventually die, and a new generation grows up that is familiar with it'.

NOTES

1. See the manifesto available at http://www.cato.org/special/stimulus09/cato_stimulus.pdf. This url was last accessed on 21 September 2012.

2. Among them C. Goodhart, M. Desai, J. Vickers, D. Newbery, H. Pesaran, K. Rogoff, and T. Sargent.

3. *Sunday Times* (2010).

4. Among them M. Miller, V. Chick, P. De Grauwe, B. DeLong, S. Dow, J.P. Fitoussi, G.C. Harcourt, A. Kirman, R. Rowthorn, M. Sawyer.

5. Among them D. Hendry, A. Blinder, R. Solow, D. Vines.

6. A copy of the letter is available at http://www.ft.com/intl/cms/s/0/75b2481e-1cb5-11df-8d8e-00144feab49a.html. This url was last accessed on 21 September 2012.

7. A copy of the letter is available at http://www.ft.com/intl/cms/s/0/7 beb9b0e-1cdd-11df-8d8e-00144feab49a.html. This url was last accessed on 21 September 2012.

8. For instance, it is acknowledged that the present situation of Britain, Greece, Spain (in 2010 running a deficit of over 13 per cent and 11 per cent. respectively), Ireland, Portugal, and Italy (with figures of over 12 per cent, 8 per cent, and 5 per cent) may stand in the way when invoking public expenditure to sustain aggregate demand.

9. In December 2009, Spanish unemployment rose to 19.3 per cent (the highest in more than a decade), the nation's jobless rate soaring to twice the Eurozone average. Unemployment in Greece reached 9.8 per cent in October 2009. See http://www.banknoise.com/en/2009/12/la-disoccupazione-in-italia-confrontata-con-gli-altri-paesi-europei-usa-e-giappone.html.

10. The countries within the European Union have agreed to a 'Stability and Growth Pact' (SGP), which arbitrarily limits national government deficit spending to 3 per cent of gross domestic product (GDP), whilst limiting overall public debt as a percentage to GDP of 60 per cent.

11. The contemporary 'austerity debate' is summarized in the *Financial Times*, 18 July 2010. This article is available at http://www.ft.com/intl/cms/s/0/dc3ac844-9010-11df-91b6-00144feab49a.html. This url was last accessed on 21 September 2012.

12. A recent study relative to 30 countries concluded that 'there is mixed evidence on the effectiveness of fiscal stimulus packages in generating employment gains in a recession' (Jha 2009: 25).

13. "'Loan expenditure" is a convenient expression for the net borrowing of public authorities on all account, whether on capital account or to meet a budgetary deficit. The one form of loan expenditure operates by increasing investment and the other by increasing the propensity to consume' (CWK VII: 128n).

14. In Minsky's words, 'the intrinsically irrational fact of uncertainty is needed if financial instability is to be understood' (1982: 120).

15. According to Roncaglia (2009: p. 496n18), the distinction between risk (cases involving quantitative probabilities) and uncertainty (cases in which probabilities are non-measurable) is to be found in Knight rather than in Keynes.

16. According to Bordo et al. (2001), between 1945 and 1971 the world experienced only 38 financial crises, while from 1973 to 1997 it went through 139 such crises.

17. The NK model, 'which has largely replaced the IS-LM model as the basic model of fluctuations in graduate courses' (Blanchard 2008: 10) is made up of three equations. Aggregate demand, derived from maximization condition of consumers, is set equal to consumption (no investment) and made a function of interest rate and future expected consumption. The price equation gives inflation as a function of expected inflation and of the output gap, that is, the actual output minus what output would be absent nominal rigidities. The third is a reaction function—Taylor's rule—giving the real interest rate chosen by the central bank as a function of inflation and the output gap.

18. Colander et al. (2009). Available at http://www.debtdeflation.com/blogs/
wpcontent/uploads/papers/Dahlem_Report_EconCrisis021809.pdf.

19. The names mentioned in the Report are Walter Bagehot, Axel Leijohnufvud,
Charles Kindleberger, and Hyman Minsky.

20. 'Both the New Classical and New Keynesian complete markets macroeco-
nomic theories not only did not allow questions about insolvency and illiquidity
to be *answered*. They did not allow such questions to be *asked*.' in Buiter (2009).
Available at http://blogs.ft.com/maverecon/2009/03/the-unfortunate-uselessness-
of-most-state-of-the-art-academic-monetary-economics/.

21. Posner (2009).

22. Mankiw (2008).

23. Becker (2009).

24. See Wray's nice description of the 'message':

> Entrepreneurs produce what they expect to sell, and there is no reason to pre-
> sume that the sum of these production decisions is consistent with the full-
> employment level of output, either in the short run or in the long run. Moreover,
> this proposition holds regardless of market structure—even where competition
> is perfect and wages are flexible. It holds even if expectations are always fulfilled,
> and in a stable economic environment. In other words, Keynes did not rely on
> sticky wages, monopoly power, disappointed expectations, or economic insta-
> bility to explain unemployment. While each of these conditions could certainly
> make matters worse, he wanted to explain the possibility of equilibrium with
> unemployment. (Wray 2007: 3)

25. 'In the short run one does not win by picking the company most likely
to succeed in the long run, but by picking the company most likely to have high
market value in the short run' (Akerlof and Shiller 2009: 133).

26. A preliminary inquiry can be found in Fantacci et al. (2012) and in
Fantacci et al. (2010).

REFERENCES

Akerlof, G. and R. Shiller. 2009. *Animal Spirits. How Human Psychology Drives
the Economy, and Why It Matters for Global Capitalism*. Princeton: Princeton
University Press.

Barba, A. and M. Pivetti. 2009. 'Rising Household Debt: Its Causes and Macro-
economic Implications—A Long-Period Analysis', *Cambridge Journal of
Economics*, 33(1): 113–37.

Becker G. 2009. 'How to Increase Employment'. Available at http://www.becker-
posner-blog.com/2009/11/how-to-increase-employment-becker.html. This url
was last accessed on 29 November 2009.

Blanchard, O. 2008. 'The State of Macro', Working Paper 08–17. Cambridge: MIT
Press.

Bordo, M., B. Eichengreen, D. Klingsbiel, and M. Martinez-Peria. 2001. 'Is the
Crisis Problem Growing More Severe?', *Economic Policy*, 16(32): 51–82.

Bresser-Pereira, L.C. 2009. 'The Global Financial Crisis and After: A New Capitalism?' Working Paper 240. São Paulo, Brazil: Escola De Economia De São Paulo da Fundação Getulio Vargas.

Brittan, S. 2010. 'The Impoverished Fiscal Debate', *Financial Times*, 8 October. A copy of the letter is available at http://www.ft.com/intl/cms/s/0/f31f0188-d241-11df-8fbe-00144feabdc0.html#axzz276Np71sF.

Buiter, W. 2009. 'The Unfortunate Uselessness of Most "State of the Art" Academic Monetary Economics', *Financial Times*, 3 March.

Colander, D., H. Föllmer, A. Haas, M. Goldberg, K. Juselius, A. Kirman, T. Lux, and B. Sloth. 2009. 'The Financial Crisis and the Systemic Failure of Academic Economics'. Report of the 98th Dahlem Workshop, 2008.

De Cecco, M. 2010. 'Keynes and Modern International Finance Theory', in B.W. Bateman, T. Hirai, and M.C. Marcuzzo (eds), *The Return to Keynes*. Cambridge: Harvard University Press, pp. 225–40.

De Grauwe, P. 2010. 'The Return of Keynes', *International Finance*, 13(1): 157–63.

Fantacci, L., M.C. Marcuzzo, A. Rosselli, and E. Sanfilippo. 2012. 'Speculation and Buffer Stocks: The Legacy of Keynes and Kahn', *European Journal for the History of Economic Thought*, 19(3): 453–73.

Fantacci, L., M.C. Marcuzzo, and E. Sanfilippo. 2010. 'Speculation in Commodities: Keynes's Practical Acquaintance with Future Markets', *Journal for the History of Economic Thought*, 32(3): 397–418.

Jha, V. 2009. 'The Effects of Fiscal Stimulus Packages on Employment', Employment Working Paper No. 34. Geneva: ILO.

Keynes, J.M. 1971–89. *The Collected Writings of John Maynard Keynes* (CWK), edited by D.E. Moggridge, 30 vols. London: Macmillan; volumes are identified as CWK followed by volume number in Roman numerals.
  CWK VII. *The General Theory of Employment, Interest and Money.*
  CWK VIII. *A Treatise on Probability.*
  CWK IX. *Essays in Persuasion.*
  CWK XIV. *The General Theory and After*. Vol. 2: *Defence and Development.*
  CWK XXVII. *Activities 1940–1946. Shaping the Post-War World. Employment and Commodities.*

Kirman, A. 2009. 'Economic Theory and the Crisis', VoxEU.org, 14 November, available online: http://www.voxeu.org/article/economic-theory-and-crisis. This url was last accessed on 27 April 2012.

Kregel, J.A. 2010. 'Keynes's Influence on Modern Economics: Some Overlooked Contributions of Keynes's Theory of Finance and Economic Policy', in B.W. Bateman, T. Hirai, and M.C. Marcuzzo (eds), *The Return to Keynes*. Cambridge: Harvard University Press, pp. 241–56.

Krugman, P. 2010. 'The Strange Death of Fiscal Policy', *New York Times*, 3 November. A copy of the article is available at http://krugman.blogs.nytimes.com/2010/11/03/the-strange-death-of-fiscal-policy/.

Lawson, T. 1985. 'Uncertainty and Economic Analysis', *The Economic Journal*, 95(380): 909–27.

Mankiw, N.G. 2008. 'What Would Keynes Have Done?', *The New York Times*, 28 November. Available at http://www.nytimes.com/2008/11/30/business/economy/30view.html?_r=1. This url was last accessed on 21 September 2012.

Marcuzzo, M.C. 2011. 'Reason and Reasonableness in Keynes. Rereading *The Economic Consequences of the Peace*', in A. Arnon, J. Weinblatt, and W. Young (eds), *Perspectives on Keynesian Economics*. Berlin: Springer, pp. 35–52.

Minsky, H. 1982. 'Financial Instability Revisited', in *Inflation, Recession and Economic Policy*. Armonk: Wheatsheaf Books, pp. 117–61.

Planck, M. 1950. *Scientific Autobiography, and Other Papers*. (English translation by F. Gaynor.) London: Williams and Norgate.

Posner, R.A. 2009. 'How I Became a Keynesian: Second Thoughts in the Middle of a Crisis', *The New Republic*, 23 September. Available at http://www.tnr.com/article/how-i-became-keynesian. This url was last accessed on 21 September 2012.

Roncaglia, A. 2009. 'Keynes and Probability: An Assessment', *European Journal of the History of Economic Thought*, 16(3): 489–510.

Skidelsky, R. 2009. *The Return of the Master*. London: Allen Lane.

Sunday Times. 2010. 'UK Economy Cries Out for Credible Rescue Plan', 14 February, p. 26.

Svetlova, E. and M. Fiedler. 2011. 'Understanding Crisis: On the Meaning of Uncertainty and Probability', in O. Dejuán, E. Febrero, and M.C. Marcuzzo (eds), *The First Great Recession of the 21st Century: Competing Explanations*. Cheltenham: Edward Elgar, pp. 42–62.

Wolf, M. 2008. 'Keynes Offers Us the Best Way to Think about the Financial Crisis', *Financial Times*, 23 December. Available at http://www.ft.com/intl/cms/s/0/be2dbf2cd113-11dd-8cc3-000077b07658.html

Wray, R.L. 2007. 'The Continuing Legacy of John Maynard Keynes', Levy Economics Institute Working Paper 514. Annandale-on-Hudson, NY: Levy Economics Institute of Bard College.

2

The Dog Called Investment

ROGER E. BACKHOUSE AND BRADLEY W. BATEMAN

James Meade (1975: 82, 1988: 343), a member of the younger gen-
eration who helped bring about the 'Keynesian Revolution', summed
up that revolution with a familiar metaphor: 'Keynes' intellectual
revolution was to shift economists from thinking normally in terms
of a model of reality in which a dog called *savings* wagged his tail
labelled *investment* to thinking in terms of a model in which a dog
called *investment* wagged his tail labelled *savings*.'

This was, Meade claimed, the Keynesian Revolution in economic
theory. He went on to argue that it was a short step from this to
recognition that investment was not the only injection into the
income-generating cycle and that savings were not the only leakage.
The Keynesian Revolution in economic policy could then be said to
have centred on the inference that governments could and should sta-
bilize the level of aggregate demand through adjusting leakages and
injections (Meade 1988: 348). If the only significance of consumption
and investment is their role in determining aggregate demand, all
leakages and injections have equal status in making economic policy,
which means that investment loses its unique status.

After the financial crisis, it is important to draw attention to the dis-
tinction between consumption and investment. It is once again being
argued that we cannot afford to undertake stabilization policy, even
when confronted with falling aggregate demand and rising unem-
ployment because government deficits are creating a burden that will

rest on future generations. However, this critique of Keynesian policy rests on ignoring the crucial difference between consumption and investment, namely that investment creates assets that can compensate for, if not outweigh, the costs of any debt created in the process of building it up. Thus, if we were, today, to follow the type of policy Keynes himself advocated, building up assets for the future rather than a 'Keynesian' stimulation of current spending, the argument about debt being a burden on future generations would not have any credence. In addition, when we look at Keynes's attitude towards government investment, we find that he was motivated, in large part, by a concern not to frighten the markets, something that has enormous resonance today. His solutions, a capital budget and organizing public investment so as to buttress the confidence of private investors, might not work today, for the world has changed, but given the need for new ideas, they are worth re-examining.

Our contention is that Keynes never reduced the dog called investment to the same status as other leakages and injections. He did not make the jump to seeing investment as merely one among several injections into the circular flow of income but continued to view it as being uniquely important. He always believed that there was a need for higher investment: even during the Great Depression, when much productive capacity was lying idle, investment needed to be increased. The importance of a high level of investment was made especially clear at the end of *The General Theory*, where, in working out the social philosophy towards which his work might lead, he explored the implications of a world where capital was no longer scarce.

Keynes (CWK VII: 372) opened the final chapter of *The General Theory*, Chapter 24, with a statement that whilst the relevance of his theory to society's failure to achieve full employment was obvious, the theory was also relevant to the problem of income distribution. It was, he argued, common to defend an unequal distribution of income on the grounds that it encouraged saving and hence capital accumulation. However, his theory led to the conclusion that 'in contemporary conditions the growth of wealth, so far from being dependent on the abstinence of the rich, as is commonly supposed, is more likely to be impeded by it' (Ibid.: VII: 373). There was, therefore, no case for an unequal distribution of income. He then went on to argue that the rate of interest should be kept low to stimulate enough employment to

generate full employment. If that were achieved, because the demand for capital was strictly limited, it would be possible to achieve a position where capital was no longer scarce and the return on capital covered simply depreciation and compensation for risk-taking. Because the capitalist would no longer be able to 'exploit the scarcity value of capital' this would mean the 'euthanasia of the rentier' (CWK VII: 376). Keynes's belief was that 'a somewhat comprehensive socialisation of investment' might be necessary to ensure full employment, but that, beyond that there was no case for 'State Socialism'. In other words, capitalism had one defect, which could be controlled by state control over the level of investment, but apart from that, individualism, with all its advantages, could prevail.

Thus, contrary to the received view of what constitutes 'Keynesian' economic policy, Keynes generally did not advocate using consumption (private or public) to stabilize demand, but argued that it was investment that needed to be stabilized at an appropriate level. He was not entirely consistent in this, for some of his statements about public works spending (such as burying banknotes in the ground so that there would be work to be done digging them up) did focus purely on aggregate demand, but he never abandoned his concern with investment. If the government did have to run a deficit in order to finance public investment (for example, building infrastructure), it should be on capital account, with the current account remaining in balance. He was thus not a 'deficit spender' as the term has come to be understood.

These issues have not always been neglected. Keynes's focus on the importance of increasing and stabilizing investment to the functioning of capitalism surfaced in a debate which took place in the early 1990s between Patinkin (1990, 1993) and Meltzer (1988, 1992). Though their main concern was with the interpretation of Keynes, which may account for why it is not better known, its focus on the role of investment makes it highly relevant for discussions of economic policy. Patinkin, whose *Money, Interest and Prices* (1956) had virtually defined the theoretical basis for the 'neo-classical synthesis', and which was the dominant graduate macro textbook for a generation, opened the debate with his Keynes Lecture 'On Different Interpretations of the General Theory' (1990). This was taken up by Meltzer (1992) who, together with Karl Brunner, is usually accredited with coining the term 'monetarism', and whose recently published *Keynes's Monetary Theory: A Different Interpretation* (1988) had been

sharply criticized in Patinkin's article. In his book, Meltzer argued that Keynes's central message in *The General Theory* had been that the main cause of unemployment in capitalist economies is low levels of investment.

A central plank of Patinkin's criticism of Meltzer was that '*The General Theory* was written at a time not only of idle men, but of idle factories; so it is surely far-fetched to think that a major concern of Keynes' [sic] at that time was to increase capital investment in order to further increase the stock of idle plant and equipment' (1990: 226). Meltzer had argued that Keynes's primary argument about macroeconomic policy in *The General Theory* had been the need to use it for stabilizing (and increasing) private investment to stimulate growth. Patinkin's argument against Meltzer, on the other hand, was that it is government expenditure, not private investment, which matters in stabilizing the economy and ensuring growth.

Delving into this disagreement between Meltzer and Patinkin further illustrates Meade's original point about the importance of the 'dog named investment'. Drawing on an unpublished report by Keynes, written for N.V. Philips, the Dutch electric appliance maker, in May 1930, when it was clear that unemployment *and* excess capacity were rising, we show that Keynes argued for exactly the position that Patinkin claims he could not possibly have meant; namely that increases in investment, despite idle capacity, are exactly what would help bring about recovery. The way Keynes framed his statement also contradicts Patinkin's claim that Keynes's final chapter (on the social philosophy towards with *The General Theory* might lead) is not important in understanding the rest of the book. Patinkin denied that this chapter shows that Keynes thought that stabilization of private investment was more important to long-term prosperity than activist fiscal policy; but Keynes's report of May 1930 shows that, just as he was beginning the work that would eventually become *The General Theory*, he was, in fact, thinking much more about the importance of stabilizing investment than he was about activist fiscal policy. This is not a new claim (Clarke 1988; Bateman 1996, 2006), but his 1930 report lends further credence to the arguments that, while Keynes saw the potential for public works projects to help stimulate and stabilize private investment, he was *not* an advocate of activist fiscal policy as the term is commonly understood. Management of investment, not consumption, was the key.

THE DEBATE BETWEEN PATINKIN AND MELTZER

Patinkin's interpretation of Keynes was based on identifying what he called his 'central message'. Following his own injunction that one should be guided by an author's intention, as revealed in what he wrote, Patinkin looked at the text of *The General Theory*, augmented by correspondence and other writings, to identify this central message. Thus, Patinkin attached weight to the overall structure of *The General Theory*, to passages in which Keynes said that he was summarizing his main ideas, and to sentences where he stated what he considered to be novel in his work. If Keynes described something as a 'digression' or 'supplementary notes', then this was clear evidence that it was not part of the central message.

On the basis of such evidence, Patinkin (1990: 209–10) concluded that Keynes's central theoretical message was three-fold. (1) The level of aggregate demand (determined by the marginal propensity to consume, the marginal efficiency of investment, and liquidity preference) need not be equal to aggregate supply. (2) Saving and investment were brought into equality by variations in output, not changes in the rate of interest. (3) Because it might create perverse expectations, a fall in money wages would leave the level of aggregate demand unchanged. *The General Theory*'s main policy conclusion followed directly: there was no reason to believe that either wage policy or open-market monetary policy could, unaided, achieve continuous full employment. Patinkin's description of Keynes's main policy message continued:

> Consequently government must take 'an ever greater responsibility for organising investment' (*The General Theory* [CWK VII: 164; see also p. 378]) in order to assure that total expenditures on investment in the economy—augmented by the multiplier effect—will supplement expenditures on consumption to the extent necessary to bring aggregate demand to its full employment level. (Patinkin 1990: 210)

In this passage it is worth noting that the statement that government had to organize investment comprises Keynes's own words, but Patinkin constructed an interpretation of their meaning that is dependent upon what he took to constitute Keynes's central message. The important point about this interpretation of Keynes is that, on Patinkin's reading, investment is fulfilling a role that could, as Meade

argued in the quotation with which this essay started, equally be taken by government consumption or any other type of autonomous expenditure. This is the basis for the Keynesianism of Abba Lerner (1944) or Alvin Hansen (1953) which focused entirely on aggregate demand and the use of deficit financing to stabilize the economy at full employment, paying scant attention to investment and capital accumulation.

Meltzer, both in his book and in his subsequent comment on Patinkin, can be seen as trying to rescue Keynes from the Keynesians, making him an advocate of something other than an argument that can be read as an apology for constantly expanding the public sector in the face of poor economic performance. This explains why he argued that Keynes was more sympathetic towards rule-governed policies than Patinkin had admitted, for this undermined the connection between Keynes and discretionary management of the economy. However, for our purpose, what is more significant is his argument that Keynes attached great importance to raising the capital stock (Meltzer 1988, 1992; cf. Patinkin 1990: 225). A major part of Meltzer's evidence was his claim that Keynes's views on many subjects changed little between the 1920s and *The General Theory*.

> Keynes's broad policy views, particularly the state's role as manager or director of state investment, his support for managed capitalism as opposed to laissez-faire, his insistence on the importance of avoiding variability and instability, and others that a reader can find in Meltzer (1988, chapter 2). These views are traced, in part, to Keynes's philosophy of government and his beliefs about the role of intellectuals like himself in leading society. A finding that a position is consistent with his basic philosophy and restates an earlier position is, I believe, evidence about an author's commitment to that position. *On that basis, I concluded that Chapter 24 is the policy conclusion of the book of which it is a part, and therefore important for interpretation, whereas Patinkin believes that the chapter 'could have been omitted without affecting its* [the book's] *central message'.* (Meltzer 1992: 153) [emphasis added]

Chapter 24 of *The General Theory* comes in Book VI, 'Short Notes Suggested by the General Theory', and is entitled 'Concluding Notes on the Social Philosophy towards which the General Theory Might Lead'. Meltzer claims that this chapter is central to understanding the

book's message for economic policy, whereas Patinkin argues that it is not.

Setting aside their disagreement over rules versus discretion, the key difference between Patinkin and Meltzer concerns Keynes's attitude towards investment. Meltzer used Chapter 24 to argue that Keynes's central concern was for increasing investment so that society achieves its optimal capital stock (where the return, after allowing for necessary expenses such as depreciation, is zero). In contrast, Patinkin took Keynes's central concern what eventually became the standard Keynesian position on macroeconomic policy: that what mattered during times of high unemployment was to raise aggregate demand, and this could be achieved by raising consumption as well as by raising investment.

As has been mentioned already, an important part of Patinkin's argument was that the discussion of reducing the rate of interest to zero came in a chapter that was described as a supplementary note, not part of the main text. However, he also offered an argument that, in the Great Depression, where there was surplus capital as well as unemployment, it would not have made sense for Keynes to have attached importance to increasing the capital stock. The paragraph merits quoting in full.

> That here and in other writings Keynes considered it desirable to increase the stock of capital is a point of Meltzer's (1988: 186) that is well taken. But to contend that this was a major theme of the *General Theory* is to tear this book out of the historical context in which it was written, and to tear Chapter 24 out of its context in the book. For the *General Theory* was written at a time not only of idle men, but of idle factories; so it is surely far-fetched to think that a major concern of Keynes' at that time was to increase capital investment in order to further increase the stock of idle plant and equipment. Instead the crucial role of investment expenditures was to supplement consumption expenditures in order (with the help of the multiplier) to raise aggregate demand to its full employment level. In brief, the passage in Chapter 24...has to do not with the major role of investment in the *General Theory*, but with its role (incidental to the central message of the book) in ultimately bringing about Keynes's version and vision of the classical stationary state. (Patinkin 1990: 226)

Patinkin here uses the argument that because there was idle capital, it would be 'far-fetched' to think that Keynes wanted to increase the capital stock, and therefore it cannot have mattered to Keynes

whether the additional spending needed to achieve full employment took the form of investment or, say, government consumption.

ON INVESTING DURING A DEPRESSION: KEYNES'S UNPUBLISHED REPORTS FOR N.V. PHILIPS

During this period, Keynes acted as an adviser to the Dutch company N.V. Philips, sending them monthly reports on the economic situation. On 24 June 1930, H. du Pré wrote to Keynes, making the point that, given the level of excess capacity, raising investment will exacerbate the problem of excess capacity, asking him to respond to this in his next letter.

> These last months many articles in the economic press, analysing the position, consider that the world is suffering—amongst others—from an excess of productive capacity in many trades; in other words that the world has first to grow into a productive apparatus which is too big for immediate needs. If this should be true, can a renewed investment-activity soon be hoped for, and if it soon comes, would it really do good? Of course there would be less unemployment in a number of industries; but would not prices for consumptive commodities, and so cost of living rise? And especially it might turn out after some time, that the new activity has only added to the—supposed—actual over-investment, so that the disequilibrium would only be greater. It may of course be that entirely new industries are going to take the lead, but we do not yet see any that they are very likely to do so.
>
> We should be much obliged if you would solve this puzzle for us or at least give your views on the pretended overcapacity and its probable effects on future developments in your next letter. (Keynes Papers, File BM5)

This letter has been quoted at length, because it shows that Keynes in the letter which follows was responding to exactly the argument that Patinkin made: that in a condition of unused capital, to increase investment would be counter-productive.

In his reply, his 'July letter', hand-dated 11 July 1930, Keynes started by explaining why the timing of any recovery was difficult to forecast, before turning to the question of investment.

> In previous letters I have emphasized the point that recovery will probably have to be preceded by a substantial fall in the long-period rate of interest and a strong bond market, leading in due course to the recovery of investment. But perhaps I should explain that I mean in

this connection, by a recovery of investment, not primarily investment in manufacturing industry, the world's capacity for which is probably quite ample for the present, but mainly in building, transport, and public utilities. Indeed, the capital requirements of industry are never, even at the best of times, of more than trifling amount compared with world savings. For example, in Great Britain to-day the maximum estimates made by anyone as to the total costs of rationalising British manufactured plant and bringing it thoroughly up to date would not use up the country's savings for more than, say, three months. Moreover, when expected profits are satisfactory the rate of expenditure by manufacturing industry in fixed plant is not very sensitive to the rate of interest.

On the other hand, the borrowing requirements for building, transport, and public utilities are not only on a far greater scale, but are decidedly sensitive to the rate of interest. If I were asked to put my finger on the prime trouble to-day, I should call attention to the very high rate of interest for long-term borrowers. Although the world is better equipped than it was before the war, the long-term rate of interest is higher today than it has been in time of peace for a long time past. When, at the same time, there is a big business depression and prices are falling, it is not surprising that new enterprise is kept back at the present level of interest. It may be that a very substantial fall will be required before enterprise revives. If so, this goes to confirm the view that some time may elapse before a recovery sets in. (Keynes Papers, File BM5)

The significance of this passage is that, although it echoes what Keynes was saying elsewhere (for example, in *Can Lloyd George Do It?*, CWK IX [1929]: 86–125, or his Harris Lectures in Chicago in June 1931, CWK XX: 343–67), he was responding specifically to the question of whether there is any scope for useful investment during recovery. His argument here is that though business may not need further investment, business investment is only a small proportion of total investment even in the best of times, and there is still a need for investment in what could be called infrastructure. The problem was a high long-term interest rate (the reference to falling prices suggests he is thinking of a high real rate) and that investment in building, transport, and public utilities was being held back.

KEYNES'S POLICY PRESCRIPTIONS

The central policy prescription Keynes drew from his *General Theory* was that governments should raise and stabilize the level of investment. To complete our argument about the importance he attached to

investment, it is necessary to step back to consider the theoretical basis that he offered for this prescription and to examine what he said about economic policy following the book's publication.

The reason for Keynes's belief that the remedy for mass unemployment was to raise and stabilize the level of investment is not far to seek: the deleterious effect of uncertainty. Keynes identifies two fundamental problems caused by uncertainty: it causes capitalists to pull back on their investment plans and it causes portfolio managers to drive up interest rates. As regards interest rates, Keynes argued that portfolio managers who are facing an uncertain future are likely to demand to hold much of their funds as cash; cash provides them with a hedge against the future, as well as with the ability to act quickly should the outlook suddenly improve. They would invest in bonds only if they were offered a high interest rate as compensation for their loss of liquidity.

The offshoot of Keynes's concern with the effects of uncertainty on interest rates was his focus on monetary policy in *The General Theory*. For those whose knowledge of Keynes comes only from macroeconomics textbooks, the very idea that Keynes was concerned with monetary policy does not make sense, for several generations of economists have embraced the canard that *The General Theory* is about fiscal policy, rather than monetary policy. However, *The General Theory* says more about monetary policy than fiscal policy. Keynes argued repeatedly in the book that monetary authorities need to keep interest rates low to maintain high levels of investment. Because he had overseen the portfolio management of a large insurance company, Keynes knew the bond markets well. His argument for keeping interest rates low hinged on his experience as a buyer and seller of bonds: if the Treasury could effectively manage expectations of future interest rates through auctions and re-financings, it could keep interest rates low.

Keynes had seen careful monetary management of interest rate expectations, of precisely the type that he was recommending, after Britain left the Gold Standard in 1931. Prior to leaving the Gold Standard, Britain had been forced to use interest rates to sustain the value of sterling against other currencies; but after leaving the Gold Standard, interest rates were free to fluctuate in the free market. Keynes realized, however, that the authorities still had the ability to influence their level through sales and re-financings of bonds. He wrote widely

about what he saw happening in the bond markets and he captured this in his theoretical work in *The General Theory* (Bateman 1996).

Keynes had a similar hope for the government's ability to influence private investment, although he realized that influencing investment would be more difficult than influencing interest rates. As indicated earlier, Keynes was not interested in nationalizing companies or in government ownership of the means of production. Instead, he hoped to stabilize private investment by using government investment as a counterweight for swings in private investment. Moreover, this would not merely stabilize investment: it could increase it, for if private investors came to trust that the government would increase its investment in new roads, new ports, and other kinds of infrastructure when the economy began to slow, then their fears about the future would be assuaged. They would then be able to depend on a steadier stream of profits and hence would not cut back their own investment plans as drastically when economic growth began to slow. In Chapter 12 of *The General Theory* ('The State of Long-Term Expectation'), Keynes offered a well-articulated explanation of the instability of private investment in a capitalist economy; in Chapter 22 ('Notes on the Trade Cycle') he went on to argue that instability in private investment was the cause of the business cycle. Neither his explanation of why investment is unstable nor the fact that he saw that instability of investment as the cause of the business cycle are in doubt, for the chapters in which he makes these points are clear and widely known. The ambiguity comes in his final Chapter 24, the focus of the disagreement between Meltzer and Patinkin. Here Keynes made his widely discussed statement, cited earlier, about the need for the state to control the volume of investment, while simultaneously stating that he did not mean that the state should nationalize industries (that is, establish a form of state socialism).

As Meltzer suggested, however, it is important to look at the long arc of Keynes's ideas to understand his policy recommendations in *The General Theory*, for there is much about Keynes's policy ideas that remained consistent through the years. Two of the most important ideas that he developed in the 1920s and which he never abandoned are his arguments for reforming the way that the government presented its budget expenditures and the need for a national investment board. These two ideas help to explain how he understood the possibilities for influencing the volume of investment.

Before Keynes became actively interested in public works projects as a policy tool, he was interested in correcting what he believed to be a serious problem with the government budgeting process. The British government did not report a separate capital budget, as a corporation would do. Instead of keeping a capital budget to track the funds borrowed for investment and the collection of revenue from those investments that could be used to pay off the borrowed money, all the borrowing and all the revenue streams were reported in the annual ('ordinary') exchequer budget as expenditures and receipts. Keynes's view was that this distorted the regular budget and he argued for using a better budget process that would break out the capital budget from ordinary transactions.

Keynes's views on the organization of the government's budget are important for understanding his attitude to the use of public works projects. First, if his proposed accounting procedures were adopted, it would not be necessary to run a deficit in order to undertake public works projects, since public works projects could generate revenue streams to pay off the loans originally used to finance them. If the capital outlays and the revenue streams were all kept in the capital budget, there would be no deficit in the Exchequer (ordinary or current account) budget. Keynes still adhered to this position in the 1940s when, in a memorandum he prepared for the Treasury on the National Debt Enquiry (CWK XXVII [1945]: 405–13), he wrote: 'It is important to emphasize that it is not part of the purpose of Exchequer or the Public Capital Budget to facilitate deficit financing, as I understand the term' (Ibid.: 406).

There is a second reason why Keynes's views on the reporting of the budget are important for understanding his suggestions on the use of public works projects. Because the British government was not using a capital budget at that time, it set aside a part of its revenue stream each year in a 'sinking fund' that would eventually be used to retire a tranche of bonds. Keynes often argued for using this sinking fund to pay for public works. For instance, in the book he wrote with Hubert Henderson for the 1929 General Election campaign, *Can Lloyd George Do It?*, (CWK IX: 86–125), they proposed that contributions to the sinking fund be suspended for two years and that the proceeds be used to pay for £250 million of public works projects. This approach to public works allowed for the projects to be undertaken without running a deficit on the 'ordinary' budget. Likewise, the money spent on the public works would not be lost permanently

from the sinking fund because it was being spent on building assets that generated revenue streams for the Treasury. There would be no increase in future tax burdens.

One problem with using public investment to manage the economy, often raised by the Treasury, was the difficulty in undertaking public works projects sufficiently quickly. Keynes's remedy for this came in his recommendations, also mooted in the 1920s, that there be a national investment board (see Bateman 1996). Such a body would keep fully developed plans on hand for repairing roads and bridges, building airports, or developing other infrastructure. In modern parlance, the board would have 'shovel ready' projects on the shelf, with rates of return on each project carefully calculated beforehand. When there was a slowdown of growth or a pause in the economy, the government could quickly roll out those projects that offered the best returns on investment, financing them from the sinking fund.

Keynes did not write publicly about the problems of trying to use changes in consumption to stimulate the economy, although he did have an important exchange with James Meade about this issue during the Second World War. Meade, who was also working in the Treasury, proposed using countercyclical changes in social security taxes to stabilize the level of output. Keynes objected strongly that consumption was not as flexible as Meade supposed and that this would make his favoured scheme less effective than Meade imagined it would be.

> I have much less confidence than you have in off-setting proposals which aim at short period changes in consumption. I agree with Henderson that one has to pay attention to securing the right long-period trend in the propensity to consume. But the amount one can do in the short period is likely to be meagre. I think that it may be a tactical error to stress so much an unorthodox method, very difficult to put over, if in addition to its unpopularity, it is not very likely to be efficacious. (CWK XXVII: 326)

This followed from Keynes's idea that consumption was a fairly stable part of aggregate demand, for complex social psychological reasons. But in any case, he never shared with Meade, or other Keynesians, the idea that all leakages and injections were equally useful in stabilizing the economy. For Keynes, investment was the problem that caused the instability of capitalism and it was, likewise, the cure for the problem.

* * *

It is well known that *The General Theory* placed great emphasis on investment. He presented his difference from what he chose to call the 'classical' theory as resting on the principle of effective demand. Whilst the propensity to consume was obviously very important, the reason was that the multiplier connected the level of aggregate demand to the level of investment, not because he believed that changes in consumption were a likely lever for stabilizing the economy. Effective demand was unstable primarily because investment was unstable for reasons he explained in his famous Chapter 12, on 'The State of Long-Term Expectation', and which he reiterated in his summary of *The General Theory of Employment*, (CWK XIV: 109–23). Clearly the propensity to consume could change—it depended on both 'objective' and 'subjective' factors—but it was clear that investment was crucial. As Meade put it, the dog called investment wagged a tail called savings: investment varied for reasons that to a great extent depended on non-economic factors and, through the multiplier, savings adjusted, along with the level of output, to accommodate. This provides an important reason why, in his policy prescriptions, he focused on stabilizing investment.

If this were the only reason why Keynes believed that investment was important, Meade, Patinkin, and other post-war Keynesians would have been justified in arguing that what mattered was not investment but autonomous expenditure. But this was not Keynes's view. His report to N.V. Philips shows that Patinkin was wrong in claiming that it was 'far-fetched' to think that Keynes could have thought it important to increase investment during the Depression, for this was precisely what Keynes had argued as the world was falling into depression in 1930. There might be no need for manufacturing investment but, as he argued in his report to du Pré, there was scope for raising investment outside manufacturing industry, and this required lower long-term rates of interest than were then being experienced. Thus, lowering the long-term rate of interest was central to his beliefs about how to cure the Depression. Fiscal policy could be part of the remedy, but it is consistent with this belief that Keynes repeatedly stressed public investment, not consumption. Fine tuning through varying level of consumption or short-term interest rates may have been the Keynesians' preferred policy, but it was not Keynes's own preference (cf. Clarke 1988; Bateman 1996, 2006). When others, such as Meade, proposed measures to use consumption as a stabilizer, Keynes was sceptical.

This emphasis on investment was also apparent in his proposals for organizing the budget. If the government's accounts were organized like the accounts of most businesses, so as to separate its capital from ordinary expenditures, investment projects would be part of the capital budget and so would not impinge on the deficit. In the long term investment would be self-financing.

Keynes no doubt emphasized investment because he believed that fluctuations in investment were the main problem. However, his policy prescriptions reflected the judgement that society needed capital accumulation. The vision of a future society that he sketched in Chapter 24 was one that he had held for many years, having previously been presented in 'Economic Possibilities for Our Grandchildren', CWK IX. This essay, based on a talk that was first given in 1928, and then published in 1930, just as the world was falling into the Great Depression, and in the same year that he wrote to du Pré about the need for more investment, held out a vision of a world in which the pursuit of wealth would become less important. The real economic problem was not, as Lionel Robbins (1932) was to argue two years later, that of scarcity, but 'how to use his freedom from pressing economic cares, how to occupy his leisure, which science and compound interest will have won for him, to live wisely and agreeably and well' (CWK IX: 328). In *The General Theory*, having found an explanation of why capitalist economies failed, and hence how the path of capital accumulation could be sustained, he was able to present this vision as something that might one day be achieved.

This vision of the future in which investment was crucial was also attractive to Keynes because it was consistent with leaving as much of economic activity as possible in the hands of individuals. Once the problem of the instability of investment was solved, 'the classical theory comes into its own again' (CWK VII: 378). Reductions in inequality and social change were to be achieved through the abundance that would be brought about through capital accumulation, removing the need for more socialistic methods, his chapter containing a defence of liberty with which even Friedrich Hayek would not have disagreed.

> Individualism, if it can be purged of its defects and its abuses, is the best safeguard of personal liberty in the sense that, compared with any other system, it greatly widens the field for the exercise of personal choice. It is also the best safeguard of the variety of life, which emerges

precisely from this extended field of personal choice, and the loss of which is the greatest of all the losses of the homogeneous or totalitarian state. (CWK VII: 380)

The fact that Keynes chose, at this point in *The General Theory*, to express such strongly held views is further evidence that this vision of the future was something to which he attached great importance. It was a vision to which a high-level investment, not simply a high level of aggregate demand, was important.

At a time when the role of fiscal policy is very much at the centre of debates about how best to manage the economy, Keynes's ideas have a renewed relevance. Both the advocates of traditional activist Keynesian policies and those who argue that to increase government spending is to create an intolerable burden of debt, miss the point of what Keynes said. Keynes did not propose using government consumption expenditure or tax-induced changes in private consumption to stabilize the economy. Indeed, he was generally opposed to this approach. He advocated stabilizing investment, both directly through government investment and indirectly through influencing the expectations that drove private investment, an approach that does not result in the creation of unsustainable deficits. Keynes was an opponent of 'deficit spending' as the term is normally used. What Meade called 'the dog called investment' did more than wag the tail called saving: it was the key both to explaining why capitalist economies could plunge into depression and, contrary to Meade's view, to the policies through which the problem of instability might be ameliorated. His belief in the importance of investment led Keynes to propose a set of policies to counter depression that are not even being seriously discussed in the contemporary debates about policy. These policies, the relevance of which should be enhanced by the widely perceived need to invest heavily in green energy, are almost as distinct from much post–Second World War Keynesianism as they are from the New Classical macroeconomics.

REFERENCES

Bateman, B.W. 1996. *Keynes's Uncertain Revolution*. Ann Arbor, MI: University of Michigan Press.

———. 2006. 'Keynes and Keynesianism', in R.E. Backhouse and B.W. Bateman (eds), *The Cambridge Companion to Keynes*. Cambridge: Cambridge University Press, pp. 271–90.

Clarke, P. 1988. *The Keynesian Revolution in the Making, 1924–1936*. Oxford: Clarendon Press.

Hansen, A. 1953. *A Guide to Keynes*. London: McGraw Hill.

Keynes, J.M. 1971–89. *The Collected Writings of John Maynard Keynes* (CWK), edited by D.E. Moggridge, 30 vols. London: Macmillan; volumes are identified as CWK followed by volume number in Roman numerals.

CWK VII. *The General Theory of Employment, Interest and Money*.

CWK IX. *Essays in Persuasion*.

CWK XIV. *The General Theory and After, Part 2: Defence and Development*.

CWK XX. *Activities, 1929–31: Rethinking Employment and Unemployment Policies*.

CWK XXVII. *Activities, 1940–6: Shaping the Post-War World: Employment and Commodities*.

Keynes Papers, Kings College Cambridge.

Lerner, A.P. 1944. *The Economics of Control*. New York: Macmillan.

Meade, J.E. 1975. 'The Keynesian Revolution', in M. Keynes (ed.), *Essays on John Maynard Keynes*, pp. 82–8. Cambridge: Cambridge University Press.

———. 1988. *The Collected Papers of James Meade*, edited by S. Howson, vol. I. London: Unwin Hyman.

Meltzer, A.H. 1988. *Keynes's Monetary Theory: A Different Interpretation*. Cambridge: Cambridge University Press.

———. 1992. 'Patinkin on Keynes and Meltzer', *Journal of Monetary Economics*, 29(1): 151–62.

Patinkin, Don. 1956. *Money, Interest and Prices*. New York: Harper & Row.

———. 1990. 'On Different Interpretations of the *General Theory*', *Journal of Monetary Economics*, 26(2): 205–43.

———. 1993. 'Meltzer on Keynes', *Journal of Monetary Economics*, 32(2): 347–56.

Robbins, L.C. 1932. *An Essay on the Nature and Significance of Economic Science*. London: Macmillan.

3

Keynes, Kalecki, and the Real World

JULIO LÓPEZ-GALLARDO*

Since the beginnings of our discipline an important debate has taken place among economists about whether or not capitalist economies are endowed with an endogenous full-employment mechanism. Keynes and Kalecki, the founding fathers of the principle of effective demand, rejected the mechanism envisioned by the economic orthodoxy, which relies on the notion that the wage fall caused by unemployment expands demand, thus reabsorbing any unemployment. Therefore, they proposed that fiscal and monetary policies could, and should be implemented to bring about full employment. Kalecki added to this the idea that redistribution from profits to wages would also stimulate demand.

This essay is an attempt to take the Keynes–Kalecki view of macro-economics to the data, using modern econometric techniques, in

* I want to thank Armando Sanchez and Luis Reyes Ortiz for allowing me to use results from our unpublished papers, and to Hiroshi Nishi, who kindly gave me access to his database to carry out my econometric work for Japan. Also, I want to express my deep gratitude to Elizabeth Martínez, Moises Anaya, and Sarai Nava for their excellent research assistance, and to the participants of the International Workshop held in Florence, 20–22 March 2012, and the editors of this volume for their comments on a previous version of this essay. Last, but not least, I acknowledge the financial support from UNAM, Universidad Nacional Autonoma de México: DGAP-Papiit, Proyecto IN-305812.

order to assess their empirical plausibility. I will explore here two issues that figure prominently in their theories. The first one concerns the effects of changes in income distribution on the level of output and employment. The second one is related to the ability of economic policies to exert a lasting influence on those same variables. It will be seen that, in all the countries I consider here, the empirical evidence is strongly in favour of Keynes's and Kalecki's hypotheses. On the one hand, fiscal and monetary policy influences effective demand, both in the short and in the long run. On the other hand, the shift from wages to profits, instead of stimulating demand and output as per the conventional view, depresses them both.

The present chapter is organized as follows. In the first place, it discusses and contrasts the views of the founding fathers of the principle of effective demand on the two previously mentioned issues. The emphasis is on the association between the wage share and aggregate demand, because this point is crucial to the debate on the self-regulating properties of a capitalist economy. The discussion about economic policy will be less detailed, though hopefully sufficient for the purposes of the present work.[1]

According to a certain legend, probably the fruit of misreading Joan Robinson's (1964, 1971) enthusiastic appraisal of Kalecki's work, the latter would have anticipated most of importance of what later Keynes wrote in his *The General Theory*. While I am also convinced of the enormous theoretical achievements of Kalecki, I do not share this legend. I rather think that the two authors indeed agreed on many issues, most conspicuously that demand, not supply, shapes the overall level of economic activity, and I also believe that Kalecki anticipated some, certainly not all, of the important ideas that later Keynes proposed.[2] However, in their formulation of the principle of effective demand, they emphasized different theoretical aspects, and they had also important disagreements. This is easy to understand once we take into account that the main objectives of their theoretical research, their cultural background and political attitude, and their overall vision of the most important features of the capitalist economy were all dissimilar. Accordingly, I want to show here that while Keynes and Kalecki had a parallel stance on the issues on which I focus in this chapter, they also differed in important points.

In the second part of this work I contrast Keynes's and Kalecki's hypotheses with the real world. Thus, I will present empirical results

dealing with the issues under consideration, coming from econometric research. In the past, the debate around these questions took place typically on an analytical basis, participants adducing mostly institutional reasons and logical arguments to support their positions. Nowadays, given the larger availability of information and our greater capacity to process it, we probably can do better than then. Besides that, I am convinced that the results of economic controversies cannot be ascertained solely with a-priori considerations, since in most cases they are dependent on the specific conditions of the economy. In other words, I claim that debate on these issues, and on economics in general, cannot advance much unless they have a solid empirical support.

This is why in the second part I put emphasis on the empirical side. I will consider the case of four of the largest European countries, namely, France, Germany, Spain, and the United Kingdom, and also of Japan and the US.[3] These results come from estimating different types of individual models for each one of the economies involved. By the way, readers will probably notice that in this part of the chapter I opted for a Kaleckian rather than Keynesian approach. Kalecki was convinced of the usefulness of econometrics, and in his *Theory of Economic Dynamics* (Kalecki 1991b) he actually tried to validate his theory estimating an econometric model for the US economy. Keynes was critical of the econometric approach, and he (Keynes 1939) harshly criticized Tinbergen when the latter carried out what were, probably, the first attempts to turn the Keynesian theory into an estimable model.[4]

In the course of the theoretical discussion carried out in the first part of the chapter, I will also contrast Keynes's and Kalecki's views with nowadays ruling orthodoxy. However, I will not go too deep into this controversy because this is not the objective of this essay. Besides, I believe modern authors adhering to the orthodox view, whatever their technical skill and mathematical sophistication, are simply repeating the arguments of their predecessors. Such that, as Tobin (1980: 20) nicely put it: 'The controversy of the 1930s is being replayed today.'[5]

KEYNES AND KALECKI ON THEORY

Let us first of all discuss how Keynes and Kalecki envisioned the effect of changes in income distribution, and more specifically on

the wage share, on the level of output and employment. To proceed, I will make a small detour and bring to mind that both in the old and in the current ruling orthodoxy wage flexibility is assumed to be the endogenous full-employment mechanism triggered when unemployment appears.[6] The mechanism relies on several effects. In a closed economy the first effect is the reduction in interest rates, which arises from the increased real amount of money, brought about by falling prices when the amount of nominal money is given; the so-called 'Keynes effect'.[7] The second effect, also pertaining to a closed economy, the 'Pigou effect', is based on the idea that the wage reduction and the ensuing price decline would stimulate aggregate demand due to higher spending from creditors which, with lower prices, would feel richer and consume (and probably also spend) a larger proportion of their current income. The third effect has to do with an open economy. It is the one most frequently invoked by policymakers, supporters of the orthodoxy. It adds to the two previous effects the depreciation of the domestic currency and the enhanced competitiveness following from the wage and price fall. Superior competitiveness is claimed to provoke a demand expansion associated with the improvement in the trade balance. In a less orthodox rendition of the story, it is claimed that greater availability of foreign exchange also makes possible the implementation of expansionary policies.

Keynes surmised that upon an increase in employment, real wages would have to drop.[8] However, one of his objectives when he wrote the *General Theory* was to criticize the automatic full-employment mechanism based on the alleged expansionary effect of lower wages. He first assumed, for expository purposes, a given nominal wage, but in Chapter 19 of his opus magnum he discussed the consequences of wages falling with unemployment. We also know that, especially following the interpretation of the message of the *General Theory* encapsulated in Hicks's (1937) model, Keynes's criticism was reduced to a single idea: the 'liquidity trap'.

Of course, Keynes did have this possibility in mind, but we should not forget that he considered it to be a 'limiting case'. Writing in the middle of the world depression which started in 1929, he wrote: '...whilst this limiting case might become practically important in the future, *I know of no example of it hitherto*' (Keynes 1964: 207) [emphasis added]. To this 'limiting case' Keynes added several obstacles to the full-employment standard mechanism, of which I

mention here only a few. One was the notion that the real amount of money might not rise as a consequence of the wage and price decrease. Thus, expressing the point with the endogenous conception of money approach reminiscent of his *Treatise on Money* (Keynes 1930) he stated:

> It is, therefore, on the effect of a falling wage- and price-level on the demand for money that those who believe in the self-adjusting quality of the economic system must rest the weight of their argument; though I am not aware that they have done so. If the quantity of money is itself a function of the wage- and price-level, there is indeed, nothing to hope in this direction. (Keynes 1964: 266)

Besides that, he discussed the issue taking into account expectations, arguing: 'If...the [wage] reduction leads to the expectation, or even to the serious possibility, of a further wage reduction in prospect,... [it] will diminish the marginal efficiency of capital and will to a postponement' of both investment and of consumption' (Ibid.: 263). And he went on: 'If, moreover, the reduction in wages disturbs political confidence by causing popular discontent, the increase in liquidity preference due to this cause may more than offset the release of cash from the active circulation' (Ibid.: 263–4).

He added the argument that falling prices would raise the burden of the debt and this might discourage investment. In his words: '...the depressing influence on entrepreneurs of their greater burden of debt may partially offset any cheerful reactions from the reductions of wages. Indeed if the fall of wages and prices goes far, the embarrassment of those entrepreneurs who are heavily indebted may soon reach the point of insolvency—with severe adverse effects on investment' (Ibid.: 264). This idea is especially important from the point of view of our present circumstances. We know that Minsky (1975, 1986), one of Keynes's most innovative followers, gave special relevance to the indebtedness ratio of firms in his explanation of instability of capitalist economies. More recently, Koo (2008) provides an explanation of the US crisis of the 1930s and of Japan stagnation in the 1990s, based on deteriorating balance sheets of firms.

Keynes also took into account the consequences of a wage fall in an 'unclosed system'. In this context, he posited in the first place: '...it is evident that the change [i.e., the wage fall] will be favourable to investment, since it will tend to increase the balance of trade' (Keynes

1964: 262). In the second place, he stated: 'a reduction of money-wages...is likely to worsen the terms of trade. Thus there will be a reduction in real incomes, except in the case of the newly employed, which may tend to increase the propensity to consume' (Ibid.: 263). I must confess that here I am puzzled. On the one hand, the notion that the wage fall 'will be favourable to investment, since it will tend to increase the balance of trade' is open to two interpretations, not necessarily opposed. It may simply mean that lower wages improve the trade balance and thus imply an export of capital, in which case the second part of the sentence is redundant. Or otherwise it may mean that a higher export surplus brings about higher demand, which stimulates investment thanks to a sort of accelerator effect.[9] On the other hand, the worsening of the terms of trade need not necessarily imply a reduction in *total* real incomes, because it can bring about expansion of demand and output. Besides, if a reduction in real incomes does occur for the previously unemployed, this might actually induce a higher propensity to consume out of *their* income, but this need not be the case, and will surely not be the case, if it is workers' income, not capitalist or rentier's income, that falls. Kalecki, as we shall see, was more precise regarding the influence of falling wages on employment in an open system.

Anyway, Keynes concluded the whole discussion of the impact of flexible wages on employment in *The General Theory* as follows: 'There is, therefore, no ground for the belief that a flexible wage policy is capable of maintaining a state of continuous full employment.... The economic system cannot be made self-adjusting along these lines' (Ibid.: 267).

Kalecki also harshly criticized the alleged beneficial results of wage flexibility, expanding on Keynes's arguments and producing some of his own concoction. In the first place, setting the issue also in terms of an endogenous theory of money, he discarded the view whereby the nominal amount of money would remain constant when wages and prices fall, so that the interest rate would tend to decline (Kalecki 1991b: 336).[10] In the second place, he rejected the 'Pigou effect', arguing that a generalized price decline would make not only creditors feel richer, but would also make debtors feel poorer (Kalecki 1990b). He added that widespread and persistent wage and price decrease would likely bring about a 'crisis of confidence' which would slow down private spending.

His third objection to the wage-fall-induced full-employment mechanism was novel vis-à-vis those proposed by Keynes. He argued (Kalecki 1991a) that a wage reduction would likely imply a smaller proportional fall in prices than in wages, and that the consequent drop in the wage share would depress workers' consumption and effective demand. Given its importance, I think it may be useful to formalize the idea using some of Kalecki's equations. Let P stand for gross profits, I for gross private investment, C_k for capitalist consumption, and X for net exports (exports minus imports). ω is the relative share of wages in the value added (or output), so that under simplifying assumptions $(1-\omega)$ is the share of profits in output; k is what Kalecki labelled the 'degree of monopoly', or the ratio of aggregate proceeds to aggregate prime costs (which is also equal to the ratio of average prices to average prime costs); j is the ratio of aggregate cost of materials to the wage bill. Kalecki assumed that in a given short period capitalist expenditure $(I + C_k)$ is the result of previously taken decisions that will not normally be changed during this period.

$$P = I + C_k + X \qquad\qquad [3.1]$$

$$\omega = \frac{1}{1 + (k-1)(j+1)}; k > 1 \qquad\qquad [3.2]$$

$$Y = \frac{P}{(1-\omega)} = \frac{I + C_k + X}{(1-\omega)} \qquad\qquad [3.3]$$

Equation [3.1] is the well-known Kalecki equation for total profits in an open economy (where we abstract from workers' savings and from the budget deficit to simplify). Equation [3.2] shows that (for a given composition of output) the relative share of wages in the value added is determined by the degree of monopoly and by the ratio of the materials bill to the wage bill. Equation [3.3] encapsulates Kalecki's theory of effective demand, making total output dependent on total profits and the share of profits in output.

We may first consider the case of the closed economy so that the variable X in equations [3.1] and [3.3] disappears. Let us assume that firms reduce prices in proportion to the wage and cost fall. Then parameters k and j do not change and since total profits do not vary

(equation [3.1]), aggregate demand and thus employment, remain constant (equation [3.3]). Now, in Kalecki's view, when wages fall, firms will probably be tempted to reduce prices proportionally less than costs. Thus, both the degree of monopoly k and the j ratio rise, and the wage share ω falls (equation [3.2]). Given I and C_k, total profits do not rise (equation [3.1]). However, since ω fell, aggregate demand will fall. In other words, the wage fall and the shift from wages to profit, instead of stimulating employment as per the conventional view, depress aggregate demand and employment.

Kalecki extended the reasoning to the open economy. In this case, when wages fall, variable X, the trade balance, rises, dragging with it total profits.[11] However, domestic producers will be tempted to reduce their prices less than costs and to raise their degree of monopoly, because prices of competitive imports did not fall. Besides, since prices of imported inputs did not fall, the ratio of aggregate cost of materials to the wage bill (j) will also rise. The aforementioned changes entail a shift of factor shares from wages to profits, which may offset, or more than offset, the expansionary effect of a more favourable trade balance on output and employment (equation [3.3]).

To summarize, the two founding fathers of the principle of effective demand discarded the classical–neoclassical story, whereby the wage fall brought about by unemployment gives rise endogenously to processes that tend to restore full employment. Some of the reasons they adduced were convergent and others were different, but the assumptions of their reasoning appear realistic and the logic impeccable. It remains to be seen, however, how their final conclusion stands when confronted with the real world. But before carrying out this test, I will deal with the economic policy stance of our two authors. As anticipated, I will only briefly take up this point here.

Let us first of all discuss fiscal policy. We all know that the conventional wisdom rejects high government expenditure, especially but not exclusively when deficit financed, even more strongly than any other type of government involvement. In its milder version, the ruling orthodoxy could accept that under recessionary conditions, a fiscal impulse may stimulate an economic recovery. But it considers that such an impulse has to be purely temporary and followed by fiscal retrenchment: after all, debts must be paid. In its more radical version, under no conditions whatsoever a deficit can be accepted because it would only crowd out private spending.[12]

Keynes and Kalecki radically discarded the orthodox fiscal-policy vision.[13] Since his initial writings, the latter emphasized the expansionary role of government expenditure on demand and output, as well as on profits. He showed that the demand effect of government expenditure depends not only on its amount, but also on how it is financed. Greater government expenditure financed taxing wages does indeed crowd out private spending. However, when financed via deficit or via higher taxes on profits, it stimulates effective demand. In the former case this follows from the fact that current private income is not reduced. In the latter case, the government is taxing away income that would not have been produced if government spending had not taken place. But here the multiplier effect is smaller than under deficit financing because profits and capitalist consumption do not rise. We can see that Kalecki, probably due to his socialist penchant, emphasized the social class from which the taxes financing expenditure came.

Keynes also favoured government expenditure to overcome depressed private demand. As early as 1933, in the midst of the World Crisis, he wrote a series of articles for *The Times*, which he later published as *The Means to Prosperity* (Keynes 1933). In those essays, Keynes proposed that governments should stimulate or embark on large-scale loan-financed expenditure. However, it is as well to recall that Keynes saw the deficit only as an instrument of last resort (Kregel 1985; Carvalho 1997). Besides that, he disagreed with Kalecki with respect to the latter's notion that taxing profits would not dampen private investment.[14]

Finally, let us briefly review how Keynes and Kalecki saw the likely impact of money and finance on effective demand and output. Kalecki did not give much importance to monetary conditions and policy. Referring to a drop in the interest rate, he argued: 'this method is not very effective because the long term rate of interest changes rather slowly and (what is more important) because it cannot be reduced below a certain limit' (Kalecki 1990c: 370). Though he recognized that an interest rate fall would stimulate demand, he considered that to achieve this the interest rate fall ought to be large. This may explain why in his most detailed applied studies (Kalecki 1991c, 1997, 1991d, and 1991e), he seldom discussed how the evolution of monetary policy and the interest rate had shaped the evolution of the countries concerned.

Keynes's thought on this matter was different. He maintained that, except during particular circumstances, availability of credit and low rates of interest would stimulate the pace of investment and expand effective demand, and conversely. More specifically, he thought that open market operations should be the driving factor in monetary policy affecting the real economy, with the interest rate playing a major role. Monetary authorities carry out this type of operation by inducing private banks to substitute reserves for loans (expansionary policy), or to renew reserves (contractionary policy) (Panico 2008).

Keynes's view is the opposite of the conventional one. In its neoclassical synthesis version, the latter considers that any positive effect of monetary expansion will be only transient. It gives two reasons, both related to the alleged inflationary impact of this expansion. On the one hand, workers will recognize sooner rather than later that their inflation-deflated nominal wage does not justify a higher labour supply. On the other hand, inflation will reduce the real amount of money, and will thus nullify any intended expansion of the money supply. In its New Consensus incarnation, the conventional view accepts that monetary expansion will bring about inflation. But it postulates a less mechanical course of events. It is rather the central bank that will not accept inflation and will raise the interest rate. Finally, the more radical view, the rational expectations version, discards any positive impact of monetary policy even in the short run (see Carlin and Soskice 2006, for an overview).

I close here our theoretical discussion. As mentioned, I think economic theories cannot be proven right or wrong purely on conceptual reasoning. They have to be tested against actual facts. The main purpose of the estimated econometric models I present in the following is to carry out an empirical test of the hypotheses of the founding fathers of the principle of effective demand. Hopefully, they may also serve to shed light on the recent economic evolution of the countries involved.

FACTS AND THEORY

I this section I carry out econometric analysis. Many of the hypotheses I explore in the following have been already subjected to econometric inquiry by different authors but, due to space limitations,

I cannot discuss their works here. I will only mention that even a selective review will show a large diversity of empirical results. What may seem even more surprising is that differences can be found even among authors adopting a similar theoretical perspective and analysing comparable periods. Probably in any other discipline this situation would stimulate a thorough reflection about the rigor or otherwise of the competing underlying econometric methodologies. Unfortunately, in economics this apparently is not considered important. Since I do think this to be an important issue, I will explain with some detail the econometric approach I have used to carry out the empirical research.

There is a controversy among applied economists about the most adequate procedure to carry out empirical modelling. In a recent overview, Colander (2009), contrasts two alternative perspectives. He distinguishes on the one hand what he calls the 'European perspective', based on 'the general-to-specific Cointegrated Vector Auto Regressive (CVAR)' approach; and on the other, the currently dominant 'Dynamic Stochastic General Equilibrium (DSGE) models'. In the DSGE approach the theoretical model is supposed to be valid, because it is based on decisions taken by optimizing agents. Therefore, the probability and statistical assumptions underpinning the estimations are tested rarely, if at all. This is why Spanos (2009: 1) argues that this approach can be 'better described as a "Pre-Eminence of Theory" (PET) standpoint, where the data are assigned a subordinate role broadly described as "quantifying theories presumed adequate". In contrast, the European "general-to-specific" CVAR perspective attempts to give data a more substantial role in the theory-data confrontation'.

In the econometric work of this chapter, I have followed the European general-to-specific CVAR perspective, or more rigorously what Spanos (2009) and Juselius (2006) call 'a probabilistic approach to econometrics'. In a few words, this approach emphasizes the use of *statistically adequate* models as the basis of drawing reliable inferences; where the term *statistically adequate* refers to the validity of the *probability and the statistical assumptions* underlying the estimated model. The foundation of this approach is the notion that *all* (that is, not only the assumed exogenous) variables under consideration are random variables, characterized by certain probabilistic and sampling features, and thus endowed with given joint density function

and a certain type of dependence. Regression analysis, which is the backbone of time series econometrics, purports to estimate the conditional expectation of a variable or group of variables, where the conditional expectation follows very strict rules determined by the joint density of the variables and their type of dependence. The statistical model is thus considered to be a set of internally consistent probabilistic assumptions aimed to capture the statistical information in the data, and more specifically its chance regularity patterns.

In this approach, economic theory suggests the potential theoretical relationships and thus the relevant data should in principle be included in the model, but the statistical model is specified by viewing the observed data as a realization of a generic vector stochastic process with a probabilistic structure that would render the observed data a truly typical realization thereof. Thus, one must distinguish between the structural model, which is based on substantive subject matter information, and the statistical model, which is chosen to reflect the *systematic statistical information* contained in the particular data. The structural model has no independent entity, because it is simply a re-parameterization/restriction of an estimated well-defined statistical model.

The success of econometric modelling depends on how appropriate the postulated assumptions are in capturing the statistical information in the data. For example, for variables Y and X the regression function, namely the conditional mean of Y given $X = x$, will only be linear if the joint density function of the two variables is normal; otherwise it will not be linear. If the model imposes linearity (say, of the form: $y = a_0 + a_1 x$) and the normality assumption is rejected by the appropriate tests, any inference, such as the value of parameters (a_0 and a_1) and t and R^2 values, will be misleading. Thus, in the approach I use, misspecification testing plays a fundamental role, to ensure the statistical adequacy of the model and the reliability of the inferences based on such a model.

Accordingly, the first important feature of the empirical work carried out in this chapter is that I subject all the estimated models to a battery of misspecification tests to secure the *statistical adequacy* (the validity of their probabilistic assumptions vis-à-vis the data in question) of the model and thus the reliability of the results.

A second relevant aspect of empirical modelling that plays an important role in what follows is the use of VAR models, and of recent

developments in system-based cointegration methods. The advantage of the former is that no a priori distinction between exogenous and endogenous variables is made, and the interrelations between the variables are duly taken care of. On the other hand, cointegration analysis allows us to deal with non-stationary time series and reach multiple and single equation specifications.

I discuss now the theoretical specification of the models. As said, I want to study only if and how, distribution, fiscal, and monetary variables affect gross domestic product (GDP). Thus, for modelling purposes the main variable of interest in the empirical section of this study is GDP. Since the basic assumption is that aggregate demand determines output, I will now discuss the theoretical underpinning of the econometric model starting from the demand equation, where Y stands for output, C private consumption, I private investment, and J the trade balance (that is, net exports). G is government expenditure on goods and services.

$$Y = C + I + J + G \qquad\qquad [3.4]$$

To specify which are the most basic factors determining the right-hand side variables I will follow a somewhat eclectic approach, taking as a basis what both Keynes and Kalecki thought were those factors. I assume the trade balance (J) depends on output (Y), on external output (Y^*), and on the wage share (ω). Usually, the argument in the trade balance equation is the real exchange rate rather than the wage share. However, I take the latter because, under rather plausible assumptions the *real* exchange rate depends on (and moves in opposite direction than) the share of wages in value added for a given *nominal* exchange rate (López-Gallardo and Perrotini 2006).

Regarding private consumption and private investment, I assume they depend on output (Y), on the share of wages in the value added (ω), on what may be called the state of liquidity prevailing in the economy L, and on the interest rate (R).

Finally, I include government spending (G) as a determinant of demand. In the case of Europe and Japan I took the total amount because I did not find disaggregated figures. However, in the case of the US, where I could disaggregate government spending according to its source of financing, I decomposed government spending into spending financed via taxes on corporate profits (H), and financed

via Other Government Revenues (O). I did not separate the budget deficit from net taxes from persons because the actual budget deficit, for well-known reasons, is highly pro-cyclical, and I did not find a satisfactory variable measuring the discretionary budget deficit. Therefore, we can reduce [3.4] as follows:

$$Y = C(\omega, Y, L, R) + I(\omega, Y, L, R) + J(Y, Y^*, \omega) + G \qquad [3.5]$$

or

$$Y = C(\omega, Y, L, R) + I(\omega, Y, L, R) + J(Y, Y^*, \omega) + H + O \quad [3.5a]$$

Simplifying again, the model can be specified as:

$$Y = Y(\omega, Y^*, L, R, G) \qquad [3.6]$$

or

$$Y = Y(\omega, Y^*, L, R, H, O) \qquad [3.6a]$$

As is usually the case in applied work, lack of adequate information makes it necessary to use variables that are only imperfect proxies for the theoretical variables of interest. I explain now how I deal with this point. First, I use as a proxy for world output the GDP of the Organisation for Economic Co-operation and Development (OECD). On the other hand, I tried several variables as proxies for liquidity, and in the case of the European countries I opted for M2 or for M3, whichever gave a *statistically adequate model* (see the earlier discussion). In the case of Japan, I took M1. In the case of the US, I opted for outstanding credit C for that same reason. Also, I tried different interest rates until I found the one that resulted in a statistically adequate model. Lastly, I mention that for each country I tried many models, with different information sets.[15] I selected the models I present here because they were statistically adequate.

The final models thus were:

$$Y = Y(\omega, Y^*, M, R, G) \qquad [3.7] \text{Europe and Japan}$$

or

$$Y = Y(\omega, Y^*, C, R, H, O) \qquad [3.7a] \text{US}$$

ECONOMETRIC MODELLING[16]

As a preliminary step for the econometric work, I give a brief description of the data. The sample is on a quarterly basis, and in all cases it runs from 1980 to 2008(3), except in France where the period ends in 2007.1, in Germany where the sample begins in 1990(1), that is, after reunification, and in Japan, where the sample starts in 1988.1. All nominal variables were deflated with the GDP price index. In Figures 3.1, 3.2, and 3.3, I show the evolution of the variables selected for the models for only three countries: France, whose behaviour is somewhat typical of the European economies, Japan, and the US. For each country I plot its GDP together with all the variables included in the models. This will give us a first informal hint on how they may be associated. To render inspection easier and to see better their association with GDP, all variables were seasonally adjusted and their values were also adjusted to make the mean and range coincide with that for GDP. In the left-hand side panel I show the variables in levels; and in the right-hand side one I take each variable in deviations from their trend (Ψ_T is variable Ψ without trend).

Regarding the economic information conveyed by the graphs, the upward trend, and the cyclical association between GDP and World GDP (Y and Y^*) is apparent for all European countries, for Japan, and for the US, though in France and above all in Germany (figure not shown) the detrended variables seem less closely connected. The upward trend of government expenditure (G) and its association with Y is also clear for Japan and all European countries (though this is not the case for the UK during the period 1980–95). In the US variables H (taxes on corporate profits) and O (other sources of finance) also move together with GDP. Money (M) and GDP also move in sympathy for all European countries (except in Italy in the 1980–95 period), and much less so in Japan, while in the US credit (C) and GDP also move in parallel. The interest rate (R) has a declining trend in all the countries we study, and its association with GDP is not very clear. Finally, in all countries the wage share declined, and persistently so in France, Italy, Germany, and the UK, while in Spain and the US the long-run fall took place with ups and downs. In Japan, after a decline between the mid-1990s and the mid-2000s, the wage share recovered, with ups and downs. The positive association between the wage share and GDP is apparent in the graphs of the

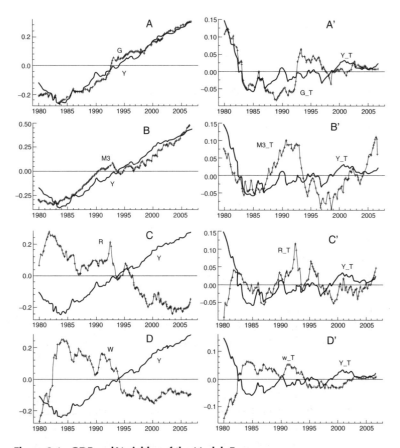

Figure 3.1 GDP and Variables of the Model: France
Source: Organisation for Economic Co-operation and Development.

detrended variables in the US, Japan, Italy, and the UK, but it is less clear in the other countries.

To test the hypotheses I want to explore in this chapter, I estimated VAR models for each country. Once I found a statistically adequate VAR, I used system-based cointegration methods (Juselius 2006), and I estimated the long-run equilibrium equation for the selected variables (Johansen 1988). Taking as the basis a VAR model, I then estimated error correction models (ECMs), and again carried out misspecification tests for each model to ensure their statistical validity.[17]

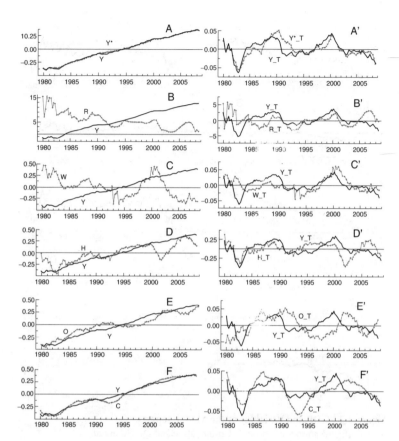

Figure 3.2   GDP and Variables of the Model: US
Source: Organisation for Economic Co-operation and Development.

Table 3.1 shows the long-run vector estimated for each country. In words, the cointegration analysis shows the existence of a stable long-run relationship between output and the variables in the right-hand side of [3.7] or [3.7a]. More precisely, in all European countries and in Japan higher output is associated with higher World GDP, with a higher share of wages in value added, and with higher money (except in Italy) and government expenditure, while lower interest rates are associated with higher output (except in Japan, where the interest rate was found to be non-significant). In the US the results are relatively similar. Higher output is associated with higher World GDP, with a higher share of wages in value added, and with higher credit

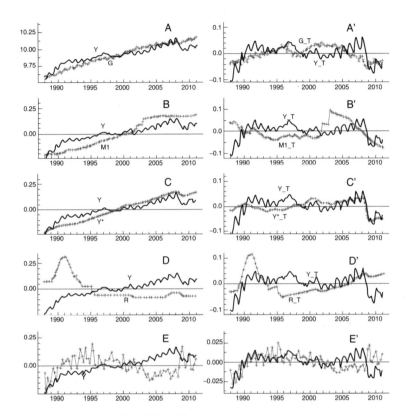

Figure 3.3   GDP and Variables of the Model: Japan
Source: Organisation for Economic Co-operation and Development.

Table 3.1   Long-run Output Equations for European Countries and Japan

Output Determinants	France	Spain	Germany	United Kingdom	Japan[18]
Y^*	0.067656	0.78617	0.15682	0.80529	0.24
G	0.83555	0.16505	0.43726	0.10921	0.09
M	0.040210	0.058313	0.34199	0.08463	0.03
R	−0.80058	−0.43346	−0.32580	−0.16140	Non-significant
ω	1.5513	1.1499	0.16696	0.20833	0.41

Source: Author's estimates.
Note: Long-run output equations for the US:
$Y = 0.83\ Y^* + 2.17\ \omega + 0.14\ C + 0.15\ O + 0.11\ H - 0.012\ R.$

and government expenditure, financed via either taxes on corporate income or other sources. Finally, lower interest rates are associated with higher output.

Now, the equilibrium relation is useful, but it does not tell the whole story we need to know. Indeed, it does not explain the dynamic pattern of association between the chosen set of variables or about how the long-run equilibrium is restored when it is disrupted. Besides, since correlation does not imply causation, it is still necessary to study whether output is indeed determined by the right-hand side of [3.7] or [3.7a]. To answer these two questions I estimated ECMs. The ECM describes the short-run association between GDP and its determinants. It also is the appropriate instrument to carry out Granger causality test when a set of variables co-integrate, and thus to check if the right-hand side variables in [3.7] or [3.7a] cause GDP. In the following I report the results of the ECMs. D before the variable denotes its first difference, $D\Psi\_i$ indicates the i_th lag of the first difference of variable Ψ. Letter d denotes a dummy variable, with the two last digits of the year, and qi stand for quarter i. V is the long-run equilibrium relation. Seas is a seasonal dummy. Note, in a multi-variate context, Granger causality of variable Ψ on variable ϑ is obtained when Ψ is contained among the regressors in the equation for ϑ, or in the cointegration vector, or both.

Error Correction Models[19]

Germany

DY = 0.027 + 0.147DY_4 + 0.497DG-0.121DG_5 + 1.13DW_2 + 0.256DM2_5 − 0.0044Seas − 0.09V_1 + 0.0161d97iv + 0.0218d00ii

Spain

DY = 0.47DY_5 + 0.74DY*_4 + 0.16DG + 0.15 DR − 0.18DR_5 − 0.00 16V_1 + 0.03d_98 + 0.03Seas

France

DY = 0.009 + 0.289DY_2 + 0.3DY_3 − 0.384DY*_1 + 0.5DY*_4 − 0.08DG_1 + 0.11DG_5 + 0.175DW_5 + 0.03DM2_1 + 0.048DM2_2 − 0.02V_1 + 0.005d83iii_85i

United Kingdom

$$DY = - 0.18 + 0.26DY\_2 + 0.18DY\_3 + 0.33DY^* + O.44DY^*\_4$$
$$- 0.14DR + 0.23DW + 0.022DG + 0.22DG\_7 + 0.01d87.3 - 0.01d90.3$$
$$+ 0.01d94.2 - 0.008d99.1$$

United States

$$DY = 0.15DY\_2 + 0.53DY^*\_1 - 0.37DY\_3 + 0.05DH + 0.02DH\_2 +$$
$$0.19DO - 0.1DO\_4 + 0.17DW\_1 - 0.001DR\_2 - 0.001V\_1$$

Japan

$$DY = 0.78 - 0.37DY\_1 + 0.18DY\_2 + 0.55DY\_4 + 0.27DY\_5 + 1.16DY^*$$
$$+ 1.03DY^*\_2 - 1.54DY^*\_4 + 0.51Dw\_2 + 0.29Dg\_2 + 0.27Dg\_3$$
$$- 0.12V\_1$$

The results from the ECMs seem rather involved at first sight but at closer look they allow us to make important inferences. In the first place, they show that variables in the right-hand side of equation [3.7] or [3.7a] do Granger-cause output.[20]

In the second place, the response of output with respect to changes of the right-hand side variables takes place in some cases contemporaneously and in other cases with a certain delay.

In the third place, we infer that output growth is path-dependent: output growth causes, with a certain delay, output growth. Thus, for example, if the government implements restrictive policies that affect growth in the current period, then future growth will be compromised. Similarly, if a fall of the wage share brings about an aggregate demand decline which contracts current output, then unless expansionary policies were undertaken, future output growth will be also negatively affected.

To finish this part of the work, I must say that the estimated model VAR and ECM are not only statistically adequate, but also incorporate a larger information set, and a more severe battery of misspecification tests to ensure the reliability of the results than any other of the available estimated models I have been able to consult.

FINAL REMARKS

The economic interpretation of the empirical results of this study is, I hope, clear. In all the countries under investigation, the statistical

findings are coincident. The same, or very similar, set of variables affect demand and output, and the nature of the associations are also analogous. I will restate the results succinctly, concentrating on the hypotheses that are the main object of this inquiry.

First, we find that a higher share of wages encourages demand and output in the short and in the long run.

Second, higher government expenditure also stimulates demand and output. Let us note here that this positive effect takes place even when such expenditure is financed with higher taxes. The implication is that not only higher government expenditure financed via deficit stimulates demand and output, but that even a balanced budget turns out to be expansionary. In the case of the US economy, we can in addition see that government expenditure financed taxing corporate profits stimulates demand and output.

Third, monetary conditions also influence demand and output, not only in the short but also in the long run. When credit conditions are relaxed and broad money grows, or when the interest rate declines, growth is stimulated.

Last, but not least, the evolution of the world economy has a strong influence on the development of each one of the national economies we have studied.

I conclude relating the aforementioned results to the theoretical debate. As extensively discussed in this essay, in the controversy about the macroeconomic effects of monetary and fiscal policy, and of changes in the wage share, Keynes and Kalecki stand in one camp, supporting the positive role of monetary and fiscal policy and of a higher wage share, on demand and output. Classical as well as Neoclassical and New Classicals, and even most of New Keynesians, oppose the previous view. I will end this work stating that for the countries I have studied at least, the empirical evidence is strongly in favour of Keynes and Kalecki.

STATISTICAL APPENDIX

In the following I show results for some misspecification tests, for the estimated VAR and ECMs. Due to the large number of results, I show only those I consider to be most important. The remainder, such as recursive stability tests and equation tests for the VARs, can be obtained from the author upon request.

Germany

VAR Tests
Vector Portmanteau(7): 238.52
Vector AR 1-4 test: $F(144,136) = 1.2343$ [0.1078]
Vector Normality test: $Chi^2(12) = 10.544$ [0.5684]
Vector Hetero test: $F(252,220) = 0.74440$ [0.9883]
Vector Hetero-X test: $F(567,141) = 0.39294$ [1.0000]

Error Correction Tests
AR 1-4 test: $F(4,44) = 0.77423$ [0.5479]
ARCH 1-4 test: $F(4,40) = 0.25331$ [0.9059]
Normality test: $Chi^2(2) = 2.1015$ [0.3497]
Hetero test: $F(15,32) = 0.61548$ [0.8404]
RESET test: $F(1,47) = 2.3257$ [0.1340]

France

VAR Tests
Vector Portmanteau(12): 458.623
Vector AR 1-5 test: $F(180,285) = 1.2705$ [0.0359]*
Vector Normality test: $Chi^2(12) = 19.431$ [0.0786]
Vector Hetero test: $F(756,567) = 0.59177$ [1.0000]

Error Correction Tests
AR 1-5 test: $F(5,85) = 0.45531$ [0.8083]
ARCH 1-4 test: $F(4,82) = 1.3537$ [0.2573]
Normality test: $Chi^2(2) = 0.77563$ [0.6785]
Hetero test: $F(21,68) = 1.8514$ [0.0299]*
RESET test: $F(1,89) = 1.4238$ [0.2359]

Spain

VAR Tests
Vector Portmanteau(12): 488.657
Vector AR 1-5 test: $F(180,315) = 1.3395$ [0.0123]*
Vector Normality test: $Chi^2(12) = 13.651$ [0.3236]
Vector Hetero test: $F(504,747) = 0.88753$ [0.9267]

Error correction tests
AR 1-5 test: $F(5,90) = 1.3484$ [0.2514]
ARCH 1-4 test: $F(4,87) = 2.2396$ [0.0712]
Normality test: $Chi^2(2) = 4.0614$ [0.1312]
Hetero test: $F(15,79) = 0.28029$ [0.9960]
Hetero-X test: $F(36,58) = 0.53968$ [0.9750]
RESET test: $F(1,94) = 0.46918$ [0.4950]

United Kingdom

VAR Tests
Vector Portmanteau(12): 430.765
Vector AR 1-5 test: $F(180,273) = 1.1973$ [0.0899]
Vector Normality test: Chi^2(12) = 8.8088 [0.7192]
Vector Hetero test: $F(756,531)= 0.54435$ [1.0000]

Error correction tests
AR 1-5 test: $F(5,80) = 0.44413$ [0.8163]
ARCH 1-4 test: $F(4,77) = 0.62543$ [0.6458]
Normality test: Chi^2(2) = 7.9172 [0.0191]*
Hetero test: $F(23,61) = 0.80190$ [0.7158]
RESET test: $F(1,84) = 0.11352$ [0.7370]

Japan

VAR Tests
Vector Portmanteau(10): 422.807
Vector AR 1-5 test: $F(180,202) = 1.1072$ [0.2403]
Vector Normality test: Chi^2(12) = 21.152 [0.0482]*
Vector Hetero test: $F(504,446) = 0.80489$ [0.9910]
Hetero-X test: not enough observations

Error correction tests
AR 1-5 test: $F(5,70) = 2.3159$ [0.0526]
ARCH 1-4 test: $F(4,67) = 0.92039$ [0.4574]
Normality test: Chi^2(2) = 1.1714 [0.5567]
Hetero test: $F(22,52) = 1.8458$ [0.0359]*
RESET test: $F(1,74) = 2.2554$ [0.1374]

USA

VAR Tests
Vector Portmanteau(12): 399.16
Vector AR 1-5 test: $F(180,250)= 0.99467$ [0.5124]
Vector Normality test: Chi^2(12) = 20.663 [0.0555]
Vector Hetero test: $F(1050,231)= 0.24489$ [1.0000]

Error correction tests
AR 1-5 test: $F(5,91) = 0.82941$ [0.5321]
ARCH 1-4 test: $F(4,88) = 0.66039$ [0.6212]
Normality test: Chi^2(2) = 2.1759 [0.3369]
Hetero test: $F(27,68) = 1.0840$ [0.3831]
RESET test: $F(1,95) = 3.0087$ [0.0861]

NOTES

1. Readers are referred to López-Gallardo and Assous (2010) for a more extensive analysis.

2. But then, we must acknowledge that, as Laidler (1999) and Toporowski (2005) have masterfully shown, most of the ideas of both Kalecki and Keynes had been proposed and had been circulating among economists from a much earlier date.

3. I could not find a statistically well-specified model for Italy. By the way, readers will notice that I am not an expert in any of the economies studied here. Thus, the econometric exercises are not intended to provide an explanation of their macroeconomic evolution, but only to test if the data support Keynes's and Kalecki's hypotheses discussed in this chapter.

4. Morgan (1990) gives a beautiful and judicious account of Keynes's criticism.

5. I think anybody having read Laidler (2004, 2009) will probably come to the conclusion that most contemporary New Classical and even New Keynesian authors have a much more rigid view than their predecessors.

6. Many contemporary authors, otherwise identified with the principle of effective demand, share the idea that a wage fall may stimulate demand and employment. For example, this was the basis of the well-known predator–prey model proposed by Goodwin (1967). More recently, and following the seminal Bhaduri and Marglin (1990) essay, the notions of profits-led and wage-led regimes have been coined. The first one denotes a situation whereby a higher profit-share stimulates output and employment, and conversely. This idea has given rise to a host of papers, of both theoretical and empirical nature. But of course none of the aforementioned authors posit that wage flexibility brings about full employment.

7. Note, the 'Keynes effect' was first put forward in print by Kalecki (1990a). But the paper was originally published in Polish, and was translated into English only when the first volume of the *Collected Works* of Michael Kalecki was published in 1990.

8. However, he did not posit that a wage fall would raise demand and employment. Rather he held the view that higher employment results in lower real wages because the marginal productivity of labour would decline with higher employment. Afterwards, and in the light of empirical evidence, he recanted from his previous opinion (Keynes 1939).

9. To check that the ambiguity of the sentence is not simply due to my reading, I consulted the point with several colleagues; their responses differed, favouring one interpretation or the other, or both.

10. He wrote:

> A long-run fall in money wages causes a fall in the money volume of transactions. If the supply of cash by banks is not proportionally reduced, this leads in turn to a fall of the long-term rate of interest. Such a fall...would cause an upward trend movement. ...

It is, however, highly doubtful whether the mechanism described will be effective in increasing output at all. The connection between the fall in turnover and the fall in the short-term rate of interest is in fact fairly uncertain in the long run. If the fall in turnover continues over a long period, the banking policy may easily adapt itself to this secular fall in such a way as to reduce the supply of balances *pari passu* with turnover and thus to sustain the short-term interest rate. (Kalecki 1991b: 336)

11. Assuming that the 'Marshall-Lerner' condition is fulfilled and that the wage and price fall do not negatively affect private investment. This latter point cannot be taken for granted because, as Keynes warned, the price fall may provoke a rise in the burden of the debt and discourage investment.

12. In the midst of the deepest world recession since the 1930s, Robert Barro, a leading member of the New Classical School, recently wrote (2009):

> The theory [underpinning the plea for a fiscal push] implicitly assumes that the government is better than the private market at marshaling idle resources to produce useful stuff. Unemployed labor and capital can be utilized at essentially zero social cost, but the private market is somehow unable to figure any of this out. In other words, there is something wrong with the price system…A much more plausible starting point is a multiplier of zero. In this case, the GDP is given, and a rise in government purchases requires an equal fall in the total of other parts of GDP—consumption, investment and net exports. In other words, the social cost of one unit of additional government purchases is one.

See also Barro (1974).

13. Of course, they were not the only ones supporting active fiscal policy (Laidler 1999; Perez Caldentey 2003). But they were the pioneers in setting the argument in the framework of a consistent macroeconomic outlook.

14. See López-Gallardo and Assous (2010) for details about the controversy between the two authors.

15. Wealth may be an important argument in the private spending equation but in the case of the European countries I did not find a good variable that I could use to measure private wealth. In the case of the US economy, I tried different variables but none of them turned out to be statistically significant.

16. This section relies on two works-in-progress co-authored by the author, López-Gallardo and Ortiz (2011) and López-Gallardo and Sanchez (2011). Data sources and details of the econometric work can be found in these two essays.

17. The models selected were subjected to, and were not rejected by, a large battery of misspecification tests. The most important of the tests are shown in the Statistical Appendix.

18. The results I obtained are different from those arrived at by Nishi (2011). Even though we both used the same database, our estimation periods and model specifications were different. By the way, in his otherwise very careful statistical analysis, Nishi does not present the results of misspecification tests.

19. All estimated values of parameters are significantly different from zero, with 95 per cent confidence.

20. Of course, bi-causality among the set of variables cannot be excluded. For example, higher output may also cause a higher wage share or higher government expenditure.

REFERENCES

Barro, R. 1974. 'Are Government Bonds Net Wealth?' *Journal of Political Economy*, 82(6): 1095–117.

———. 2009. 'Government Spending Is No Free Lunch', *The Wall Street Journal*, 22 January.

Bhaduri, A. and S. Marglin. 1990. 'Unemployment and the Real Wage: The Economic Basis for Contesting Political Ideologies', *Cambridge Journal of Economics*, 14: 375–93.

Carvalho, F.J. Cardim de. 1997. 'Economic Policies for Monetary Economies. Keynes's Economic Policy Proposals for an Unemployment-Free Economy', *Revista de Economia Política*, 17(4): 141–66.

Carlin, W. and D. Soskice. 2006. *Macroeconomics. Imperfections, Institutions and Policies*. Oxford: Oxford University Press.

Colander, D. 2009. 'Economists, Incentives, Judgement, and the European VAR Approach to Macroeconometrics', *Economics. The Open-Access, Open-Assessment E-Journal*, 3(9), 2 April, available online: http://www.economics-ejournal.org/economics/journalarticles/2009-9/version_1/count (accessed 7 May 2012).

Goodwin, R.M. 1967. 'A Growth Cycle', in C.H. Feinstein (ed.), *Socialism, Capitalism and Economic Growth*. Cambridge: Cambridge University Press, pp. 54–8.

Hicks, J. 1937. 'Mr. Keynes and the "Classics": A Suggested Interpretation', *Econometrica*, 5 (April): 147–59.

Johansen, S. 1988. 'Statistical Analysis of Cointegration Vectors', *Journal of Economic Dynamics and Control*, 12: 231–54.

Juselius, K. 2006. *The Cointegrated VAR Model: Methodology and Applications*. Oxford: Oxford University Press.

Kalecki, M. 1990a [1934]. 'Three Systems', in J. Osiatynsky (ed.), *Collected Works of Michael Kalecki*, Vol. I. Oxford: Oxford University Press, pp. 201–19.

———. 1990b [1944]. 'Professor Pigou on "The Classical Stationary State"', in J. Osiatynsky (ed.), *Collected Works of Michael Kalecki*, Vol. I. Oxford: Oxford University Press, pp. 342–3.

———. 1990c [1944]. 'Three Ways to Full Employment', in J. Osiatynsky (ed.), *Collected Works of Michael Kalecki*. Vol. I. Oxford: Oxford University Press, pp. 357–76.

———. 1991a [1939]. 'Money and Real Wages', in J. Osiatynsky (ed.), *Collected Works of Michael Kalecki*, Vol. II. Oxford: Oxford University Press, pp. 21–50.

———. 1991b [1954]. 'Theory of Economic Dynamics', in J. Osiatynsky (ed.), *Collected Works of Michael Kalecki*, Vol. II. Oxford: Oxford University Press, pp. 205–348.

Kalecki, M. 1991c [1955]. 'The Impact of Armaments on the Business Cycle after the Second World War', in J. Osiatynsky (ed.), *Collected Works of Michael Kalecki*, Vol. II. Oxford: Oxford University Press, pp. 351–73.

———. 1991d [1962]. 'The Economic Situation in the USA, 1956–1961', in J. Osiatynsky (ed.), *Collected Works of Michael Kalecki*, Vol. II. Oxford: Oxford University Press, pp. 386–401.

———. 1991e [1962]. 'Economic Aspects of West Germany Rearmament', in J. Osiatynsky (ed.), *Collected Works of Michael Kalecki*, Vol. II. Oxford: Oxford University Press, pp. 402–8.

———. 1997 [1956]. 'The Economic Situation in the USA as Compared with the Pre-war Period', in J. Osiatynsky (ed.), *Collected Works of Michael Kalecki*, Vol. VII. Oxford: Oxford University Press, pp. 279–86.

Keynes, J.M. 1930. *A Treatise on Money*, 2 vols. London: Macmillan.

———. 1933. *The Means to Prosperity: Mr. Keynes's Reply to Criticism*, as reprinted in D.E. Moggridge (ed.), *The Collected Writings of John Maynard Keynes*, (CWK), (1972), Vol. IX. *Essays in Persuasion*. London: Macmillan.

———. 1939. 'Relative Movements of Real Wages and Output', *Economic Journal*, 49(143): 34–51.

———. 1964. *The General Theory of Employment, Interest and Money*. New York: Harcourt Brace & Company.

Koo, R. 2008. *The Holy Grail of Macroeconomics: Lessons from Japan's Great Recession*. Singapore: John Wiley & Sons (Asia).

Kregel, J. 1985. 'Budget Deficits, Stabilization Policy and Liquidity Preference: Keynes's Post-war Policy Proposals', in F. Vicarelli (ed.), *Keynes's Relevance Today*. London: Macmillan, pp. 28–50.

Laidler, D. 1999. *Fabricating the Keynesian Revolution*. Cambridge: Cambridge University Press.

———. 2004. 'Woodford and Wicksell on *Interest and Prices*. The Place of the Pure Credit Economy in the Theory of Monetary Policy', EPRI Working Paper Series 2004–5, October, The University of Western Ontario, London, Ontario (Canada), Economic Policy Research Institute; available online: http://economics.uwo.ca/centres/epri/wp2004/Laidler05.pdf (accessed 7 May 2012).

———. 2009. 'Lucas, Keynes, and the Crisis', Working Paper # 2009–2, EPRI Working Paper Series 2009–2, July, The University of Western Ontario, London, Ontario (Canada), Economic Policy Research Institute; available online: http://economics.uwo.ca/econref/WorkingPapers/researchreports/wp2009/wp2009_2.pdf (accessed 7 May 2012).

López-Gallardo, J. and M. Assous. 2010. *Michael Kalecki*. London: Palgrave-Macmillan.

López-Gallardo, J. and I. Perrotini. 2006. 'On Floating Exchange Rates, Currency Depreciation and Effective Demand', *Banca Nazionale del Lavoro Quarterly Review*, 59(238): 221–42.

López-Gallardo, J. and L. Reyes Ortiz. 2011. 'Effective Demand in the Recent Evolution of the US Economy', Levy Economics Institute Working Paper 673, June, Annandale-on-Hudson, NY: Levy Economics Institute of Bard College,

available online: http://www.levyinstitute.org/pubs/wp_673.pdf. Last accessed on 7 May 2012.

López-Gallardo, J. and A. Sanchez. 2011. 'Macroeconomic Evolution in Five European Economies', mimeo, Facultad de Economia, UNAM, Mexico.

Minsky, H. 1975. *John Maynard Keynes*. New York: Columbia University Press.

———. 1986. *Stabilizing an Unstable Economy*. New Haven, CT: Yale University Press.

Morgan, M. 1990. *The History of Econometric Ideas*. Cambridge, UK: Cambridge University Press.

Nishi, H. 2011. 'A VAR Analysis for the Growth Regime and Demand Formation Patterns of the Japanese Economy', *Revue de la Regulation*, 1 and 2 semester: 1–26.

Panico, C. 2008. 'Keynes on the Control of the Money Supply and the Interest Rate', in M. Forstater and L.R. Wray (eds), *Keynes and Macroeconomics After 70 Years: Critical Assessments of the 'General Theory'*. Cheltenham, UK, and Northampton, MA, USA: Edward Elgar, pp. 157–75.

Perez Caldentey, E. 2003. 'Chicago, Keynes and Fiscal Policy', *Investigación Económica*, 62(246): 15–45.

Robinson, J.V. 1964. 'Kalecki and Keynes', as reprinted in J.V. Robinson, 1965, *Collected Economic Papers*, Vol. III. Oxford: Basil Blackwell, pp. 92–102.

———. 1971. 'Michael Kalecki', as reprinted in J.V. Robinson, 1973, *Collected Economic Papers*, Vol. IV. Oxford: Basil Blackwell, pp. 87–91.

Spanos, A. 2009. 'The Pre-Eminence of Theory versus the European CVAR Perspective in Macroeconometric Modeling', *Economics: The Open-Access, Open-Assessment E-Journal*, 3(10), 7 April, available online: http://www.economics-ejournal.org/economics/journalarticles/2009-10/version_1/count. Last accessed on 7 May 2012.

Tobin, J. 1980. *Asset Accumulation and Economic Activity*. Chicago: University of Chicago Press, and Oxford: Blackwell.

Toporowski, J. 2005. *Theories of Financial Disturbance*. Cheltenham, UK, and Northampton, MA, USA: Edward Elgar.

II
Economic Theory and the World Recession

4

The State of Macroeconomics in View of the Global Economic Crisis

ASAHI NOGUCHI

The world economic crisis, initiated by the burst of the US subprime bubble, casts doubts on the soundness of the global free market economy and the efficacy of existing macroeconomic theories. What is serious is that these doubts are held not only by outsiders—journalists, politicians, heterodox economists, and social scientists sceptical of economics—but also by insiders, namely, the economists supposedly in the mainstream. Paul Krugman, one of the outstanding contributors to the existing body of economics, went on to say that most macroeconomics of the past 30 years had turned out to be useless at best and harmful at worst.

The purpose of this chapter is to retort to the tide by undertaking the unattractive task of defending the existing macroeconomics that everyone is so eager to abuse. Recent events must have forced many economists to reconsider their customary way of thinking. However, this does not mean that they are forced to go back to the good old times when a simple Keynesian multiplier formula was worked out without any reservation.

As many critics have noted, macroeconomics has changed drastically in 30 or 40 years. Evaluations of these changes differ even among economists.[1] What is important is that there were apparent and legitimate reasons, at least internally, for changes to have been made.

This chapter is intended to defend the existing macroeconomics by showing why macroeconomics has become what it is now, more specifically why economists were urged to abandon some of the old content and accept new material.

This chapter will proceed as follows. The next section gives a brief overview and an assessment of the recent controversy on the state of macroeconomics in view of the crisis. The third section shows the reason why the monetarists' criticism of the Keynesian model was eventually accepted. The fourth explains the reason why the rational expectation idea became the consensus among macroeconomists in spite of all the opposition to it. The fifth section shows the basic elements of the real business cycle (RBC) model and its significance. The sixth section shows how the New Keynesian model adopted the theoretical elements from its rivals. The last section provides a brief conclusion.

CONTROVERSY OVER THE STATE OF MACROECONOMICS IN VIEW OF THE CRISIS

The Economist's article of 18 July (2009) on the state of economics described as follows the confusion which broke out in the economic profession after the crisis:

> To the uninitiated, economics has always been a dismal science. But all these attacks come from within the guild: from Brad DeLong of the University of California, Berkeley; Paul Krugman of Princeton and the New York Times; and Willem Buiter of the London School of Economics (LSE), respectively. The macroeconomic crisis of the past two years is also provoking a crisis of confidence in macroeconomics.

As is natural, the criticisms from the outsiders, particularly from the heterodox economists, are harsher than ever. Paul Ormerod, known as the author of *The Death of Economics* (1994) and *Butterfly Economics* (1998), declared that the current crisis has falsified 'the ideas at the heart of modern macroeconomics which provided the intellectual jus-tification of the economic policies of the past 10 to 15 years' (Ormerod 2010: 5). Robert Skidelsky, the author of a three-volume biography of John Maynard Keynes (1983, 1992, 2000), denounced the existing macroeconomics as a 'shamed subject' that must be dismantled and reconstructed on the spirit of J.M. Keynes (Skidelsky 2009).

These external criticisms, however harsh, might not have been so harmful to the insiders, since the latter know well that there would be little hope for reconciliation between the insiders and the outside critics in any way and event. They would simply dismiss these criticisms as 'the views of people who have seized on the crisis as an opportunity to restate criticisms they had voiced long before 2008' (Lucas 2009). The seriousness of recent events lies in the fact that criticisms almost undistinguishable from those of the outsiders were voiced by such a name as P. Krugman, whose contributions to existing economics are apparent. If a layman read Krugman (2009) and Ormerod (2010) successively without any background knowledge about the authors, he would be sure to regard them as being from the same camp.

The most striking thing about Krugman (2009) is that he is quite negative not only about the anti-Keynesian 'New Classical' macroeconomics, spreading from the University of Chicago since the 1970s, but also about the New Keynesian economics that was gradually constructed since the 1980s to defend the basic Keynesian vision by standing up to the New Classical attacks. The article begins with an accusation against Olivier Blanchard, one of the leading figures carving out New Keynesian economics, of his making a false statement that 'the state of macro is good' in his survey paper on recent macroeconomics (Blanchard 2009). According to Krugman, New Keynesian economists cannot be devoid of guilt since 'the self-described New Keynesian economists were not immune to the charms of rational individuals and perfect markets. They tried to keep their deviations from neoclassical orthodoxy as limited as possible'[2] (Krugman 2009: 7). Thus, Krugman concluded, in the last of his Lionel Robbins lectures at the LSE on 10 June 2009, that most macroeconomics of the past 30 years was 'spectacularly useless at best, and positively harmful at worst' (*The Economist* 2009).

Willem Buiter, a prominent monetary economist and member of the Bank of England's Monetary Policy Committee from 1997 to 2000, made a similarly severe accusation against New Classical and New Keynesian thinkers alike. Buiter maintained that 'the typical graduate macroeconomics and monetary economics training, received at Anglo-American universities during the past 30 years or so, may have set back by decades serious investigations of aggregate economic behaviour and economic policy-relevant understanding', and 'most

mainstream macroeconomic theoretical innovations since the 1970s (the New Classical rational expectations revolution associated with such names as Robert E. Lucas Jr., Edward Prescott, Thomas Sargent, Robert Barro etc., and the New Keynesian theorizing of Michael Woodford and many others) have turned out to be self-referential, inward-looking distractions at best' (Buiter 2009). In Buiter's view, the customary precepts of the New Classical and the New Keynesian models—that is, the assumption of complete markets, dynamic optimization, and linearization—are so unrealistic that economists indulging themselves with these models were doomed never to foresee the adversity developed around 2008.

The noticeable feature of this controversy on the state of macroeconomics is that it does not look like a 'controversy' at all. The existing macroeconomics, whether it is New Classical or New Keynesian, has continued to be beaten one-sidedly both from the outside and inside just like a punching bag. The only exception to this picture is a tiny but enlightening article by Robert Lucas (2009), whose purpose is to rebut criticisms that the financial crisis represents a failure of economics. Beyond this, however, any overt attempt to defend the way that an ordinary economist, who believes in the usefulness of standard macroeconomic theories, used to think about existing macroeconomics cannot be seen in the controversy. This is quite astonishing as the majority of economists conducting economic research or teaching in universities or research institutions would be included in this category.

The other noticeable feature of the controversy is that policy arguments were sometimes too carelessly mingled with theoretical ones, which could easily distort the picture. If one evaluates the state of macroeconomics, one should primarily confine one's attention to its theoretical framework. Macroeconomic policies should be referred to only in relation to the theory. Moreover, one should not infer someone's theoretical stance from his policy stance. This is because an economic policy always needs a certain value judgement in addition to theoretical justification. If the constituent members had different value judgements about the desirability of a certain policy, a division of opinion could easily be seen even within the same theoretical circle.[3]

Krugman's accusation of the existing macroeconomics, and also of Blanchard's description of it, is an apparent example that failed

to make a distinction between positive theorizing and normative policy judgement. By describing 'convergence' in macroeconomics, Blanchard is only concerned with the theoretical and methodological aspects of macroeconomics. In contrast, by saying that 'division' recently arose within the economic profession, Krugman is mostly concerned with policies, particularly with fiscal policy. In this regard, Krugman's critical reference to Blanchard is highly unlikely since theoretical 'convergence' is possible even with a wider division of policy disposition.

In the theoretical and methodological sphere, Krugman apparently went too far when he said that most macroeconomics of the past 30 years was either useless or harmful. This is the same as saying that Old Keynesian economics proliferating in the 1960s was better than any macroeconomics since then. Most economists would think of this as absurd. If this statement were true, macroeconomics would then be regarded as a curious case showing long-term scientific regress rather than progress in the history of science.

It is true that Old Keynesian economics had its own significance in its proper historical context. However, there are plentiful reasons to suppose that the larger part of the Old Keynesian economics would have been discarded sooner or later. What actually happened was simply a typical aspect of scientific progress characterized by the feature that degenerative contents, or Scientific Research Programmes (SRPs) in Lakatosian terminology, occupying a certain research field are gradually or swiftly replaced by progressive ones.

Most economists, if they are sincere, would agree with Krugman's contention that recent events have been forcing economists to shift the focus of their research, and that they should pay more attention to the actuality of an economic model than to its mathematical rigor. However, they would not agree with the statement that rather than subsequent macroeconomic theories including the New Keynesian economics, the Old Keynesian economics, dominating the field until the 1970s, could better serve as a tool to analyse the recent crisis and to provide a policy prescription.

Not all economists would think that the monetarists and the New Classicals were always right. Some would say that they were positively wrong. However, few can deny that these anti-Keynesian critics had successfully pointed out the very weaknesses residing in early Keynesian economics. Later developments in the New Keynesian

economics had evolved from an effort to overcome these weaknesses by modifying and reconstructing the model to defend it from these critics.[4] The next four sections will trace this evolution.

WHY COULD THE MONETARIST COUNTER-REVOLUTION BE ACCOMPLISHED SO EASILY?

There is already a stylized story about how this happened. The story usually begins with Milton Friedman's famous presidential address to the American Economic Association in which he criticized Keynesian interpretation of the Phillips Curve, a trade-off between inflation and unemployment, by presenting his 'natural rate of unemployment' hypothesis (Friedman 1968). According to Friedman, a trade-off between inflation and unemployment that Keynesians had supposed to exist without any suspicion does not exist in the long run. The trade-off exists only in the short run while the inflation expectation of workers is not completely adjusted to actual inflation. In the long run, there is no such trade-off since the natural rate of unemployment is said to prevail. The stylized story then proceeds to describe how Friedman's argument was accepted among the economists, sometimes by mentioning the occurrence of stagflation which Friedman's theory was supposed to be able to predict. The story usually concludes with a description of how this task of counter-revolution to Keynesian economics provoked by Friedman was seamlessly handed down to the 'rational expectation' school.

Although this stylized story is useful for understanding the general picture, it cannot sufficiently explain why the counter-revolution was accomplished so easily. To find a sufficient answer to this question, it is necessary to pay more attention to the nature of the Keynesian economics that Friedman was attempting to discredit. If we examine Keynesian economics at that time from a historical perspective, we can easily notice that it had certain apparent peculiarities. First, as a result of focusing exclusively on demand factors, the Keynesians too often forgot the simple fact that an economy was always bounded by its resource constraints, the truth that every economist had been obliged to keep in mind. Second, as a result of focusing directly on demand factors, the Keynesians tended to ignore the importance of monetary factors that generations of monetary economists from David Hume to Irving Fisher had revealed so convincingly. It is exactly

on this weakness residing in Keynesian economics that Friedman was making his attack.

In short, what Friedman had achieved was literally a counter-revolution, namely the restoration of the traditional monetary thinking that had been completely wiped out by the Keynesian Revolution. Before Keynesian economics dominated the field, the monetary economists used to treat economic fluctuation as a deviation from some type of norm, or 'natural state' in the older economic terminology. In this norm, there is no room for monetary factors to influence the real factors in an economy, which are real income, income distribution, and so forth, since the resource constraints are to be fully bounded there. The monetary factors only affect nominal variables, namely prices of goods, money wages, amongst others. This thesis has been called the 'classical dichotomy' or 'neutrality of money' depending on context. The quantity theory of money, which has a long history from Hume via Fisher to Friedman, is simply an application of this thinking.

The monetary economists had not been content with this at all. They had also investigated a 'disturbance' situation in which the neutrality of money thesis could not hold, namely the situation in which the monetary factors affected real variables as well as nominal variables. As can be confirmed by the vast amount of business cycle literature, which appeared in the pre-Keynesian age, these investigations were not at all secondary for the monetary economists. In fact, it is these investigations that paved the way for the Keynesian Revolution.[5]

Nonetheless, one can say that Keynes's *The General Theory* (1936) was revolutionary at least for the following two reasons. First, it reversed the previous notion of 'norm and disturbance' to which the preceding monetary economists have been accustomed. For Keynes, the situation that these economists had supposed to be a deviation from the norm was in fact 'general'. Second, Keynes's *The General Theory* successfully provided a tractable model describing the non-neutrality of a money situation in which aggregate demand rather than resource constraint matters. Its success is apparent when we continue to see that models such as IS-LM (Investment—Saving or Liquidity preference—Money supply) and AD-AS (Aggregate Demand–Aggregate Supply model) descended from *The General Theory* are extensively used, at least for pedagogical purposes, in most of the introductory textbooks on macroeconomics.

The problem is that a revolution, whether it is political or scientific, so often goes too far. Provoked by Keynes's criticism of 'classical' economists, subsequent Keynesians tended to consider the situation in which aggregate demand matters as the norm rather than as a deviation from the norm. In retrospect, this conception carried the apparent risk of attaching too much importance to expansionary macroeconomic policies. As actually occurred, if these policies were extended beyond the demand-deficient situation for which the policies had originally been intended, inflation would be inevitable without any gain in real income. The reminder that productive capacity is always bounded by resource constraints should not have been wiped out even after the revolution.

In view of the broader history of monetary economics described earlier, what Friedman had done was simply a return to its tradition, by correcting Keynesian extremism. Thus, Friedman restored the traditional 'norm and disturbance' relationship once more. In his framework, the norm was defined by the natural rate of unemployment concept, and a deviation from the norm was explained by maladjustment of inflation expectation to actual inflation. The subsequent course of events shows that Friedman himself could not successfully provide a business cycle theory to finally replace the Keynesian one, although his emphasis on expectation was to subsequently trigger one of the biggest waves in macroeconomics. However, by using the natural rate of unemployment concept, he could effectively criticize the surrounding Keynesian arguments that had an apparent tendency to overdose the economy with expansionary macroeconomic policies.

The other theoretical viewpoint Friedman restored from pre-Keynesian monetary economics was deliberate consideration of the role of monetary factors and monetary policy in a phase of economic fluctuation. In Keynesian thinking, what is important is aggregate demand, not money. Money is important in so far as it can influence aggregate demand. It is the same with monetary policy. Expansionary monetary policy is effective in so far as it can influence aggregate demand. The early Keynesians tended to believe, for some reason or other, that expansionary monetary policy could not be so effective. Therefore, they usually preferred fiscal policy to monetary policy, as they thought that the former could affect aggregate demand more directly than the latter.

This 'money does not matter' attitude prevalent among the Keynesians at that stage was apparently odd and unbalanced. Harry Johnson, who was one of the severest critics of these crude Keynesians, thus said: 'It is an ironical paradox that Keynesian economics, having begun with a head-on attack on the alleged classical fallacy that money is merely a veil over the workings of a barter economy, should have wound up with the attempt to persuade the public that money is in fact merely a veil' (Johnson 1972: 56). To fix such a paradox, the monetarist counter-revolution was necessary.

WHY WAS THE RATIONAL EXPECTATION REVOLUTION NECESSARY?

One of the most conspicuous elements observable in the articles critical of the existing macroeconomics is definitely the condemnation of its rationality hypothesis. These articles commonly contend that the economists' failure to predict the crisis was largely due to their inclinations towards models based on the rational individual assumption. This condemnation is quite ironical, since one of the reasons why Keynesian economics had gradually been discredited among economists was its lack of micro-foundation, namely the lack of explanation for the way in which an individual makes economic decisions rationally. Now the New Keynesian economics has been charged not because it lacks micro-foundation, but because it is based on such an ill-founded assumption.

When Robert Lucas and others first prompted economists to introduce the rational expectation concept into macroeconomics in the 1970s, dominant Keynesians at that time did not hesitate to express overt hatred towards them and their intention. These Keynesians' anger was, in some aspects, far more furious than the aforementioned critics were with the models based on rationality. Today, the picture is completely different, at least among the macroeconomists. Michael Woodford describes this as follows:

> It is now widely agreed that it is important to *model expectations as endogenous*, and in particular, that in policy analysis it is crucial to take into account the way in which expectations ought to be different in the case that an alternative policy were to be adopted. This was, of course, the point of the celebrated Lucas (1976) critique of traditional methods of econometric policy evaluation. Because of sensitivity to this issue,

it is now routine both in positive interpretations of macroeconomic data and in normative analyses of possible economic policies to assume rational expectations on the part of economic decision makers, in accordance with the methodology introduced by the New Classical literature of the 1970s. (Woodford 2009: 271–2)

The reason why such a drastic conversion could occur in the profession was, supposedly, not so much that the economists were persuaded of the righteousness of the rational expectation hypothesis, but rather that they gradually realized that assuming otherwise in a model could occasionally lead to a fatally misdirected conclusion. In a paper in which Lucas first presented his proclamation later known as the 'Lucas critique' (Lucas 1976), he revealed that almost all of the econometric models which existed then were risking this failure.

The problem is evident even in the most standard textbook Keynesian model, namely the IS-LM. The IS-LM model usually assumes the static expectation that individuals would continue to hold an existing inflation expectation into the future. This means that these individuals would not change their inflation expectations however drastically macroeconomic policies were shifted. The difficulty arises when the inflation expectations of the individuals actually shift according to the future shifts in macroeconomic policies. It is quite plausible, for example, that a new plan for a government's spending policy would raise their inflation expectations. In this case, the standard IS-LM model with the static inflation expectation will systematically underestimate the effect of such a policy by failing to take the effect on private investment into account. Since private investment in the IS-LM model is a negative function of the real interest rate, that is, the nominal interest rate minus the expected inflation rate, a higher expected inflation necessarily leads to a lower real interest rate, which in turn leads to increased private investment. Therefore, if the magnitude of government spending were determined on the basis of an econometric model similar to this static IS-LM, the policy would inevitably overheat the economy rather than stabilize it.

As to the rational expectation hypothesis itself, its general notion is quite commonplace. It simply says that individuals will utilize available information and determine expectations regarding future economic variables such as income or the inflation rate that are necessary whenever they make intertemporal economic choices such as

saving or investment. By contrast, the static expectation assumption implies that individuals will not utilize any new information they can obtain and will continue to hold certain fixed expectations regarding future economic variables when they make intertemporal economic choices. If this is a true representation of human behaviour, we must admit that a human being is much inferior to an animal that is always keen to receive new information from outside, particularly a new sign of danger, and promptly responds to it. It is quite natural that the economists who had realized its oddness could no longer believe in a model that was based on such an assumption.

Although the rational expectation is now a consensus among macroeconomists as Woodford says, it is not likely to be so among outsiders. Rather, contempt and hatred of it is very widespread. This hostility among the outsiders seems to be based on a conviction that the rational expectation presupposes a certain socially desirable consequence, categorically rejecting the inconvenient truth that the real world is facing. In fact, this conviction is not true; it is just a simple misunderstanding. The rational expectation does not presuppose a socially desirable consequence by itself at all. It says that individuals will utilize available information when determining their expectations. However, it does not say that such information, and the individuals' ways of interpreting this information, is either complete or correct. If the information were incomplete, for example, the outcome would be distorted from that which would be attained if the information were complete. This is exactly the result that Lucas (1972) obtained from his seminal model of rational expectation with incomplete information. In this paper, which Robert Hall (1996: 40) describes as 'arguably the most significant paper in theoretical macroeconomics since Keynes', Lucas showed that incomplete information on a monetary shock could be a source of economic fluctuation.

A similar misunderstanding is readily observable with regard to the 'efficient market' hypothesis presented by Eugene Fama. Robert Skidelsky made a fierce condemnation of this as follows:

> An important implication of this view (a stable and repetitive universe in which rational actors make efficient use of the information available to them) is that shares are always correctly priced. This is the basis of the so-called efficient market hypothesis that has dominated financial economics. It led bankers into blind faith in their mathematical forecasting models. It led governments and regulators

to discount the possibility that financial markets could implode. It led to what Alan Greenspan called (after he had stepped down as chairman of the US Federal Reserve) 'the underpricing of risk worldwide'. (Skidelsky 2009)

The argument made by Robert Lucas in his concise article that 'rebuts criticisms that the financial crisis represents a failure of economics' (Lucas 2009) is in sharp contrast to this. He contends that the failure of the models to forecast sudden falls in the value of financial assets such as those which occurred after the Lehman shock is not a refutation of the efficient market hypothesis at all. Far from it, it is exactly 'one of the main implications' of the hypothesis. Lucas says: 'If an economist had a formula that could reliably forecast crises a week in advance, say, then that formula would become part of generally available information and prices would fall a week earlier.' So the fact that the models could not forecast the crisis is not refuting but convincing the efficient market hypothesis. As Lucas warns against its misuse, the term 'efficient' exclusively means that individuals use information in their own private interest. It has nothing to do with socially desirable pricing.

WAS RBC ONLY A MAGNIFICENT TOY?

After the rational expectation revolution was over, the macroeconomists were largely divided into two camps, namely the New Classicals and those remaining in the Keynesian tradition. Unlike their previous leaders such as Friedman and Lucas on the one hand, and Paul Samuelson, Robert Solow, and James Tobin on the other, the economists in these two camps had been disregarding rather than criticizing each other. The cause was apparently on the New Classicals' side. A drastic shift of the research agenda that was described by Blanchard (2009: 211) as 'the Mencheviks gave way to the Bolcheviks' occurred among them. The Bolcheviks were those who cherished the RBC model under the leadership of Edward Prescott. The emblem of the Mencheviks that focuses on a monetary disturbance in line with Friedman and Lucas was completely lost.

Robert Hall (1976) called these two camps the 'fresh-water' school and the 'salt-water' school respectively, hinting at the geographic locations of most of the New Classicals and most of the Keynesians.

Blanchard (2009: 212) describes the relationship between these two groups as 'tense, and often unpleasant' such that 'the first accused the second of being bad economists, clinging to obsolete beliefs and discredited theories. The second accused the first of ignoring basic facts, and, in their pursuit of a beautiful but irrelevant model, of falling prey to a "scientific illusion"'. Blanchard even says that the situation at that time was so bad that 'one could reasonably despair of the future of macro' (Ibid.).

The RBC model begins with a model presented by Frank Ramsey (1928) that depicted the dynamic nature of an economy in which a representative consumer made an optimal intertemporal choice between consumption and saving. The RBC model is a modified version of this Ramsey model, the former adding stochastic productivity shocks and intertemporally determined labour supply into the latter. The model shows that economic fluctuations are largely due to optimal responses by individuals to random fluctuations in the productivity level exogenously caused by innovations, bad weather, imported oil price increases, stricter regulations, amongst others. A positive productivity shock would induce individuals to work more now than in the future since the future work under the normal productivity trend is likely to give them a lesser amount of products. If a negative productivity shock occurred, the result would be the reversal of this. This is exactly the way in which economists in the fresh-water school think about business cycles.

The RBC explanation of business cycles, particularly the schema that individuals are simply opting to have more leisure instead of work in a depression phase triggered by a negative productivity shock, is quite counter-intuitive, at least for economists in the Keynesian tradition. Since the model assumes perfect competition and completely flexible prices along with the Walrasian general equilibrium model, there is no room for a negative demand shock to be associated with unintended waste of resources or involuntary unemployment. Similarly, since the model assumes perfect information, there is no room for a monetary shock to have any influence on the real side of the economy. This is exactly an application of the classical 'neutrality of money' thesis, although the RBC uses this to show that money is irrelevant even for the explanation of economic fluctuations, a view which sharply contradicts traditional monetary thinking including

Friedman and Lucas in which money is supposed to be essential for explaining economic disturbances. It is extremely ironical that the result of Lucas (1972) was eventually used to justify the exclusion of money from the model with an assumption of perfect information. As a strong objection made by Lawrence Summers (1986) shows, it seemed completely impossible for Keynesians to accept the RBC model, at least in the beginning. In spite of their resistance, however, the fresh-water school had been gradually invading and successfully occupying the academia, although the actual macroeconomic policies largely remained in the hands of the salt-water economists.

Gregory Mankiw (2006) describes this confrontation between the fresh-water economists and the salt-water economists not as a conflict between two competing theoretical positions, but as a difference in roles between scientists and engineers, the former being those who want to solve practical problems and the latter those who want to understand how the world works. After categorizing the macroeconomists in this way, he proceeds to state 'new classical and new Keynesian research has had little impact on practical macroeconomists, who are charged with the messy task of conducting actual monetary and fiscal policy' (Ibid.: 29–30). Michael Woodford (2009: 275–7) makes a strong objection to this appraisal by Mankiw through citing actual empirical models that have been constructed in line with a theoretical frame called the dynamic stochastic general equilibrium (DSGE), a category initiated by RBC but wider than this since it also contains the New Keynesian models as long as they are based on dynamic optimization.

Mankiw is probably right on the point that the engineers usually prefer the applicability of a model to its consistency. However, this does not mean that engineers do not care for the consistency of the model they are applying to actual policies. Inconsistency apparently would make them less confident about policy conclusions of the model. Eventually, they would look forward to a more consistent model that could replace the existing one. This is exactly the situation that economists who were working with the Old Keynesian model faced.

For a long time, the Old Keynesian model had been criticized for its lack of micro-foundation. The weakness is apparent if we compare it with the RBC model. The latter inherited the rigid foundation of optimal intertemporal choice, a condition usually expressed

by the Euler equation from the Ramsey model. The Old Keynesian counterpart for this is the Keynesian consumption function, whose ground was supposed to be problematic even in the heyday of Keynesianism. Many economists questioned why the current consumption depended solely on current income, and why current consumption depended neither on wealth already accumulated nor on income attainable in the future. There was no plausible answer for this, except that it was for convenience sake.

The reason why the legitimate ground for the Keynesian consumption function was particularly needed is because the greater part of Keynesian policy conclusions depended on the specific property of the Keynesian consumption function. At the earlier stage of the Keynesian era, it was widely believed that the core of Keynesianism lay in its fiscal multiplier theory. The commercial success of Paul Samuelson's *Economics* (1948), the second Keynesian textbook in the US following *The Elements of Economics* (1947) by Lorie Tarshis, might have contributed to such an understanding. In these Keynesian textbooks, the fiscal multiplier theory was explained using a simple algebraic formula as if fiscal policy had a magical power to magnify income several times as much as the initial fiscal spending. These textbooks never mentioned that the theory could be true only if the Keynesian consumption function held true, a condition that was actually not at all obvious either theoretically or empirically. In this sense, the Keynesian fiscal multiplier theory might lead to the undesirable effect that people expected too much of the power of fiscal policy, even if this actually had some decent power. The case of Japan, which resorted to fiscal policy rather than monetary policy every time a depression occurred, might exemplify this.[6]

Although the Keynesian consumption function and the associated fiscal multiplier remain at the core of elementary macroeconomics textbooks, they gradually have been displaced from serious economic research. It was again Milton Friedman who triggered the trend, followed by Franco Modigliani, Albert Ando, and others.[7] Unlike the Keynesian consumption function, their theories of consumption and saving were solidly micro-founded, in the sense that households are always supposed to make optimal intertemporal choices between consumption and saving. The most noticeable property of their dynamic optimization theories is consumption smoothing, meaning that consumption is less volatile than income. It is

apparent that consumption smoothing undermines the inference from the Keynesian fiscal multiplier theory, since the sensitivity of current income to consumption in the dynamic optimization model cannot exceed that in the Keynesian consumption function models. In retrospect, the reason why the RBC model successfully dominated academia and led the fashion in the 1980s and the 1990s might not have been its explanatory power as a theory. Rather, it offered a theoretical consistency that rivalling Keynesian models supposedly lacked. Superiority in logical coherence, however, does not establish superiority as a scientific theory. Whatever its focus, science is always a framework of human knowledge that facilitates understanding a mechanism dominating actual phenomena. That means a scientific theory always should be related to the actual world; thus, the greater the potential for explaining actual phenomena, the better the theory. In this scientific sense, the superiority of the RBC model to the traditional Keynesian model is quite dubious, since the scientific scope of the former apparently had been narrower than the latter. The RBC model categorically rejects the possibility that a demand shock or a monetary shock can be associated with macroeconomic fluctuations. That also means the RBC model has no connection with the commonly held roles of monetary and fiscal policy in macroeconomic stabilization, which long had been the supreme focus of macroeconomics. This situation explains why the salt-water economists of the 1980s and the 1990s, who were mainly concerned with macroeconomic policies, mostly disregarded the ongoing development of the RBC model.

However, it became apparent that the RBC model's central advantage was not its specification of labour supply fluctuations, but its incorporation of dynamic optimization. It also became apparent that the RBC model was primarily useful not as a tool for macroeconomic estimation but as a benchmark that offered multiple possibilities for extension. Although the initial RBC model assumed perfect and flexible markets, there was no convincing reason for these assumptions other than simplicity. Rather, the model with these assumptions was apparently too restricted to be applied directly to the actual world. In fact, efforts to incorporate market imperfections or restrictions into the model started afterwards.[8] The economic model resulting from these efforts eventually came to be called the DSGE model.

WHY WERE NON-KEYNESIAN NOTIONS EVENTUALLY ACCEPTED AS THE CONSENSUS?

As described in Blanchard (2009) and Woodford (2009), the present-day macroeconomists have certain definite theoretical and methodological consensus among themselves. These papers show that this is largely due to the acceptance by the New Keynesians of the notions that were initially thought to be non-Keynesian in nature, namely the rational expectation and the DSGE framework. The reason why economists were forced to accept them has already been shown in the previous sections. As for the New Keynesians, they realized in due course that these notions were not actually contradictory to the Keynesian core that 'demand matters'. Moreover, they gradually realized that these notions could be utilized to reinforce the reliability of their models by removing their weaknesses, thus presenting better models that have more rigid foundations.

In fact, the main motivation of the New Keynesian economics was to reconstruct the framework to effectively defend the Keynesian core from the criticism cast by the New Classical economists. This project began in the 1980s; it followed the collapse of the research project called the general disequilibrium approach founded by Robert Clower in the 1960s. Although what comprises of the Keynesian core is a subject of immortal controversy, it is usually recognized that some form of nominal rigidities in the goods market and/or in the labour market makes the indispensable core of Keynesian economics. As to the structure of the model, most of the static Keynesian models were simply 'fixed price general equilibrium models', in which at least one of the variables, that is, the price or the nominal wage, is fixed, which means that the variable is exogenously determined instead of endogenously solved. This setting necessarily leads to a disequilibrium solution, namely one with excess demand or excess supply, since the price or the wage cannot be adjusted to clear the market. If this resulting disequilibrium turns out to be excess supply of labour, it is simply the involuntary unemployment, a phenomenon that the Keynesians were focusing on consistently. The textbook IS-LM model is a representative example of such a model, in which the nominal wage is fixed and the resulting solution of the model would be unemployment equilibrium if there were not sufficient aggregate demand. The general disequilibrium approach, in other words the fixed price general

equilibrium approach, was intended to investigate the nature of these disequilibrium solutions using the general equilibrium analysis.

When Lucas and his colleagues began to criticize Keynesian economics for its lack of micro-foundation in the 1970s, such fixed price setting itself came to be a target of their attack. Once fixed price was assumed, disequilibrium would be inevitable. What is important, however, is why it is fixed. What the Keynesians, including the general disequilibrium theorists at that time, were doing was simply to assume a fixed price without any reasoning behind this. Apparently, the Keynesians needed a micro-foundation for the maladjustment of price, namely a reasoning to explain why price failed to be adjusted to clear the market.

The New Keynesian economics that has been shaped into that of today simply began from here. Various types of hypotheses were presented and explored. One of the most important points elucidated in the course of this was that the model capturing the Keynesian core should inevitably diverge from perfect competition. Imperfect competition was needed because price setters can set price and quantity simultaneously to maximize their benefits only in such a setting. Since monopolistic competition is the most tractable among the various cases of imperfect competition, assuming monopolistic competition became the norm in the New Keynesian models thereafter.[9] In such a setting, Mankiw (1985) pointed out that the existence of menu costs, that is, the costs to firms to change prices, would induce the firms to prefer quantity adjustment to price adjustment if the menu costs were large enough to offset the gains that would be obtained by the adjustment without the menu costs. Although the actual importance of the menu costs for economic fluctuation is not agreed upon among economists, it can at least provide a micro-founded reasoning to explain why a demand shock is largely transferred into a supply change without much change in price.

If viewed from today's criterion, the New Keynesian models in the 1980s were not fully micro-founded since they were basically static in nature. More specifically, these models were lacking the dynamic optimization structure with which the rival RBC models were equipped. This might be the reason why advanced education on macroeconomics around the beginning of the 1990s was based on the RBC model rather than the New Keynesian model in most cases.

The situation began to change after the mid-1990s, specifically after Tack Yun published an article (Yun 1996) in which he presented a model introducing staggered price setting as devised by Guillermo Calvo (1983) into the dynamic model commonly used in the RBC. His model provided the basic structure for what we now call the New Keynesian model, and triggered the proliferation of literature along this line. Theoretical results of these investigations were collected extensively by Woodford (2003) and intensively by Gali (2008).

* * *

For a long time, the word Keynesian was thought to be a category of economists who focused on demand and not money. Furthermore, rational expectation was thought to be incompatible with Keynesian thought. Moreover, the Keynesian consumption function was thought to be an essential component of the Keynesian model. The course of events since the monetarist counter-revolution proved all of these to be false. The Keynesians as well as the monetarists should have paid more attention to monetary factors and monetary policy, as the recent, New Keynesians do. The evolution of the New Keynesian economics since the 1980s has proved that such a notion as the static expectation, or the Keynesian consumption function, was not the essential component of the Keynesian core at all. Far from it, they were actually the weakest link of the older model.[10] If merely some type of nominal rigidity was introduced into it, the model would display a feature of the Keynesian core that demand and money matters. Introducing rational expectation and dynamic optimization into the model only makes the model more reliable.

In recent times, many economists have been undertaking research on macroeconomic policies using the New Keynesian model. They are largely motivated by the intention to provide better policy guidance to save the economy that has been under the most troublesome adversity.[11] It would be unrealistic to say that the older Keynesian model used in the 1960s could have served better for this purpose. Moreover, an economist making such statements and criticizing others who are seriously thinking about macroeconomic policies would be just like a soldier shooting fellow soldiers from behind. This kind of cynicism would eventually hurt the profession as a whole, and injure the hope for it to contribute to the real world.

NOTES

1. It is inevitable that evaluations of each change in economic science differ among economists with different theoretical perspectives. As seen in comments by J. Tobin, F. Modigliani, and R. Solow in their interviews (Snowdon and Vane 1999), traditional Keynesians were quite critical of what had become dominant in macroeconomics during these 30 or 40 years. In contrast, G. Mankiw and O. Blanchard, who represent the New Keynesian School, expressed qualifiedly positive views of these developments in modern macroeconomics (Ibid.). Despite this difference, 'Old' and 'New' Keynesian economists apparently had the common agenda of modelling Keynes's ideas within the neoclassical framework (see Arena 2010). Fundamentalist Keynesians inevitably saw these departures from Keynes's original thinking, which began shortly after his death, as nothing more than degenerate.

2. As was readily expected, Ormerod's comments about New Keynesian economists are more destructive. In addition to O. Blanchard, Ormerod (2010) also accused Michael Woodford, the other prominent figure of the New Keynesian economics, of saying 'convergence in macroeconomics' (Woodford 2009) in the midst of the crisis.

3. As reported in *The Economist* (2009), there emerged a fierce controversy among the US economists as to the power of fiscal policy to pull the US economy up from the bottom. It is understandable that New Classical economists like Lucas and Robert Barro are almost entirely negative with regard to fiscal policy. The economists positive about fiscal policy are, quite naturally, Keynesians or New Keynesians. What is interesting is that some New Keynesians, for example, John Taylor and Gregory Mankiw, are not positive about fiscal policy at all.

4. In interviews with leading macroeconomists (Snowdon and Vane 1999), G. Mankiw was asked a question about what papers or books he thought had the biggest impact on the development of macroeconomics over the last 25 years. His answer was as follows:

> The biggest impact has undoubtedly come from Lucas. He put the cracks into the Keynesian consensus that existed in the 60s. He really pulled macroeconomics apart by proposing new and intriguing ideas. The disagreements today among macroeconomists have largely arisen from the critiques of Lucas and of his followers. As you know, I do not agree with Lucas's solutions, but I take the problems that he pointed out very seriously. A lot of the work that I and other new Keynesians have done is a response to the problems he pointed out in the old Keynesian ideas. (Ibid.: 107)

5. David Laidler describes the situation quite convincingly. By examining a vast amount of inter-war literature, Laidler (1999) concludes that Keynes's *The General Theory* (1936) should be treated not so much as a revolution but as an evolution of preceding economic thinking on money, unemployment, and the business cycle.

6. The deep-rooted tendency of Keynesian economists to opt for fiscal rather than monetary policy was most conspicuous in Japan. For a long time, it was

widely believed that Keynesian policy exclusively meant expansionary fiscal policy and that monetary policy had nothing to do with the Keynesian policy. This belief began to change only after the mid-1990s when Japan's economy first fell into long-lasting deflation. Around that period, certain economists began to argue that not only expansionary fiscal policy but also drastic and unconventional monetary policy, such as quantitative easing, was needed for Japan's economy to overcome deflation.

7. Krugman (2007) describes the situation quite accurately:

> In his 1957 book *A Theory of the Consumption Function*, Friedman argued that the best way to make sense of saving and spending was not, as Keynes had done, to resort to loose psychological theorizing, but rather to think of individuals as making rational plans about how to spend their wealth over their lifetimes. This was not necessarily an anti-Keynesian idea—in fact, the great Keynesian economist, Franco Modigliani simultaneously and independently made a similar case in work with Albert Ando.

8. A comment by Blanchard concerning the RBC model appropriately summarized the situation:

> The real business cycle approach gave us a natural starting point. It has become clear that one cannot stop there, but we now have a structure in which we can introduce imperfections, be it in the goods, the labour, or the credit and financial markets, and see where that leads us. While Keynes gave us a way of thinking about the world but without any specific technical tools, proponents of the real business cycle approach have done just the opposite. They have given us nice tools. (Snowdon and Vane 1999: 233)

9. The basic model of this type was presented by Blanchard and Kiyotaki (1987).

10. Krugman's assessment of Keynes and Friedman seems fair in this regard: 'Keynesian theory initially prevailed because it did a far better job than classical orthodoxy of making sense of the world around us, and Friedman's critique of Keynes became so influential largely because he correctly identified Keynesianism's weak points' (Krugman 2007).

11. Blanchard et al. (2010) and the papers referenced in it provide good examples.

REFERENCES

Arena, R. 2010. 'From the "Old" to the "New" Keynesian–Neoclassical Synthesis: An Interpretation', in B.W. Bateman, T. Hirai, and M.C. Marcuzzo (eds), *The Return to Keynes*. Cambridge, MA: Harvard University Press, pp. 77–93.

Blanchard, O. 2009. 'The State of Macro', *Annual Review of Economics*, 1: 209–28.

Blanchard, O. and N. Kiyotaki. 1987. 'Monopolistic Competition and the Effects of Aggregate Demand', *American Economic Review*, 77(4): 647–66.

Blanchard, O., G. Dell'Ariccia, and P. Mauro. 2010. 'Rethinking Macroeconomic Policy', *Journal of Money, Credit and Banking*, 42: 199–215.

Buiter, W. 2009. 'The Unfortunate Uselessness of Most "State of the Art" Academic Monetary Economics', *Willem Buiter's Maverecon*, 3 March, available online: http://blogs.ft.com/maverecon/2009/03/the-unfortunate-uselessness-of-most-state-of-the-art-academic-monetary-economics/ Last accessed on 27 April 2012.

Calvo, G. 1983. 'Staggered Prices in a Utility-Maximizing Framework', *Journal of Monetary Economics*, 12(3): 383–98.

Friedman, M. 1968. 'The Role of Monetary Policy', *American Economic Review*, 58(1): 1–17.

Gali, J. 2008. *Monetary Policy, Inflation, and the Business Cycle*. Princeton: Princeton University Press.

Hall, R. 1976. 'Notes on the Current State of Empirical Economics', an unpublished paper presented at the one-day workshop of the Institute of Mathematical Studies in Social Sciences, Stanford University.

———. 1996. 'Robert Lucas, Recipient of the 1995 Nobel Memorial Prize in Economics', *Scandinavian Journal of Economics*, 98(1): 33–48.

Johnson, H. 1972. *Inflation and the Monetarist Controversy*. Amsterdam: North Holland.

Keynes, John Maynard (1936), *The General Theory of Employment, Interest and Money*, London: Macmillan.

Krugman, P. 2007. 'Who Was Milton Friedman?' *The New York Review of Books*, 15 February. Available at http://www.nybooks.com/articles/archives/2007/feb/15/who-was-milton-friedman/ Last accessed on 27 April 2012.

———. 2009. 'How Did Economists Get It So Wrong?' *The New York Times Magazine*, 2 September, p. 7.

Laidler, D. 1999. *Fabricating the Keynesian Revolution: Studies of the Inter-war Literature on Money, the Cycle, and Unemployment*. Cambridge: Cambridge University Press.

Lucas, R. 1972. 'Expectations and the Neutrality of Money', *Journal of Economic Theory*, 4(2): 103–24.

———. 1976. 'Econometric Policy Evaluation: A Critique', *Carnegie–Rochester Conference Series on Public Policy*, 1(1): 19–46.

———. 2009. 'In Defence of the Dismal Science', *The Economist*, 8 August.

Mankiw, G. 1985. 'Small Menu Costs and Large Business Cycles: A Macroeconomic Model of Monopoly', *Quarterly Journal of Economics*, 100(2): 529–37.

———. 2006. 'The Macroeconomist as Scientist and Engineer', *Journal of Economic Perspectives*, 20(4): 29–46.

Ormerod, P. 1994. *The Death of Economics*. London: Faber and Faber.

———. 1998. *Butterfly Economics*. London: Faber and Faber.

———. 2010. 'The Current Crisis and the Culpability of Macroeconomic Theory', *Contemporary Social Science: Journal of the Academy of Social Sciences*, 5(1): 5–18.

Ramsey, F. 1928. 'A Mathematical Theory of Saving', *Economic Journal*, 38(152): 543–59.

Samuelson, Paul A. 1948. *Economics: An Introductory Analysis*. New York: McGraw-Hill.

Skidelsky, R. 1983. *John Maynard Keynes: Hopes Betrayed, 1883–1920*. London: Macmillan.

———. 1992. *John Maynard Keynes: The Economist as Saviour, 1920–1937*. London: Macmillan.

———. 2000. *John Maynard Keynes: Fighting for Britain, 1937–1946*. London: Macmillan.

———. 2009. 'How to Rebuild a Shamed Subject', *Financial Times*, 6 August.

Snowdon, B. and H. Vane. 1999. *Conversations with Leading Economists: Interpreting Modern Macroeconomics*. Cheltenham, UK and Northampton, MA: Edward Elgar.

Summers, L. 1986. 'Some Skeptical Observations on Real Business Cycle Theory', *Federal Reserve Bank of Minneapolis Quarterly Review*, 10(4): 23–7.

Tarshis, Lorie. 1947. *The Elements of Economics: An Introduction to the Theory of Price and Employment*. Boston: Houghton Mifflin.

The Economist. 2009. 'The State of Macroeconomics', 18 July.

Woodford, M. 2003. *Interest and Prices: Foundations of a Theory of Monetary Policy*. Princeton: Princeton University Press.

———. 2009. 'Convergence in Macroeconomics: Elements of the New Synthesis', *American Economic Journal: Macroeconomics*, 1(1): 267–79.

Yun, T. 1996. 'Nominal Price Rigidity, Money Supply Endogeneity, and Business Cycles', *Journal of Monetary Economics*, 37(2): 345–70.

5

Keynes and Capitalism

The Case of Japan

COLIN ROGERS

To many economists alive today, Keynes was a socialist and as such an enemy of capitalism. But like almost everything else about Keynes in contemporary mainstream literature, this view is at best misleading and at worst plain wrong. Those who have read Keynes's *Collected Writings* or the excellent biographies by Skidelsky (2003) or Davidson (2007) will surely know that Keynes offered a 'middle way' between the extremes of National Socialism or Communism and the faith in laissez-faire capitalism. Keynes was a pragmatist who recognized that capitalism, with all its flaws, was the only economic system compatible with the maintenance of individual freedoms essential to the enjoyment of a good life. Capitalism, like democracy, has flaws that need to be managed to temper its extremes and protect the freedoms it bestows. By contrast, the confusion apparent in modern macroeconomics means that many policymakers are incapable of understanding the flaws in capitalism and consequently they put individual freedoms at risk.

The theoretical basis for Keynes's ultimate vision of how to manage capitalism was presented in *The General Theory*, where the principle of effective demand is presented as a generalization of classical theory. The principle of effective demand explains how monetary and real theory can be integrated and reveals all the special assumptions that

are required to generate the classical special case of unique natural long-run equilibrium at full employment. *The General Theory* therefore offered a theoretical framework that Keynes imagined would change the way economists thought about the behaviour of the aggregate economy. Unfortunately he was wrong in that belief and contemporary macroeconomics and monetary theory is floundering in its attempts to understand current events.[1] One reason for this confusion is that even Keynesian economists have failed to understand Keynes's principle of effective demand and his general theory[2]—the generalization of classical theory. As a consequence, they have failed to understand the transformation that occurred to most economies in the post–Second World War period, and more recently the implications of the surge in globalization and the rise of 'managed' capitalism in Asia and particularly China. The improved economic performance of the West in the post–Second World War period and the emergence of Asia in recent decades convinced many in the economics profession that this improved performance is as a result of laissez-faire capitalism (Lucas 2011). Any crises are then interpreted as random shocks that leave the objective reality of the classical vision intact. Hence their classical special case is interpreted as the general case of universal applicability. But as Keynes explained, this is a fundamental conceptual mistake.

The difference between Keynes's vision and that of contemporary macroeconomics represented by old and new schools of various shades of macroeconomic thought is that Keynes generalizes the useful insights of classical theory while contemporary macroeconomists select special, and in some cases bizarre or imaginary, cases of classical ideas. The irony of this intellectual failure on such a grand scale is that it leads to policy mistakes that accentuate and magnify the failings of capitalism that opens it to attack from its old enemies on the left and the right.[3] For, if individual freedoms are to be protected, capitalism must be seen to work in a manner that is consistent with universal notions of fairness and justice. But if management of the capitalist system is based on a flawed vision, it inevitably results in mismanagement bringing the capitalist system into question.

To illustrate the importance of Keynes's vision for the management of a capitalist system the following discussion will outline the key elements of his general theory. The general theory will then be employed to assess the analyses of Japan's Great Recession offered by

McKinnon, Krugman, and Koo. Each focuses on different aspects of Japan's predicament but each contains insights that can be explained using Keynes's general theory.

KEYNES'S GENERAL THEORY

The structure of Keynes's general theory and the importance of the principle of effective demand were sketched in Rogers (2010, 2011), so here only a brief outline will be provided before I examine the policy implications of the theory.

Essentially Keynes's general theory explains why and how laissez-faire capitalist monetary economies can become trapped for decades in positions of sub-par performance; there exists a continuum of long-run equilibria. In general, this happens because in a world of incomplete stochastic knowledge laissez-faire capitalism can easily impart an upward bias to the rate of interest and a downward bias to the marginal efficiency of capital, relative to the rate of interest. Keynes (1936), in generalizing Wicksell, stresses the importance of these *two rates of interest* (the rate of interest and the marginal efficiency of capital) in determining long-run equilibrium. The principle of effective demand then replaces Say's Law by demonstrating how a limit to the profitable expansion of output can occur before full employment is achieved. Contra Say's Law unilateral increases in supply beyond the point of effective demand will *not* increase employment unless the increased output can be sold for at least a normal profit, that is, something shifts the point of effective demand. The principle of effective demand explains why this will generally not be the case and so classical equilibrium, equality between the rate of interest and the marginal efficiency of capital, can occur at less than full employment and no amount of flexibility in wages and/or prices will automatically produce full employment by shifting the point of effective demand as required.

Furthermore, in an uncertain world the rate of return on the safer more liquid asset rules the roost; classical equilibrium, defined as equality between the rate of interest and the marginal efficiency of capital, is determined by the rate of interest. Note that the money rate of interest and the marginal efficiency of capital can be compared in nominal or real (inflation-adjusted) terms but obviously the nominal rate of interest should not be compared with the real (inflation-adjusted)

marginal efficiency of capital. So even if the money rate of interest falls to zero, when the structural marginal efficiency of capital is negative, it is the money rate that determines the equilibrium rate of return. *Depreciation and contraction of the capital stock then occurs until the marginal efficiency of capital rises to zero in the long run.* However, like the rate of interest and the propensity to consume, the marginal efficiency of capital is an independent variable in a capitalist economy, so is not determined *only* by the forces of productivity and thrift. The marginal efficiency of capital can move independently of the rate of interest, and the marginal productivity of capital, and in a globalized world with a high degree of capital mobility it may be subject to forces external to national economies.

The tragedy for Keynes's contemporaries and contemporary macroeconomics is that they failed to recognize that he was simply offering a generalization of classical theory. In particular it was a generalization that exposed the limitations of several restrictive assumptions embedded in the classical vision in the 1930s. More extreme versions of this vision are now popular in contemporary macroeconomics.

Three key assumptions that Keynes abandoned in *The General Theory* were:

1. Complete stochastic knowledge
2. The neutrality of money
3. Uniqueness of long-period aggregate equilibrium

Many Keynes scholars outside of the mainstream have recognized and stressed the importance of one or more of these issues but mainstream macroeconomists have largely proceeded by re-defining macroeconomics to preclude them. Laidler (2009) provides a good discussion of these issues. But once all these issues are acknowledged, Keynes's generalization of classical theory comes into clearer focus. The principle of effective demand is based on the realization that in a world of incomplete stochastic knowledge money is a real phenomenon on a par with the real variables recognized by classical theory. How money, as a variable on a par with traditional real variables of classical theory, interacts with these traditional real variables then depends on the institutional arrangements that apply to the existing national and international monetary and financial systems; financial structure matters. For example, under the gold standard where domestic money supplies are effectively exogenous, Keynes

applies the principle of effective demand to explain how under these conditions in a laissez-faire economy the lack of stochastic certainty would inevitably produce a rate of interest that was too high and a marginal efficiency of capital that was too low for full employment; in a world with a high uncertainty index (a common occurrence in a laissez-faire economy) liquidity preference forces up the rate of interest when the supply of money is constrained while an elevated state of uncertainty depresses 'animal spirits' and the marginal efficiency of capital. In such a system monetary policy would, in effect, be in the hands of the public and the private banks. With the rate of interest on average too high and ruling the roost, the point of effective demand would in general be insufficient to ensure full employment. In short it was quite possible in a real laissez-faire monetary economy with incomplete stochastic knowledge to face decades of growth below potential.[4]

Thus in a laissez-faire monetary economy with incomplete stochastic knowledge, the two elements of Keynes's principle of effective demand, the rate of interest and the rate of return on capital (the marginal efficiency of capital), can be biased—the rate of interest upwards and the return on capital downwards. The end result is classical long-period equilibrium with unemployment that flexibility of wages and prices can eliminate only by chance. Unemployment results because the rate of interest rules the roost so rates of return on other assets adjust to the money rate as the less risky rate and investment will inevitably be insufficient to fill the gap left by saving at full employment in any laissez-faire economy with a propensity to spend of less than unity. Say's Law fails because any increases in aggregate supply beyond the point of effective demand cannot be sold at a normal profit unless some fortuitous event shifts the point of effective demand. Say's Law in fact requires the classical theory of the rate of interest to ensure that the point of effective demand always occurs at full employment in the long run. All this is explained in *The General Theory* but from an aggregate Marshallian perspective that has escaped most post-Keynes macroeconomists.

POLICY IMPLICATIONS OF *THE GENERAL THEORY*

Based on his analysis of the potential pathological tendencies of laissez-faire capitalism, aggravated in the 1920s and 1930s by the

perverse constraints imposed by a misguided attempt to return to the gold standard, Keynes made two key policy proposals in *The General Theory* that apply to national economic policy and later, at Bretton Woods, a proposal for the international monetary system that would avoid the flaws of the gold standard. All these policy proposals are based on his theoretical framework applicable to the global system as a 'closed economy'.

At the national level Keynes made two proposals, both of which were adopted in the post-war period by many governments to manage what they called 'mixed economies'. Minsky (1986), in particular, provided a comprehensive discussion of Keynes's policy proposals relating to the role of 'bigger government' and the 'big bank'. Unfortunately, the rationale for the adoption of these structural changes to the role of government and the central bank and the objectives of this structural change has now been largely forgotten. Fiscal policy is now justified on the basis that public works can temper unemployment, as many classical economists argued, and Laidler (1999) pointed out.

By contrast, Keynes's objective for 'bigger' government through public investment was to increase the marginal efficiency of *private capital* by reducing uncertainty and improving profitability. Thus, although Keynes's proposal for the 'socialisation of investment' accounts for his label as a 'socialist' in some quarters, his intention was clearly to increase government participation in the economy so as to induce or 'crowd-in' sufficient private sector investment and preclude the decades of sub-par growth that was possible, or even inevitable, under laissez-faire capitalism. In other words, the intention of Keynes's 'bigger' government role in the otherwise capitalist economy is not to replace capitalism with socialism but to save capitalism from itself. Specifically, Keynes envisaged a role for 'bigger' government to calm the volatility of 'animal spirits' evident under laissez-faire and still evident to some extent under 'managed' or 'free' market capitalism. So Keynes intended 'bigger government' to stabilize and lift estimates of the private marginal efficiency of capital. By reducing uncertainty and increasing the profitability of private investment Keynes's policy proposal aimed to *permanently* increase the marginal efficiency of capital and move the point of effective demand closer to that consistent with full employment. The growth path around which the economy would inevitably fluctuate would then generate a lower

average level of unemployment. In other words, Keynes offered a rationale for managed capitalism.

The other blade to Keynes's principle of effective demand was the rate of interest on money (as a proxy for the cost of capital). To escape the upward pressure on interest rates from the inelastic and possibly erratic supply of gold, Keynes advised that the gold be abandoned and replaced by 'green cheese'.[5] The intention here was to bring monetary policy and the rate of interest in particular, under government control by creating an elastic supply of *state money*. The mandate of the central bank was then to ensure that interest rates were kept 'low'. The recommendation for public control of the central bank has escaped the attention of contemporary macroeconomists entirely as they seem unaware that many central banks were nationalized in the 1940s or only created in the 1950s or later. (The Federal Reserve is an interesting exception and that partly explains its current predicament.)[6] Furthermore, the collapse of the peg between gold and the US dollar in 1971 surely ushered in the era of unfettered state monies. Such systems give national governments more power to achieve domestic macroeconomic goals by keeping real money interest rates lower but they pose particular problems for the international monetary system that are only now coming into clear focus.

The principle of effective demand simply explains why in a monetary economy there is no basis to the belief that laissez-faire capitalism would automatically gravitate to full employment in the long run. Keynes's policy proposals were therefore intended to ensure that governments could improve the aggregate performance of what was otherwise a capitalist system. Current policy proposals should be, from this perspective, evaluated in terms of their impact on the relationship between the marginal efficiency of capital and the rate of interest. Or, in other words, the relationship between the return on real capital investment and the cost of capital is the key macroeconomic relationship to be influenced by macroeconomic policy. Different economies may be in different states, and for those economies where the marginal efficiency is too low and the rate of interest too high, the challenge will be to increase the marginal efficiency of capital while simultaneously keeping interest rates low.

But as the experience with the failed return to gold in the 1930s revealed, national economic policy cannot operate in a global vacuum. Domestic macroeconomic policies must be compatible with the

pressures emanating from the rest of the world and are therefore dependent on the 'rules of the game' that apply to global trade, exchange rates, and capital flows. Here Keynes's vision was compatible with his views on the properties of real monetary capitalist economies. In particular, he saw no reason to believe that freely floating exchange rates would automatically find their natural long-period equilibrium levels compatible with full employment in all economies, particularly as domestic interest rates are independent variables; or that free portfolio capital mobility would inevitable produce an efficient allocation of capital across economies. If capitalism required management at the national level, then it inevitably required management at the international level. But who would do this and what should be the rules of the game? Keynes made a proposal to address these questions but the proposal was never adopted. Keynes's International Clearing Union (ICU) proposal (Keynes 1980) was intended to eliminate global imbalances, as had occurred under the gold standard and which imposed deflationary pressure and unemployment on economies with external deficits. The intention was to have an international monetary system that allowed all economies to operate without external constraints on the domestic point of effective demand. The properties of the system have recently attracted attention at the United Nations (UN) (2009) and elsewhere, but as I have argued (Rogers 2009) there is little chance that the global economy will wean itself off the US dollar standard in the foreseeable future. The existence of the international monetary non-system under the de facto US dollar standard is therefore an important institutional feature to bear in mind when applying Keynes's analytical framework to current events. The global economy is currently in a distinctly nth best state—a long way from equilibrium—and consequently finds itself trapped by the huge cost of adjustment required to restore some semblance of equilibrium.

To illustrate some of the aforementioned points, I will apply Keynes's analytical framework to examine the performance of the Japanese economy over the past two decades. Japan is of particular interest to macroeconomists because it has suffered from a long period (18 years) of below par growth (relative to the post–Second World War boom) and has therefore attracted much attention. The diagnoses of Jap ı's 'illness' by McKinnon, Krugman, and Koo are of particular interest as each has something of merit to add but lacks a general theoretical framework in which their different insights can be reconciled. In what

follows I will attempt to explain how their important insights can be explained by Keynes's general theory.

LEADING ASSESSMENTS OF JAPAN'S POST-BUBBLE PERFORMANCE

Three analyses of Japan's lost decade(s) have been offered by Krugman (1998a, 1998b, 1998c, and 1999), McKinnon (2006), and Koo (2009). Although the analysis is not presented in terms of Keynes's general theory, all offer interesting insights when their analysis is interpreted from that perspective.

Krugman (1998a, 1998b, 1998c, and 1999) argued that Japan is caught in a liquidity trap and that textbook macroeconomics suggests a simple way out—the Bank of Japan (BOJ) should generate expectations of inflation (and inflation to back up those expectations) to produce a negative real rate of interest. Looking at Krugman's analysis from Keynes's perspective, we see that he makes the classical mistake of conflating the real rate of interest and the marginal efficiency of capital—a mistake about which Keynes (1936) complained. Once this mistake is removed, the merit in Krugman's argument is clearer. However, he does not explain why Japan's marginal efficiency of capital has fallen so dramatically and not recovered since the bubble period of the early 1990s.

The international dimension to Japan's liquidity trap is presented by McKinnon (2006) who argues that the ever-appreciating yen relative to the US dollar over the period 1973–90 has, in Keynes's terminology, reduced the marginal efficiency of capital on Japanese investment and thereby imposed continuous deflationary pressure on Japan. To remove these negative forces on the Japanese economy, McKinnon argues that Japan needs a stable peg to the US dollar. That will remove the pressure on the marginal efficiency of capital *and* ensure the solvency of Japanese financial institutions.

Koo (2009) also focuses on Japan's financial structure and argues that Japan suffered from a 'balance sheet' recession in the early 1990s that seriously distorted the usual relationship between the banking system, households, and government. In many respects Koo is closest to Keynes's analytical framework but somewhat surprisingly is critical of Keynes for neglecting the idea of a balance sheet recession. In this respect he seems to be unaware of Minsky's work, and once this

oversight is corrected it is clear that Koo's analysis can be reconciled with that of Minsky and Keynes and as such is further confirmation of the usefulness of the general theory for the analysis of the instabilities inherent in capitalist finance.

Thus, each of the three theses has some merit that is revealed by Keynes's general theory. In what follows we examine each in more detail.

Krugman's Liquidity Trap

To place Krugman's analysis in perspective it is necessary to recall that the classical vision of equilibrium assumed, for any national economy, a unique natural rate of interest that acted as an attractor for the market or money rate, with any discrepancy between the two to be corrected by movements in the price level that forced the money rate back into equality with a natural rate consistent with full employment. This is in essence the classical notion of unique long-run equilibrium characterized by a uniform risk-adjusted rate of return. Full employment was automatically attained in the long run, and if aggregate unemployment occurred in the short run it was due to sticky wages.[7] In contrast, Krugman applies the Fisherian distinction between nominal and real (inflation-adjusted) interest rates and then compares a nominal money rate with the real rate (the same inflation-adjusted nominal rate); so strictly speaking he lacks the two rates that characterize the classical equilibrium of Wicksell and therefore he misses Keynes's generalization. For example, Keynes, like Wicksell, has a money rate and the marginal efficiency of capital (a generalization of Wicksell's notion of the natural rate of interest) and both can be compared in nominal or real terms. Everyone agrees that nominal rates should not be compared with real rates, so Krugman's application of Fisher obfuscates Keynes's (and Wicksell's) analysis.

This is apparent when he argues that the inflation-adjusted nominal rate of interest (a real rate) in Japan has become negative while the nominal rate of interest is stuck at the zero lower bound. A moment's reflection will reveal, however, that Krugman is comparing a nominal rate with the Fisherian real rate and thereby missing the Wicksell and Keynes's distinction between the rate of interest (real or nominal) and the marginal efficiency of capital (real or nominal). Krugman's argument is therefore easily corrected if recast in Keynes's terminology.

From the perspective of Keynes's principle of effective demand, Krugman's diagnosis of Japan's predicament can be explained as follows. Something caused a collapse in the marginal efficiency of capital (elements of Japanese capital stock were redundant and a *contango* existed in some capital goods markets as Marshallian demand prices fell below long-run supply prices). So in Japan in the 1990s in the post property-bubble period, the point of effective demand collapsed and could not recover until the surplus capital stock was worked off and/or other factors changed to stimulate use of that capital. This state of the Japanese economy in the late 1990s and most of the twenty-first century can be illustrated in a suitably amended version of Krugman's liquidity trap Investment—Saving/Liquidity preference—Money supply (IS-LM) story as presented in Figure 5.1.

Notice that Figure 5.1 now incorporates some important elements of Keynes's general theory omitted from most versions of the IS-LM model, in particular the following.[8]

First, there are two rates of return—the marginal efficiency of capital and the rate of interest (cost of capital). Second, the principle of effective demand applies so there is nothing to ensure that the marginal efficiency of capital is positive at full employment. Third, the point of effective demand is determined by the cost of capital, in this case what the model calls the rate of interest, i. Fourth, the LM curve is treated as horizontal because the model describes a state money

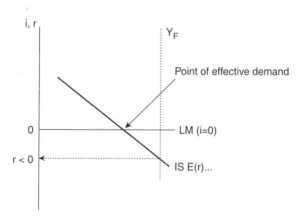

Figure 5.1   Keynes's Version of IS-LM Illustrating Japan in Krugman's Liquidity Trap

system in which the central bank (the 'green cheese factory' suggested by Keynes) sets the rate of interest. Fifth, and more formally, all variables in the model are forward-looking so expectations are important but best analysed as *rational beliefs* based on incomplete knowledge (as opposed to rational expectations based on complete stochastic knowledge). That is why the behavioural foundations of Keynes's key concepts such as the propensity to consume, liquidity preference, and 'animal spirits' have recently come back into focus. These behavioural and *Marshallian microeconomic foundations* of Keynes's analytical framework are more general than those of traditional Keynesian (classical or Walrasian) interpretations of the IS-LM model. Finally, the point where the LM curve cuts the IS curve corresponds to what Keynes called the point of effective demand, and as the model deals with aggregate behaviour the fallacy of composition applies.

Unlike Keynesian explanations, aggregate unemployment does not arise in this model because wages and/or prices are sticky. Unemployment can persist because there are no markets that can *automatically* ensure that equality between i and r occurs at full employment or that the structural marginal efficiency of capital is inevitably positive. In Keynes's general theoretical framework the long-period equilibrium depends on the relationship between the rate of interest and the marginal efficiency of capital given a propensity to consume that is less than unity. Classical theory avoided consideration of this possibility by introducing additional assumptions to ensure that the constellation of these independent variables, the rate of interest, the marginal efficiency of capital, and the propensity to consume, is such as to always and automatically ensure full employment in the long run. Keynes argued that there was no basis for the use of those assumptions.

With Japan in a state illustrated by Figure 5.1, Krugman proposed an inflation target to lift inflationary expectations and inflation. From Keynes's perspective, Krugman's inflation policy is aimed at increasing the marginal efficiency of capital. Would this policy work? Maybe—if it could produce a marginal efficiency of capital that is positive at full employment, that is, shift the IS curve sufficiently. For example, the adoption of an inflation target by Japan might work in the short run as Krugman suggested, but if and only if, domestic prices rose faster than wages, increasing the marginal efficiency of real investment in Japan. But as Keynes warned about reliance on

changes in prices and wages to restore full employment, there is no basis for expecting that they will move as required to shift the point of effective demand in the desired direction. In this case, if wages and prices rose in tandem, then there would be no increase in the marginal efficiency of capital and no increased incentive to real investment in Japan, so the point of effective demand does not shift as required. Thus, what Krugman's proposal requires is inflation with prices rising ahead of wages to lift the demand price of capital goods above their normal supply price and thereby stimulate real investment *in Japan*. This seems to be what Krugman has in mind and *it would probably work in a closed economy*.

However, in an open economy with free capital mobility there is an additional margin of comparison to consider—what is the marginal efficiency of capital elsewhere? Japanese entrepreneurs will not invest for a positive real return *in Japan* even if the real cost is negative, if greater positive returns are available offshore. Hence, Krugman's inflation solution would probably be ineffective as Japan is an open economy with free capital mobility; so the international dimension to Japan's predicament is also crucial to understanding what can be done.

McKinnon's Liquidity Trap

McKinnon (2006) has consistently pointed out that Asian economies on the US dollar standard have an incentive to peg to the US dollar and follow an export-led growth strategy. Essentially, Japan followed this strategy until the 1970s when, under US and G7 pressure, the yen started a trend appreciation that stopped only in the late 1990s. Steady appreciation of the yen then exerted persistent negative pressure on the return on capital in Japan and this pressure was intensified by negative shocks in the late 1980s and early 1990s that lowered the real rate of return on investment in Japan relative to the rest of the world (Ibid.: 107). McKinnon is not specific about these shocks but they would, I assume, include not only the bursting of the property bubble and the collapse in domestic private demand, but also increasing competition from emerging Asia. This competition was given further impetus by the unilateral devaluation of the yuan in 1994 and the de facto undervaluation of several other Asian currencies after the crisis of 1998. From a Keynes perspective,

these shocks would indeed deflate the marginal efficiency of capital *in Japan* and deflate animal spirits for domestic investment.

McKinnon (2006) also argues that given the state of interest parity that applies to portfolio equilibrium when Japan is in a liquidity trap, the BOJ is periodically forced to intervene in the foreign exchange market to prevent expected appreciation of the yen and an increasing risk premium on foreign currency denominated assets. McKinnon argues that both of these factors keep downward pressure on Japanese interest rates, a pressure that is exacerbated when foreign interest rates also fall towards zero, as occurred in response to the dot-com recession in 2000–1 and the global Great Recession starting in 2007. The downward pressure in Japanese interest rates emanating from international portfolio balance is then said to compresses interest rate spreads in the Japanese banking system, which inhibits lending. As McKinnon (Ibid.: 126) puts it: 'macroeconomic phenomena have compressed bank lending (as well as deposit) rates towards zero so as to take away the "normal" margin of profitability on new lending.' McKinnon therefore has a 'reluctance to lend' element to his diagnosis of Japan's predicament.[9]

McKinnon's (2006) proposed solution to this liquidity trap is to eliminate the downward pressure on Japan's interest rates emanating from the expected appreciation of the yen and the rising risk premium attached to foreign currency denominated assets. The way to do this, he argues, is to find a credible peg of the yen to the US dollar as this will eliminate both sources of downward pressure on Japan's interest rates. However, he acknowledges that this is not a solution that Japan can reach on its own—it will require international cooperation, at least with the US.

Koo and the Balance Sheet Recession

Koo offers what looks like a Minsky analysis of a demand-driven recession, but in contrast to Minsky (1975, 1986: 172) he regards this as a serious omission from Keynes's analysis. See, in particular, Koo (2009: 172) where he suggests that Keynes never offered a convincing explanation of why the marginal efficiency of capital could fall, failed to note that the liquidity trap was a borrower's phenomenon, and generally failed to appreciate the negative impact of what he calls a balance sheet recession. Koo is here understandably following

a largely Keynesian (that is, classical) interpretation of Keynes and is not aware of Minsky's analysis (there is no reference to Minsky in his book).[10] Consequently, once these oversights are corrected, Koo's analysis is far more compatible with Keynes than perhaps he realizes. The essence of Keynes's principle of effective demand is that demand-constrained long-period equilibria can exist in a monetary economy and Koo offers aspects of one such case.

Specifically, Koo stresses that Japan has suffered from a lack of domestic demand and not from structural impediments on the supply-side of the economy or the banking sector. Instead, the collapse of the property bubble produced a balance sheet recession that has forced Japanese firms to pay down debt even when interest rates were at zero. As a consequence, and as Keynes would expect, when Japanese firms do this on mass the paradox of thrift is revealed as aggregate demand contracts. The fallacy of composition applies to aggregate analysis as Keynes (1936) stressed. As the economy contracts, it takes longer for firms and households to restore their balance sheets in the face of a significant collapse in asset values and this accounts for the sluggish recovery. The Japanese economy remains in a slump so long as firms continue to repay debt and the demand for borrowed funds has collapsed—there are no willing borrowers even at zero interest rates. This is Koo's take on the liquidity trap.

Koo then argues correctly that without the fiscal spending by the Japanese government the contraction would have been much worse. However, fiscal policy in Japan cannot relieve the external and persistent negative pressure on the marginal efficiency of capital *in Japan* so it is ineffective in restoring Japan to its previous growth path. Nevertheless, the Japanese government and to a lesser extent the Japanese consumer stepped in to fill the gap left by the collapse in domestic investment by the corporate sector. All this is what Keynes would expect, although Koo retains the classical view that household saving finances corporate investment and the banking sector simply intermediates this process. He also argues that in the face of a balance sheet recession, monetary policy becomes ineffective because of a dearth of borrowers. This contrasts with McKinnon's view that reluctance to lend was also a problem. The recession then persists until households and firms have repaired their balance sheets, and as time is required to repair balance sheets and as this process is aggravated by the paradox of thrift, this explains why balance sheet–induced recessions are prolonged.

JAPAN FROM KEYNES'S PERSPECTIVE: SUMMING UP

The assessment of Japan's problems by Krugman, McKinnon, and Koo clearly all raise relevant issues that can be reconciled with Keynes's general theory. When looked at from Keynes's general theory perspective the challenges facing policymakers in Japan come into clearer focus and can be contrasted with the conventional interpretation of Japan's policy objectives as largely supply-side driven, as presented recently by the governor of the BOJ, Masaaki Shirakawa (2011).

Both Krugman and McKinnon identify downward pressure on the marginal efficiency of capital as a major contributing factor to Japan's liquidity trap. McKinnon attributes the negative pressure on the marginal efficiency of capital to shocks and it is apparent that these are both external and internal. The external shocks in the post-bubble period come from increasing competition from emerging economies, particularly those with undervalued exchange rates, while the domestic shocks come from the collapse in domestic investment. The external pressures intensified during the post-bubble period in the 1990s and this accounts for some of the delayed recovery in Japan during that time. The deflationary pressure on wages and prices coming from yen appreciation, stressed by McKinnon, compounded by balance sheet rebuilding, stressed by Koo, then results in a vicious cycle of contraction and delay in domestic investment familiar from the history of debt deflations as outlined by Fisher (1933). Contra Pigou, Patinkin, or Friedman, deflation is not a route that a monetary economy can follow to full employment.[11] Japan, of course, did not fall into a Fisherian debt deflation because, as Koo stresses, fiscal spending, no matter how badly executed, did step into the breach and the BOJ (Japan's green cheese factory) and other central banks also played a role in preventing collapses in the financial system. All acted as Keynes intended.

The point I need to stress here is that Keynes's analytical framework, particularly as applied by Minsky and, even if inadvertently, by Koo, clearly integrates the financial structure as an integral *real* component of the capitalist system and the behaviour of the economy cannot be understood by assuming money and the financial structure are somehow neutral. Keynes, Minsky, and Koo are as one on this. What is perhaps not so widely appreciated is that the same conclusion applies to international monetary arrangements.

International monetary arrangements are not neutral and they have played a major role in influencing the distribution of global growth and therefore the growth outcomes in Japan. This is where I think that Keynes's analytical framework throws more light on the issues raised by McKinnon.

In particular, Keynes's international monetary perspective suggests that Japan finds itself 'trapped' on the US dollar standard in much the same way that Britain was trapped on the gold standard in the 1920s and 1930s—committed by the power of convention to stay on the US dollar standard even though that commitment puts it at a strategic disadvantage because it depresses the structural marginal efficiency of capital and the domestic point of effective demand. In Japan's case, not because it forces domestic interest rates up, as was the case with Britain on the gold standard, but because the post–Bretton Woods non-system has allowed the US to induce an ever appreciating yen, and also allowed some countries to hold exchange rates for sustained periods of time at undervalued rates.[12] Furthermore, the constraint on Japan is perhaps more extreme than that on Britain in the 1930s because the existing de facto US dollar standard has no formal 'rules-of-the-game', so there is effectively no mechanism through which Japan can negotiate or take action to escape the downward pressure on the domestic marginal efficiency of capital emanating from these sources. Thus, although McKinnon is right to stress that some forces holding Japan in the liquidity trap are external, his proposal to stabilize the yen to the US dollar is not sufficient to spring the liquidity trap. That conclusion is reinforced by the fact that although the yen–US dollar rate has been loosely stabilized since the mid-1990s, the liquidity trap has remained in place. McKinnon nevertheless correctly recognizes that Japan cannot easily take unilateral action to solve this problem. What is required here is a new international monetary arrangement along the lines of Keynes's ICU proposal as recently considered by the UN (2009). But as I argued elsewhere (Rogers 2009), progress on reform of the international monetary system is almost non-existent so it seems to me that Japan should put more effort into supporting proposals along the lines of Keynes's ICU as it has much to gain from such a scheme.

An assessment of Japan's predicament in the 1990s using Keynes's analytical framework therefore clarifies what Krugman and McKinnon are getting at but questions the efficacy of their proposals for pulling

Japan out of its slump. The key element of Japan's predicament in the 1990s was indeed the collapse of the marginal efficiency of capital or what we might call more generally the rate of return on real investment (new factories and production lines). However, it seems that this collapse had largely external causes as other Asian economies caught up with Japan in the technology race, and post 1994–8 this catch-up was accelerated as several key economies, including China, had significant competitive devaluations against the yen. The net effect was, as Krugman argues, a negative rate of return on much real investment in Japan—a negative structural marginal efficiency of capital.[13] But this is something more than a negative technology shock.[14] Japan is paying a high price for a dysfunctional international monetary system.

Thus, Keynes's analytical framework leads to the correct diagnosis of Japan's lost decade(s), explains why the traditional policy responses failed to restore Japan to its previous growth trajectory, and also suggests what policies should be adopted to effectively restore the point of effective demand in Japan. Unfortunately, the insight that Keynes's analytical framework offers for Japan is that the economy remains trapped on the dysfunctional international monetary system, that is, the US dollar standard. From Japan's perspective that system is long past its use-by date. However, so long as there is no international mechanism through which exchange rates can be managed to ensure that Japan's (and all other countries') point of effective demand can be maintained at a level consistent with full employment, Japan remains trapped on a below potential growth path.

* * *

Keynes's general theory, *The General Theory*, augmented by his wartime and post-war policy proposals on the international monetary system, provides the basic principles to guide the economic management of capitalist democracies. If democracy is to be protected, then capitalist economies must be managed in accordance with universal notions of fairness and equity. Keynes's analytical framework provides an understanding of how those objectives can be achieved.

Japan, like other members of the G7, has failed to take advantage of Keynes's insights and consequently failed to make the correct diagnosis of its predicament. Koo is on the right track here. Instead, by adopting a Panglossian view of capitalism, too many economists

and governments are unaware of the risks associated with financial markets and monetary policy in general. Few had heard of Minsky before the Great Recession of 2007–9 and this is a major reason why they failed to see it coming. But more generally, contemporary macroeconomic theory has led democratic governments to implement policies that undermine confidence in democracy that may induce voters to look for more extreme solutions to their distress. Fortunately, Japan has escaped much of that stress this time. That is the good news. The bad news is that the difficulties facing Japan, and other members of the G7, require elements of international cooperation that in the present environment seem out of reach.

Specifically, in the case of Japan, Keynes's analytical framework leads to the conclusion that in the post-bubble period of the early 1990s, the country found itself in a predicament not unlike that of Britain after its loss of export markets and the return to gold at an overvalued parity in 1925. Under these conditions, domestic monetary and fiscal policy can provide support to domestic effective demand but they cannot eliminate the external factors that depressed the marginal efficiency of capital in Japan. However, Japan had an advantage over Britain of the 1930s on the gold standard because Japan could, and it did, deploy domestic demand policies. But, on the other hand, Japan faces a greater hurdle in that there is no effective international institutional mechanism through which the pressure on the marginal efficiency of capital can be relieved. Japan cannot unilaterally abandon the US dollar standard or induce China and other Asian economies to revalue their exchange rates. In the current non-system, described by some as the G-0 rather than the G-20, Japan remains trapped on the US dollar standard and this accounts for the persistence of Japan's lost decade(s) and the inability to restore its lost vitality.

NOTES

1. See the conference organized by Blanchard at the International Monetary Fund [IMF] (2011) and Blanchard (2011).

2. In this chapter, *The General Theory* (italic, initial capital letters) refers to the 1936 book; the expression 'the general theory' (not italic, lower case letters) includes the 1936 book plus Keynes's proposals for reform of the international monetary system.

3. In a similar vein, Rogers (2011) explains how the failure to understand Keynes's principle of effective demand led the designers of the euro to implement a governance structure that was bound to fail.

4. *The General Theory* is therefore *not* just a theory of the trade cycle as the structure of the book makes clear and any careful reader would realize.

5. Keynes describes the problems associated with the gold standard and the need for state money and a central bank in the following terms:

> Unemployment develops, that is to say, because people want the moon—men cannot be employed when the object of their desire (i.e. money) is something which cannot be produced and the demand for which cannot be readily chocked off. There is no remedy but to persuade the public that green cheese is practically the same thing and to have a green cheese factory (i.e. a central bank) under public control. (1936: 235)

6. See the discussion of the history of the Federal Reserve by Johnson and Kwak (2010) and Minsky's (1986: 253) perceptive observation on the operating procedures of the FED.

7. That Keynes saw sticky wages as the classical explanation for aggregate unemployment is apparent in *The General Theory* (1936: 257).

8. For a discussion of Keynes's version of IS-LM, see Rogers (2011).

9. Woodford (2010) has proposed how these factors can be incorporated into the IS-LM type structure illustrated in Figure 5.1, but they will not be examined further here.

10. By contrast, Koo's (2009: Appendix) thoughts on the flaws in modern macroeconomic theory are right on the mark.

11. As Minsky (1986: 177) put it: 'In a world with complicated financial usage, if there is a road to full employment by way of the Patinkin real-balance effect, it may well go by way of hell.'

12. Michael Mussa has been scathing in his critique of the failure of the IMF to implement its post-1978 mandate to ensure stability of the international monetary system. He makes the following telling observation:

> Although it has evolved considerably over six decades, there is still an international monetary system. *The notion that this system can always be relied upon to work perfectly smoothly on its own*, and individual nations safely be allowed to distort and disrupt the operation of [the system in] whatever manner they choose, without any official over-sight from a competent international institution backed by the will of the international community, *is, to put it bluntly, a gross stupidity*. (2007: 37) [emphasis added]

Keynes would surely have agreed.

13. As noted previously, Krugman calls for a negative real rate of interest to stimulate borrowing. Although it may do that, it will not stimulate investment *in Japan* until the structural marginal efficiency of capital becomes positive.

14. Hayashi and Prescott (2002) offer such an interpretation.

REFERENCES

Blanchard, O. 2011. *The Future of Macroeconomic Policy: Nine Tentative Conclusions*. Washington, DC: IMF. Availbale at http://blog-imfdirect.imf.

org/2011/03/13/future-of-macroeconomic-policy/ Last accessed on 27 April 2012.

Davidson, P. 2007. *John Maynard Keynes*. London: Palgrave, Macmillan.

Fisher, I. 1933. 'The Debt-Deflation Theory of Great Depressions', *Econometrica*, 1(4): 337–57.

Hayashi, F. and E.C. Prescott. 2002. 'Japan in the 1990s: A Lost Decade', *Review of Economic Dynamics*, 5(1): 206–35.

International Monetary Fund (IMF). 2011. *Macro and Growth Policies in the Wake of the Crisis*. IMF, 7–8 March 2011, Washington, DC. Available at http://www.imf.org/external/np/seminars/eng/2011/res/index.htm Last accessed on 27 April 2012.

Johnson, S. and J. Kwak. 2010. *Thirteen Bankers: The Wall Street Takeover and the Next Financial Crisis*. New York: Pantheon Books.

Keynes, J.M. 1936. *The General Theory of Employment, Interest and Money*. London: Macmillan.

———. 1980. *The Collected Writings of John Maynard Keynes* (CWK), edited by D.E. Moggridge, vol. XXV, *Activities 1940–1946. Shaping the Post-War World: The Clearing Union*. London: Macmillan.

Koo, R.C. 2009. *The Holy Grail of Macroeconomics: Lessons from Japan's Great Recession*. Singapore: Wiley.

Krugman, P. 1998a. 'Japan's Trap', May. Available online: http://web.mit.edu/krugman/www/japtrap.html (accessed 27 April 2012).

———. 1998b. 'It's Baaaack! Japan's Slump and the Return of the Liquidity Trap', *Brookings Papers on Economic Activity*, 2: 137–205.

———. 1998c. 'Japan: Still Trapped', November. Available at http://web.mit.edu/krugman/www/japtrap2.html. Last accessed on 27 April 2012.

———. 1999. 'Thinking about the Liquidity Trap', December. Available at http://web.mit.edu/krugman/www/trioshrt.html. Last accessed on 27 April 2012.

Laidler, D. 1999. *Fabricating the Keynesian Revolution. Studies of the Inter-War Literature on Money, the Cycle, and Unemployment*. Cambridge: Cambridge University Press.

———. 2009. 'Keynes, Lucas and the Crisis', The University of Western Ontario, Research Report 2009–2.

Lucas, R.E. 2011. 'The U.S. Recession of 2007–201?', Millman Lecture, University of Washington, 19 May.

McKinnon, R.I. 2006. *Exchange Rates under the East Asian Dollar Standard: Living with Conflicted Virtue*. Cambridge, MA: The MIT Press.

Minsky, H.P. 1975. *John Maynard Keynes*. New York: Columbia University Press.

———. 1986. *Stabilizing an Unstable Economy*. New Haven: Yale University Press.

Mussa, M. 2007. 'IMF Surveillance over China's Exchange Rate Policy', paper presented at the Conference on China's Exchange Rate Policy, Peterson Institute for International Economics, Washington, 19 October. Available at http://iie.com/publications/papers/mussa1007.pdf. Last accessed on 27 April 2012.

Rogers, C. 2009. 'Is International Monetary Reform Possible or is the Global Economy Trapped on the US Dollar Standard?' Conference at University of Adelaide on 6 July 2009.

———. 2010. 'The Principle of Effective Demand: The Key to Understanding the *General Theory*', in R.W. Dimand, R.A. Mundell, and A. Vercelli (eds), *Keynes General Theory After 70 Years*, IEA Conference Volume No. 147: 136–156. London: Palgrave-Macmillan.

———. 2011. 'Back to the Future: 75 Years of Misunderstanding Keynes', paper presented at the 40th Conference of Economists, ACE2011, ANU, Canberra, 12 July.

Shirakawa, M. 2011. 'Towards a Revitalization of Japan's Economy', speech at the Foreign Correspondents' Club of Japan, Tokyo, 7 February. Available at http://www.bis.org/review/r110207b.pdf. Last accessed on 27 April 2012.

Skidelsky, R. 2003. *John Maynard Keynes 1883–1946: Economist. Philosopher. Statesman.* London: Penguin.

United Nations (UN). 2009. *United Nations Conference on the World Financial and Economic Crisis and Its Impact on Development,* Report of the Commission of Experts of the President of the United Nations General Assembly on Reforms of the International Monetary and Financial System. New York, 24–26 June. Available at Please provide the date when this url was last accessed. http://www.un.org/ga/econcrisissummit/docs.shtml.

Woodford, M. 2010. 'Financial Intermediation and Macroeconomic Analysis', *Journal of Economic Perspectives,* 34(4): 21–44.

6

Keynes and the Case for Europe

TOSHIAKI HIRAI*

Keynes entered the world stage at Versailles, at a time that saw the world endeavouring to restore the 'Pax Britannica' which had collapsed with the First World War. But this endeavour came to grief. Instead, as confusion and conflict deepened, the world was engulfed by the Second World War. It was during the closing days of that war that Keynes emerged as the figure exerting the greatest influence as economist, economic policymaker, and, most of all, international system planner.

From Versailles to Bretton Woods, Keynes worked both for the rescue and relief of a Europe ruined by war, and also for the rehabilitation and reconstruction of a new and more solid Europe on the foundations of the old. In this latter respect, Keynes can be seen as a visionary precursor of the modern European Union (EU), a project that today is facing its greatest challenge since inception. Were Keynes alive today, there is no question he would be at the very centre of things, once again urging proposals both for rescue from the errors of the past and reconstruction for the possibilities that lie yet in the future.

* The author would like to express his deep gratitude for invaluable suggestions and comments by M.C. Marcuzzo, P. Mehrling, F. Ranchetti (University of Pisa, Italy), S. Nisticò (University of Cassino, Italy), and J. Obata (Rissho University, Japan).

But Keynes is not alive today. All we have of him is the record of his response to previous crises. The central purpose of this chapter is to bring that record up to light, as a lens through which to examine the current crisis in Europe. Keynes is not himself alive, but his ideas and his way of approaching problems are. We can therefore legitimately ask: What would Keynes have said?

First, Keynes's relief and reconstruction plan for ruined Europe after Second World War is examined. Second, we come to Keynes's response to the United Nations Relief and Rehabilitation Administration (UNRRA) advocated by the US for ruined Europe, and finally we go on to deal with what moved ahead thereafter for Europe.

KEYNES'S RELIEF PLANS FOR RUINED EUROPE

Immediately after resigning as Treasury representative for the Versailles Peace Conference, disappointed by the proceedings conducted there, in 1919, Keynes published *The Economic Consequences of the Peace*. It is famous, among other things, for the acid description of the 'Big Three' (Wilson, Lloyd-George, and Clemenceau) and his calculation of reasonable reparations as paid by Germany. What concerns us here, however, is Chapter 7, 'Remedies', where he shows his bold and creative flair as a planner.

After proposing to cancel out all the war debts (including abandonment of 2 billion pounds for the US and 0.9 billion pounds for the UK), Keynes put forward the following grand design for ruined Europe, proposing: (i) to reorganize the Coal Commission into a sort of cooperative system for supplying and allocating coal and iron ore throughout Europe; (ii) to set up a 'Free Trade Union' for Europe, including the UK; (iii) to make an 'international loan' for the rebirth of Europe, consisting of loans to be used to obtain food and materials from the US, plus a 'Guarantee Fund'. The latter was to be set up by the contributions (either in cash or kind) of the member countries of the League of Nations. Keynes considered the Guarantee Fund to be the foundation for the general reorganization of currency.[1]

The 'cooperative system' for coal is a prototype of the European Coal and Steel Community (ECSC 1952); the Free Trade Union is a prototype of the European Community (EC 1967); and the Guarantee Fund is a sort of international monetary organization—a project that could be even said to belong to the same sphere as the Euro system.

But Keynes was too early. Instead, the attention of statesmen was distracted by problems of reparations and war debts—legacies of the War that was past—rather than was directed towards the future. The result was the Second World War, which Keynes seized as a second chance to do what should have been done after the First World War.

In July 1940, Keynes was appointed member of the Chancellor of the Exchequer's Consultative Council which was set up 'to help and advise the Chancellor on special problems arising from war conditions' (Moggridge 1992: 636). Thereafter he was to be engaged on a range of important assignments. Two fields are relevant here.

The first field concerns external war finance and the balance of payments crisis; Keynes played a key role in the negotiations with the US over the Lend-Lease arrangements, and indeed in the Anglo-American Financial Agreement[2] of 1945 for support in the UK's balance of payments crisis.

The second field, which is relevant to this essay, concerns the shaping of the post-war world economic order. Here Keynes's unexcelled ability in designing international systems emerged in all evidence. Viewing a problem in the worldwide context, he was able to devise excellent plans for dealing with it. Three plans in particular are worth considering here—(i) an international buffer stock plan, (ii) an international relief and reconstruction plan named Central Relief and Reconstruction Fund (CRRF), and (iii) an international monetary system. Keynes himself negotiated with the US as chief British representative for these issues, which were closely connected in Keynes's mind.

Let us take the three cases in order.

1. *The Commodity Problem.*[3] Keynes designed international organizations named 'Commod Control' and 'General Council for Commod Controls' for buffer stock operations, with the purpose of stabilizing the short-term prices, while allowing for gradual changes in the long-term prices, of various primary commodities, and of ensuring due income to the producers concerned. The fundamental principle on which the buffer stock plan is based is his view of the market economy as emerges clearly in *The End of Laissez-Faire* (Keynes 1926a)—if left to the law of supply and demand, the market economy cannot attain an optimum allocation of resources. Because a

competitive market system abhors buffer stock, violent fluctuations in prices are caused; so in order to avoid them, some sort of international organization for buffer stocks is required. This idea can be traced back to 'The Control of Raw Materials by Governments' (Keynes 1926b).

2. *The Relief and Reconstruction Problem*. Keynes designed the CRRF for the management of a joint fund comprised of money donations or contributions in kind from various countries. The basic principle here was to create an ideal international organization for the efficient distribution of goods with humanitarian criteria among countries in need of relief. It was predominantly Europe which preoccupied Keynes here, for he believed that without the rebirth and reconstruction of Europe there would be no hope for the future of the world.

Although we will examine the CRRF in more detail later, it should be noted in advance that the CRRF could be taken in relation to the Organization for European Economic Cooperation (OEEC) in the Marshall Plan, which aimed at relieving and reconstructing Europe in crisis through central institutions.

3. *International Monetary System*. Keynes proposed an 'International Clearing Union'—a multilateral clearing system among the central banks to which all the foreign exchange transactions were to be transferred. For this purpose an international organization named Clearing Union would be set up with each central bank opening its account. Every international transaction was to be recorded in the account of the nation concerned in terms of 'bancors' as an international currency used only among the central banks. The Clearing Union would be endowed with credit creation facility (each nation should fix its exchange rate in terms of bancor). The bancor was to stand as international currency, gold giving way to it while the existing currencies such as the dollar and pound sterling remained as local currencies. The foreign exchange markets' function would dwindle and credit could be created in accordance with the growth of the world economy. International financial transactions would be concentrated on the Clearing Union, while international transactions of goods and services were to

be left to the free activities of firms and individuals. Keynes stated that the Clearing Union plan could be said to be an international version of a domestic banking system. The basic principle upon which the Clearing Union plan is founded is an international monetary system which, if needed, could increase or decrease the amount of bancors so that either deflationary or inflationary trends in the world economy could be adjusted, and world trade could grow accordingly. He expressed the view that each government should pursue prosperity and stability for its own economy by means of economic policy, criticizing the Gold Standard because it could deprive governments of scope for economic policy, as is clearly seen in *A Tract on Monetary Reform* (1923) and *The General Theory* (1936).

Having explained how Keynes worked out international institutions in the context of the world order during the inter-war period, we would concentrate on the relief and reconstruction phase for Europe, for the main purpose of this chapter is to examine Keynes's involvement in both the past and present Europe in crisis. (Table 6.1 shows the relation between Keynes's vision and Europe in reconstruction and crisis. Readers should preferably refer to it throughout the chapter.)

KEYNES'S RELIEF AND RECONSTRUCTION PLAN FOR EUROPE AFTER THE SECOND WORLD WAR

At the outbreak of the Second World War, Britain made a desperate effort to prevent strategic commodities from falling into the enemy's hands. To this end the UK needed to buy up large quantities of primary commodities, as a result of which it later found itself in possession of excessive stockpiles. Thus, the prime minister stated in August 1940 that Britain should be committed to 'a policy of building up stocks of food and raw materials for post-war relief purposes' (Keynes 1980: 3). In November, Frederick Leith-Ross[4] was appointed to represent Britain in the necessary negotiations. As we already said, Keynes also became the Treasury representative on the official committee set up to advise him. Keynes insisted that any plan should be drawn up in complete collaboration with the US and that it should be based on the principle of internationalism.

Table 6.1 Keynes's Vision and Europe in Reconstruction and Crisis

	After First World War	Reparation and war debt problems in the 1920s	During Second World War	1950s	1960s–1990s	1990s
Europe towards EC	Coal Corporation* Free Trade Union* International Loan*		CRRF* →UNRRA	ECSC (1952) Marshall Plan OEEC (1948)	→EEC (1957) EC (1967)	→EU (1993 Maastricht Treaty)
Europe and Monetary System		Criticism of the Gold Standard*	ICU* vs White Plan	EPU (1950–8) EMA (1958–72)	EMS (1979–98)	→EURO (ECB)
Time	After First World War	Reparation and war debt problems in the 1920s	During Second World War	1950s	1960s–1990s	1990s

Note: * Keynes's proposal or involvement.

CRRF–Central Relief and Reconstruction Fund; EC–European Community; ECA–Economic Cooperation Administration; ECB–European Central Bank; ECSC–European Coal and Steel Community; EEC–European Economic Community; EMA–European Monetary Agreement; EPU–European Payments Union; ICU– International Clearing Union; OEEC–Organization of European Economic Cooperation; and UNRRA–United Nations Relief and Rehabilitation Administration.

On a visit to Washington in May 1941, Keynes discussed the surpluses problem with Dean Acheson, Assistant Secretary of State. Keynes took this opportunity to set out his ideas on the problems that could be anticipated after the war. The solutions Keynes anticipated, and upon which Acheson concurred to a degree well beyond his expectations, included an outline of a post-war relief and reconstruction programme for Europe (this could be a blueprint for the CRRF[5]) and that of an 'ever-normal granary' as a comprehensive plan for the unification of primary commodity prices throughout the world.

Keynes believed that the accumulation of commodity surpluses which was developing throughout the world could be turned to advantage in the task of putting Europe back on its feet once the war was over. In other words, the solution to the commodity problem could help solve the relief problem. Evidently, then, in mid-1941 there was acknowledged agreement between Keynes and the US government on the issues of post-war relief and surplus commodities.

The plan for Europe Keynes had sketched out to Acheson was succeeded by a proposal to carry out relief and reconstruction operations through the establishment of a Central Relief and Reconstruction Fund[6] (CRRF). This was set out in the 'Treasury Memorandum on Financial Framework of Post-War European Relief' (24 October 1941; Keynes 1980: 46–51; hereafter the CRRF Plan or the 'Keynes Plan', for Keynes was its chief author).

The central idea of the Keynes Plan was that the CRRF should operate a joint fund comprised of money donations or contributions in kind from many countries. The basic principles of the CRRF were that it should be responsible for collecting and distributing all required relief materials (it should be authorized to buy the commodities required at fair prices from any country); moreover, it should determine, on the basis of some appropriate principle yet to be established, the proportion of the relief materials which a country should receive gratis or should be liable to pay. All the transactions were to be booked in the joint fund. To allow the CRRF to estimate the scale of transactions, the CRRF should request allied governments to produce lists of their requirements, while at the same time taking the enemy countries, as well as France and China, into account. Second, the CRRF should make estimates of the quantities of commodities available to it and it should investigate the financial position of each of the countries concerned, knowledge of which would be prerequisite

for equitably determining the proportions in which assistance should be granted free of charge or made payable.

Keynes considered the CRRF, conceived as mentioned, greatly superior to the idea of having various countries giving relief in kind separately, and sincerely wished to see it set up. He argued that establishing the CRRF would obviate the need to make separate financial arrangements for each commodity, whilst the alternative idea would result in the distribution of commodities becoming a messy affair, due to the absence of any necessary correspondence between the commodity quantities available and an appropriate financial burden.

Keynes put forward the buffer stock plan, the CRRF plan, together with the ICU plan as representing his vision for the post–world war system. However, none of them were adopted, partly because of the changed circumstances of the British economy and partly because of the predominance of the US in both military and economic terms.

KEYNES'S RESPONSE TO THE UNRRA

After the CRRF plan, in fact, the relief problem went through a long, zigzag process (Hirai 2011). We will not go into its details here but move on to the problem of the UNRRA, which shifted the initiative in the relief problem to the US with Harry White,[7] Assistant Secretary of the Treasury, as a leader.

The UNRRA was established in November 1943 at a 44-nation conference at the White House. The task was to provide economic relief to Europe after the War and to rescue the refugees. More than 70 per cent of the UNRRA's fund was provided by the US government.

Keynes's response to the UNRRA changed over time, tracing a convoluted contour. Although he went on calling it a 'chimera', around September 1943 he began to approach the idea more favourably. He commented on the 'White Plan' in a memorandum of 17 September to Ronald Campbell and R. Law, entitled 'Finance of European Relief' (Keynes 1980: 90–2), referring to several tenets of the plan.

1.   Irrespective of whether free or payable, all supplies should be given to recipient countries along with invoices expressed in value, and should be dealt with on a commercial basis as soon as possible. In the case of gifts, supplying countries should withdraw the amount involved from the contributions to relief finance. Keynes agreed to this.

2. Prices should be inclusive of freight charges, for which supplying countries should pay. Keynes judged that, financially speaking, this would be advantageous to Britain.

3. The plan aims at establishing the principle that loans made by a given country should be used by the recipient country only for the commodities of the donor country (that is, all loans should be tied aid). Keynes remarked that the US administration would, in this way, be able to use their funds to provide for cash purchases outside the US.

4. The standard of contributing 1 per cent of national income to UNRRA should be established. Keynes commented that if this were agreed to, the US administration would obtain a stronghold in negotiations with the Congress.

Here we see Keynes displaying a positive attitude towards the White Plan which laid the groundwork for the UNRRA. At the beginning of 1945, however, he was highly critical of it. He thought the best option for the UK now would be:

> To carry on with the present military basis in the very small number of non-paying non-enemy countries and persuade the U.S.A. to revise the terms of this to UNRRA proportions, which, if UNRRA appropriation was to be released would be very easy for them. Through the disappointment with UNRRA we have been led along a path of nonsense. The sooner we take any opportunity to retrace our steps… the better. (Keynes 1980: 95)

The words 'present military basis … non-enemy countries' appear to indicate the Lend-Lease.[8] Keynes suggests that Britain should seek to return to the *status quo ante* through the dissolution of the UNRRA, try to get the Lend-Lease continued in certain countries, and make efforts to get the US to improve the terms of the Lend-Lease by making use of contributions which had so far gone to the UNRRA. The UNRRA's liquidation was determined in August 1946 (it was, in fact, made in 1949).

AFTER THE SECOND WORLD WAR

Keynes died in 1946 before seeing the developments in the relief and reconstruction problem for Europe. However, as emerges in all evidence from the aforementioned, Keynes would surely have been

involved and interested in it if he could have seen it. It was, in the end, under the Marshall Plan (the 'European Recovery Program'), which took effect in 1948, that relief and reconstruction for Europe were carried out. Loans were systematically allocated, by the Economic Cooperation Administration (ECA) of the US, through the OEEC.[9] Roused from complacency by the onset of the Cold War, the US, which even in the immediate post-war period had been extremely reluctant to get involved in European affairs, became—well aware of the role it was taking on—the leader of the West in the new international order from 1949 on. The world in which Britain, now suffering from a hugely adverse balance of payments and massive war debts, had been able to assume leadership had gone (it was, in fact, Britain that was to receive the largest share of the Marshall Plan).

The ECA and the OEEC could be said to correspond to the CRRF as a central organization allocating resources among the countries in Europe in order to, as first stage, relieve and then reconstruct them. The main difference lies in the fact that in the former it was the US that was willing to make the whole loan. The OEEC started its activities by setting up the ECSC (1952), which was to lay the foundation of the EEC (1958; this comes from the customs union plan by P. Henri Spaak), followed by the EC (1967) as integrated from the EEC, the European Atomic Energy Community (EURATOM), and the ECSC.

How would Keynes have acted if he had lived long enough to see the development of the Marshall Plan? In a word, the Marshall Plan, which made a great contribution to the path leading up to the EU,[10] might be related to Keynes's three ideas expressed in his *The Economic Consequences of the Peace* (1919) and the CRRF plan.[11] He would probably have endorsed the Marshall Plan (the principal architects of which were Clayton and Acheson, who were on good terms with Keynes), and might have led the planning and management of the OEEC (remember that it was Bevin, Foreign Secretary of the Attlee Government, UK, who led the initiative on the European side). This seems clear-cut.[12]

Before trying to answer this question let us take a look at the integration project Europe had successfully carried out over the years. Although the details are different, in effect the European integration project has followed the broad lines anticipated by Keynes.

The movement for European integration, which initially aimed at the formation of an economic community as typified by the

EEC (1958) proceeded towards setting up a more comprehensive community inclusive of monetary integration, common foreign security, and so forth, as represented by the Maastricht Treaty of 1993. As for monetary integration, although there was some concern over the hazards it might give rise to, it soon gave way in the face of the economic growth evident in the area subsequent to adoption of the Euro in January 1999 (complete changeover in 2002). Soon the Euro was to be highly evaluated as an international currency, practically the equal of the Dollar, of which the EU was rightly proud. Then the EU moved forward in the direction of boosting its influence on the world economy as well as world politics by admitting a series of nations to membership. It was to be highly evaluated as a gigantic economic zone which could be equal to the US—up until the spring of 2009.

THE EURO CRISIS

It was with the Lehman Shock of 2008 that the danger and fragility embedded in the Euro system came to light. Through the shockwave of the Lehman bankruptcy, one year later, in the fall of 2009, the Euro crisis started with the fiscal crisis in Greece. The critical situations hit the Euro zone from May 2009 to March 2012.[13]

The bailouts to Greece (twice, May 2010 and July 2011), Ireland (November 2010), and Portugal (May 2011) were implemented by the EU (European Commission), the ECB, and the International Monetary Fund (IMF)—the Troika—with the condition that the countries concerned should pledge to carry out austerity measures. In the Euro System, a member country concedes monetary policy as well as foreign exchange policy to the ECB, relinquishing its own currency, which means that the only economic policy tool should be fiscal policy. In order to prevent a member country from implementing fiscal policy flightily, the Euro system ruled the so-called 'Stability and Growth Pact'. However, it was no more than a gentlemen's agreement, for it entails no sanctions against any country breaking the pact. This turned out to be a fatal drawback for the system when the shockwave of the Lehman Shock hit Europe.

When the Lehman Shock came to Europe, the member countries experienced a sharp economic downturn. In order to tackle this state of affairs, each member country resorted to stimulus measures—the

only economic policy tool at its disposal. However, the bubble burst and the budgetary situations grew progressively worse and worse.

Investors who were worried about the bond markets of the countries concerned (Greece, Ireland, Portugal, and so on) demanded prohibitively high interest rates. The countries coming up against the difficulty of raising funds in the bond markets were forced to ask for bailout, which resulted in the aforementioned rescue packages by the Troika. In return, these countries were called upon to implement austerity measures, implying a sharply deflationary policy. These economies are plunging into a deflationary spiral.

The measures implemented by the Troika to quell the Euro crisis are, in a nutshell, mere stopgaps, far from offering a fundamental solution to the crisis. The Troika provided the ailing members with bailout money on condition that they pledge the austerity measures, which, the Troika believes, is the only way to get over the crisis. The proposal for European Financial Stability Facility (EFSF) enlargement is also a stopgap in preparation for similar emergencies.

The main objective of these bailouts is, of course, to prevent contagion from spreading throughout Europe and to defend the Euro system. The German and French banks, among others, have been deeply involved in these financial matters as the big holders of the sovereign debts of the ailing member countries as well as lenders to the private sectors there. Thus, once a contagion spread there would be catastrophic consequences not only for the Euro system but also for the world economy—a second Lehman Shock. This type of contagion reminds us of the contagion seen in Europe in the 1930s, which was finally to bring about blocked economy throughout the world.

KEYNES'S LIKELY RESPONSE TO THE EURO CRISIS

Now we come to the last question. How would Keynes have evaluated the Euro system and responded to the Euro crisis? Here are our some considerations.

Keynes would have supported the European Payments Union (EPU, 1950–8), which had operated in the 1950s and drew great inspiration from Keynes's ICU plan.[14] In the case of the EPU, Keynes would have said that inasmuch as each central bank's independence is maintained, it can implement its own monetary policy and foreign

exchange rate policy. The EPU is, moreover, a kind of clearing union so that it can prevent chronic imbalance. To be correct, the EPU, created by OEEC, was a clearing system with credit facilities, but did not have something like bancor. The EPU was succeeded by the European Monetary Agreement (EMA, 1958–72).

Keynes would have endorsed the EC as a free trade zone (or a customs union) and he would have believed it could contribute to economic growth there.

It is likely that Keynes would have been against the Euro system and its inflexibility;[15] he would have questioned the shift from the EPU to the Euro system and would not have regarded it as an evolution in the right direction. The reason is, as is now well known, that the Euro system is burdened with a fatal drawback—a member country has ceded monetary policy and foreign exchange policy to the ECB. Although the only policy at its disposal is fiscal policy, this cannot be implemented in defence of the Euro system, but rather the country is forced to take austerity measures which constitute, by their very nature, a deflationary policy. This could lead up to the collapse of the Euro system per se.[16]

Keynes would have opposed the austerity measures. They are not so much a proposition dictated by economics as a kind of 'belief'. The system should be constructed in such a way that any member country could achieve economic growth without falling into liquidity shortage. The Euro system, which makes any such state of affairs impossible, incorporates fundamental defects.

Keynes would have opposed the phenomenon that sees the financial markets and commodity markets turning into a great casino. That is, he would have been against the financial globalization backed by neo-liberalism over the last two decades, if not against milder financial liberalization. Keynes championed the ICU plan, which is so structured that, by means of the international clearing system rather than a single currency system, the liquidity required for the growth of each economy is secured, while international imbalance (especially a tendency of a certain country constantly having a surplus) could be prevented. Keynes would have been critical of the present dollar system, of course.

This chapter tried to clarify what kind of planning Keynes proposed and would have proposed for Europe in crisis. To this end, two aspects were examined. These are, of course, no more than conjectures, and

yet not mere fruits of the imagination, for we may with a fair degree of certainty consider them to be the kind of remarks that would have emerged through his own vision and planning for Europe in crisis in the inter-war period and during the Second World War.

NOTES

1. Earlier Keynes had advocated an international monetary system at Amsterdam (and at the same time at Cambridge), for which see Markwell (2006: 92–3, 106).

2. President Truman announced the immediate termination of Lend Lease on 17 August 1945. The principal negotiator leading up to the Anglo–American Financial Agreement was William Clayton, for which see Keynes (1979: Chapter 4). Clayton was to be the 'intellectual architect of the [Marshall] Plan'. In March 1946, Clayton insisted that '[we] must go all out in this world game.... Assistance should take the form not only of financial aid, but of technical and administrative assistance' (from Behrman 2007: 54).

3. This idea was often to be referred to, as seen in Common Fund (1989). At present, however, the prices of commodities have been violently fluctuated by Index Speculation enabled by the Commodities Futures Modernization Act (CFMA 2000).

4. Leith-Ross visited Japan in 1935 in order to bring the Japanese government round to an aid programme for China but in vain. See Imamura (1948: 237–8).

5. It should be noted that Acheson together with Clayton was to be a major architect of the Marshall Plan, as can be seen in his famous address of 1947 insisting that 'a coordinated European economy ... was a fundamental objective' (from Behrman 2007: 58).

6. The term 'relief' is used to cover a period of six months to one year immediately after the end of the war, while 'reconstruction' refers to a longer period of three to five years.

7. White is also famous as the main architect of the IMF. For his activities in the 1930s, see Laidler and Sandilands (2002).

8. According to the Lend-Lease Act, the US would supply munitions to the Allies with payment to be discussed later. Keynes played a central role in the negotiations, one result of which was the Anglo-American Mutual Aid Agreement. In the negotiations, it was Acheson who represented the American side. Article VII of the Agreement that includes 'discrimination' became a hot issue.

9. The law concerned is the Foreign Assistance Act of 1948. The total sum of aid to the OEEC composed of 15 countries amounted to $13 billion, 89 per cent of which was gratis. Although the Marshall Plan ended in 1951, it was the starting point of the long road towards the EU.

10. It seems unfair to regard the Marshall Plan as the victory of capitalism over communism, for the Marshall Plan itself was based on elaborate planning.

11. For an interesting reference to the relation between the Marshall Plan and Keynes, see Markwell (2006: 266–7).

12. What remains uncertain is how he would have dealt with the position of the UK in the power politics of the world. To what degree would he have reacted to a certain element recognizable in the Marshall Plan—lack of consideration for the UK in terms of the British Empire? Taking the subsequent developments—the deteriorating situation of the UK, the emergence of the two hegemons (the US and the USSR), and the Suez Crisis—into account, he could not have done anything to prevent the British Empire from disintegrating, as it finally came to disintegrate with the Macmillan government.

13. A rough sketch for this runs as follows. May 2009: spread to the PIGS (which stands for Portugal, Ireland, Greece, and Spain) leading up to the Euro crisis; November 2010: the bailout to Ireland; May 2011: the bailout plan to Portugal; July 2011: the second-round bailout plan to Greece, and enlargement of the EFSF on 26 October 2011: the EU summit; on 11 December 2011 the EU summit, the main theme of which was to establish the 'Fiscal Union'. Standard & Poor's (S&P) arguably remarked that the EU summit determined only a long-term matter (Fiscal Union), without considering the short-term one; on 21 December 2011, the ECB announced a drastically easy monetary policy ('Long Term Refinancing Operation') which contributed to keep the financial market calm; at the beginning of 2012, there emerged Euro crisis in various countries; on 25 January 2012, Merkel clearly referred to 'Political Union'; on 30 January and 2 March 2012, the EU summit, the main theme of which was, again, the 'fiscal compact'; as of mid-March 2012, Greek hair cut negotiation (debt swap deal) was finally agreed. However, it does not mean that Greece and the Euro zone escaped from the Euro crisis. For these measures are directed at quelling the financial sector without any consideration to difficulties of the PIIGS (Portugal, Ireland, Italy, Greece, and Spain) economies.

14. For this, see Amato and Fantacci (2011) and Fantacci's chapter in this volume.

15. Concerning the relation between the EMU (the Economic and Monetary Union of the EU) and Keynes's ICU plan, see Trautwein (2010). For a critical view of the Euro system from Keynes's ICU point of view, see Paus and Troost (2011).

16. Merkel and the Troika believe that collapse of the system can be prevented by going further with 'Fiscal Union' or 'Economic Government', reaching a higher level of integration. But this would ultimately prove pie in the sky. Above all, the political divide is so acute, not only among the Euro member countries but also within each member country, that there is no room for such a view.

REFERENCES

Amato, M. and L. Fantacci. 2011. *The End of Finance*. Cambridge: Polity Press.

Behrman, G. 2007. *The Most Noble Adventure: The Marshall Plan and the Time When America Helped Save Europe*. New York: Free Press.

Hirai, T. 2011. 'International Design and the British Empire. Keynes on the Relief Problem', paper presented at the Annual ESHET Conference, 'Competition, Innovation and Rivalry', Istanbul, 19–22 May, Bogazici University.

Imamura, T. 1948. *Takahashi Korekiyo*. Tokyo: Jiji-Hyoronsha.

Keynes, J.M. 1919. *The Economic Consequences of the Peace*. London: Macmillan.

———. 1923. *A Tract on Monetary Reform*. London: Macmillan.

———. 1926a. *The End of Laissez-Faire*. London: Hogarth Press.

———. 1926b. 'The Control of Raw Materials by Governments', *The Nation and Athenaeum*, 12 June; as reprinted in D.E. Moggridge (ed.), *The Collected Writings of John Maynard Keynes* (CWK) (1981), Vol. XIX. *Activities 1922–29. The Return to Gold and Industrial Policy. Part I*. London: Macmillan, pp. 546–52.

———. 1936. *The General Theory of Employment, Interest and Money*. London: Macmillan.

———. 1979. *The Collected Writings of John Maynard Keynes* (CWK), edited by D.E. Moggridge, Vol. XXIV. *Activities 1944–6: The Transition to Peace*. London: Macmillan.

———. 1980. *The Collected Writings of John Maynard Keynes* (CWK), edited by D.E. Moggridge, Vol. XXVII. *Activities 1940–6: Shaping the Post-War World: Employment and Commodities*. London: Macmillan.

Laidler, D. and R. Sandilands. 2002. 'An Early Harvard Memorandum on Anti-Depression Policies: An Introductory Note', *History of Political Economy*, 34(3): 515–52.

Markwell, D. 2006. *John Maynard Keynes and International Relations. Economic Paths to War and Peace*. Oxford: Oxford University Press.

Moggridge, D. 1992. *Maynard Keynes: An Economist's Biography*. London: Routledge.

Paus, L. and A. Troost. 2011. 'A European Clearing Union. The Monetary Union 2.0', mimeo, available online: http://www.transform-network.net/uploads/media/A_European_Clearing_Union_March_2011_02.pdf (accessed 29 April 2012).

Trautwein, H-M. 2010. 'European Macroeconomic Policy: A Return to Active Stabilization?' in B.W. Bateman, T. Hirai, and M.C. Marcuzzo (eds), *The Return to Keynes*. Cambridge, MA: Harvard University Press, pp. 51–75.

III
Money and International Liquidity

7

Was Keynes's Monetary Policy, à *outrance* in the *Treatise*, the Model for ZIRP and QE?

JAN KREGEL

KEYNES'S CHALLENGE TO MONETARY AUTHORITIES IN 1930: INTRODUCE ZIRP AND QE

At the end of 1930, as the US stock market crash was starting to have a negative impact on the real economy in the form of falling commodity prices, falling output, and rising unemployment, John Maynard Keynes, in the concluding chapters of his *Treatise on Money*, launched a challenge to monetary authorities: take 'deliberate and vigorous action' to reduce interest rates and reverse the crisis. He argued that until 'extraordinary', 'unorthodox' monetary policy action 'has been taken along such lines as these and has failed, need we, in the light of the argument of this treatise, admit that the banking system can *not*, on this occasion, control the rate of investment, and, therefore, the level of prices' (Keynes 1930a: 387).[1] The 'unorthodox' policies that Keynes recommends are virtually identical to the Japanese central bank's experiment with zero interest rate policy (ZIRP) in the 1990s and the US Federal Reserve's experiment with ZIRP, accompanied by quantitative easing (QE1 and QE2), during the recent crisis. While too late to be considered a response to Keynes's challenge, these modern policy measures provide a clear test of Keynes's belief in the

power of monetary policy to counter financial crisis. This modern response to Keynes's challenge would appear to be a clear admission of the inability of monetary policy to influence the rate of investment as a means of responding to the crisis. Indeed, Keynes himself seems to have modified his position as his thinking evolved towards the analysis of *The General Theory*.

THE OBJECTIVES OF MONETARY POLICY

In the penultimate chapter of volume 2 of the *Treatise*, Keynes raises 'the crux of the whole matter' of monetary policy: '[D]oes it lie within the power of a central bank in actual practice to pursue a policy which will have the effect of fixing the value of money at any prescribed level?' (Keynes 1930a: 339).[2]

Despite some residual doubts,[3] Keynes nonetheless answers his own question in the affirmative, urging central bankers to adopt 'extraordinary', 'unorthodox' measures to reduce interest rates to near zero in an attempt to counter the deepening recession.

THE *TREATISE* AND THE ALTERNATIVE DETERMINATION OF PRICES

Keynes's proposal is built on his explanation of price determination provided in the *Treatise*. His approach was based on the formulation of 'fundamental equations' for the prices of what he called 'available' and 'non-available' output. In simple terms, Keynes argued that prices would be determined by unit labour costs (efficiency wages) and the pressure of demand caused by a divergence of savings from investment driving profitability of production. The focus of recovery policy should thus be to increase investment in order to drive up the demand for output, absorbing excess production and encouraging entrepreneurs to again expand employment and output. Keynes points out that his approach is substantially different from that of the quantity theorists, in that there is no direct impact of money on prices; rather it is investment that is the crucial factor. Since Keynes believed that banks had the power to determine the terms of credit, they could influence the rate of investment, which would then determine the price level.

Although Keynes attributed 'to the banking system much greater power to *preserve* investment equilibrium than to force the prevailing

rate of money incomes away from the existing level or from the level produced by spontaneous changes, to a new and changed level imposed by conditions abroad or by arbitrary decree at home' (Keynes 1930a: 352), he nonetheless urged central bankers to attempt to do so in response to the crisis.

SHORT-TERM RATES OF INTEREST AND LONG-TERM RATES

Keynes notes a major difficulty in his proposal that while 'the main direct influence of the banking system is over the short-term rate of interest', the control of the rate of investment will primarily depend on the long-term rate of interest. It is thus necessary to 'be sure that the long-term rate of interest will respond to the wishes of the currency authority which will be exerting its direct influence, as it must, mainly on the short-term rate' (Ibid.).

Keynes's 'experience shows that, as a rule, the influence of the short-term rate of interest on the long-term rate is much greater than anyone who argued on the above lines would have expected' (Ibid.: 353). In support of this position Keynes refers to statistical studies by the Federal Reserve Board (Riefler 1930) showing that 'all the important movements in short-term rates from 1919 to 1928 were reflected in bond yields' (Keynes 1930a: 353). Keynes emphasizes that the surprising fact 'is not that bond yields are relatively stable in comparison with short-term rates, but rather that they have reflected fluctuations in short-term rates so strikingly and to such a considerable extent' (Ibid.: 355–6).[4]

In further support of this relationship Keynes raises an issue that would take on greater importance in *The General Theory*: the predominant impact of short-term realizations on long-term expectations.

In truth—he writes—we know almost nothing about the more remote future.... The ignorance of even the best-informed investor about the more remote future is much greater than his knowledge.... But if this is true of the best informed, the vast majority... know almost nothing whatever about what they are doing. They do not possess even the rudiments of what is required for a valid judgment, and are the prey of hopes and fears easily aroused by transient events and as easily dispelled. This is one of the odd characteristics of the capitalist system under which we live, which, when we are dealing with the real world, is not to be overlooked. (Ibid.: 359–61)

SHORT-TERM MONEY: QUANTITY IS AS IMPORTANT AS PRICE

Having established the importance of the short term in formulating long-term expectations, and thus the possibility that short-term interest rates could be used to influence long-term capital investment decisions, Keynes goes on to admit:

> I do not believe...that the volume of investment either in working capital or in liquid capital is sensitive to changes in the short-term rate of interest by itself.... On the other hand, the direct effects of cheap money operating through changes, even small ones, in the bond market... on the volume of new investment is probably of more importance. (Keynes 1930a: 364).

EXTRAORDINARY MEASURES: ZIRP AND QE

But Keynes goes on to note that these arguments apply to 'normal and orthodox methods by which a central bank can use its powers for easing (or stiffening) the credit situation to stimulate (or retard) the rate of new investment'. But, if the central bank has not acted peremptorily 'more extreme measures will have to be invoked'. (Ibid.: 369)

These extreme measures involve

> the purchase of securities by the central bank until the long-term market rate of interest has been brought down...to any figure at which it is itself prepared to buy long-term securities.[5] ...Thus I see small reason to doubt that the central bank can produce a large effect on the cost of raising new resources for long-term investment, if it is prepared to persist with its open-market policy far enough. (Ibid.: 371)

Thus, Keynes recommends not only pushing the rate of interest down towards zero, but also dealing in the long-term market to set long rates.

Keynes notes that there may be implementation difficulties. For example, many central banks have restrictions on the type of securities acceptable for purchase or discount, so that if the bank

> continues such purchases beyond a certain point, it may create an entirely artificial position in them relatively to other securities. It is to provide against the contingency of insufficient ammunition for the carrying on of open-market operations *à outrance* that I have suggested...

that the central bank should have power to vary within limits the reserve requirements of its member banks. (Keynes 1930a: 369–72).

An alternative would be to vary the eligibility of the assets that the bank can acquire, which is precisely what the Federal Reserve did in invoking Section 13(3) of the Federal Reserve Act to create special facilities for lending against alternative types of collateral and to non-member institutions.

Keynes also notes that the central bank may be purchasing securities at rates 'far beyond what it considers to be the long-term norm', *and* that when the central bank reverses strategy it 'may show a serious financial loss'. But this should be accepted since the central bank, representing the public interest, should 'be ready to run the risks of the future prospects when private interest reckons these risks to be unusually high'.[6]

The conclusion for policy is that, 'if my diagnosis is correct, we cannot hope for a complete or lasting recovery until there has been a very great fall in the long-term market rate of interest throughout the world towards something nearer pre-war levels. Failing this, there will be a steady pressure towards profit deflation and a sagging price level' (Ibid.: 384). Without these extraordinary policies, 'the thing will never cure itself by the lack of borrowers forcing down the rate; for it absorbs just as much savings to finance losses as to finance investment' (Ibid.).

> The remedy should come, I suggest, from a general recognition that the rate of investment need not be beyond our control, if we are prepared to use our banking systems to effect a proper adjustment of the market rate of interest. It might be sufficient merely to produce a general belief in the long continuance of a very low rate of short-term interest. The change, once it has begun, will feed on itself. (Ibid.: 386)

Again, it is interesting to note that the Federal Reserve has made a public commitment to the preservation of the ZIRP for a sustained period.

It would appear that the Bank of Japan, by introducing a ZIRP, experimented with Keynes's recommendation that interest rates be set as low as possible, and that the Federal Reserve, through its programme of quantitative easing has followed his recommendation in full by purchasing long-term securities to bring down the long-term rate of interest and satiate the desire to hold deposits. Keynes notes

that these policies are not at all different from normal open-market policies, and that the central bank possesses the power to set any interest rate, short or long, at any level it desires. It also appears as if Keynes's expectation that the public would become willing buyers of government securities upon a sharp reduction in short rates, aiding the policy of lowering the long-term rate, was accurate. In addition, in response to Fed policy, there has been the recovery of stock prices that Keynes would have expected.

What has not been borne out in the current experiment is the expected impact on the rate of investment. Businesses have indeed increased their borrowing, particularly low grade credits, and the spread between corporate junk bonds has fallen to near-historic lows as companies seek to borrow at historically low interest rates. However, these funds are not being used to finance new investment. Similarly, banks have accumulated record levels of excess reserve deposits at the Fed, earning the short-term interest rate, which is nearly zero. Thus, the policy has been successful in influencing the spectrum of interest rates in the way Keynes's predicted, but it has not had the impact on investment that he outlined in the *Treatise*.

SCEPTICISM BETWEEN THE *TREATISE* AND *THE GENERAL THEORY*

Keynes progressively modified his belief in the efficacy of monetary policy in the interim between the publication of the *Treatise* and the completion of *The General Theory*. The first indications came during a visit to the United States in 1931 in which he gave policy lectures at the New School for Social Research in New York and at the Harris Foundation in Chicago.

His lectures at the New School in mid-June were entitled 'Do We Want Prices to Rise?' and 'What Can We Do to Make Prices Rise?' There is some controversy over the exact content of the second lecture; contemporaneous press reports appear to contradict the truncated version that appears in the *Collected Writings* published under the auspices of the Royal Economic Society (see the discussion in Kent 2004). Kent surmises that Keynes changed his presentation from the prepared written version due to his discussions with policymakers in New York. He notes that in the version of the second lecture published in the *Collected Writings of John Maynard Keynes* (CWK), Keynes does

not recommend government intervention and repeats his analysis of the *Treatise*: 'if…the rate of interest can be brought down sufficiently, I do feel confident that the demand for loans will in due course develop for buildings, for transport and for public utilities' (CWK XX: 553).

Kent cites local news reports that suggest in his oral presentation he added two new points: restoring confidence and direct government action. 'Recommending government action in the United States was a very significant change for Keynes [who] was an advocate of government intervention in Great Britain, but that was because of Great Britain's ability to reduce interest rates was restricted by concerns about the outflow of gold that it was thought would occur if this were done' (Kent 2004: 204). Keynes did not believe that the US was so constrained, suggesting a softening of his confidence in the willingness or the ability of central banks to produce interest rate reductions sufficient to generate recovery.

This interpretation finds support in Keynes's lectures to the Harris Foundation in Chicago at the beginning of July. In Lecture I Keynes identifies the 'leading characteristic' of the crisis as 'an extraordinary willingness to borrow money for the purposes of new real investment at very high rates of interest—rates of interest which were extravagantly high on pre-war standards, rates of interest which have never in the history of the world been earned, I should say, over a period of years over the average of enterprise as a whole' (CWK XIII: 345). As a result Keynes says he can 'see no hope of a recovery except in a revival of the high level of investment'. He thus directs his analysis to the 'causes of the collapse of investment and the means of reviving investment' (Ibid.: 349). He concentrates on the 'variability of the rate of investment' since it is 'the element of the economic situation which is capable of sudden and violent change' (Ibid.: 354–5). In Lecture 3, 'The Road to Recovery', he notes that this is 'essentially a technical banking problem. The practical means by which investment can be increased is, or ought to be, the bankers' business, and pre-eminently the business of the central banker' (Ibid.: 363).

He then outlines three channels of attack, restoring confidence, government action, and a reduction in the rate of interest. Here he reiterates scepticism concerning the possibility of sufficient action on the interest rate:

> I am ready to believe that a small change in the rate of interest may not be sufficient. That, indeed, is why I am pessimistic as to an early

return to normal prosperity. I am ready enough to admit that it may be extremely difficult both to restore confidence adequately and to reduce interest rates adequately. (CWK XIII: 365).

He amplified this position in a Round Table following his presentation: 'I am in favour of an admixture of public works...I should use the public works program to fill in the interegnum (sic) while I was getting the interest rate down' (Harris Foundation 1931: 494). However, in the September 1932 issue of *The Economic Journal* he reaffirms his position: 'A reduction of the long-term rate of interest to a low level is probably the most necessary of all measures if we are to escape from the slump and secure a lasting revival of enterprise' (Keynes 1932: 415).

A SHIFT OF POSITION IN *THE GENERAL THEORY*?

However, Keynes's position changed with his development of *The General Theory*.

Keynes tells his readers that one of the basic differences from the earlier book is the separation of the analysis of investment in financial assets and capital assets through the separation of their determinants via liquidity preference and the marginal efficiency of capital. While the *Treatise* made a distinction between industrial and financial circulation, the prices of both assets and liabilities were treated in a single fundamental price equation and financed by the financial circulation.

In his *General Theory* analysis, Keynes amplifies the explanation of determinants of investment, stating that 'current investment will depend...on what we shall call the inducement to invest; and the inducement to invest will be found to depend on the relation between the schedule of the marginal efficiency of capital and the complex of rates of interest on loans of various maturities and risks' (Keynes 1936: 27). 'The schedule of the marginal efficiency of capital may be said to govern the terms on which loanable funds are demanded for the purpose of new investment; whilst the rate of interest governs the terms on which funds are being currently supplied' (Ibid.: 165).

Another novel feature of *The General Theory* is its emphasis on the conditions of a monetary economy as 'one in which changing views about the future are capable of influencing the quantity of employment and not merely its direction' (Ibid.: vii). In particular, Keynes

notes that the major determinant of the rate of interest will be 'largely governed by the prevailing view as to what its value is expected to be' (Keynes 1936: 203), while 'the schedule of the marginal efficiency of capital is of fundamental importance because it is mainly through this factor (much more than through the rate of interest) that the expectation of the future influences the present' (Ibid.: 145). The current long-term rate of interest is thus no longer the sole or direct determinant of investment.

Echoing his views in the *Treatise*, he writes:

> It would be foolish, in forming our expectations, to attach great weight to matters which are very uncertain. ...For this reason the facts of the existing situation enter, in a sense disproportionately, into the formation of our long-term expectations; our usual practice being to take the existing situation and to project it into the future, modified only to the extent that we have more or less definite reasons for expecting a change. [Thus,] there is no clear evidence from experience that the investment policy which is socially advantageous coincides with that which is most profitable. It needs *more* intelligence to defeat the forces of time and our ignorance of the future than to beat the gun. Moreover, life is not long enough;—human nature desires quick results, there is a peculiar zest in making money quickly, and remoter gains are discounted by the average man at a very high rate. (Ibid.: 148–57)

As a result, Keynes modifies his prior belief in the positive impact of lower interest rates on the rate of investment. For example,

> an expectation of a future fall in the rate of interest will have the effect of *lowering* the schedule of the marginal efficiency of capital; since it means that the output from equipment produced to-day will have to compete during part of its life with the output from equipment which is content with a lower return. This expectation will have no great depressing effect, since the expectations, which are held concerning the complex of rates of interest for various terms which will rule in the future, will be partially reflected in the complex of rates of interest which rule to-day. Nevertheless there may be some depressing effect, since the output from equipment produced to-day, which will emerge towards the end of the life of this equipment, may have to compete with the output of much younger equipment which is content with a lower return because of the lower rate of interest which rules for periods subsequent to the end of the life of equipment produced to-day. (Ibid.: 143)

Keynes also modifies his position on the ability of the central bank to influence the lending practices of financial institutions through a reduction in interest rates:

> We must also take account of the other facet of the state of confidence, namely, the confidence of the lending institutions towards those who seek to borrow from them, sometimes described as the state of credit. A collapse in the price of equities, which has had disastrous reactions on the marginal efficiency of capital, may have been due to the weakening either of speculative confidence or of the state of credit. But whereas the weakening of either is enough to cause a collapse, recovery requires the revival of *both*. For whilst the weakening of credit is sufficient to bring about a collapse, its strengthening, though a necessary condition of recovery, is not a sufficient condition. (Keynes 1936: 158)

Further, Keynes argues that there may be difficulty in pushing interest rates down to extremely low levels due to extreme liquidity preference:

> We have seen...that *uncertainty* as to the future course of the rate of interest is the sole intelligible explanation of the type of liquidity-preference...which leads to the holding of cash. ...It follows that... what matters is not the *absolute* level of r but the degree of its divergence from what is considered a fairly *safe* level of r, having regard to those calculations of probability which are being relied on. (Ibid.: 201–2)

Keynes then goes on to give a precise definition of the liquidity trap:

> Every fall in r reduces the market rate relatively to the 'safe' rate and therefore increases the risk of illiquidity; and, in the second place, every fall in r reduces the current earnings from illiquidity, which are available as a sort of insurance premium to offset the risk of loss on capital account, by an amount equal to the difference between the *squares* of the old rate of interest and the new. ...*This, indeed, is perhaps the chief obstacle to a fall in the rate of interest to a very low level.* Unless reasons are believed to exist why future experience will be very different from past experience, a long-term rate of interest of (say) 2 per cent leaves more to fear than to hope, and offers, at the same time, a running yield which is only sufficient to offset a very small measure of fear. (Ibid.) [emphasis added][7]

Although Keynes continues to maintain that the 'short-term rate of interest is easily controlled by the monetary authority, both because it is not difficult to produce a conviction that its policy will not greatly

change in the very near future, and also because the possible loss is small compared with the running yield (unless it is approaching vanishing point)', he also observes that

> the long-term rate may be more recalcitrant when once it has fallen to a level which, on the basis of past experience and present expectations of *future* monetary policy, is considered 'unsafe' by representative opinion. For example, in a country linked to an international gold standard, a rate of interest lower than prevails elsewhere will be viewed with a justifiable lack of confidence; yet a domestic rate of interest dragged up to a parity with the *highest* rate (highest after allowing for risk) prevailing in any country belonging to the international system may be much higher than is consistent with domestic full employment. (Keynes 1936: 203)

Thus, the introduction of the influence of the marginal efficiency of capital on the rate of investment independent of the impact of the rate of interest and the introduction of expectations and liquidity preference as the independent determinant of the rate of interest leads Keynes to modify his *Treatise* analysis of the impact of 'extraordinary' monetary policy on the long-term rate of interest:

> A monetary policy which strikes public opinion as being experimental in character or easily liable to change may fail in its objective of greatly reducing the long-term rate of interest, because M_2 may tend to increase almost without limit in response to a reduction of r below a certain figure. The same policy, on the other hand, may prove easily successful if it appeals to public opinion as being reasonable and practicable and in the public interest, rooted in strong conviction, and promoted by an authority unlikely to be superseded. (Ibid.)

'FOR MY OWN PART I AM NOW SOMEWHAT SCEPTICAL'

Thus, in *The General Theory*, Keynes, 'after giving full weight to the importance of the influence of short-period changes in the state of long-term expectation as distinct from changes in the rate of interest', further modifies his belief in the efficacy of monetary policy to influence the rate of investment, noting that 'we are still entitled to return to the latter [that is, the rate of interest] as exercising, at any rate, in normal circumstances, a great, though not a decisive, influence on the rate of investment. Only experience, however, can show

how far management of the rate of interest is capable of continuously stimulating the appropriate volume of investment' (Keynes 1936: 164). He then goes on to state:

> For my own part I am now somewhat sceptical of the success of a merely monetary policy directed towards influencing the rate of interest. I expect to see the State, which is in a position to calculate the marginal efficiency of capital-goods on long views and on the basis of the general social advantage, taking an ever greater responsibility for directly organising investment; since it seems likely that the fluctuations in the market estimation of the marginal efficiency of different types of capital, calculated on the principles I have described above, will be too great to be offset by any practicable changes in the rate of interest. (Ibid.)

* * *

While Keynes can be considered the true father of the 'unorthodox' monetary policies introduced by the Bank of Japan and the Federal Reserve, these policies also provide the test of their efficacy that Keynes called for. They suggest that Keynes's *Treatise* optimism was misplaced, and that his more nuanced, sceptical, position in *The General Theory* was more appropriate; in particular, his emphasis on the need to provide an external source of demand through government expenditure. Finally, in comparison with the current period, Keynes did not take into account the impact of capital loss on the inducement to invest and the propensity to consume, factors that in all likelihood would have led him to place even greater emphasis on the role of government spending in bringing about recovery.

NOTES

1. Already in May 1930 Keynes expressed this view in an article in *The Nation* that reflects the conclusions of the *Treatise*:

> The fact is—a fact not yet recognised by the great public—that we are now in the depths of a very severe international slump, a slump which will take its place in history amongst the most acute ever experienced. It will require not merely passive movements of bank rates to lift us out of a depression of this order, but a very active and determined policy. (Keynes 1930b)

2. The question is considered in the context of a proposal to amend the Federal Reserve Act 'to lay upon the Federal Reserve Board the duty of using all the powers at its disposal to "promote a stable price level for commodities in general"' (Keynes 1930a: 340).

3. Raised by Congressional hearings on the proposal that surveyed the difficulties of using monetary policy to counter the impact of international conditions on commodity prices, and thus on domestic prices, and the difficulty of using monetary policy to counter declining prices in a depression.

4. Keynes does not, however, report Riefler's (1930: 123) caveat that this is more the result of the impact on the stock of existing long-terms bonds than on the prices of newly issued long-term securities.

5. If the central bank supplies the member banks with more funds than they can lend at short term, in the first place the short-term rate of interest will decline towards zero, and in the second place the member banks will soon begin, if only to maintain their profits, to second the efforts of the central bank by themselves buying securities. This means that the price of bonds will rise until there are many persons to be found who, as they see the prices of long-term bonds rising, prefer to sell them and hold the proceeds liquid at a very low rate of interest.

6. In Keynes (1932: 421–2) he notes that in the US 'the fear of the Member Banks lest they should be unable to cover their expenses' may have provided an 'obstacle to the adoption of a whole-hearted cheap money policy'.

7. Keynes also notes that the classical theory proposed an alternative method of lowering the rate of interest, by 'reducing wages, whilst leaving the quantity of money unchanged'. Just as a moderate increase in the quantity of money may exert an inadequate influence over the long-term rate of interest, whilst an immoderate increase may offset its other advantages by its disturbing effect on confidence; so a moderate reduction in money-wages may prove inadequate, whilst an immoderate reduction might shatter confidence even if it were practicable. 'There is, therefore, no ground for the belief that a flexible wage policy is capable of maintaining a state of continuous full employment;—any more than for the belief that an open-market monetary policy is capable, unaided, of achieving this result. The economic system cannot be made self-adjusting along these lines' (Keynes 1936: 267).

REFERENCES

Harris Foundation. 1931. *Reports of Roundtables: Unemployment as a World Problem*. Chicago.

Kent, R.J. 2004. 'Keynes's Lectures at the New School for Social Research', *History of Political Economy*, 36(1): 195–206.

Keynes, J.M. 1930a. *A Treatise on Money*. Vol. II: *The Applied Theory of Money*. London: Macmillan.

———. 1930b. 'Monetary Policy Alone Will Not End Depression', *The Nation*, 10 May.

———. 1932. 'A Note on the Long-Term Rate of Interest in Relation to the Conversion Scheme', *The Economic Journal*, 42(167): 415–23.

———. 1936. *The General Theory of Employment, Interest and Money*. London: Macmillan.

Keynes, J.M. 1971–89. *The Collected Writings of John Maynard Keynes* (CWK), edited by D.E. Moggridge, 30 vols. London: Macmillan; volumes are identified as CWK followed by volume number in Roman numerals.

CWK XIII. *The General Theory and After.* Vol. 1: *Preparation.*

CWK XX. *Activities, 1929–31: Rethinking Employment and Unemployment Policies.*

Riefler, W.W. 1930. *Money Rates and Money Markets in the United States.* With an Introduction by E.A. Goldenweiser. New York and London: Harper & Brothers.

8
Liquidity Preference of Banks and Crises

FERNANDO J. CARDIM DE CARVALHO*

In one of his few replies to the critics of *The General Theory of Employment, Interest and Money*, Keynes (1937a) stated that the book contained two main theoretical novelties. One of them was the concept of propensity to consume and the multiplier. The other was liquidity preference. Judging by the literature that seems to have originated from *The General Theory*, it may be difficult to understand what Keynes meant. Liquidity preference, among mainstream economists, including mainstream Keynesians, to this day is nothing more than a fancy name for money demand.[1] This was, in fact, the way the concept was taught in the old macroeconomics textbooks of the twentieth century, when they still presented Keynesian theories.

Although it can be argued that it was an honest mistake given the way liquidity preference was introduced in *The General Theory*, a more attentive reading of that text and a better general knowledge of Keynes's works make it clear that liquidity preference is in fact a theory of asset pricing. Reduced to its most essential terms, Keynes proposed that asset returns include two types of reward: (a) a monetary return (either in the form of incomes, such as interest, profits,

* The author thanks without implicating the comments of Anna Simonazzi, Luca Fantacci, Roger Backhouse, and Julio López-Gallardo. Financial support from CNPq is gratefully acknowledged.

dividends, and rents, or as capital gains or losses, net of carrying costs); and (b) a liquidity premium, represented by the implicit insurance an asset offers its holder in the form of easiness of disposal. In his argument, Keynes (1937a) pointed out that to properly assess the value of liquidity, one had to realize that the future was not only risky, but fundamentally uncertain, which he took to mean that not only are we subject to adverse developments in the future, but also that we may not know enough about them to allow us to buy an actual insurance policy against them. In this case, the possession of liquid assets, among which money counts as the asset with the highest liquidity premium, worked like a form of insurance against 'unknown unknowns', those adverse developments that were not defined by their low probability but by their actual unpredictability at the moment of decision.[2] Varying degrees of uncertainty at different moments of time are reflected in changing liquidity preferences and, therefore, in the relative prices of assets (including money) as they offer 'general' insurance in different degrees, according to how liquid each class of assets is. In particular, when uncertainty rises to very high levels, as it is supposed to happen during serious crises, a flight to liquidity would explain the frequently observed collapse of the prices of illiquid assets.

Liquidity preference was one of those early components of what Schumpeter (1996) would call Keynes's *vision*. Its final form is presented in *The General Theory*, but Keynes had mulled around the concept at least since the First World War. In his *A Treatise on Money*, Keynes had applied the notion (although not the name) even to banks' portfolio choices, but this latter discussion disappeared from *The General Theory*, a most unfortunate development.[3]

The purpose of this chapter is to argue in favour of, first, the proper understanding of liquidity preference theory and, second, its extension to explain portfolio choices of banks and their consequences. Among the latter, one counts the possibility of adding some notion of financial dynamics to the operation of entrepreneurial economies described in *The General Theory*, which is essential to the understanding of financial crises. We proceed therefore by re-examining, in the second section, the concept of liquidity preference as a theory of asset pricing instead of merely a theory of money demand. The third section reconstructs the concept of liquidity preference as applied to banks, before and beyond *The General Theory*, to arrive at a form of

the theory useful to analyse contemporary events. The fourth section addresses directly the reasons why banks should also exhibit liquidity preference even when it is acknowledged that they are also creators of money. The last section concludes.

THE MEANING OF LIQUIDITY PREFERENCE: LIQUIDITY PREMIUM AND ASSET PRICES

In the decades that followed the publication of *The General Theory*, liquidity preference was interpreted by the majority of economists as the specification of the demand function for money that Keynes wanted to substitute for the prevailing (in England) Marshallian version of the quantity theory of money. This seemed, in fact, to be Keynes's project before *The General Theory*, most clearly when writing the *Tract on Monetary Reform*, or still, with some ambiguity, during the preparation of *A Treatise on Money*.[4] The Marshallian version of the quantity theory of money stated that the demand for money was a relatively stable function of income, but Marshall admitted that the velocity of money circulation could vary as a result of changes in the opportunity cost of holding money between receipt and payment dates. Economists trained in the Marshallian tradition tended to interpret Keynes's liquidity preference as a more 'modern' presentation of the theory, where the role of the interest rate, the main measure of the opportunity cost of holding money, was formally acknowledged. What Keynes called in *The General Theory* the *speculative demand for money*, where money is held in anticipation of a future rise in interest rates that will depress the prices of securities, could be accepted even by Milton Friedman (1956) in his restatement of the quantity theory of money. Nevertheless, Friedman expected the impact of rises in money supply on the price of debt securities to be much smaller than that expected by Keynesian economists like James Tobin.[5]

In at least two senses Keynes may have been responsible himself for this misinterpretation. First, for most of central chapters of *The General Theory*, where Keynes actually builds his effective demand model on the three pillars of the concepts of propensity to consume, marginal efficiency of capital, and liquidity preference, assets are aggregated in two groups: a short-term, liquid, capital-risk-free asset, called *money*, and a longer-term, illiquid asset exposed to capital risk, called *bonds*.[6] In such a setting, the model determines the price

of bonds in terms of money, that is, 'the' interest rate.[7] 'The' interest rate measures the opportunity cost of liquidity, which is embodied in 'money'. If 'bonds' were disaggregated into a larger number of classes (and the same could be done with 'money'), the model would not produce 'the' interest rate, but the *set* of interest rates (and asset prices) corresponding to the specified classes of assets. This disaggregation is precisely what Keynes did in Chapter 17 of *The General Theory*, a chapter long neglected in conventional readings of that work, to show how prices of assets in general are determined. The interpretation that prevailed, however, was the one proposed by Hicks (and, to be fair, following Keynes's footsteps in his restatement of employment theory in Chapter 18 of *The General Theory*), whereby liquidity preference theory became just a new way to present the same old money demand and supply analysis. In this line of interpretation, the 'novelty' offered by *The General Theory* was that Keynes used the money market supply and demand equations to determine 'the' interest rate instead of 'the' price level, as the old quantity theory of money would have them to do. Even that, however, was not really such a radical change when it was determined by orthodox theorists—such as Franco Modigliani (1944)—that Keynes's approach could only be accepted on the assumption of rigid prices (and wages).

Keynes can also be blamed for the second way liquidity preference theory was emptied of its content. In *The General Theory*, 'money', as defined before,[8] is demanded for three reasons, two of which refer to its role as means of payment. One can demand money because one plans to buy goods (the transactions demand) or because one plans to buy securities (the speculative demand). In neither of the two cases money is being demanded as such but as temporary abodes of purchasing power, as Milton Friedman would later put it. Money is held today because one wants to buy goods or securities tomorrow and will have to deliver means of payment in exchange for the items one wants to acquire.

Money is demanded for *itself*, as a liquid asset, only for the third reason, as a defence against unpredictable adverse events. When one does not know what can happen in the future, one holds money because money allows its holder to buy specific forms of protection if and when a threat materializes or the future perspectives are somehow clarified. Money is fungible and can be transformed into anything very quickly. This is what having the highest liquidity

premium means. That is the reason why holding money 'lulls our disquietude', as Keynes (1937a) put it in defence of his theory. The name given to this reason to hold money was the *precautionary* demand. In *The General Theory*, however, the precautionary demand for holding money takes a backseat to the speculative demand, and in fact disappears from the model soon after it was introduced, subsumed in the transactions demand for money.[9] As a consequence, liquidity preference lost its meaning as portfolio choice analysis (which was relegated to the almost-never-read Chapter 17), and only the two roles of money as means of payment were highlighted in the rest of the work and the model that was extracted from it.

In the perspective shared by this essay, liquidity preference is a theory of asset accumulation in which it is proposed that asset returns, in the eyes of the asset buyer, comprise both a money reward (incomes generated by the asset or changes in its market price between purchase and re-sale) and an implicit insurance or liquidity premium. Under fundamental uncertainty, where not only one cannot predict what *is going to* happen but one cannot predict even what *can* happen, assets that allow a wealth-holder to react efficiently to new information are more valuable than those that do not have this property. Liquidity preference theory is based on the idea that asset-holders prefer liquid assets and will only part with liquidity if they are compensated for this loss in the form of higher money rewards. As Keynes put it, according to liquidity preference theory, the interest rate is the reward for parting with liquidity, not for abstaining from consumption (as proposed by classical theories of interest).[10]

Keynes built a particular model to illustrate the working of liquidity preference as a theory of portfolio choice in Chapter 17 of *The General Theory* with the concept of *own-rates of interest*. In this model, expected total returns for each asset comprise the incomes it is expect to generate, expected changes in its market price between the acquisition and the sale of the asset, its carrying costs (with a negative sign), and its liquidity premium, defined as a measure of the power of disposal over the asset. The sum of the four attributes defines the *own-rate of interest*, or, which is the same, the *marginal efficiency* of each asset. Asset buyers are assumed to prefer those assets that offer the highest own-rates of interest, while they try to sell those that are expected to pay lower total returns. The interaction

between supply of and demand for each type of asset determines their prices (which in equilibrium should be those that equalize their own-rates of interest). For reproducible assets, market prices reached in this process are compared with their reproduction costs. If market prices are higher than reproduction costs, new quantities of the asset will be produced; if not, existing stocks will be reduced through wear and tear.[11]

Liquidity preference theory, therefore, consists in the proposition that supply and demand for assets determine their prices, where demand for each asset is explained as a combination of expected money returns and its liquidity premium. Given its (stock and flow) supply, liquidity preference theory is expected to explain prices (and money rates of return) rather than available amounts of assets because some forms of wealth are non-reproducible. Its fundamental starting point is that under uncertainty wealth-holders value not only how much they can earn when buying an asset but also what kind of insurance it can offer if unexpected adverse events take place.

In *The General Theory*, the banking sector is a ghost. We can find consumers and entrepreneurs, savers and investors, workers and firms, but banks are mentioned only in the context of references to specific concrete events. There are debts, of course, but one does not know who issued them. In fact, the own-rates of interest model is developed as if wealth-holders were financing their asset acquisitions with unlimited resources of unspecified origin. As presented in *The General Theory*, liquidity preference is a model of asset choice, not of balance sheet choice.

The approach would be completed, however, with Hyman Minsky's (1975) extension of the own-rates of interest model to include the issuance of liabilities. Now, wealth-holders should consider not only expected returns from the purchase of asset but also the cash outflow commitments that the issuance of liabilities represented. As Minsky put it, the fundamental decision now was how to reconcile cash inflows expected to result from the purchase of assets with the cash outflows committed with the issuance of liabilities and the margins of safety to be adopted in the reconciliation between the two to guarantee that debts could be paid (and bankruptcy avoided) even when asset revenue expectations were disappointed to some degree. In the extended model, prices of assets still depend on supply and demand, but demand is now more complex, comprising not only the attributes

of the assets themselves but also of the financing channels available to their buyer.

LIQUIDITY PREFERENCE OF BANKS

Keynes's first suggestion of a specific behaviour of banks towards liquidity seems to have been his analysis of the turbulences generated by the First World War on London capital markets.[12] London was the main financial hub of the world economy. Investors and borrowers turned to the City to do their deals and local brokers worked as intermediaries, assuming debts with banks to make short-term loans to securities buyers. When the war began, payments were disrupted and brokers had to settle their debts with banks while being unable to collect their loans to clients. To prevent the market's collapse, the Bank of England extended a line of credit to banks to induce them to roll over brokers' loans. Given the increased uncertainties created by the war as to when markets would in fact return to normality, banks did borrow from the Bank of England but refused to roll over brokers' debts or to extend them new loans. Uncertain about the prospect of actually recovering their credits to brokers, they preferred to hold low-earning or non-earning liquid assets to buying paying assets. As a result, credit supply contracted and fresh difficulties were created for the overall economy.

The issue seems to have re-emerged, which is not entirely surprising, only in the context of the crises of the late 1920s and early 1930s. Two works stand out in this respect. A short article, reprinted in *Essays in Persuasion*, developed the idea of *safety margins* adopted by banks in their function as intermediaries between lenders and borrowers, which exposed them to credit and market risks.[13] Banks would react to changes in the level of uncertainty by strengthening their safety margins (which led to a reduction in credit supply). Sometimes, however, banks would be surprised by an adverse shock too strong to be neutralized by their margins, and a financial collapse would ensue.

The other piece, more pertinent for the present discussion, was contained in volume two of *A Treatise on Money*, *The Applied Theory of Money*. In that work, Keynes proposed a typical balance sheet to characterize banks' choices, where banks issued one liability, deposits, and bought three classes of assets: bills of exchange and call loans,

investments, and advances to customers. Assets differed in their liquidity premia and money returns. Call loans were more liquid and less remunerative than investments, and investments kept a similar relationship to advances to customers. Given the amount of resources a bank could retain in the form of deposits, which were supposed to be given for an *individual* bank, the problem it had to address was to structure the asset side of their balance sheets in such a way as to reach a desired overall liquidity premium and desired money return. When uncertainty increased, choices would be biased towards more liquid assets at the cost of reducing the profitability of the bank, and the converse. When rising uncertainty affected the banking sector as a whole, the result of rising uncertainty would be the reduction of credit (that is, a reduction in the advances to customers) in favour of an increase of call loans and investments.[14]

It may be more than a little surprising that one of Keynes's first followers down this path seems to have been Milton Friedman. Friedman and Schwartz (1963) relied on the idea of a rising liquidity preference of banks after the bank runs of the beginning of the 1930s to explain the perseverance of the post-depression stagnation in the US and attributed to the failure by the Fed to understand it the adoption of a tough monetary policy in 1936 that helped to cause the 1937 recession.[15] The evidence utilized by Friedman and Schwartz was, in fact, of the type suggested by Keynes, the evolution of *prices* of liquid and relatively illiquid assets, rather than merely the accumulation of reserves (Ibid.: 453). Based on the price evidence, Friedman and Schwartz (1963) concluded that reserve accumulation was not due, as conventionally accepted then and since, to the inexistence of willing and able borrowers, but to a conscious drive by banks to increase their liquid positions in the highly uncertain environment of the American economy in the 1930s.[16]

Hyman Minsky brought the subject back to the economics of Keynes through his stress on the importance of considering balance sheet maturity mismatches to explain asset accumulation strategies and their consequences combining both the idea of safety margins and liquidity preference of banks. Minsky's argument is, by now, well-known: the decision to purchase assets depends on expected yields and on the nature of the liabilities that will be issued to finance the operation. Ultimately, asset revenues have to be enough to validate debt commitments when they come due. An asset buyer has to

be *solvent* (which is the case when the net present value of assets is at least as large as the net present value of liabilities) but he/she also has to be *liquid* (to be able to honour his/her debts when they come due). Building illiquid positions, as it happens in the cases of what Minsky (1982) called speculative and Ponzi portfolios, is the essential bet that asset holders have to make in capitalist economies. In Minsky's model, asset buyers are exposed to insolvency risk when they leverage their investments, and to illiquidity risk when they accept maturity mismatches between assets and liabilities. These risks are hedged when adequate safety margins are maintained between the value of assets and liabilities and liquidity cushions are created in one's portfolio.

Banks, *as they exist in modern capitalist economies*, face similar dilemmas to those suffered by households and non-financial firms but, in contrast to the latter, cannot avoid being illiquid.[17] Issuing shorter-term liabilities to buy longer-term assets is essential to banks whose reasons to exist include liquidity and maturity transformation. Financial fragility is a non-negotiable condition of modern banking systems. For Minsky, the dilemmas are similar to the ones suffered by households, but the impacts on the economy are far more important:

> The essential liquidity preference in a capitalist economy is that of bankers and businessmen, and the observable phenomena that indicate the state of liquidity preference are the trends of business and banker balance sheets. (Minsky 1982: 74)

After Minsky, other authors relying on liquidity preference theory to explain the behaviour of banks include Jan Kregel (1984–5), Dow and Dow (1989), and Cardim de Carvalho (1999). In these works, more emphasis is given to implications of the hypothesis, particularly with respect to the debate around the controllability of the money supply (which opposes 'verticalists' to 'horizontalists'). Taking liquidity preference of banks into consideration leads to the acknowledgement that banks may not be just the transmission belt linking the general public and monetary authorities, as it is assumed both by verticalists and horizontalists (although with opposite causality relations). Keynes acknowledged that banks could 'sterilize' expansive policies initiated by the central bank, as he argued had happened during the First World War. However, Keynes's approach to liquidity preference cannot be compatible with perfectly elastic

money supply curves, as the father of horizontalism, Nicholas Kaldor (1990), acknowledged.

WHY DO BANKS HAVE LIQUIDITY PREFERENCE?

Households and firms accumulate liquid assets, including money, despite their normally low yields, first, because they recognize that their expectations as to the future returns of assets can be disappointed, but also because debts contracted to finance the purchase of those assets will have to be honoured no matter whether their revenue expectations have or have not been disappointed. Since households and firms do not produce money, to make sure that their debts will be honoured they have to make sure they will accumulate, or ensure timely access to, the necessary amounts of means of payment. If they were allowed to pay their debts freely in IOUs, there would be no need to store money as a reserve of value or to hold any highly liquid asset.

The reason for banks to have liquidity preference may be less obvious. After all, the largest component of the stock of means of payment outstanding in any modern entrepreneurial economy is represented by demand deposits at commercial banks. Bank liabilities are part of the money supply, so it would seem that banks can actually pay debts with IOUs. Or can they?

Post Keynesians explain the *moneyness* of bank deposits through their closeness to legal tender. It is government debt which is the bedrock of liquidity in a capitalist economy. As Minsky (1982: 9) observed:

> The ultimately liquid assets of an economy consist of those assets whose nominal value is independent of the functioning of the economy. For an enterprise economy, the ultimately liquid assets consist of the domestically owned government debt outside government funds, Treasury currency, and specie.

Bank deposits became money because of the support structures that were created to guarantee their prompt convertibility at par into legal tender. Moneyness is not a natural attribute. It is conferred to an asset by those support structures. The public came to accept bank deposits as a close (or even superior, given its higher convenience of use) substitute to legal tender because it trusts those

support structures. The state has in fact shared its power to create money with the banking sector by extending its guarantees to the latter's demand liabilities, thereby ensuring their convertibility into currency at fixed prices.[18] That is why banks can make payments to households and firms by issuing their own IOUs, that is, by creating deposits, when they buy earning assets from the public.[19]

Banks cannot, in contrast, pay each other or, more importantly, the central bank with these IOUs. They need an *outside* form of money to do it. Even more important, should the public lose confidence on the state support structures for any reason and demand redemption of deposits, banks have to be prepared to honour them not with other IOUs, but with legal tender. As Keynes pointed out in the *Treatise on Money*, banks too have to consider the likelihood of having to make these payments when they decide the composition of their asset portfolios.[20]

An implication of acknowledging liquidity preferences is to consider that portfolio (or balance sheet) choices are sensitive not only to variations in the relevant interest rates but also to changes in perceived uncertainties. As uncertainty rises, low-yield liquid assets increase in demand in detriment of less liquid assets that are forced to increase their offered money returns if they are to remain in demand. If one traces a liquidity preference schedule in the traditional interest rate/money demand space, an autonomous increase in liquidity preference of this kind is represented as a shift upwards of the whole function. Since demand for liquid assets is strengthened, demand for illiquid assets will fall below supply, reducing their prices. As some of the most illiquid assets are reproducible goods, as in the case, notably, of capital goods, excess supplies will lead to reduced production and, thus, lower output and employment. Through the Keynesian multiplier, this negative impulse is amplified into an even larger loss of aggregate income. This is a central proposition of the economics of Keynes, no matter *who* is demanding assets, whether households and non-financial firms or banks themselves.[21]

A key factor, therefore, to determine the dynamics of such a situation is how far banks can count on the public accepting deposits as perfect substitutes for legal tender. The public will accept those liabilities as perfect substitutes for money to the extent they trust government institutions to timely honour the guarantees they extend to bank deposits. If depositors suspect that these guarantees may not be

honoured, or even not honoured timely, bank runs may take place, as it happened in the case of Northern Rock bank in the UK in 2007.

Of course, when the economy is prosperous, supporting institutions lose their visibility and immediacy since there prevails the expectation that banks' investments will pay and allow redemption of deposits out of their own resources if needed. But in times like that, when confidence is strong, the influence of liquidity preference on behaviour can only be weak. During crises or other moments of heightened uncertainty, however, ignoring variations in the demand for liquid assets motivated by an autonomous rise in liquidity preference eliminates the possibility of understanding the defensive portfolio strategies that tend to dominate the operation of the financial system and to strengthen whatever contractive tendency the economy may be already exhibiting. For banks, in these moments, credit risks tend to sharply increase, compromising at the eyes of the depositors the trustworthiness of their liabilities.

Can we take modern banks to be immune to collapses of confidence? The question is in part rhetorical since the current crisis has unequivocally shown they are not. Of course, in the case of bank deposits there are many elements of support for their moneyness, such as the action of central banks as lenders of last resort and deposit insurers. Decades of financial innovations, however, have dramatically changed the structure of bank liabilities, away from the reliance on deposits.

Most analysts would probably agree, at least until recently, that the institutions created in reaction to the bank runs of the Great Depression had all but eliminated the problem of confidence in the convertibility of deposits and, by implication, in the solidity of banks themselves. As a consequence, banks' liquidity preference should also have been largely attenuated, perhaps to the point of becoming irrelevant. Particularly for banks that are *too big to fail*, survival seems to be taken as a given, not as a concern. Their liabilities, therefore, and not only deposits, should be considered very good substitutes for legal tender, equally able to satisfy the public's demand for liquid assets.

The financial crisis initiated in the US in 2007 shattered these views. 'Classic' bank runs, of course, remained a rare (but not unheard of) phenomenon. Amid abundant news about bank problems in 2007 and 2008, depositors did not seem to panic, apparently trusting the

ability of the authorities to safeguard deposits. In contrast, confidence collapsed *within* the financial system. The sudden realization that all classes of financial institutions were much more vulnerable to adverse shocks than initially imagined led to a sudden increase in liquidity preferences that not only caused a widespread collapse of prices for less liquid assets (including some that became less liquid in the occasion) but also led to strong credit rationing among financial entities.[22]

The dramatic shift upwards of the liquidity preference schedule of financial institutions responded to at least five sources of increased uncertainty: (i) doubts about the willingness and the ability of central banks to act as lenders-of-last-resort given the recent adherence of monetary authorities in many countries to inflation-targeting regimes; (ii) doubts about the eligibility of shadow banks' liabilities to access government guarantees; (iii) the cost of appealing to government support being interpreted as signalling weakness; (iv) disruptions in the interbank market for reserves; and (v) doubts about preserving access to securitized markets as sources of funding.

The first source of uncertainty related to the extent to which banks could count on the support of central banks in the case of a sudden need for large injections of liquidity. With the major exception of the Federal Reserve, the overwhelming majority of central banks in the largest or most important economies have adopted in the years preceding the crisis some form of inflation-targeting, acknowledging no other goal than keeping inflation under control. Particularly remarkable, the European Central Bank (ECB) did not even possess the mandate or the instruments to intervene in favour of maintaining financial stability in the euro area. Moreover, the chairmen and executive boards that directed the ECB since its creation had been remarkably consistent in the defence of an extremely conservative view of the bank's mission. Could this institution be relied upon to understand how much liquidity was needed when the financial crisis broke out and to act as needed to preserve financial stability?

During most of 2011, the same doubt returned as the ECB resisted calls to provide the necessary liquidity to deal with the crash of the sovereign debt market of the Eurozone. It was only in December 2011, after Chairman Trichet was replaced by Mario Draghi, that the Bank finally intervened to contain and, at least temporarily, revert the liquidity crisis in public debt securities in the European Union. By providing three-year funding at low interest rates to European banks

and accepting public debt securities as collateral, the ECB in fact increased the liquidity of securities that had lost this attribute in the eyes of private investors. Banks can now keep them in their portfolios because they became perfect substitutes to cash itself, assets that could easily be transformed into cash if necessary.

The second source of uncertainty was fed by the acknowledgement that even if the monetary authorities were in fact willing to intervene to try and preserve financial stability, it was far from obvious how to accomplish it given that a major share of the liabilities under threat had been issued by institutions that populated the so-called *shadow* banking system, not eligible, in principle, for government support. The shadow banking system comprises divisions of existing institutions, such as investment banks, as well as other entities, some of which were created precisely to circumvent regulatory constraints, that did not qualify for support. Special purpose vehicles, conduits, etc., they all operated alongside banks and investment banks, oftentimes in close relation with them, exposing the latter to risks generated by those shadowy institutions, but beyond the reach of both regulatory and supporting institutions.

The third source of uncertainty sprang from the possible consequences for a financial institution of appealing for government support. Besides the usual aversion to attracting the attention of regulators to one's institution and to practices and innovations that financial firms perhaps preferred to keep opaque to supervisors, it was also necessary to consider how clients, investors, and the general public would take the news that government support was needed amid an already volatile environment. The stigma that is assumed to mark every appeal for help could be catastrophic in the middle of a situation already verging on panic.

The fourth source of uncertainty was the operation of the interbank markets for reserves which became an important source of resources for banks in recent years. As the crisis showed how opaque were the data about individual banks, as banks judged to be solid by the market and by regulators showed themselves to be, in reality, extremely fragile, trust among banks crashed. Banks exhibiting high capital coefficients and praised for their risk management practices were brought out in a few days when interbank liquidity dried down.

Finally, in recent decades even *commercial* banks had come to rely more and more on the issuance of securities instead of accepting

deposits as sources of funding for their asset purchases. Commercial papers, asset-backed securities, and other types of securities had become increasingly important classes of liabilities for banks as well as for investment banks and the collapse of those markets in the aftermath of the subprime crisis threatened to close their access to liquidity sources precisely in the moments it was needed the most. These types of securities did not count on government guarantees. Banks themselves were the guarantors of securities and this did not seem enough anymore. In other words, central banks respecting the traditional boundaries of their jurisdictions would be doubly ineffective: on the one hand, they would not reach the so-called shadow banking system, because it is constituted by financial entities other than commercial banks; but even if the monetary authority restricts its action to commercial banks, it could be unable to stabilize even the traditional banking system, since modern commercial banks funded their activities through commercial paper issuance rather than by deposit acceptance.

The strong increase in liquidity preference by banks and other financial institutions as a reaction to these uncertainties should not be surprising. It manifested itself in a sharp increase in the demand for the most liquid assets, reserves and Treasury securities, with the concomitant attempts to dump illiquid assets, practically at any price. This caused the re-emergence of a Fisher-type debt deflation process in which asset prices collapsed leading to contagion to other, until then healthy, financial institutions that held similar assets in their balance sheets. In the language of Keynes in the *Treatise on Money*, banks tried to dump both advances to customers and investments, to increase their holdings of fully liquid assets. The result was credit rationing to non-financial borrowers and the transformation of the financial crisis into an economic crisis.

The macroeconomic impact of rising liquidity preferences of banks was to be the way through which rising uncertainties imparted deflationary tendencies on the overall economy, causing a rise in unemployment and a contraction of output. This is a process where a plethora of feedback effects reinforce the initial contractive impulse. A recession increases credit risks, accentuates existing uncertainties, and strengthens banks' liquidity preferences, initiating a new round of deflationary pressures. Even when the feedback effects are eventually contained as a result of some exogenous intervention (or of a natural

exhaustion of the process of contraction), the memory of risks and losses may be enough to keep banks' liquidity preferences high, preventing economic recovery, as Friedman and Schwartz (1963) argued to have happened in the 1930s.

The action of monetary authorities in the US and the European Union at the initial stages of the 2007–8 financial crisis was swift and avoided the potentially large number of bankruptcies among financial institutions that could have happened if debt-deflation was allowed to proceed unchallenged. Nevertheless, while financial institutions were preserved, the near-death experience seems to have moved their liquidity preference schedule up to a new level from which they are reluctant to come down. On the other hand, as recovery has shown itself elusive so far, both in the US and in Western Europe, and new threats have emerged, central banks have suffered strong pressures to extend their intervention. These pressures have been heeded reluctantly in both areas. The ECB has been at the receiving end of a particularly strong pressure to maintain liquidity conditions in sovereign debt securities markets of Euroland members. Dissent in its governing board is strong and support policies are adopted only after painful episodes of political conflict. No matter who is right in this debate, the result can only be increased uncertainty, not only in financial markets. It should not be surprising that evidence is still accumulating that despite the implementation of monetary easing policies in the US and Western Europe, banks still cling to liquid assets in detriment of less liquid investments and advances to customers, securities markets are unable to properly recover, and other, less important, financing channels remain clogged.

* * *

Rising liquidity preferences could explain a collapse of the demand for illiquid assets that may trigger a crisis. Alternatively, it could explain why, after a crisis or adverse shock, it may be so difficult for an economy to recover its normal production and employment levels or rates of growth. Keynes, in *The General Theory*, seemed to think that crises were seldom due to rising liquidity preferences or interest rates. His bet was on collapses of the marginal efficiency of capital as the likely cause of downturns in modern entrepreneurial economies (see Keynes 2007: 317–18). A rise in liquidity preference would strengthen the contractive impulse, pushing the economy

farther downwards, and could also make recovery more difficult while asset holders preferred liquid to illiquid (particularly reproducible capital) assets. A rise in the liquidity preferences of banks would act in the same direction, possibly making them more intractable for policymakers.

Some of the original critics of the liquidity preference theory argued that the theory was unconvincing because they could not find evidence of an increase in the holdings of liquid assets. Keynes pointed out that this was not the effect he expected since a higher demand for liquid assets would not increase their existing stocks; it would instead raise their prices. Changes in liquidity preferences should thus explain *prices* of assets, rather than their amounts unless mechanisms of new asset creation were also made part of the theory (as some authors, notably Paul Davidson [1978, Chapter 4], actually did for reproducible assets).

The extension of the theory to banks' portfolio choices does not change the principle in any essential way. Price data are still the main sort of information required to test the model validity. Of course, the price of the most liquid of assets, bank reserves, is policy-controlled and not necessarily sensitive to liquidity demands. However, particularly during the worst period of the 2007–8 financial crisis, a good indicator of rising liquidity preferences was given by the ratio between policy-controlled and market-controlled prices of reserves, such as, the LIBOR. As more and more institutions were struggling to reconstitute their liquidity reserves in private markets, prices of reserves in private markets tended to surge in comparison to policy-controlled rates.

An even more direct evidence of the shift towards liquid assets was the comparison between the yields on securities widely acknowledged as being highly liquid, such as United States Treasury Securities, and less liquid assets, like private securities or even public securities issued by less trusted governments. Again, during the 2007–8 crisis, the spread between these classes of securities reached dimensions that spoke eloquently of the flight to safety that followed in particular the bankruptcy of the Lehman Brothers investment bank. Similar, and related, effects could also be found in the movements of exchange rates that follow like a shadow changes in the demand for safe assets, like United States Treasury Securities, away from riskier securities.

Of particular interest is the behaviour of prices for assets that were considered highly liquid before the crisis and rapidly became illiquid afterwards. Securities like Collateralized Debt Obligations (CDOs) suffered a rapid change in public's appreciation simultaneously with the slowdown or downright paralysis of their secondary markets, allowing the estimation of the impact of sudden loss of perceived liquidity on their market values.

In a longer-term perspective, however, one can go beyond price data to include also quantitative data. In particular, the accumulation of voluntary reserves has increased its importance, leading some analysts to question the efficacy of policy initiatives of the quantitative easing type. Of course, proper analysis of data showing an increase in reserve accumulation has to distinguish between the speculative demand for reserves and the precautionary demand for reserves. The speculative motive refers to expectations that paying assets will have their market prices lowered even further than they have already had, so that the accumulation of reserves is just *money in waiting*, not a demand for money as such. The precautionary demand for reserves, on the other hand, is the core of the concept of liquidity preference of banks, the demand for money to hold when the future is so uncertain that no commitment to particular investments is advisable. The ability to get rid of assets in the case the future turns out different from what was expected when they were bought, for whatever reason, is a plus when uncertainty increases. Be it as it may, data already made public by public and private institutions (such as the Institute for International Finance) suggest that banks have been (and still are) accumulating reserves instead of making more profitable (but also less liquid) investments and advances to customers, which indicate that liquidity preference remains strong. One of the most fundamental propositions advanced by Keynes in *The General Theory*, that the demand for liquid assets by private agents in the face of rising uncertainty seems efficient for the individual but is socially perverse, applies to banks as well as to households and non-financial firms. In the same sense, only the intervention of an *external* agent, free from the fears that plague private agents who are vulnerable to illiquidity and insolvency, can put a stop to liquidity crises. The need for the intervention of governments and central banks in these situations is as strong now as it has ever been.

In sum, the concept of liquidity preferences of banks seems to be alive and well, with its usefulness unequivocally demonstrated by the events that have characterized not only the financial crisis of 2007–8 but also its aftermath, which as a matter of fact is still unfolding. Conventional monetary theories had converged with some non-orthodox approaches, such as Kaldor's, to minimize the role of banks, and of their liquidity preference, in the dynamics of modern capitalist economies, contrary to what Keynes proposed in 1930 in his *Treatise on Money*. Important crises have always influenced deeply the path of evolution of economic thought, burying false or obsolete theories and opening new vistas on important subjects. It is very likely that a new look at the relevance of a theory of banks' liquidity preference will be one of the legacies of the present crisis in the near future.

NOTES

1. More than one critic complained about Keynes's alleged proclivity to claim originality by giving new names to old concepts. Myrdal (1965: 8) and Ohlin were among the first to raise this criticism. Harry Johnson (1971) argued that in the case of *The General Theory* this was not an accident but a conscious attempt to establish his ideas as revolutionary. According to Johnson, Milton Friedman did the same later with his 'monetarist counter-revolution'.

2. An American authority was much ridiculed because of his proposed distinction between known unknowns and unknown unknowns but in fact this is the fulcrum of what Keynes meant by the distinction between risk and uncertainty.

3. Apparently, the operation of banks, extensively discussed in *A Treatise on Money*, but never analysed in *The General Theory*, was one of the 'technical monetary details' that fell 'into the background' as Keynes explained in the preface to *The General Theory* (cf. Keynes 2007: xvi).

4. Cf. Kahn (1984: 53): 'Keynes showed himself in his *Tract on Monetary Reform* as a fanatical believer in the Quantity Theory, in the full causal sense of the determination of the price-level by the quantity of money.'

5. Don Patinkin in fact accused Friedman of caving in to Keynes's theory of liquidity preference with his restatement, arguing that all Friedman did was to include the speculative demand for money in the demand-for-money function (cf. Patinkin 1975).

6. See, for instance, Keynes (2007: 167n1) where the boundary is defined between money and debts.

7. If one considers a perpetuity (a bond with no redemption date), the price of the bond is related to the interest rate according to the equation: $P = A/r$, where

P is the price of the bond, Annuity the value of the (fixed) coupon paid by the bond, and r the going rate of interest. Since A is fixed, when P goes up (down), r goes down (up).

8. See note 7.

9. See Cardim de Carvalho (2010) for a more detailed discussion of this point.

10. Thus the rate of interest at any time, being the reward for parting with liquidity, is a measure of the unwillingness of those who possess money to part with their liquid control over it. The rate of interest is not the 'price' which brings into equilibrium the demand for resources to invest with the readiness to abstain from present consumption. It is the 'price' which equilibrates the desire to hold wealth in the form of cash with the available quantity of cash. ... (Keynes 2007: 167)

11. Davidson (1978, 2011) describes the same process using spot and future prices.

12. The oldest discussion I am aware of was published in *The Economic Journal* in September 1914. It is reproduced in CWK XI, pp. 238–71. Sections 2 to 4 of that 1914 article touch more directly the issues being discussed in this chapter.

13. The article is 'The Consequences to the Banks of the Collapse of Money Values', included in Keynes (2010). This article was to become one of Hyman Minsky's central references when building his own theory of financial fragility and instability.

14. Of course, advances to customers in Keynes's time included mostly loans to firms, since consumer credit was very incipient. Nowadays, consumer credit is very important and probably even less safe and liquid than loans to firms.

15. No doubt changes in the demand for loans and in the supply of investments, and the large increase in available reserves produced by the gold inflows—all of which constituted changes in the supply of assets for banks to hold—played a role in the shifts in asset composition. *However, the major factor was not those but rather a shift in the liquidity preference of commercial banks, that is, a change in the demand by banks for assets, which is to say, in the portfolio composition they sought to attain for any given structure of yields.* (Friedman and Schwartz 1963: 453) [emphasis added]

16. The shift in liquidity preferences of banks was destined to be temporary. To judge by the experience of earlier episodes, the passage of time without any extensive series of bank failures would have dulled the fears of bank managers, leading them to set a lower premium on liquidity. In any case, the establishment of FDIC, which was accompanied by a dramatic reduction in the rate of bank failures, provided additional assurance against the occurrence of 'runs' of the kind that produced the shift in liquidity preferences. Such assurance, while by no means clear at the start of the FDIC, eventually became increasingly clear, but still it took time for banks to adapt their behaviour to that new fact. It is therefore not surprising that the ratio of cash assets to total assets continued rising until 1940. (Friedman and Schwartz 1963: 458–9)

A student of Milton Friedman's, George Morrison, wrote a PhD dissertation on the same subject, adding some evidence and strengthening the argument. See Morrison (1967).

17. Many proposals have been advanced through the years to restructure the banking industry, through financial regulation, in such a way as to eliminate the intrinsic illiquidity of banks. Perhaps the best known of these proposals, advocated by many economists at one point or another, is the so-called 100%-reserve banks, depository institutions that would give up making loans. I thank Anna Simonazzi and Luca Fantacci for raising the point.

18. These guarantees are extended as central banks act as *lenders of last resort* to the banking system. The way a lender of last resort should work was originally codified by Bagehot (1994: 99) when he stated that, when there were risks of panic, 'advances [from the Bank of England] should be made on all good banking securities' although 'these loans should only be made at a very high rate of interest'. Since the principle was stated, two important changes were incorporated. First, it was generally agreed that, at least under normal circumstances, these guarantees should be extended only to demand deposits, instead of 'all good banking securities'. Second, that panic could be created if there were no good banking securities available for rediscount by the central bank. In this case, the answer was defined in the 1930s with the development of demand deposit insurance schemes, which guaranteed the possibility to cash those deposits even when the bank which accepted them went bankrupt, at least up to a certain limit. So demand deposits were perfect substitutes to currency because they are safe against illiquidity *and* solvency risks. It may be also important to stress that if financial panic risks are strong enough, central banks may go back to Bagehot view that financial securities should be eligible for support in a wider sense than just bank deposits (or even good banking securities, for that matter). As shown in the financial crisis of 2007–8, the Federal Reserve extended its guarantees to a much larger set of financial instruments than just banks' demand deposits as a means to avoid financial market collapses.

19. Tobin (1963), based on Gurley and Shaw (1960), argued that it was a mistake to consider that creating means of payment would give banks any special 'power' to issue deposits because they would still have to convince savers to hold those deposits in their portfolios. Tobin seemed to assume that deposits are only held by savers in their portfolios, forgetting that most of the deposits created by banks would be used for transaction purposes when banks create them to finance investment in working and fixed capital.

20. See Keynes (CWK VI: 47): 'The problem before a bank is not how much to lend … but what proportion of its loan can be safely made in the relatively less liquid forms.'

> …what banks are ordinarily deciding is, not *how much* they will lend in the aggregate…
> but in what *forms* they will lend—in what proportions they will divide their resources
> between the different kinds of investment which are open to them. Broadly there are
> three categories to choose from—(i) bills of exchange and call loans to the money market,
> (ii) investments, (iii) advances to customers. As a rule, advances to customers are more
> profitable than investments, and investments are more profitable than bills and call loans;
> but this order is not invariable. On the other hand, bills and call loans are more 'liquid'
> than investments, i.e., more certainly realizable at short notice without loss, and invest-
> ments are more 'liquid' than advances. (Ibid.: 59)

21. As Keynes (1937b: 665, 666) observed:

> In order that the entrepreneur may feel himself sufficiently liquid to embark on the transaction, someone else has to agree to become, for the time being at least, more illiquid than before. ...In a simplified schematism, designed to elucidate the essence of what is happening, but one which, in fact, is substantially representative of real life, one would assume that 'finance' is wholly supplied during the interregnum by the banks; and this is the explanation of why their policy is so important in determining the pace at which new investment can proceed. Dr Herbert Bab has suggested to me that one could regard the rate of interest as being determined by the interplay of the terms on which the public desires to become more or less liquid and those on which the banking system is ready to become more or less unliquid. This is, I think, an illuminating way of expressing the liquidity-theory of the rate of interest; but particularly so within the field of 'finance'.

22. Alan Greenspan (2010) judged the 2007–8 financial crisis to have been worse than that of the early 1930s precisely because the former completely disrupted short-term interfinancial lending, something he argued did not happen in the Depression.

REFERENCES

Bagehot, W. 1994. *Lombard Street: A Description of the Money Market*. Gloucester, UK: Dodo Press.

Cardim de Carvalho, F.J. 1999. 'On Banks' Liquidity Preference', in P. Davidson and J. Kregel (eds), *Full Employment and Price Stability in a Global Economy*. Cheltenham: Edward Elgar, pp. 123–38.

———. 2010. 'Uncertainty and Money: Keynes, Tobin and Kahn and the Disappearance of the Precautionary Demand for Money from Liquidity Preference Theory', *Cambridge Journal of Economics*, 34(4): 709–25.

Davidson, P. 1978. *Money and the Real World*. London: Palgrave MacMillan.

———. 2011. *Post Keynesian Macroeconomic Theory*. Cheltenham: Edward Elgar.

Dow, A. and S. Dow. 1989. 'Endogenous Money Creation and Idle Balances', in J. Pheby (ed.), *New Directions in Post Keynesian Economics*. Cheltenham: Edward Elgar, pp. 147–64.

Friedman, M. 1956. 'The Quantity Theory of Money: A Restatement', in M. Friedman (ed.), *Studies in the Quantity Theory of Money*. Chicago: University of Chicago Press, pp. 3–25.

Friedman, M. and A. Schwartz. 1963. *A Monetary History of the United States*. Princeton: Princeton University Press.

Greenspan, A. 2010. 'The Crisis'. Available at http://www.brookings.edu/~/media/Files/Programs/ES/BPEA/2010_spring_bpea_papers/spring2010_greenspan.pdf. Last accessed on 27 April 2012.

Gurley, J. and E. Shaw. 1960. *Money in a Theory of Finance*. Washington, DC: Brookings Institution.

Johnson, H. 1971. 'The Keynesian Revolution and the Monetarist Counter-Revolution', *American Economic Review*, 61(May): 1–14.

Kahn, R. 1984. *The Making of Keynes' General Theory*. Cambridge: Cambridge University Press.

Kaldor, N. 1990. *The Scourge of Monetarism*. Oxford: Oxford University Press.

Keynes, J.M. 1937a. 'The General Theory of Employment', *Quarterly Journal of Economics*, 51(2): 209–23.

———. 1937b. 'The "ex-ante" Theory of the Rate of Interest', *The Economic Journal*, 47(188): 663–9.

———. 1971–89. *The Collected Writings of John Maynard Keynes* (CWK), edited by D.E. Moggridge and E. Johnson for the Royal Economic Society. 30 vols. London: Macmillan and Cambridge: Cambridge University Press; volumes are identified as CWK followed by volume number in Roman numerals. CWK VI. *A Treatise on Money: II. The Applied Theory of Money*. CWK XI. *Economic Articles and Correspondence: Academic*.

———. 2007 (1936). *The General Theory of Employment, Interest and Money*. London: Palgrave MacMillan for the Royal Economic Society.

———. 2010 (1931). *Essays in Persuasion*. London: Palgrave MacMillan.

Kregel, J. 1984–5. 'Constraints on the Expansion of Output and Employment: Real or Monetary', *Journal of Post Keynesian Economics*, 7(2): 139–52.

Minsky, H.P. 1975. *John Maynard Keynes*. New York: Columbia University Press.

———. 1982. *Can 'It' Happen Again?* Armonk: M. E. Sharpe.

Modigliani, F. 1944. 'Liquidity Preference and the Theory of Interest and Money', *Econometrica*, 12(1): 45–88.

Morrison, G. 1967. *Liquidity Preference of Commercial Banks*. Chicago: University of Chicago Press.

Myrdal, G. 1965. *Monetary Equilibrium*. New York: Augustus M. Kelley (first edition in 1939).

Patinkin, D. 1975. 'Friedman on the Quantity Theory and Keynesian Economics', in R. Gordon (ed.), *Milton Friedman's Monetary Framework. A Debate with his Critics*. Chicago: University of Chicago Press, pp. 111–31.

Schumpeter, J. 1996. *History of Economic Analysis*. New York: Oxford University Press.

Tobin, J. 1963. 'Commercial Banks as Creators of Money', in D. Carson (ed.), *Banking and Monetary Studies*. Homewood: Richard Irwin Inc, pp. 1–11.

9

Why Not Bancor?

Keynes's Currency Plan as a Solution to Global Imbalances

LUCA FANTACCI

'The problem of maintaining equilibrium in the balance of payments between countries has never been solved, since methods of barter gave way to the use of money and bills of exchange.... The failure to solve this problem has been a major cause of impoverishment and social discontent and even of wars and revolutions' (Keynes [1941] CWK XXV: 21).

When John Maynard Keynes wrote these lines, in September 1941, he knew what he was talking about. The world was at war for the second time before one single generation had lapsed after the end of the Great War. And the issue of unsettled balances between countries had played no small part in the outbreak of the second global conflict.

Keynes had denounced the risk well before it eventually material-ized. Already in 1919, in writing *The Economic Consequences of the Peace*, he had insisted on the need to reabsorb global imbalances in an equitable and orderly manner, so as to avoid the build-up of potentially explosive international tensions:

> The war has ended with everyone owing everyone else immense sums of money. Germany owes a large sum to the Allies; the Allies owe a large sum to Great Britain; and Great Britain owes a large sum to the

United States...The whole position is in the highest degree artificial, misleading, and vexatious. We shall never be able to move again, unless we can free our limbs from these paper shackles. A general bonfire is so great a necessity that unless we can make of it an orderly and good-tempered affair in which no serious injustice is done to anyone, it will, when it comes at last, grow into a conflagration that may destroy much else as well. (Keynes [1919] CWK II: 177–8)

Unfortunately, Keynes's appeals remained unheeded. Reparations imposed on Germany were seen by European Allies as a way not only to humiliate the defeated enemy but also to repay the war debts to the US. The vindictive logic of the Versailles Treaty was to prove a short-sighted miscalculation, in both political and economic terms. Germany's capacity to pay had been grossly overestimated. As a consequence, European debts remained unpaid, and international capital markets were dried up by 'distressed borrowers' who demanded money only to pay back previous debts. This, in turn, caused interest rates to remain high, crowding out productive investments that would have been essential to boost post-war recovery and alleviate 'social discontent'. Hence, not only did global imbalances persist, but they clearly failed to reflect an efficient allocation of capital, according to prospective returns on real investments. In other terms, they were not fresh funds to revitalize enterprise, but were on their way to becoming dead loans, 'as dead as mutton, and as distasteful as stale mutton' (Keynes [1932] CWK XXI: 41).

Freedom from these 'paper shackles' was sought for, not by reducing all debts for them to be repaid, but rather by increasing the quantity of money for the debts to be refinanced—in other terms, by producing even more paper. This was made possible by the establishment of the gold exchange standard at the Genoa Conference in 1922. The international monetary base was duplicated, by including among central bank reserve assets not just gold but also foreign exchange convertible into gold. The sudden abundance of credit finally managed to buttress growth, even beyond expectations. The duplication of international money allowed to finance investments on both sides of the Atlantic, fuelling, at the same time, the 'Roaring Twenties' in America and the 'Goldene Zwanziger' in Germany. However, this occurred at the price of producing ever larger imbalances that were reflected in the accumulation of foreign exchange reserves and other, mostly short-term, liabilities.

The sudden deleveraging caused by the stock market crash in 1929 found in these imbalances a channel of virulent contagion. In the words of Jacques Rueff (1972: 28 [1971: 31]): 'It was the collapse of the house of cards built on the gold-exchange standard in Europe that turned the recession of 1929 into a Great Depression.' The repatriation of funds invested abroad caused a contraction of credit worldwide, a global deflation, and, ultimately, a generalized resort to protectionist measures, retaliations, and competitive devaluations. Trade wars, military expenditure, and economic nationalism contributed together to exacerbating political tensions and to precipitating the outbreak of the Second World War.

In 1941, therefore, there were good reasons for Keynes to urge his country and its allies to plan ahead for a post-war economic order and to avoid the mistakes that had been made after the First World War: 'The authors of the Peace Treaty of Versailles made the mistake of neglecting the economic reconstruction of Europe in their preoccupation with political frontiers and safeguards. Much misfortune to all of us has followed from this neglect. The British Government are determined not to make the same mistake again' (Keynes [1940] CWK XXV: 11).

Indeed, Keynes was entrusted by the Treasury with the task of drawing up a plan for a new international economic order to discuss with the Americans. The centrepiece of his plan was the International Clearing Union (ICU), a monetary system expressly designed to facilitate international trade and to avoid the creation of systematic balance of payments disequilibria. Keynes drafted seven different versions of the plan in over two years, in the attempt to meet criticisms at home and to win support abroad.[1] A compromise with the Americans was struck in April 1944 with the Joint Statement, which represented the point of departure for the Bretton Woods Conference held in July, where the foundations were laid of the post-war economic order.

Today, after almost 70 years, we still cannot claim to have solved the problem to which Keynes understandably assigned such great importance. Despite the ongoing crisis, global imbalances persist and net international credit and debit positions continue to accumulate, threatening to fuel diplomatic tensions. The issue has come back to the fore, both at the global level, where it was put at the top of the agenda of the G-20 under the recent French presidency, and within the Eurozone, where it underlies the ongoing debt crises of peripheral countries.

In this essay, I intend to revisit Keynes's proposal, paying particular attention to the way in which the Clearing Union was designed to address global imbalances. I will show that, in this respect, the Bretton Woods system was based on principles and prescriptions that operated in a different, indeed in an opposite manner than what Keynes had proposed. Moreover, I will argue that the international monetary system inaugurated at Bretton Woods contributed decisively to broaden balance of payments disequilibria and that the Keynes plan would have been far more appropriate to avoid the build-up of global imbalances. Finally, I will suggest that the principles of the Clearing Union could contribute to reform financial institutions today with a view to face international imbalances, not only globally, but also regionally within the euro area.

The chapter is divided in seven sections that try to answer the following questions: 1. How are global imbalances related to the current crisis? 2. When are global imbalances good and when are they bad? 3. Where do global imbalances come from? 4. How did Keynes's plan cope with global imbalances? 5. Why was it not adopted? 6. What were the consequences? 7. What can be done today?

HOW ARE GLOBAL IMBALANCES RELATED TO THE CURRENT CRISIS?

The relationship between global imbalances and the current financial crisis is not obvious, and deserves to be discussed at the outset. My claim is that there is indeed a close relationship between the two phenomena, which, however, cannot be reduced to a univocal causal relation; that global imbalances are of a more structural character; that they have not caused the financial crisis, but they have made it possible as a global crisis; that, therefore, they should receive more attention than they have so far, because overcoming the crisis without reabsorbing global imbalances would mean leaving open the possibility of further crises in the future.

That global imbalances have a more structural character with respect to the contingent nature of the crisis is made clear enough by their sheer persistence: they started to accumulate well before the outbreak of the crisis and they have continued undisturbed until today—representing perhaps the only certitude in an age

of uncertainties. It is by now widely acknowledged that large trade deficits, and corresponding massive capital inflows, preceded, and indeed contributed to fuel the 'irrational exuberance' on US asset markets (spanning from derivatives to real estate). What is less obvious is that the imbalances that inflated the bubble should persist, only on a slightly lower scale, even after the bubble has burst.

Traditionally, crises have at least the merit of reducing the overall level of indebtedness, since most bad loans are normally written down, cancelled, or inflated away. Hence, crises have been viewed as a necessary evil, or as an 'unavoidable concomitant' of the ordinary functioning of financial markets (Eichengreen 2002: 4). They have acted as a sort of jubilee: however involuntary and accidental, they have appeared to reduce a debt burden that had become intolerable and to restore some sort of equilibrium, if not of justice. Something like a fever which is necessary, from time to time, to eliminate toxins and restore the health of the economic body. Unfortunately, it is difficult to hold this view in the face of the legacy of debts that the last crisis is leaving in its wake. What has occurred, since the summer of 2007, is not so much a cancellation or restructuring of non-performing loans, but a substitution of unpayable debts with other unpayable debts: from private debts, to public debts, to foreign debts. It is worth taking a closer look at this transformation since it can be seen as a gradual unveiling of the true nature of the debts on which the global economy is precariously floated.

The crisis started from private debts: securitized mortgages, bank loans, corporate liabilities of various sorts. Governments were compelled to intervene through bail-outs, relief programmes, and outright nationalizations, supported by special facilities and massive liquidity injections of central banks. Thus, private debts were substituted by public debts (Figure 9.1).

But the reason why governments were forced to intervene is because those apparently private debts had in fact a public character from the very outset. This is quite evident in the case of the securitized mortgages that benefited from an implicit guarantee by the Government Sponsored Enterprises. It is less evident, but not less substantial, in the case of the liabilities of those institutions that were considered too big or too interconnected to fail. It was their systemic relevance that demanded state intervention as a way of defending national interests. The very liquidity of credit markets had assumed

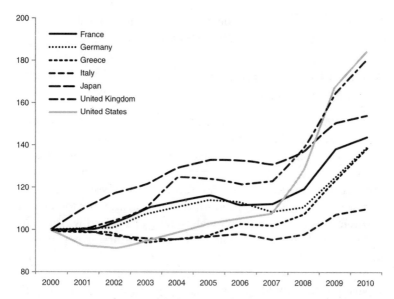

Figure 9.1 Growth of Public Debt/GDP Ratios (Index 2000 = 100)

Source: Extrapolations from IMF (2010).

the character of a public good, for which no private institution could be held accountable and that ultimately required to be preserved by monetary authorities at all costs. Private debts became public because, in a sense, they were public from the very beginning.

Today the problem appears to be the sovereign debts of potentially insolvent states. Yet, even here there is a fundamental ambiguity. Since their invention, in the early modern era, public debts were never meant to be paid out, but merely floated on the secondary markets for Treasury bills and bonds. The issue is hence not of solvency, but of sustainability. And sustainability, unlike solvency, is not a matter of accountancy but of expectations. Any level of public debt is sustainable, as long as there are investors willing to purchase it on the market. Now, the possibility of selling their debts on liquid international markets, at stable or fixed exchange rates, is exactly what has allowed certain states to accumulate more debts than they could ever have dreamed of financing domestically. This is true for the US as it is for Greece. And this is what makes the sustainability of these debts not a domestic issue of public debts, involving considerations of intergenerational equity in view of dampening social tensions, but an

international issue of foreign debts, involving international negotiation and coordination in an effort to stave off potential conflicts.

WHEN ARE GLOBAL IMBALANCES GOOD AND WHEN ARE THEY BAD?

At this point, a clarification is needed. I have hitherto referred to global imbalances as a major source of economic and political instability. This contrasts sharply with the established theory of the international economy that views capital movements in a rather positive light, as a way of ensuring the efficient allocation of savings worldwide.

Indeed, there are situations in which it may make sense for a nation as whole, just as for an individual, to lend or to borrow. Typically, nations may find it reasonable to be net creditors or net debtors, according to whether they are 'old' or 'young' in both economic and demographic terms. If a nation has a mature economy and an aging population, it may wish to save, that is to earn more than it spends, and to invest the positive balance abroad, where it promises to yield higher returns, in the prospect of suffering a reduction in its productive capacity and an increase of its needs. On the contrary, if a nation has a young population and a developing economy, it may wish to invest more than it is capable of saving, in the prospect of catching up, making innovations, increasing productivity and capacity, and eventually repaying capital and interest.

Now, as these examples show, global imbalances only make sense as long as they are temporary. If they are really for the sake of precaution and self-improvement, credits and debts necessarily have a limited time span. In strictly economic terms, just as for an individual, it makes sense for a nation to accumulate credits, only if, sooner or later, it intends to spend them; and it makes sense for a nation to negotiate a debt, only if, in due course, it expects to be able to repay it.

In actual fact, however, we observe that global imbalances tend to acquire a permanent character: credits and debts are accumulated, without any connection with real investments and beyond all prospect of repayment. International reserves are hoarded without ever being spent, and international debts are granted without any possibility of being repaid from the proceeds of actual investments.

Chinese foreign exchange, and particularly dollar, reserves exceed any reasonable amount that can be justified on the grounds of the economic motives for the demand for money: they are not held for

the purpose of transactions, since the US balance of trade towards China has now been negative for years and cannot expect to turn positive in the foreseeable future; they are not held for the purpose of precaution, since their amount is greater than any conceivable capital outflow against which they should provide protection; they are not even held for the purpose of speculation, since it is difficult to imagine that such a long position in dollars is held in anticipation of a prospective appreciation. Hence, we are left with the assumption that dollar accumulation on the part of China is intended merely to counter potential dollar depreciation, which amounts to saying that China has to continue to buy dollars, because she bought dollars in the past. Rather tautological.

On the other hand, it is difficult to explain the massive amounts of savings flowing towards the US in terms of a greater profitability of American investments. Foreign assets in the US have yielded system- atically less than US assets abroad over the past 10 years (Figure 9.2). And this has not withheld huge amounts of capital from seeking to be invested in the US (Figure 9.3). What attracted them was clearly not

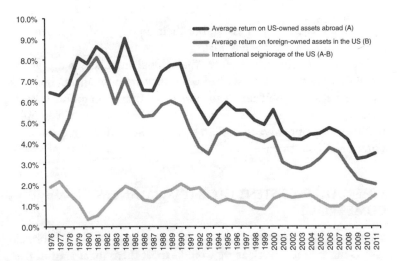

Figure 9.2   Returns on Foreign Assets
Source: Extrapolations from US Department of Commerce, Bureau of Economic Analysis, US International Investment Position (version released 27 June 2008) and US International Transactions Account Data (version released 17 September 2008). Data available online at: http://www.bea.gov/international/index.htm (accessed 27 April 2012).

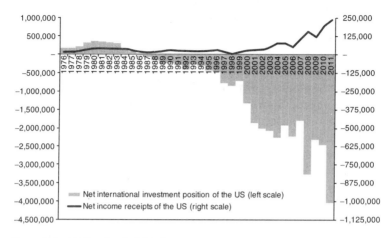

Figure 9.3   US Foreign Indebtedness
Source: Extrapolations from US Department of Commerce, Bureau of Economic Analysis, US International Investment Position (version released 27 June 2008) and US International Transactions Account Data (version released 17 September 2008). Data available at: http://www.bea.gov/international/index.htm. Last accessed on 27 April 2012.

the returns on American assets, but their liquidity, which, however, is once again quite self-referential.

We may conclude, therefore, that global imbalances are good when they are temporary and bad when they are permanent. The distinction between 'good' and 'bad' here is not drawn on moral, but on strictly economic grounds. Permanent imbalances are 'bad' simply because it is impossible to explain them on the basis of an economic criterion of convenience.

WHERE DO PERSISTENT GLOBAL IMBALANCES COME FROM?

Why, then, do permanent imbalances arise? Why do international capital markets not work as we would expect them to, at least in the long run? Three main reasons have been indicated to give account of present and past imbalances: only the first has to do with an obstruction in the smooth functioning of market forces, while the second depends on a peculiar configuration of the international

monetary system, and the third follows from the very existence of capital markets as such. Let us review them in turn.

One popular explanation (particularly in the US) traces the cause of global imbalances (specifically of the US trade deficit) in maladjustments of the exchange rates (namely between the dollar and the renminbi) that are impeded to fluctuate freely (by Chinese monetary authorities). According to a theory of international trade that goes back at least to David Hume, any disequilibrium will eventually be reabsorbed by automatic adjustment mechanisms (Hume 1752). In a system of freely fluctuating exchange rates, a trade surplus ought to determine an appreciation of the currency of the surplus country, thus reducing its competitiveness and contributing to rebalance its foreign trade. If a country throws sand in the mechanism, for example, by piling up foreign exchange reserves in order to keep its exchange rate low and thereby enhance its competitiveness, this will obviously hinder the correction and perpetuate the imbalance (at least until a rebalancing is achieved, more slowly and indirectly, by a greater inflation in the surplus country, or by a greater deflation in the deficit country, so as to eventually devalue the currency of the latter in real terms, if not in nominal terms).

Another reason for maladjustments derives not from the violation of the rules of the game within a system of flexible exchange rates, but from the application of the rules of the game within a system of fixed exchange rates. Perhaps for this very reason, fixed exchanges have enjoyed a decreasing popularity, both in theory and in practice, over the past few decades.[2] And yet, there are two instances of huge practical importance that go exactly in the direction of stabilizing rates—in fact, even more strongly than in a regime of fixed exchange rates. This occurs when an international currency is used as a national currency (as in the Eurozone or in developing countries that have opted for dollarization, eurization, or currency boards) and when a national currency is used as an international currency (as in the case of the dollar ever since Bretton Woods). In fact, when nominal exchange rates are fixed, or indeed when two areas use the same currency, the only possible adjustment is in real exchange rates, through different price dynamics. This can be very painful, particularly for the deficit country that is forced to deflate, and hence may have a strong interest in postponing the adjustment. The identification of national and international currency is thus

another, perhaps even more important, factor of structural global imbalances, as paradigmatically described by the Triffin dilemma in relation to the role of the US dollar as a global currency. The argument finds strong support in the data that shows how global imbalances have exploded in the world since the adoption of the dollar as the international standard (Figure 9.3) and in Europe since the introduction of the euro (Figure 9.4).

A third reason for persistent imbalances is of a completely different nature, and has to do with the functioning of international capital markets *as markets*. The very fact that imbalances are funded by surplus countries at a cost, in the form of credits that have to be remunerated, puts the whole burden of adjustment on the shoulders of the deficit country, which is, in most cases, the weakest party and the least capable of bearing the weight. The relationship between creditor and debtor countries is greatly asymmetric: the debtor pays an interest on its debts, while the creditor earns a return on its investments; the debtor may be forced to borrow, while the creditor is never compelled to lend; the debtor faces a limit on the

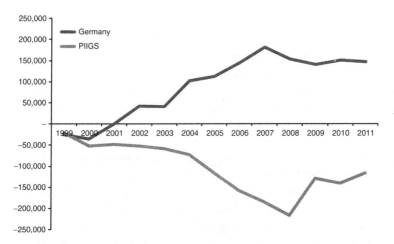

Figure 9.4   Trade Imbalances in EMU (Current Account as Per Cent of GDP), 1999–2009
Source: Altomonte and Villafranca (2010).
Notes: EMU refers to European Monetary Union; PIIGS refers to Portugal, Ireland, Italy, Greece, and Spain.

sustainability of its liabilities, while the creditor can go on indefinitely accumulating reserves and assets; the adjustment is more painful for the debtor, who is compelled to enforce restrictive monetary and fiscal policies, than for the creditor, who is asked to adopt expansionary policies. Clearly, all these asymmetries play against a convergence of international positions and contribute to the perpetuation of imbalances.[3]

HOW DID KEYNES PROPOSE TO COUNTER GLOBAL IMBALANCES?

The plan drawn up by Keynes for the post-war monetary system aimed expressly at contrasting the creation of permanent disequilibria in the balance of payments between countries. To be sure, it shared this goal with the plan concocted by Harry Dexter White on behalf of the US Treasury, and indeed with the institutions that were eventually set up at Bretton Woods. The Articles of Agreement that were signed at the Conference clearly indicated as one of the main goals of the International Monetary Fund (IMF) 'to shorten the duration and lessen the degree of disequilibrium in the international balances of payments of members'.[4] That the Bretton Woods system failed to accomplish this task is quite evident from the situation of persistent and widening disequilibrium that has characterized the 65 years since its inception. My claim is that the Clearing Union proposed by Keynes would have been more appropriate and more effective in achieving the desired purpose. This claim is based on the fact that the international monetary system envisaged by Keynes, unlike the one that was established at Bretton Woods, radically overturned the causes of structural imbalance outlined in the previous section. This stands out clearly from the distinctive features of the Clearing Union: an international unit of account, distinct from all national currencies; a symmetric distribution of the burden of readjustment between debtor and creditor countries; a criterion to detect chronic disequilibria and to correct exchange rates accordingly. Let us see what kind of international monetary architecture Keynes planned to build on these three pillars.

The Clearing Union was conceived as a bank with the task of financing temporary disequilibria in the balance of trade between countries. In this respect, it shared the same purpose as the IMF.

Yet, unlike the IMF or an ordinary commercial bank, it would not grant credit on the basis of deposits or capital previously entrusted to it by its members. Member countries would not be required to commit any amount of money in any form to the Clearing Union. They would be simply assigned a current account denominated in a new, international unit of account called 'bancor'. Not having deposited anything into its account, the initial balance of each country would be equal to zero. The par value of the currency of each member would be expressed in terms of bancor.

The Clearing Union would grant credit in the form of overdraft facilities. In other terms, each member would have the possibility of financing a trade deficit up to a predetermined limit simply by entering a negative balance on its account. Symmetrically, a country with a trade surplus would have a positive balance credited to its account. Hence, for example, an export from country A to country B financed by the Clearing Union would give rise to the simultaneous registration of two entries of equal amount: a credit to the account of A and a debit to the account of B. Thanks to the centralization of all accounts at the Clearing Union, however, the credit and debit would not be bilateral, but multilateral positions, of each country vis-à-vis all the other members as a whole. In other terms, the surplus country A could spend its credit in bancor not only with B, but with any other member country; and B could reduce its debit by exporting towards any other country. In this way, the Clearing Union would be able, in principle, to finance international trade and its expansion, without the need of any given amount of money.

For this reason, Keynes's proposal has been accused of being inflationary. However, this criticism depends on a misunderstanding of its logic and functioning. Bancor is not a fiat money. Indeed, it is created *ex nihilo*. And yet its creation does not depend on the decision of a central authority.[5] The actual amount of bancor balances is not decided by the Clearing Union: it results, instead, from the autonomous behaviour of private market participants that gives rise to the transfer of real goods from a surplus country to a deficit country.

Moreover—and this is a second difference with respect to a fiat money—bancor does not only come from nothing, but it also goes back to nothing; it is not only created, but it is also destroyed every time a transfer of goods occurs in the opposite direction, from a

deficit to a surplus country. Hence, bancor really is made to comply with the definition of money that Keynes had given 20 years before in his *Tract on Monetary Reform*: 'a mere intermediary, without significance in itself, which flows from one hand to another, is received and is dispensed, and disappears when its work is done from the sum of a nation's wealth' (Keynes [1923] CWK IV: 124).

The destruction of bancor reflects reabsorption of imbalances. The ideal situation is one in which all bancor balances have returned to zero, since this would imply that each country would have given to other countries an amount of goods exactly equivalent to those received in return. In the words of D.H. Robertson, the British economist who participated with Keynes in the Anglo-American currency talks:

> It is arguable that the proudest day in the life of the Manager of the Clearing Union would be that on which, as a result of the smooth functioning of the correctives set in motion by the Plan, there were no holders of international money—on which he was able to show a balance sheet with zero on both sides of the account. (Robertson 1943: 359, quoted in Cesarano 2006: 150)

Of course, however, this outcome is not guaranteed. For this reason, Keynes introduced in his scheme a series of corrective mechanisms. This leads us to the second distinctive feature of the plan: the burden of adjustment is distributed symmetrically between debtors and creditors. In fact, exactly the same rules would apply to positive and negative balances with the Clearing Union. First, both would be subject to maximum levels of imbalance (or 'quotas'), so that it would be impossible to increase a country's debt indefinitely, but also to indefinitely accumulate credits. Second, and even more significantly, both debtors and creditors would be subject to the payment of a charge, in proportion to their imbalance. It is as if, in this sort of international bank designed by Keynes, not only debtors would have to pay an interest on their debts, but also creditors would have to pay an interest on their credits.

For this reason, bancor cannot be considered a reserve asset. Bancor is not intended to serve as a store of value. Positive bancor balances accumulated by surplus countries do not preserve their value indefinitely. On the contrary, they are subject to periodical charges that act as a sort of 'carrying cost' on money, such as that advocated

by Keynes in *The General Theory* as a countermeasure against the deflationary effects of the preference for liquidity.[6]

This might appear startling and vexatious towards creditors, since we are used to seeing them as virtuous savers that deserve to be rewarded. Yet, this is contrary to the logic of Keynes's plan, and on strictly economic, not moral, grounds. First of all, the creditors within the Clearing Union have not deposited any money, and hence do not have to be compensated for not spending it. In fact, their credit remains perfectly liquid, and they are free to spend it, in any direction and at any moment they please. So, if they refrain from doing so, it is only for their free decision not to spend. This is perhaps enough to explain why creditors do not earn anything. But why do they have to pay? Because, indeed, they receive a benefit from the possibility of running credits with the Clearing Union that it is worth paying for. Just as the Clearing Union allows deficit countries to purchase goods that they otherwise would not have been able to afford, in exactly the same way and in the same measure it allows surplus countries to sell goods that they would have otherwise not have been able to sell. Hence, the creditors may be happy to pay a charge for the opportunity of gaining access to a wider market, especially in economic systems that are chronically affected by overproduction, where demand is often the most difficult good to find.

The symmetric charges would have the further benefit of facilitating the return to a balanced position for all members. Insofar as creditors have an incentive to spend their positive balances, it will be easier for deficit countries to reduce their negative balances. This would facilitate the repayment of debts and the reduction of global imbalances in the interest of all, and hence the achievement of the main purpose of the Clearing Union.

Despite the incentives to converge towards a clearing of all balances (whence the name of the Union), it may occur that a country still experiences a persistent imbalance. Here comes into play the third distinctive feature of Keynes's proposal: the correction of exchange rate misalignments. In case a country should have a systematic deficit (or surplus), its currency would be devalued (or revalued) accordingly, in order to increase (or reduce) its competitiveness and hence to restore the equilibrium of its foreign trade. The fact of restricting the possibility of devaluating to deficit countries is sufficient to rule out 'competitive devaluations', that is, the indiscriminate

recourse to this sort of measure as a way to boost exports. In fact, the disequilibria that would justify such corrections would be clearly defined in terms of a certain proportion of the quota for a certain number of years.

Even in this respect, Keynes's plan differs from the Keynesian proposals that are convincingly criticized by Spahn in his contribution to this volume. The exchange rate regime envisaged by Keynes for the Clearing Union was a system of adjustable pegs, and not of fixed exchange rates. The logic of the realignments admitted within the Clearing Union was coherent with its purpose of avoiding the build-up of chronic imbalances. Indeed, if 'the key problem in fixed-exchange-rate systems is a wrong fixed exchange rate', as Spahn concludes, then a system of adjustable exchange rates may well be the solution. This was, in fact, the kind of exchange-rate regime envisaged, not only in Keynes's proposal, but also, at least in principle, in the Bretton Woods system. The difference was that, as we shall see later, only the former univocally specified the conditions for realignments.

Given this peculiar way of creating (and destroying) international money, the Clearing Union differs radically from a world central bank, such as those envisaged in the Keynesian proposals criticized by Spahn. Unlike the Clearing Union, a world central bank would control the creation of international money, but would have hardly any possibility of ensuring that the money created was actually used up in circulation.[7] On the other hand, since it does not arbitrarily determine the quantity of international money, the Clearing Union could not be said to exercise a monopoly on monetary policy as a world central bank would do. Thanks to the distinction between international currency (bancor) and national currencies, member countries would be left free to lead an autonomous monetary policy. The discretionary powers of the Clearing Union would essentially concern the determination of quotas, charges, and exchange rate adjustments. And the criterion for such decisions would be economic, and not political. This does not mean, of course, that the managers of the Clearing Union would always make independent and informed decisions, but that they could be held responsible for their decisions on the basis of a purely economic criterion, measured by the appropriateness of their action in relation to the objective of ensuring international clearing.

WHY WAS THE KEYNES PLAN NOT ADOPTED?

In the light of this analysis, however sketchy, it appears that the Keynes Plan contained measures that would have presumably allowed it to pursue much more effectively the goal of containing global imbalances, on which there was general consent. It is therefore only natural to ask why the proposal was eventually set aside, in favour of the American scheme.

The most immediate answer would seem to be that it failed to reflect existing power relations. After all, by the end of the Second World War, the US was by far the leading industrial power of the world, it had accumulated massive credits towards its European allies, and it was the owner of almost all the official gold reserves of the entire world. Why should it have been willing to enter a plan on a level of parity with all the other countries? It might seem obvious that no reason at all could induce the Americans to enter the Clearing Union. And yet, at a closer look, there were indeed good reasons. First of all, Keynes was not so naïf to believe that the world economy could restart from scratch after the war. He envisaged the possibility that the wealth previously accumulated in the form of gold could be paid into the Clearing Union and credited to the account of the owner. However, this was conceived by Keynes as a one-way convertibility: gold would be convertible into bancor, but bancor could not be converted back into gold. The rationale for this provision, in the logic of Keynes's proposal, is quite evident: the possibility of taking positive balances out of the Clearing Union would have allowed creditor countries to escape the charge, and to refrain from reducing their position. Keynes was convinced that such behaviour was to be avoided, in the interest even of the creditor countries, since it would have exerted a contractionist pressure on world trade, to their own detriment. Of course, one might argue that the US might not have subscribed to this view. However, the scale of US aid, particularly under the Marshall Plan, testifies that indeed the Americans did share the belief that a substantial redistribution of wealth was necessary, and in their own interest.

It is then perhaps more accurate to say that the true aim of the American government was not to preserve the existing distribution of power and money, but to maintain control of the source of money and power, by establishing the use of their national currency as an

international means of payment. Indeed, this endowed the US with 'the secret of a deficit without tears', which, as shown by Jacques Rueff (1972: 23 [1971: 24]), 'allowed the countr[y] in possession of a currency benefiting from international prestige to give without taking, to lend without borrowing, and to acquire without paying'.

To be sure, the gold dollar standard that was established at Bretton Woods as the new international monetary system provided an invaluable thrust to the political and financial power of the US, supporting it with a potentially unlimited purchasing power. And yet, the dollars flowing conspicuously out of the US into the rest of the world also served, more broadly, the purpose of defending the interests of capitalist democracies in the confrontation with the Soviet bloc, and of promoting the steady expansion of international trade and investment that was to prove even more strategic than open military conflict in winning that confrontation. Hence, it cannot be stated that such system was imposed unilaterally by the US as a means of preserving power. Rather it was willingly accepted by all Western powers, as the most effective means of pursuing an indefinite increase of power, where productive and destructive capacity are inextricable, and where economic growth and military escalation are just two equally essential and mutually enforcing faces of the mobilization of resources.

WHAT WERE THE CONSEQUENCES OF THE BRETTON WOODS SYSTEM?

The system established at Bretton Woods owes its strength and its resilience to the apparent capacity of serving simultaneously all purposes and all nations in their quest for growth and empowerment. It is apparently a win-win game for all participants. And, yet, we might ask: Is it true that nothing is lost in the process? What are the actual consequences of the Bretton Woods system? What are its costs? The most important one, on which this whole chapter is focused, is indeed the chronic build-up of global imbalances, together with the financial, economic, and political instability that they entail. And, if we compare the IMF with the Clearing Union, it is not difficult to understand why: the statute of the Fund failed to adopt all three distinctive features that Keynes had designed as mainstay of his proposal and as bulwark against the formation of persistent imbalances.

First, the treatment of creditor and debtor countries by the Fund was greatly asymmetric. Deficit countries faced severe limits, charges, and interest payments on their debts towards the Fund. On the contrary, surplus countries did not have to pay any charges whatsoever, and could go on accumulating surpluses indefinitely. In fact, the systematic surplus of a country would imply that, as the other countries would be purchasing its currency from the Fund for the purpose of funding their deficits, the currency of the surplus country would eventually be declared by the Fund to be scarce. In that case, the 'scarce currency' clause would come into effect. It has often been said that the reason why surplus countries did not share the burden of readjustment within the Bretton Woods system was because that clause was not applied. Considering its provisions, it might as well not have been written. In face of persisting surpluses, in fact, all it states is that the Fund can borrow or purchase the scarce currency from the surplus country. Far from putting surplus and deficit countries on an equal footing, therefore, the Articles of Agreement of 1944 actually give an advantage to surplus countries, not only with respect to deficit countries, but in relation to the Fund itself, since the latter may be forced to borrow the currency of the surplus country at an interest.

Second, the statute of the Fund did not present adequate measures to correct exchange rate misalignments. In principle, the Bretton Woods system established a regime of adjustable pegs, just as the one envisaged by the Keynes plan. And yet, the conditions at which the exchange rates were to be adjusted were not equally clear. The Articles of Agreement stated that 'A member shall not propose a change in the par value of its currency except to correct a fundamental disequilibrium.' And yet nowhere in the entire document was a definition of 'fundamental disequilibrium' to be found. In the absence of a definite and agreed criterion according to which exchange rates ought to be adjusted, the adjustment did not take place, the Bretton Woods system came to be seen as a system of fixed exchange rates, and the ensuing imbalances could not but persist.

Third, and most important, the Bretton Woods adopted a national currency as international money. Systematic balance of payments deficits for the country issuing the international money were an inevitable consequence of this arrangement. Those deficits became essential as a source of money supply for the rest of the world, and

as a means to finance the expansion of international trade and investments. And, as Triffin (1960) has pointed out in formulating the dilemma that goes under his name, running deficits in the interest of growth can only jeopardize stability.[8]

WHAT CAN BE DONE TODAY?

The Triffin dilemma has been recently quoted as a reason of major concern in a paper by the governor of the People's Bank of China, Zhou Xiaochuan. If it is read between the lines, the remark also seems to suggest the reason why China might not be so eager to take over America's dubious privilege of issuing the global currency. The paper indicates the identification of the international money with a national currency as the main cause of the global imbalances, in which the People's Bank of China is in up to the neck under the weight of its foreign reserves. The governor, then, sets out to propose a way of overcoming the dilemma. The proposal consists in '[t]he creation of an international currency unit, based on the Keynesian proposal' (Zhou 2009).

The explicit reference to Keynes's plan, as a model for reforming the international monetary system, is all the more significant and encouraging as it comes not from a large debtor country, as was Britain in 1944, but from the greatest creditor country worldwide. Unfortunately, however, the Chinese proposal only maintains one of the three distinctive features of the Clearing Union: the international currency. And it misinterprets it as a reserve currency, whereas bancor was a pure unit of account. As a consequence, the other pillars of the Clearing Union fall. The Chinese proposal consists in extending the use of Special Drawing Rights (SDRs), issued by the IMF, as a means of international settlement and as a reserve asset. This would definitely alleviate the pressure on the US balance of payments to provide international liquidity, but it would transfer the entire burden on the frail shoulders of the IMF. Moreover, SDRs are created as a fiat money by the IMF, and they are lent out at interest, thus producing a clear dissymmetry between debtors and creditors. The use of SDRs as a global currency, in lieu of the dollar, may not require global imbalances, but it certainly also does nothing to reabsorb them.

What, then, can be done? One option could be to transform the SDR in a pure unit of account (or to establish another monetary unit), to be used by a special department of the IMF (or by another international financial institution created ad hoc) to grant overdraft facilities to states for the settlement of their international payments on current account, according to the principles of multilateral and intertemporal compensation devised by Keynes for the Clearing Union. A similar clearing system could be set up in Europe to face the current sovereign debt problems. As I have already observed, the whole debate concerning the so-called 'sovereign debts' is biased by an obsessive concern for public debts, whereas the problem really concerns that part of public and private debts which is financed abroad. In other terms, the real problem of the euro today is the persistent disequilibrium in the balance of payments of participating countries. And the European monetary unification bears itself a responsibility for the build-up of such imbalances, since it has encouraged international capital movements to expand at bay from exchange risk, in fact inhibiting the correction of exchange rate misalignments. The ensuing economic and political tensions have been exacerbated by a consolidated expert and public opinion that views a trade surplus as a virtue and a deficit as a vice, whereas they are in fact the two sides of the same medal. The imbalances within the Eurozone would be more appropriately and effectively tackled if they were financed through a clearing system, with a more balanced distribution of the burden of adjustment between debtor and creditor countries.[9] Such institution could be drawn up along the lines of the European Payments Union, that actually allowed Europe to clear 75 per cent of its trade in the 1950s and that, in turn, was largely inspired by Keynes's plan for an International Clearing Union.[10]

NOTES

1. All versions are collected in CWK XXV.
2. See the compelling arguments provided in this sense by Peter Spahn in his contribution to this volume.
3. The argument is clearly spelled out by Keynes ([1941] CWK XXV: 27–8). It obviously does not apply to the case when the deficit country is also the provider of the international currency, for rather apparent reasons that will be discussed later.

4. Articles of Agreement of the International Monetary Fund, 27 December 1945, in Peaslee (1956: 259–87, at p. 259).

5. As we shall see, the Clearing Union decides the 'quota', that is, the maximum amount of positive or negative balance attainable by each member. And quotas are assigned to each member country in proportion to the volume of its foreign trade, that is, on the basis of economic criteria, consistent with the purpose of the Clearing Union to finance temporary balance of trade disequilibria. This is another point where Keynes's plan is not affected by the criticism that may be rightfully raised (as Spahn does in this volume) against certain Keynesian proposals that allow a distribution of international reserves according to political priorities.

6. Keynes ([1936] CWK VII). See, in particular, Chapter 17 on the introduction of artificial carrying costs on money as a possible remedy against the accumulation of excessive money balances, and Chapter 23 on the practical experiments in this direction represented by the stamped money of Silvio Gesell.

7. The difficulty of central banks to induce the actual use of the money they create is testified, for instance, by the Long term refinancing operations (LTRO) undertaken by the European Central Bank in December 2011 and in February 2012, which together have expanded the money supply by approximately 500 billion euros. Most of these have been re-deposited at the central bank, and it is not clear how the latter can ensure that the new money may be actually circulated and eventually destroyed through appropriate exit strategies (see Fantacci 2013, forthcoming).

8. In his contribution to this volume, Spahn appropriately distinguishes two cases, according to whether the deficits of the country providing international money are on capital account or on current account. Indeed, for such a country, it makes a great difference if it is accumulating international credits (like Britain during the classical gold standard) or debts (like the US today). However, for the world economy as a whole, it is the accumulation of creditor and debtor positions as such, regardless of which country is on one side or the other, that represents a factor of economic disequilibrium and political tension. For the stability of the global economy, it is no better if the leading country is a chronic creditor than if it is a chronic debtor. Not by chance, Triffin formulated his concerns when the US was still running a trade surplus with the rest of the world (Triffin 1960).

9. The introduction of symmetric charges within the TARGET2 settlement system is mentioned as a possible step in this direction by Spahn, in his contribution to this volume. The proposal of introducing limits on trade imbalances in lieu of budget constraints in the Stability Pact goes in the same direction.

10. See Amato and Fantacci (2011: Part 2, Chapter 5, 'The European Payments Union'). In particular, on the importance of the Clearing Union proposal in the conception of the European Payments Union, see Kaplan and Schleiminger (1989: Appendix 1).

REFERENCES

Altomonte, C. and A. Villafranca. 2010. 'Not Only Public Debt: Towards a New Pact on the Euro', ISPI Policy Brief 198, October, Milano: Istituto per gli Studi di Politica Internazionale. Available at http://www.ispionline.it/it/documents/PB_198_2010.pdf. Last accessed on 27 April 2012.

Amato, M. and L. Fantacci. 2011. *The End of Finance*. Cambridge: Polity Press.

Cesarano, F. 2006. *Monetary Theory and Bretton Woods. The Construction of an International Monetary Order*. Cambridge: Cambridge University Press.

Eichengreen, B. 2002. *Financial Crises and What to Do about Them*. Oxford: Oxford University Press.

Fantacci, L. 2013 (forthcoming). 'Why Banks Do What They Do. How the Monetary System Affects Banking Activity', *Accounting, Economics, and Law*.

Hume, D. 1752. 'On the Balance of Trade', published in *Political Discourses*, and republished in W.B. Robertson (ed.) 1906. *Hume's Political Discourse*. London: Walter Scott Publishing Co., pp. 51–66.

International Monetary Fund (IMF). 2010. *World Economic Outlook, Recovery, Risk, and Rebalancing*. Washington: IMF.

Kaplan, J.J. and G. Schleiminger. 1989. *The European Payments Union. Financial Diplomacy in the 1950s*. Oxford: Clarendon Press.

Keynes, J.M. 1971–89. *The Collected Writings of John Maynard Keynes* (CWK), edited by D.E. Moggridge, Vol. XXV. *Activities 1940–44: Shaping the Post-War World: The Clearing Union*. London: Macmillan.

———. 1919. *The Economic Consequences of the Peace*, as reprinted in D.E. Moggridge (ed.), *The Collected Writings of John Maynard Keynes* (CWK), Vol. II. London: Macmillan.

———. 1923. *A Tract on Monetary Reform*, as reprinted in D.E. Moggridge (ed.), *Collected Writings of John Maynard Keynes* (CWK), Vol. IV. London: Macmillan.

———.1932. 'The Economic Prospects 1932', as reprinted in D.E. Moggridge (ed.), *The Collected Writings of John Maynard Keynes* (CWK), Vol. XXI. London: Macmillan, pp. 39–48.

———. 1936. *The General Theory of Employment, Interest, and Money*, as reprinted in D.E. Moggridge (ed.), *The Collected Writings of John Maynard Keynes* (CWK), Vol. VII. London: Macmillan.

———. 1940. 'Proposals to Counter the German "New Order"', as reprinted in D.E. Moggridge (ed.), *The Collected Writings of John Maynard Keynes* (CWK), Vol. XXV. London: Macmillan, pp. 7–10.

———. 1941. 'Post-war Currency Policy', as reprinted in D.E. Moggridge (ed.), *The Collected Writings of John Maynard Keynes* (CWK), Vol. XXV. London: Macmillan, pp. 21–33.

Peaslee, A.J. 1956. *International Governmental Organizations. Constitutional Documents*. The Hague: M. Nijhoff.

Robertson, D.H. 1943. 'The Post-War Monetary Plans', *Economic Journal*, 53(212): 352–60.

Rueff, J. 1972. *The Monetary Sin of the West*. London: Macmillan [original edition 1971. *Le Péché monétaire de l'Occident*. Paris: Plon].

Triffin, R. 1960. *Gold and the Dollar Crisis. The Future of Convertibility*. New Haven: Yale University Press.

Zhou X. 2009. 'Reform the International Monetary System', Speech by the Governor of the People's Bank of China, 23 March. Available at http://www.bis.org/review/r090402c.pdf. Last accessed on 23 April 2012.

10

In a Keynesian Mood?

Why Exchange Rate Systems Collapse

PETER SPAHN

Whenever international monetary relations are in trouble, Keynes's proposal of establishing an International Clearing Union (ICU) and more far-reaching plans for building a world central bank that issues a true world money are at stake again. In a way, the world monetary system is still in its infancy. While we have succeeded in introducing a two-tier banking system at the national level,[1] market agents 'choose' the international money of account and means of payment from the pool of national currencies. It is less clear how to interpret this state of affairs. Maybe the evolutionary process of search for efficient institutions simply is time consuming. Or, economic and political interests that take advantage of the status quo block the transition to a welfare-enhancing solution. Or, the idea of a world central bank has severe drawbacks. Probably, an answer might embrace all three aspects.

One important caveat surely is related to the political risk of having a monopolistic monetary authority or an International Monetary Fund (IMF) with enlarged power 'at the centre of world macroeconomic policy management' (Ocampo 2010: 309). For the very reason of disapproving a powerful body that seemed difficult to control, the US did not even allow the emergence of a national central bank before the beginning of the twentieth century. It is hard to imagine how the governing council of a world central bank should look

like; which countries should have the right to appoint members of the council; and who should lay down the principles that guide the council's decisions. Whereas at the moment, mainly market forces determine the latitude of each national economy, that is, its possibilities of drawing credit and resources from abroad, the 'progress' of politicization of these relations will boost the discontent felt in many countries with regard to their 'budget constraint'.[2]

These remarks maybe suffice to allow the following tentative conclusion: it is highly improbable that a substantial number of important nations will agree to found a supranational monetary authority and promise to submit themselves to its decisions. National governments fear to lose political autonomy and room for manoeuvre with regard to macro stabilization policies; they know that they are able to leave a key-currency system, whereas this is hardly an option if the world economy is organized as an hierarchical monetary system. If a supranational central bank ever should be established, this reform of world monetary relations might easily turn out to be a nightmare, rather than a step towards more welfare and peaceful relations, given the ponderous procedures to reach agreement on the bank's statute and its policy rules.

On the other hand, even if these critical arguments about the institution of a world central bank are assessed to be valid, this is not to deny that the constellation of a national central bank that performs the double task of issuing a national currency with international money functions is far from efficient. There are well-known deficiencies of a world monetary 'non-system' where the key-currency money supply is the by-product of national policy-making of a large country:

1. First of all, there is the big privilege of the home country being exempt from any liquidity problem in its cross-border economic transactions.
2. If the provision with key-currency reserves follows via net capital exports, the leading country easily accumulates economic power and foreign assets as the capital-importing countries are motivated to keep additional reserves. This represents an obvious case of privatizing the social benefits that accrue from running a bank.
3. If the increase of key-currency units held abroad flows from the leading country's trade deficit, markets may speculate on the sustainability of that deficit.

4.   Also, political observers might complain about the unfair transfer of resources from member countries to the leading nation.

5.   Putting the focus on member countries, their incentive to earn reserves by way of net exports may cause deflationary tendencies in the world economy.

6.   Finally, fixed-exchange-rate systems in general are said to put asymmetric pressure upon (trade) surplus and deficit countries: whereas the former gain additional latitude, the latter are forced to a painful adjustment process with higher interest rates and lower employment. Trade-deficit countries are forced to run high-interest-rate policies in order to dampen imports via reduced income dynamics, and to attract financial capital that provide necessary finance to balance money flows on the foreign exchange market.

Some of these arguments may raise doubts on their validity. Looking at point 1., one may wonder whether the privilege of disposing of a key currency is a blessing or a curse. From a long-term perspective, this privilege might mislead government and market agents in their behaviour; the reduced market pressure that emanates from a diminished liquidity problem may well undermine the nation's productive supply-side forces over the decades. With respect to the last point, one may surmise that it is the essence of a market society that there is more adjustment pressure on agents who show a low performance compared to others.

It is hardly appropriate, however, to speculate on the issues of the aforementioned list without looking at specific examples. This will be done in the following sections. We will ask to what extent historical exchange rate systems were affected by the points listed earlier, and what main reason can be given for their downfall. Finally, a short summary will be given indicating what directions may be taken in order to reform world monetary relations.

LOOKING BACK AT THE GOLD STANDARD

The gold standard is a natural starting point for our analysis for two reasons: it was the first important fixed-exchange-rate system and it formed the empirical background for Keynes's reasoning. He truly was an internationally oriented economist, but obviously also interested

in the welfare of his home country. Thus, he was deeply concerned about the terms of Britain's re-entry into the gold standard in 1925. Though there were strong 'signalling' arguments for keeping to the old nominal parity, the real exchange rate made Britain's gold reserves its cheapest export product. Restoring competitiveness via nominal wage adjustments proved to be a slow and sluggish expedient. Whereas the US experienced a golden decade, the UK fell into stagnation.

Given this troubled situation, it would have been particularly beneficial for Britain if the US had lived up to David Hume's Rules of the Game that obliged trade surplus countries to increase their money supply in line with the inflow of gold reserves. In that case, the ensuing monetary expansion would also have drawn higher imports from the UK. But actually, monetary policy in open economies not always obeyed to Hume's prescription so that the alleged 'automatic' stabilization of the balance of payments did not assert itself. The international monetary system thus was not characterized by gold flows, triggering parallel movements of each nation's quantity of money, but rather by the norm of *minimizing* gold flows:

- For a central bank in a deficit country, it makes no sense to allow gold losses via the foreign exchange, restrict the money supply as a by-product, and suffer from a macroeconomic downturn in the end. It is more rational to initialize the slump (that cannot be avoided anyway) via restrictive interest rate policies 'voluntarily', but defend the stock of gold reserves.
- Surplus countries likewise might prefer to sterilize gold inflows, if they occur, in order not to overheat macro activity in the national economy.

Of course, Keynes was well aware of monetary policy practice in the 'managed' gold standard from his intimate relation with the Bank of England. Nevertheless he complained (even before the resumption of the old gold parities) about the inadequate and 'unfair' sterilizing policy of the Fed as if he were a naive adherent of Hume's textbook model of the gold standard:

> In practice the Federal Reserve Board often ignores the proportion of its gold reserve to its liabilities and is influenced, in determining its discount policy, by the object of maintaining stability in prices, trade, and employment. Out of convention and conservatism it accepts gold.

Out of prudence and understanding it buries it.... For the past two years the United States has *pretended* to maintain a gold standard. *In fact* it has established a dollar standard. (Keynes 1923, CWK IV: 197–8)

This statement is all the more noteworthy as Keynes himself in that very book, *A Tract on Monetary Reform*, had proposed the primacy of internal over external equilibrium as a rational guide for monetary policy, that is, exactly that kind of policies that the Fed was pursuing during the 1920s. Formally, this meant that central banks ought to be more interested in interest rate levels (stimulating investment and employment), and less in interest rate differences (inducing capital movements). But the implication was that England was cut off from the stabilizing demand effect that David Hume's Rule would have set in motion. As a consequence, the British economy got caught in the unfavourable position of a deficit country that was confronted with an asymmetric adjustment pressure. This degrading experience constituted the origin of Keynes's (1942, CWK XXV: 176) claim of transferring 'the onus of adjustment from the debtor to the creditor position' and his more general recommendation of pursuing symmetric macro adjustment policies in both deficit and surplus countries (on this issue, also see Fantacci, Chapter 9, in this volume).

The question whether to respond to world macro imbalances in a symmetric or asymmetric fashion should be answered after a thorough analysis of the situation, but in the history of monetary policy the reaction often was driven by old-fashioned principles or wounded vanities—or both.[3] In the case of the British deficit in relation to the US, surely a more expansive American macro policy would have provided some relief to the UK balance of payment, but this would have come at the cost of losing control over internal macro dynamics in the US; and the asset price bubble that developed towards the end of the 1920s indicated a need for stabilization.

The asymmetric adjustment rules prevalent in the gold standard blocked a more easy recovery for the UK, but the root of the British dilemma was the decision to enter the post-war gold standard at an overvalued exchange rate, a step that simply could not be healed at low costs[4] (interestingly, the UK fell into the same mistake when entering the European Monetary System [EMS] in 1990). Just because France and the US gained from the competitive gift implied by

re-establishing the old parities, and experienced a boom, they could not afford an easy-money policy that would have destabilized the domestic price level. This is the fallacy of an unconditional call for symmetric demand policies in the case of severe trade imbalances: export-surplus countries surely have enough external leeway that would allow further demand expansion, but strong export demand at the same time causes inflationary risks that preclude a further (monetary or fiscal) stimulus.

If thus a major central bank like the Fed pursues both an external and an internal target, that is, defending a fixed exchange rate and maintaining price stability, an export surplus of that country transmits a deflationary impulse to its trading partners if export proceeds are sterilized from the monetary circulation. This follows from the relentless zero-sum logic of reserve distribution in the gold standard. Keynes therefore insisted on the duty of any surplus country to redirect funds into the world market, for example, by way of long-term foreign investment, which was the favoured British strategy. He called for establishing

> a system of general and collective responsibility, applying to all countries alike, that a country finding itself in a creditor position *against the rest of the world as a whole* should enter into an obligation to dispose of this credit balance and not to allow it meanwhile to exercise a contractionist pressure against the world economy and, by repercussion, against the economy of the creditor itself. (Keynes 1941, CWK XXV: 47; cf. Carabelli and Cedrini 2010)

However, it cannot be taken for granted that this zero-sum logic of reserve distribution applies to all fixed-exchange-rate systems alike. It was a peculiar feature of the gold standard where also the leading central bank was subject to a liquidity problem. Things were different in other key-currency systems.

THE GOLD-PAPER STANDARD OF BRETTON WOODS I

The Bretton Woods System designed in 1944 was a half-way house between a gold-based and a paper standard. This kind of ambiguity also was reflected in the question whether the famous Triffin Dilemma really was a severe menace to the sustainability of Bretton Woods, or not. When the French in the late 1960s threatened to convert dollar reserves into gold, this no doubt added to the expectation of dollar

devaluation, but it also became evident that an orderly managed key-currency system does not need to be resource-based. The necessary condition of providing a nominal anchor for the international monetary system could be met more efficiently by maintaining price stability in the US, compared to the duty of defending a constant gold price. Without a gold backing, but with a successful policy of inflation control, the dollar standard according to McKinnon (1993) could have continued indefinitely. But it did not.

The US heaped dollar reserves on the rest of the world via its capital export, but the current account did not turn negative before 1971. The hypothesis (put forward by Fantacci in this volume) that the US right from the inception of the Bretton Woods System aimed at a 'trade deficit without tears', that is, acquiring foreign goods and services in exchange for dollars kept abroad, appears questionable; the Marshall Aid project proves an interest in promoting American exports. Nevertheless the privilege of the US, the ability of acquiring foreign assets without bearing any liquidity problem, became an issue in international political relations, but did not cause any macroeconomic distortions. By absorbing the excess supply of US dollars on the foreign exchange in order to keep the parity, central banks around the world, in the first place, withdrew dollar from the global circulation. But that was immediately undone by investing these funds into interest-bearing dollar assets in the US banking system. Even if they had decided to hoard dollar notes as liquid reserves, this would not have brought about any dollar shortage; by disregarding the limit posed by the Triffin Dilemma, the Fed simply could easily create the dollar supply that supported its implicit interest rate targets.

On the other hand, by purchasing US dollars on the foreign exchange, Bretton Woods member central banks involuntarily engaged in monetary expansion in their home countries that finally led to a rate of inflation that was even higher than in the US. The Bretton Woods System finally collapsed because the key country pursued a too expansive monetary policy. The US exported inflation into the world economy, an attack that only could be deterred by letting domestic currencies float against the dollar. The system was ill-designed: either the Fed should have been obliged to defend the dollar on the foreign exchange (this had been the gold standard solution where the key central bank was exposed to a liquidity problem), or to maintain price stability on the American goods market. This latter U-turn of US

monetary policy did not occur before the famous Volcker Revolution in 1979, six years after Bretton Woods I had collapsed.

THE REPRISE OF THE PLAY IN BRETTON WOODS II

Bretton Woods II in a way is a detour, a special case. Actually, one may say that it is no exchange rate 'system'; there was no crisis; and it did not collapse. To begin with, there are no treaties that oblige member countries to fix parities, but of course, there were no such treaties in the classical gold standard either. The 'system' consists but of unilaterally fixing an undervalued exchange rate of the national currency vis-à-vis the dollar; this pegging behaviour can be suspended at any time if that appears to be convenient. There were mutual benefits that made this arrangement acceptable also for the US as the passive player: the net flow of resources from, say, China[5] to the US brings to mind the 1960s debate on the American privilege of 'buying' abroad by means of ever expanding credit lines, which was so nicely captured by Rueff and Hirsch (1965: 3): 'If I had an agreement with my tailor that whatever money I pay him returns to me the very same day as a loan, I would have no objection at all to ordering more suits from him.'

The benefits on the part of emerging countries are twofold:

- By acquiring dollars (or euros) on the foreign exchange, home currency is created against a first-rate backing.
- By pursuing an export-led growth strategy, the country follows the only workable and successful path of development.

The second point is much under dispute. Traditional neoclassical development theory holds that a country exporting a net flow of resources foregoes the opportunity of investing at home, that is, building up its capital stock. But this argument is based on the typical neoclassical assumption of full employment, whereas an emerging country like China (just like West Germany after Second World War) easily can engage in export and investment growth *at the same time*.[6] Frenkel and Rapetti (2010) rightly emphasize the Keynesian view that growth also in emerging countries is demand-constrained; therefore an agreement on real exchange rates that allow export-led development would be much more useful than paying development aid.

What comes as a surprise is that authors from roughly the same camp accuse the current international monetary system of being 'unfair' as emerging countries are led to transfer resources to rich countries, thereby creating an 'inequity bias' (Ocampo 2010). Given the enormous progress in terms of income and wealth that cannot be overlooked in economies that practise export-led growth, this line of attack against Bretton Woods II is hard to swallow. Emerging countries are able to increase employment, receive a lot of technical knowledge via foreign direct investment, and build up a creditor position against the rest of the world. Finally, they are free to terminate this policy at any time.

Another large issue of concern is the involvement of world macro imbalances, which went along with Bretton Woods II, in the great financial crisis of 2007–8. There is the hypothesis of a Triffin Dilemma II: just as US dollar indebtedness in the 1960s grew too large with respect to its gold stock, its capital import from foreign creditor countries (including Japan) after 2001 grew too large compared to solid investment opportunities in the US. Thus, so the story goes, the US financial market was swamped with a huge amount of funds that simply could not be processed properly. Like any other producer who is confronted with excess demand, American banks were led to create low-quality products, that is, high-risk dollar assets. The paradox here is that foreigners were interested in keeping high-quality (dollar) reserves, but their supply of funds to the US banking system fed the creation of 'toxic waste'.[7]

This scenario deserves some comments:

- The problem was not the high-risk feature of many of the newly created financial products, rather, they were mispriced, a notorious failure of the rating agencies.
- If US financial agents really had succeeded to distribute packed pieces of bad risks, at whatever price, to portfolios of savers all over the world, there would have been no financial market crisis in the US. The latter event occurred just because the banks *failed* to sell the 'toxic waste' abroad and kept these assets on their books. 'Far from passing on the bad loans to the greater fool next in the chain, the most sophisticated financial institutions amassed the largest exposures to the bad assets' (Shin 2010: 2).

- Only one half of US capital import can be seen as covering the current account deficit, the other half was 'used' to finance American capital export. This 'over-funding' of the current account deficit emphasizes the banking function of the US capital market, and it also allows the hypothesis that the American banking system might have had difficulties to allocate capital inflows efficiently even in the case of a balanced current account.

- Thus, the alleged link from macro imbalances to the world financial crisis (also mentioned by Fantacci in this volume) tends to ignore that the unsustainable creditor–debtor relations in the US financial market were built up by gross, not by net, capital flows (Borio and Disyatat 2011). A large part of effective finance supply was provided by banks in Europe whose current account basically was balanced.

These types of arguments lead many professional observers to conclude that the world financial crisis basically was not caused by world macro imbalances, but mainly by a malfunctioning of US financial markets (Stiglitz 2009; Clarida 2010). The financial crisis was no currency crisis. The often-predicted run on the dollar did not show up. Balance-of-payment disequilibria might increase again for cyclical reasons. In other words: Bretton Woods II is still alive (Dooley et al. 2009; European Central Bank [ECB] 2010).

If that is taken to be the case, there are two further issues which have been raised as critical points. One is the reprise of Keynes's main attack against the gold standard: export-surplus countries are imposing a deflationary pressure upon the world economy; this finding should justify, in a future international monetary system, to oblige these countries to stimulate domestic spending. It was argued earlier that Keynes's argument was well founded in the setting of a gold standard where *all* central banks, in principle, suffer from a liquidity problem. Greenwald and Stiglitz (2010: 331) argue that also the current international system is deflationary because of the accumulation of dollar reserves in emerging countries: 'Reserve accumulation represents a subtraction from global purchasing power.'

A comprehensive investigation of the supposed link between a nation's export surplus and the path of macro dynamics in the world economy should scrutinize the origins of increased net exports,

the use of export proceeds as seen from a balance-of-payment view, and the nature of the reserve supply function. We have to confine the analysis to the Bretton Woods II case instead. The rhetoric of the Saving Glut Hypothesis suggests that China's additional exports originate from a decision favouring a different use of a full-employment income: 'In practice, these [emerging] countries increased reserves through the expedient of issuing debt to their citizens, thereby mobilizing domestic saving, and then using the proceeds to buy U.S. Treasury securities and other assets' (Bernanke 2005: 9). Actually it was the other way round: by purchasing dollars on the foreign exchange, the People's Bank of China initiated and maintained an exchange-rate-induced export surplus that created a flow of income and saving that otherwise would not have existed (Bibow 2009: Chapter 8). The impact of Chinese monetary policy in the domestic economy is clearly expansive, regardless whether the central bank buys home bonds or foreign currency.

The effects on other countries are less clear. For keeping things simple, let the rest of the world be represented by the US. Chinese exchange rate policy prevents an appreciation that otherwise would follow from a low-wage-induced export surplus. Accordingly, these products conquer a segment of the US goods market, increase American real wages, and lower the production of competing US goods. If the Fed follows a Taylor Rule, both impacts on the inflation gap and on the output gap provoke an expansive monetary policy response. As Chinese monetary authorities purchase dollar assets, we have excess demand on the US capital market. Again, this has an expansive effect via higher asset prices and lower long-term interest rates.[8] The conclusion is: it is a myth that Chinese net exports produce a deflationary, contractive impulse in the world economy.

This leaves a final topic: is Bretton Woods II an example of a viable long-term international monetary system? The answer is no because ever-increasing current account imbalances are not sustainable and thus cannot be tolerated. Emerging countries should be allowed to pursue export-led growth policies for a while, including the acquisition of foreign reserves, but this kind of policy has been excessive in the past decade. Things would have worked more smoothly if China, besides the dollar, also had oriented its currency and trade policies towards the euro so that the burden of the key-currency country would be shared.

The question is whether the euro—or some other important national currency—will ever live up to the hope of becoming a competitor of the dollar. Before, however, the current euro crisis can be addressed, a look at the forerunner of European Monetary Union (EMU), the European Monetary System (EMS), is advisable.

THE EUROPEAN FIXED-RATE SYSTEM

At a first glance, the EMS came down in the early 1990s for a similar reason as the old Bretton Woods I, but with an inverted sign. American leadership no longer was accepted because US monetary policy was too inflationary; German leadership was undermined because the Bundesbank embarked on a restrictive course that maybe was adequate for Germany, but not for the rest of Europe.

During the 1980s, the system worked quite well, despite—or we should say due to—various realignments. Here we find the constellation that is addressed by the Keynesian critique of asymmetric fixed-rate systems: the surplus country, that is Germany, exerted macroeconomic pressure upon deficit countries; they had to adjust wage costs in order to regain competitiveness. But according to the majority of observers, this enforced pattern of following the German nominal-wage standard was the very reason for the existence of the EMS. The system was interpreted as a device for pursuing disinflation policies in high-inflation countries. The aim was to reduce disinflation costs by borrowing monetary credibility by means of a fixed exchange rate vis-à-vis the German mark, that is, by 'tying the hands' of national policymakers (Giavazzi and Pagano 1988). It would have hardly made sense to modify the architecture of the EMS towards more symmetry as this would have meant less disinflation in southern countries and more inflation in Germany.

It is noteworthy that the EMS in no way got into systemic trouble due to the quite substantial inflation differences during the 1980s; frequent realignments provided necessary adjustments without diminishing the pressure for continuous disinflation in southern member countries. The experience of these realignments no doubt undermined the credibility of the fixed-rate arrangement; thus, the rational-expectation promise of an easy, quick, and low-cost changeover to a German inflation regime did not come true. But seen as a whole, the EMS period up to the crucial event of German reunification was an economic success.

This workable fixed-exchange-rate arrangement nevertheless suffered from two drawbacks: member countries had delegated the power to decide on European monetary policy matters to a foreign entity, which might wound political vanity. A more serious problem was that the Bundesbank quite naturally was concerned with the German, but not the European, rate of inflation. This was bound to raise a serious problem when German inflation, instead of providing an anchor to wage and price formation abroad, had to be stabilized itself. This type of shock hit the EMS in the wake of German reunification, which meant a massive demand expansion, more precisely: an asymmetric demand shock that obviously could not be dampened by only one monetary policy instrument. There were several ways out, but in the end a response was chosen that implied the collapse of EMS (see Box 10.1):

1. The first best solution would have been a symmetric increase of interest rates in all member countries, in order to compensate the general demand expansion, accompanied by a *revaluation* of the mark, in order to neutralize the asymmetric part of the demand shock. This was rejected mainly for political reasons: some smaller countries preferred to maintain their perfect pegging to the mark, and larger countries did not want to bear the loss of reputation that was supposed to be the by-product of devaluation.
2. Without a realignment, an asymmetric policy response might have come about by a relatively stronger monetary restriction in Germany. But the implied interest rate differential between the mark area and financial markets abroad required a *devaluation* expectation with respect to the mark (or a risk premium), in order to be compatible with constant exchange rates. Although there were many reasons that might have caused such a bad-reputation effect (high inflation, mounting public debt, a current account deficit, and the massive problem of restructuring the German Democratic Republic [GDR]), financial-market agents held on to their positive views with regard to the mark. Thus, any interest rate differential was precluded.
3. If all central banks had engaged in moderate, but symmetrical interest rate increases, German inflation only could have been dampened by additional fiscal or wage policies. But the efficiency of these instruments was rather low from the point

Box 10.1   Blowing up the EMS by the Bundesbank's Stabilization Policies

From a standard macro model, a condition for price stability in Germany can be derived and visualized as the *PS* line in an interest–exchange rate space (Spahn 2001: Chapter 7.3). It exhibits a positive slope as a rise in the exchange rate and a rise in the rate of interest have contrary effects on demand; thus both variables have to move in line if some demand-determined level of prices is to be maintained. The curve shifts with autonomous shocks: changes in interest or exchange rates are required to offset their immediate price effects. Points above *PS* represent a deficiency of effective demand causing deflationary tendencies and rising unemployment. Likewise, a full employment condition *FE* in the foreign country can be derived, the slope of which necessarily is negative.

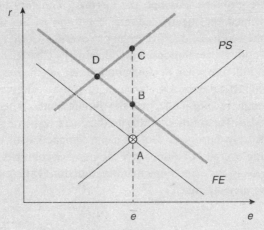

Asymmetric Demand Shock in the EMS

A domestic demand shock requires *PS* to shift upwards, more than *FE*. The efficient macro solution consists of higher interest rates in both countries and a mark revaluation (A ⇒ D). The political failure to reach a realignment decision left B and C as feasible solutions. But they could not be realized at the same time as financial market agents did not expect the mark to devalue. The dominating German interest rate (C) was too high for other countries (B), where unemployment ensued, which triggered the final EMS crisis.

of view of the Bundesbank; and the latter disliked the idea of simply accepting a heavy dose of German inflation (although this might have been helpful for internal restructuring).

4. The mirror image of this last scenario was realized: a strong interest rate reaction by the Bundesbank that had to be replicated

by other central banks, in order to keep external equilibrium abroad. But this was inappropriate for internal equilibrium in countries like France where unemployment already was high. The French macroeconomic constellation was not credible for political reasons: why should France (with inflation lower than in Germany!) import further monetary restriction? There was no way out for the Banque de France.[9]

Speculation quickly detected the fragile stability of the fixed-rate arrangement and brought it down. The notorious German export surplus was not the culprit (it had turned negative), but the impact of a double problem: although the German monetary policy actually determined the macroeconomic condition in the whole EMS (just like the Fed had a decisive influence over the world economy in Bretton Woods I), the Bundesbank following its Charter only looked at German inflation when deciding on interest rate moves; and other member countries were not able to agree on a realignment of the mark (though recommended by the Bundesbank) when this was utterly needed. The solution of this predicament was straightforward: establish a truly European central bank equipped with the task of safeguarding overall inflation,[10] give all member countries a share in the bank's decisions— and hope that inflation differentials remain low in the new currency area.

THE EUROPEAN NO-RATE SYSTEM

Having no exchange rates, one may convincingly argue that EMU is not an exchange rate system at all. Some professional observers, however, regard EMU as an extremely *tough* variant of the gold standard, where no temporary leave is possible, no policy cooperation exists, and no regular emergency lending is agreed upon (Eichengreen and Temin 2010). Considering the EMU project in comparison to the EMS, substantial expected improvements can be detected:

1. As monetary policy is now geared to European inflation, stabilization in single countries no longer can the put the whole system under stress.
2. Closing foreign exchange markets in Europe removed a source of financial stress and speculation.

3. This also signalled a final, extreme step within the 'tying one's hands' strategy mentioned earlier, as the credibility of exchange-rate fixing now is definite.

Hardly any one of these hopes came true, and new problems arose. EMU's history so far can be divided into three periods.

(1) 1999-2007

The first simple finding is that removing exchange rates did not also dissolve the reasons of former European exchange rate crises; rather, the absence of exchange rates implied that there were no solutions for upcoming macroeconomic distress that emanated from continuing (and partly diverging) macroeconomic cycles on the national level. Whereas financial markets were integrated quickly, leading to an EMU-wide capital-market rate of interest with very small differences between the national segments, national wage policies still went separate ways; thus, instead of a gold standard there was a wage standard in each country. This had the most unfavourable effect that actually unions determined the real rate of interest in each national macro economy; and the threat of dynamic instability stemmed from the fact that nominal wage increases in a boom *lowered* real interest rates (see Box 10.2).

Southern member countries thus enjoyed a strong boom that was supported by the new experience of having unlimited access to a large European financial market with low interest rates, nominal and real; and capital flows to these countries partly were misused to finance consumption and real estate bubbles. Deficit countries did not suffer from lacking 'reserves', they received ample credit from surplus countries just like Keynes would have liked to have it (Carabelli and Cedrini 2010). The problem was not that deficit countries were restricted by a shortage of transnational credit flow—it was the cheap excess supply of finance that caused the destabilizing boom in Spain and other countries. On the other hand, large countries like Germany and France suffered from stagnation, so that ECB policies, controlling average inflation, were helpful in neither case: one size did *not* fit all (Wickens 2007; Giavazzi and Spaventa 2010). Trade imbalances mounted to unprecedented size, clearly some countries suffered from low competitiveness.

Box 10.2   EMU Member-country Macro Model

The supply side, that is, the rate of inflation p_t is given by

$$p_t = \mu p^E + (1-\mu)\, p_{t-1} + a\, y_t + w_t$$

The demand side, that is, the output gap y_t is

$$y_t = \theta\, y_{t-1} + g_t - \beta\,(i^E - p_t) + \tau\,(p^E - p_t)$$

Expected, and given, euro-wide inflation is denoted by p^E, the constant euro-wide nominal interest rate by i^E. Domestic supply and demand shocks are w_t and g_t, respectively. Dynamic instability ensues if $\beta > \tau$, and

- demand persistence θ is high, or
- belief μ in domestic relevance of ECB inflation is low.

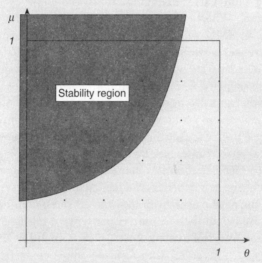

Region of Convergence with Varying Belief in EMU Inflation Target
and Varying Domestic Output Persistence

Problems of competitiveness necessarily are a two-sided issue. The German export surplus, which might have been useful to exert a disciplinary impact on high-inflation countries in the EMS, now shows as a force apt to blow up the system. Whereas nominal unit labour costs in southern countries outstripped the boundaries given by national productivity growth and the ECB inflation target, particularly

German wage costs seemed to indicate that Germany continued its mercantilist tradition and made a trade war against its European partners. Export-promoting wage restraint surely exerts deflationary pressure within the common market (this case is different from Chinese-US relations in Bretton Woods II).

(2) 2008–10

The aftermath of the world financial crisis revealed the lacking sustainability of the macroeconomic relations in EMU. Creditors became more risk-sensitive again and denied to supply funds at easy terms, which were required to revolve private and public debt. The immediate consequence was a balance-of-payment shock: trade flows to deficit countries no longer were matched by private capital flows; the concomitant bookkeeping entries emerged as (TARGET2) imbalances within the European System of Central Banks (ESCB). At the same time, commercial banks in deficit countries encountered liquidity problems. The policy reaction revealed that—contrary to the opinion of Eichengreen and Temin (2010)—EMU in fact resembles a *soft* gold standard:

1. Deficit-country central banks are not forced to settle their balances within the ESCB. Likewise, surplus-country central banks cannot convert their positive euro claims (that they hold basically against deficit-country central banks) into some 'final' means of payment.
2. National central banks use the possibility of issuing euros on their own account, to support their stressed national commercial banking systems (Buiter et al. 2011). This 'Emergency Liquidity Assistance' (hardly known in EMU's early years), if compared to the rules of the gold standard, comes down to printing forged gold reserves, a behaviour that can only be prohibited by a two-thirds vote of the ECB board.

TARGET2 balances in a way resemble 'bancor' claims and debts that, according to Keynes's proposal, would emerge within a Clearing Union (see Fantacci in this volume). The old idea to restrict the extent of trade imbalances, if necessary by means of interest costs on intra-ESCB balances, for both debtors *and* creditors, appears to be in

line with an agenda of fighting against forces of divergence among EMU member countries.

(3) 2010–?

Quickly rising interest rates in some countries raised the threat of bankruptcy.[11] None of the national governments that got under heavy financial stress had the classical option of resorting to its central bank and begging for Lender-of-Last-Resort services, or of devaluing the currency. The irony here is that exactly the abolition of these possibilities was one of the key arguments favouring the introduction of the euro as a supranational currency. The former chairman of the German Council of Economic Advisors once celebrated the almost constitutional reform that deprived national governments of their last way out of monetizing their debts: 'The history of money ... is the eventful history of the improper use of the right to issue money. ... The decisive point is that in a currency union each single nation has to pay its public debt in units of a currency that cannot be issued by its national authorities' (Sievert 1993: 14, 18; my translation). Many observers expected that the exclusive dependence on private financial-market agents' readiness to buy public bonds would exert a strong disciplinary force on national governments; but they were wrong.

Financing public debt under EMU conditions reveals a structural weakness of national governments because, by definition, it is *foreign* public debt in each case (debt contracts written in terms of the supranational currency; no resorting to a domestic central bank; no devaluation). Therefore, the missing Lender of Last Resort for European governments raises an element of instability and panic in the market for the stock of national public debt (De Grauwe 2011). In principle, this financial-market defect arises regardless whether a country suffers from a current account deficit or not. But of course, such a deficit ranks high among the criteria that are used by asset holders when assessing the quality of governments bonds. Therefore, the divergence of competitiveness across EMU members moves into centre stage again.

An agenda of reforming EMU should include—besides a powerful European Monetary Fund with large financial and regulative powers—the establishment of norms for current account imbalances. They could replace the budget-deficit rules stipulated in the Stability

and Growth Pact as both types of (im–)balances are connected via the flow-of-funds identity. A large budget deficit thus can be healed by a private-sector surplus, originating from the difference between saving and investment. The use of public-budget balances to counter undesirable trade imbalances is less efficient. Surely, it is the duty of surplus countries to expand in a crisis (Eichengreen and Temin 2010), but given the current situation in EMU, additional fiscal spending in Germany would only add to German debt (that rather should be lowered in an upswing) without necessarily helping the Greek to reduce their trade deficit that basically is driven by real-exchange-rate differentials. The wage rate is the most appropriate substitute for an exchange rate that no longer exists. Hence, if EMU is not to collapse in the medium run, appropriate wage guidelines should be established.

SYNOPSIS: WHAT WENT WRONG?
WHAT CAN BE DONE?

It may appear a strange diagnosis to say that the key problem in fixed-exchange-rate systems is a wrong fixed exchange rate; and yet this is the finding for the gold standard, the EMS, and also the EMU, although in the latter case it is wage policy that fails to deliver the required constant real exchange rate. Of course, we do not know how the gold standard could have survived even if the British had chosen a more suitable nominal rate when re-entering the system in the 1920s; the limitations of a resource-based reserve system sooner or later would have become apparent.

It is interesting to speculate on the sustainability of an EMS, as a 'Deutsche Mark Club' (Dornbusch 1987), after a hypothetical realignment of the mark in the early 1990s. German trade surplus was mounting before the historical shock of the collapse of East German socialism. Without continuous realignments reflecting diverging wage-cost dynamics, EMS would not have been viable in the long run. But what a flexible and low-cost adjustment procedure are occasional realignments, compared to the nightmare of debt crises in the EMS follow-up system. True, in a European DM Club system, politicians outside Germany would have had no chance to influence German, and thus European, monetary policy. But German politicians had no large influence either; and political independence of

the central bank is the mantra of modern theory of monetary policy after all.

Instead of tolerating the Bundesbank solution, Europe now has advanced to a regime where market constraints are substituted by political rules and negotiations, a system that up to now appears as an attempt to maximize systemic instability and political transaction costs. The existence of EMU, however, is one of the obstacles to the realization of the vision of a true world monetary system. Despite its various shortcomings, European politicians will cling to EMU as a cornerstone of political integration. It is equally unthinkable to close down the ECB and then let European nations obey to a world central bank, or to subordinate the ECB to the directives of a world monetary authority, which lets European economies be trapped in a two-stage dependency. Hence, the collapse of EMU is the precondition for far-reaching plans of reforming world monetary relations.

Looking at Bretton Woods I and II teaches us that we must not get misled by the idea of a given stock of reserves that was a legitimate principle when analysing the gold standard. In modern paper-standard systems, key-currency reserves are both hard to define and to control. Base money is supplied elastically, following the needs of the markets; and interest-bearing papers are close substitutes to the whole spectrum of financial and real assets. Excessive demand for reserves, under these conditions, tends to be inflationary on a world scale, rather than deflationary. It also distorts real exchange rates and contributes to the build-up of large macroeconomic imbalances that are unsustainable in the long run, that is, give rise to destabilizing expectations. Maybe China now has started to embark on an internal-demand strategy and thus supports the world economy (Bibow 2010), but its exchange rate policy in the past should not set an example for other emerging countries.

Recent experiences also shed a new light on the widely shared opinion that the current international monetary system, in general, places too much burden upon trade-deficit countries. But in Bretton Woods II, the key deficit country was the US. In EMU, building up trade deficits was far too easy for those member countries that benefited from the new access to the large euro capital market. And the remedy for poor developing countries is not facilitating imports by more credit supply on easy terms, but designing an agenda of structural reform.

The prospects for Keynes's plan of an International Clearing Union, let alone a true world central bank, are dim. The larger the authority and powers of an international monetary institution, the less probable is an agreement of yet autonomous governments towards the foundation of such an institution. Keynes's bancor concept seems to rest upon the assumption of capital controls that have to be embodied in the first place.[12] If such a far-reaching regulation cannot be reached, and private capital investments cover current account imbalances, the aim of avoiding 'holdups' in worldwide monetary circulation is fulfilled. Hence, there is no money hoarding and no shortage of finance; yet the short history of EMU shows that such a state of affairs does not preclude macroeconomic instability.

A modest reform of world monetary relations should instruct the IMF to monitor and ban excessive reserve keeping (which of course implies that countries agree to report data to the IMF in the first place). There should be limits to the volume of reserves in relation to GDP or trade, and there should also be a prescription of a minimum diversity of reserve holding with regard to the currencies involved. To put it differently: partly dethroning the dollar is no threat, but offers the chance of moving to a competitive system where we have two or three reserve currencies (Eichengreen 2011). Holding reserve assets denominated in these currencies provides a perfect hedge in case of relative exchange rate changes between them. A basket of reserve currencies also implies that there is a burden-sharing between rich countries: providing a ready market for emerging countries' export-led growth efforts, that is, accepting a trade deficit, should not be the task of just one country.

The obvious candidate of a second world reserve currency besides the dollar is, of course, the euro, provided that it survives the severe troubles originating from the European debt crisis. If the euro should experience appreciation due to increased reserve keeping abroad, European economies, and Germany in particular, will be challenged by the task of strengthening internal demand. It is less clear which further national currency will qualify for the role of a reserve currency. Contrary to the opinion widely shared in the press, a nation's financial strength does not result from the amount of foreign assets held in its central bank's books, but rather from foreign agents' willingness (and permission) to acquire and hold assets denominated in that nation's domestic currency. Thus, opening its capital market and abolishing

exchange rate controls is the precondition for China to gain the status of a reserve currency country.

These are huge tasks for Europe and China; moreover, finding an agreement on the regulation of reserve-keeping requires enormous progress in the sphere of world politics. But if we do not reach consent and power for small steps on the reform agenda, how can we hope to establish a word central bank?

NOTES

1. This innovation unfolded after the famous Peel Act of 1844 (Spahn 2001: Chapter 4.5).

2. Proponents of a world central bank proposal involuntarily emphasize the wide field of political conflict that opens up, for example, with respect to the distribution of reserves: Ocampo (2010: 307) suggests that 'a larger proportion of allocations would be given to those countries with the highest demand for reserves' and seems to assume that the council easily agrees on the candidates that should be favoured.

3. In the late 1920s, the Banque de France possessed an amount of sterling assets that matched the whole gold stock of the Bank of England, and was in a position to threaten the British balance of payment. In view of the British deficit,

> Paris had the power to force upon London a Bank Rate increase, but Norman [Governor of the Bank of England] suggested to Moreau [Governor of the Banque de France] the alternative of a reduction in the Paris rate. The French, suspicious always of what Moreau referred to as 'the imperialism of the Bank of England', maintained that the responsibility for corrective measures rested with the deficit country. (Eichengreen 1984: 80)

4. Eichengreen and Temin (2010: 378) hint to Keynes's hidden adherence to the gold standard: during the Depression he considered restrictions of trade and foreign lending, national impositions on wages, profits and rents—but not suspending the gold standard.

> Keynes…had opposed Britain's return to gold at the pre-war parity,…but once the decision was made he reconciled himself to it. He was unwilling to recommend going off gold in 1930, which he saw as the linchpin of the international financial system and essential for financial stability. Only when he grew convinced that the gold standard was doomed, in the summer of 1931, did Keynes recommend bowing to the inevitable and abandoning convertibility.

5. The explorers of the Bretton Woods II idea, Dooley et al. (2003), rightly stress that the role of China can well be taken up by other peripheral countries, so that the play does not depend on the willingness of single actors.

6. China's large net foreign asset position is at odds with the predictions of the neoclassical theory. A country where the capital-to-labour ratio is relatively low should enjoy high returns on capital and, with increasingly integrated financial markets, receive net

capital inflows. Capital should flow from rich countries (the north) to poor countries (the south), and the process should continue until the return on investment is equalised in all countries. In practice, this is not the case. The fact that the direction of capital flows is not in line with the prediction of neoclassical theory has become known as the 'Lucas Paradox'....China fits the paradox well: by structural endowment, it is a candidate net international borrower, but in fact it is a net lender. (Cappiello and Ferrucci 2008: 46)

Also Fantacci (in this volume) sees China, due to its investment–saving gap, as a typical trade-deficit country.

7. Over the last decade, the US has experienced large and sustained capital inflows from foreigners seeking US assets to store value. ...Excess world savings have looked predominantly for safe debt investments. ...First, during a period of good shocks...the growth in asset demand pushes up asset prices and lowers risk premia and interest rates. It is interesting to observe that the value of risky assets rises despite the fact that the increase in demand is for riskless assets. Second, foreign demand for debt instruments increases the equilibrium level of leverage of the domestic financial sector. In order to accommodate this demand, the US financial sector manufactures debt claims out of all types of products, which is the reason for the wave of securitization. Third, if shocks turn negative...the foreign demand now turns toxic; bad shocks and high leverage lead to an amplified downturn and rising risk premia. ...The US sells riskless assets to foreigners and in so doing raises the effective leverage of its financial institutions. ...As global imbalances rise, the US increasingly specializes in holding its 'toxic waste'. (Caballero and Krishnamurthy 2009: 584)

8. Even if the Chinese central bank would keep dollars instead of dollar assets, this hardly would produce a dollar shortage because the Fed adjusts the supply of base money endogenously. Therefore, already in Bretton Woods I foreign central banks did not pursue a policy of dollar hoarding (in order to dampen domestic inflationary pressure) as they knew that this easily would be overruled by an elastic money supply on the part of the Fed (Spahn 2001: Chapter 6).

9. An increase in the unemployment rate raises the costs to the government of continuing to pursue policies of price stability. When the public observes unemployment, it revises upward its forecast of the probability that the authorities will deviate in order to reflate the economy; this in turn requires the authorities to raise the discount rate to defend the currency, which only serves to aggravate their unemployment problem. (Eichengreen et al. 1995: 260–1)

10. The ECB would not have responded to German reunification by increasing interest rates if average European inflation was not affected by excess demand in that region.

11. If the market perceives a higher default risk, it raises interest rates on the debt to compensate for the extra risk. Higher debt-service payments, however, worsen the budget deficit, and—if the government does nothing—this pushes the nation towards the edge of sustainability. If this precipice is already close to start with, the higher interest rates themselves can magnify default fears, thus yielding even higher interest rates and so on; the spiral inexorably drags the nation towards default. ...Government must slash non-interest spending programmes and/or raise tax rates. But even this may backfire. This type of fiscal contraction may slow growth thereby undermining sustainability. If it does, default risk and interest rates can rise, which then requires further cuts or higher taxes. But cutting and taxing cannot go on forever—eventually

the people will revolt. In the end, the government may find default to be the least bad option. (Baldwin and Gros 2010: 8)

12. On this topic, see the instructive analysis of Fantacci (in this volume) who traces back the origin of bancor units to a transfer of real resources, so that bancor corresponds to Keynes's early vision of money as a transaction-facilitating medium (a vision that was modified substantially in his later writings, however).

REFERENCES

Baldwin, R. and D. Gros. 2010. 'Introduction: The Euro in Crisis—What to Do?' in R. Baldwin, D. Gros, and L. Laeven (eds), *Completing the Eurozone Rescue—What More Needs to Be Done?*, pp. 1–23. London: Centre for Economic Policy Research/VoxEU.org Publication. Available at http://www.voxeu.org/reports/EZ_Rescue.pdf. Last accessed on 27 April 2012.

Bernanke, B.S. 2005. 'The Global Saving Glut and the U.S. Current Account Deficit', Sandridge Lecture, Virginia Association of Economists, Richmond, Virginia, 10 March. Available at http://www.federalreserve.gov/boarddocs/speeches/2005/200503102/default.htm. Last accessed on 27 April 2012.

Bibow, J. 2009. *Keynes on Monetary Policy, Finance and Liquidity Preference.* Abingdon and New York: Routledge.

———. 2010. 'How to Sustain the Chinese Economic Miracle? The Risk of Unravelling the Global Rebalancing', Levy Working Papers 617, Annandale-on-Hudson, NY: Levy Economics Institute of Bard College.

Borio, C. and P. Disyatat. 2011. 'Global Imbalances and the Financial Crisis—Link or No Link?' BIS Working Papers 346, Basel: Bank for International Settlements.

Buiter, W.H., J. Michels, and E. Rahbari. 2011. 'ELA—An Emperor without Clothes?' Citi Economics, Global Economics View, an online distribution of Citibank, 21 January.

Caballero, R. and A. Krishnamurthy. 2009. 'Global Imbalances and Financial Fragility', *American Economic Review, Papers and Proceedings*, 99: 584–8.

Cappiello, L. and G. Ferrucci. 2008. 'The Sustainability of China's Exchange Rate Policy and Capital Account Liberalisation', ECB Occasional Papers 82, European Central Bank, Frankfurt.

Carabelli, A.M. and M.A. Cedrini. 2010. 'Global Imbalances, Monetary Disorder, and Shrinking Policy Space—Keynes's Legacy for Our Troubled World', *Intervention, European Journal of Economics and Economic Policies*, 7(2): 303–23.

Clarida, R.H. 2010. *What Has—and Has Not—Been Learned about Monetary Policy in a Low Inflation Environment? A Review of the 2000s.* New York: Columbia University.

De Grauwe, P. 2011. 'The European Central Bank—Lender of Last Resort in the Government Bond Markets?' CESifo Working Papers 3569, CESifo, Munich.

Dooley, M.P., D. Folkerts-Landau, and P. Garber. 2003. 'An Essay on the Revived Bretton Woods', NBER Working Papers 9971, National Bureau of Economic Research, Cambridge, MA.

———. 2009. 'Bretton Woods II Still Defines the International Monetary System', NBER Working Papers 14731, National Bureau of Economic Research, Cambridge, MA.

Dornbusch, R. 1987. 'Prosperity or Price Stability', Oxford Review of Economic Policy, 3(3): 9–19.

Eichengreen, B. 1984. 'Central Bank Cooperation under the Interwar Gold Standard', Explorations in Economic History, 21: 64–87.

———. 2011. Exorbitant Privilege—The Rise and Fall of the Dollar and the Future of the International Monetary System. Oxford and New York: Oxford University Press.

Eichengreen, B. and P. Temin. 2010. 'Fetters of Gold and Paper', Oxford Review of Economic Policy, 26(3): 370–84.

Eichengreen, B., A.K. Rose, C. Wyplosz, B. Dumas, and A. Weber. 1995. 'Exchange Market Mayhem—The Antecedents and Aftermath of Speculative Attacks', Economic Policy, 10(21): 249–312.

European Central Bank (ECB). 2010. 'Prospects for Real and Financial Imbalances and a Global Rebalancing', Monthly Report, April, pp. 91–100.

Frenkel, R. and M. Rapetti. 2010. 'Economic Development and the International Financial System', in Stephany Griffith-Jones, José Antonio Ocampo, and Joseph E. Stiglitz (eds), Time for a Visible Hand—Lessons from the 2008 World Financial Crisis. Oxford and New York: Oxford University Press, pp. 253–68.

Giavazzi, F. and M. Pagano. 1988. 'The Advantages of Tying One's Hands—EMS Discipline and Central Bank Credibility', European Economic Review, 32: 1055–82.

Giavazzi, F. and L. Spaventa. 2010. 'Why the Current Account May Matter in a Monetary Union—Lessons from the Financial Crisis in the Euro Area', CEPR Discussion Papers 8008, London: Centre for Economic Policy Research.

Greenwald, B. and J.E. Stiglitz. 2010. 'A Modest Proposal for International Monetary Reform', in Stephany Griffith-Jones, José Antonio Ocampo, and Joseph E. Stiglitz (eds), Time for a Visible Hand—Lessons from the 2008 World Financial Crisis. Oxford and New York: Oxford University Press, pp. 314–44.

Keynes, J.M. 1923. A Tract on Monetary Reform, as reprinted in D. Moggridge (ed.), The Collected Writings of John Maynard Keynes (CWK), Vol. IV, (1971). London: Macmillan.

———. 1941. 'Proposals for an International Currency Union', as reprinted in D.E. Moggridge (ed.), The Collected Writings of John Maynard Keynes (CWK), 1980, Vol. XXV. Activities 1940–1944. Shaping the Post-War World: The Clearing Union. London: Macmillan, pp. 42–66.

———. 1942. 'Proposals for an International Clearing Union', as reprinted in D.E. Moggridge (ed.), The Collected Writings of John Maynard Keynes (CWK),

Vol. XXV, (1980). *Activities 1940–1944. Shaping the Post-War World: The Clearing Union*. London: Macmillan, pp. 168–95.

McKinnon, R.I. 1993. 'The Rules of the Game—International Money in Historical Perspective', *Journal of Economic Literature*, 31: 1–44.

Ocampo, J.A. 2010. 'Reforming the Global Reserve System', in Stephany Griffith-Jones, José Antonio Ocampo, and Joseph E. Stiglitz (eds), *Time for a Visible Hand—Lessons from the 2008 World Financial Crisis*. Oxford and New York: Oxford University Press, pp. 289–313.

Rueff, J. and F. Hirsch. 1965. 'The Role and the Rule of Gold—An Argument', Princeton Essays in International Finance 47, Princeton University International Finance Section, Princeton.

Shin, H.S. 2010. 'Financial Intermediation and the Post-Crisis Financial System', BIS Working Papers 304, Bank for International Settlements, Basel.

Sievert, O. 1993. 'Geld, das man nicht selbst herstellen kann—Ein ordnungspolitisches Plädoyer für die Europäische Währungsunion', in Peter Bofinger, Stephen Collignon, Ernst-Moritz Lipp (eds), *Währungsunion oder Währungschaos? Was kommt nach der D-Mark?* Wiesbaden: Gabler, pp. 13–24. English translation produced in the chapter 'Money That We Cannot Produce Ourselves—A Constitutional Plea for European Monetary Union', in *Currency Uinion or Currency Chaos—What Comes After the German Mark?*

Spahn, P. 2001. *From Gold to Euro—On Monetary Theory and the History of Currency Systems*. Berlin and Heidelberg: Springer.

Stiglitz, J.E. 2009. 'Interpreting the Causes of the Great Recession of 2008', Contribution to Eighth BIS Annual Conference: 'Financial System and Macroeconomic Resilience—Revisited', BIS Papers 53 (2010), Bank for International Settlements, Basel.

Wickens, M.R. 2007. 'Is the Euro Sustainable?' CEPR Discussion Papers 6337, Centre for Economic Policy Research, London.

IV
Finance and International Economic Disorder

11

Uncertainty and Speculation in the Keynesian Tradition

Relevance in Commodity Futures

SUNANDA SEN*

THE ROOTS OF SPECULATION UNDER UNCERTAINTY: SOME CONCEPTUAL ISSUES

It is common knowledge that the possibility of moving funds over time and space can add to the incentives for speculation. Uncertainty and risk in deregulated markets make for financial innovations to handle the unknown prospects relating to returns on assets. Financial instruments as are innovated in the process include derivatives which often consist of forwards, futures, options, and swaps, all contracted on the basis of what is described as the 'underlying', one which relates to financial assets backed by physical assets, currency, commodities, or even real estates.

Agents who operate in these markets require different types of professional skill and expertise. As a consequence, there emerges a

* Earlier versions of this essay were presented at a workshop organized by the Advanced Academic Centre, Jawaharlal Nehru University, in November 2009. Comments received from the participants and from the unknown referees of this volume are gratefully acknowledged. None of them, however, are responsible for the limitations that may have remained in this essay.

division of responsibilities—between those who mobilize and deploy (physical as well as financial) resources at their command in trade and businesses, and others who complement by managing risks in the face of uncertainty. Actions by the latter category of agents to sustain and maximize returns on those financial assets in uncertain times, often entail financial engineering in the handling of derivatives. Strategies as aforementioned include hedging by balancing of risks with returns, which, however, may not always materialize.

While operations in uncertain markets generate demand for risk-management and use of derivatives, reliance on these instruments contributes to transaction costs for each such financial deal, which in turn are pitted against the capital gains/losses on these transactions. However, in terms of the standard convention relating to national accounts, capital gains/losses as aforementioned are reckoned as pure transfers which are not included in computations of gross domestic product (GDP). It may be recalled here that the multiplicity of financial investments as rely on derivatives, while originating from the *same* base in terms of specific spheres of real activities (or 'underlying'), do not expand the base itself. Instead, these amount to a piling up of claims which in turn are linked to the same set of real assets. *Finance in its gyrations thus becomes increasingly remote from the real economy; while financial innovations proliferate within the economy, to hedge and insulate financial assets in the presence of uncertainty.* We point out that contrary to what is postulated in the rational expectations approach (which underlies the mainstream doctrines), capital markets hardly serve as an informational/signalling agency in the economy (Shackle 1974, cited in Sen 2003: 25). It will thus be argued that the free capital (financial) markets including the use of instruments like derivatives do not necessarily contribute to efficiency in the financial sector or material growth in the real economy.

Let us now dwell on the notion of uncertainty in the literature. We refer here to Keynes in his writings on uncertainty and related matters. Uncertainty lay at the heart of Keynes's explanation as to why economies fail to be self-correcting, following a disturbance which, for example, happened with the Great Depression that hit the world in 1929 (see Sen 2011). As Keynes had emphasized, wages and prices do not adjust when the economy has already started to slide because *no one knows* what the correct wages and

prices are. Thus, economic theory needs to start from an assumption of uncertainty, and not one of perfect information.

Keynes's interest in the problems relating to uncertainty can be traced back to his personal acquaintance and involvements with the stock market, with commodity futures, as well as with his role as the bursar of Kings College in Cambridge during the 1920s. It is interesting how Keynes initially subscribed to an objective account of probability which finally gave way to a subjective notion as an acceptable notion under uncertainty, thus moving all the way from 'relative frequency' approach in the *Treatise on Probability* (1921) to 'animal spirits' in his magnum opus, *The General Theory of Employment, Interest and Money* (1936).

Looking back, Keynes considered *three* types of probability: First, cardinal or measurable probability, where probabilities can be counted by comparing the distances between numbers and their absolute values. However, a notion as above can hardly be verified, not with standing its widespread use in theories relating to the 'efficient financial markets', and in the risk-management apparatus, especially in terms of a bell-shaped normal distribution of the universe of probabilities. Second, there is one ordinal probability which falls between statistical frequency and irreducible uncertainty; representing what one might call 'vague knowledge'. The third type of probability according to Keynes lies in the domain of irreducible uncertainty which always remains unknown. Here it becomes rational to allow 'caprice' to determine probability. Incidentally, 'caprice' here is not irrational: it is rational to act on caprice when we have no way of telling what the future will hold.

In the 'relative frequency' position which he held in the *Treatise on Probability* (1921), Keynes was considerably influenced by G.E. Moore, the contemporary philosopher. Moore, in his book *Principia Ethica* (1993 [1903]), had contested 'utilitarianism', which was the most influential school of thought around the time. Influenced considerably by Moore's objective reasoning, Keynes in 1921 settled to a 'logical-objective' approach to probability. Defined as a 'degree' of belief based on observations where the *degree of belief* 'α' was spelt out in terms of the ratio a/h where 'a' is related to observations based on the knowledge of 'h', Keynes here relied on an objective understanding of uncertainty as well as probability. Here the 'knowledge' of 'h' justified a 'rational' degree of belief, which was 'α' in 'a'. In this

228 KEYNESIAN REFLECTIONS

Keynes's main contention was that probability is not statistical, but logical. Keynes thus made, in *Treatise on Probability* (1921), a crucial distinction between our expectations about the future and the confidence with which we hold them, especially under uncertainty. His notion of the 'logical theory of probability' followed as closely as possible the way people used terms like 'probably', 'likely', 'I don't know'.

Laying stress on the fact that probability was based on a 'rational belief', Keynes also pointed out that such beliefs were very different from what could be viewed as 'caprice'. In this Keynes, while deviating from the dominant utilitarianism under the influence of G.E. Moore in his *Principia Ethica*, was, however, not inclined to accept the notion of 'relative probability' in Moore which was based on the statistical frequency of events. Nor was he inclined to what his contemporaries under the influence of Moore had conceived as 'rules' which followed the highest 'frequency' of 'good' performances.

The 'caprice' of the *Treatise* (1921) became 'animal spirits' in *The General Theory* (1936), as rational or at least reasonable, given the state of knowledge. The shift was consistent with Keynes's view that luck plays a much greater role in success or failure as compared to the explicable causes which we invent afterwards. Incidentally, Keynes consistently treated individuals as rational, not irrational.

'Uncertainty' as viewed by Keynes was thus consistent with holding either optimistic or pessimistic beliefs about the future. He also argued that faced with varying degrees of uncertainty, it is rational to fall back on conventions in forming our expectations and deciding how to act.

However, the notion of rational belief under 'objective' conditions to define probability, as spelt out in Keynes's 1921 book (*Treatise on Probability*), was critiqued by the mathematician-philosopher F.P. Ramsey between 1921 and 1926. Ramsey in his article, 'Truth and Probability' (written in 1926, published in 1931), was the first to lay out the theory of subjective probability with a beginning to axiomatize choice under (subjective) uncertainty. Questioning Keynes's information—theoretic notion of probability in the *Treatise on Probability*—Ramsey successfully influenced Keynes's position on probability as the latter switched to a subjective notion in his book *Essays in Persuasion* (1931) where he re-introduced probability from a subjective point of view.[1] This led to the eventual formulation of the notion in 1936 with the publication of *The General Theory* where the 'weight'

of events, viewed on a 'subjective' basis, was to determine probability under uncertainty. While such 'weight' of the argument relied on observations (h), it was the subjective 'belief' in it which mattered. And in case the 'weight' happened to be too small, uncertainty was considered as irreducible while probability could not be ascertained. Keynes's position as above connects to 'animal spirit' which remains unpredictable as a subjective element in market economies. Keynes reiterates the point in his article of 1937 with the statement that 'About these matters there is no scientific basis on which to form any calculable probability whatever. We simply do not know.' (Keynes 1937)

FUTURE MARKETS IN COMMODITIES: KEYNES AS A SPECULATOR

The notion of uncertainty and risks in markets is of much relevance in analysing the current scenario of financial instability as well as the fluctuations in global commodity markets. We introduce here the role of future contracts in commodity markets, which are run on principles similar to the use of derivatives (see Sen and Paul 2010) in financial markets, especially in their role in fetching short-run profits. These contracts are entered between parties which mutually agree to fix the terms of transactions (prices as well as quantities) on a future date. In case such contracts take place outside the formal exchange, described as 'over the counter' (OTC), these are described as 'forwards', as distinct from 'futures' which are mediated via the formal exchanges.

We recall here Keynes's direct involvement in commodity future markets during his time, both as a bursar to Kings College and also in managing his personal portfolio. In trying to formulate a general principle for movements in commodity prices which are subject to future markets, Keynes made some significant contributions. These related to markets which are cleared under 'normal' conditions and also for those subject to excess supply (described as 'backwardation'), a phenomenon which was common during the post-war years of the 1920s. Keynes here drew a distinction between professional speculators who are paid a sum ('return') for insuring against risks and others who were involved in the physical transactions, including the producers/sellers/traders, etc., in the market.[2]

The issue of rising and fluctuating commodity prices as were common during the inter-war years drew attention from Keynes. This led to his advocacy for a state-level buffer stock, to be used to control fluctuations in commodity prices. Keynes's convictions, based on his first-hand familiarity with future markets, convinced him of the need to stabilize prices, which, as he pointed out, was in the interest of direct producers and consumers rather than that for the speculators. The notion of risks under uncertainty and the difficulties of estimating movements in future prices for assets such as stocks of commodities, prompted Keynes to this advocacy for buffer stocks, suggesting state-level speculation as a public good as against private speculation for personal profits.[3]

Following the Keynesian tradition, it can be held that uncertainty (and knowledge) is subjective and hence 'non-ergodic'. Accordingly, uncertainty is thus not a natural phenomenon which is time invariant. Rather it is ontological and is embedded in social reality which, as described by Shackle (1974), is 'kaleidoscopic' and relates to what Joan Robinson called 'historic time' (Pressman 1996). From this angle, speculation in markets does not necessarily work in continuing to sustain higher profits, if any, nor does it generate growth via efficiency, as can be witnessed from the current turmoil in the global economy.

With high stakes in markets subject to uncertainty, risks often turn out to be disproportionately high as compared to their realized returns. This subverts efforts to hedge assets, and in effect failing to secure a stream of income flows to cover related liabilities. It even can negate the possibility of refinancing by rolling back loans by using 'speculative finance', as spelt out by the Post-Keynesian economist Hyman Minsky (1986). In such cases the agent is left with no option other than to borrow additional amounts to meet the liabilities. Transactions as the last one are identified in the literature as 'Ponzi' deals, which, as described, are unsustainable as well as hazardous, especially when compared to acts of simple hedging (or even speculation) on asset prices. It may be stressed that Ponzi deals are different from hedge finance or speculation, both of which keep the business going by offsetting the possible losses. Even speculatory finance, which takes on more risks than those under hedging, can only be sustained until it becomes Ponzi, with borrowings at high rates no longer generating compensating returns (Davidson 1988, 1991); a situation which of late has plagued the global financial markets from 2008.

CURRENT SCENARIO OF RISING COMMODITY PRICES IN THE GLOBAL MARKET: FINANCIALIZATION OF COMMODITY MARKETS UNDER FUTURE TRADING

As mentioned earlier in this chapter, there have been sharp increases in commodity prices and a related spread of future trading in the global commodity markets. In principle, future trading is supposed to transfer price risk from market participants having direct interest in transactions of physical commodities to other agents with speculative interests and who are ready to assume risks. However, the role of future markets in terms of 'price discovery' can work only with access to full information on part of those operating in the market and also when none of the agents has the capacity to influence prices by exercising their influence in the market in terms of large size.

For those who believe that forward and future trading can be beneficial by imparting efficiency in pricing, the arguments centre around a process known as 'price discovery' which, subject to a competitive market and full information, provides a direction to price formation in the spot market via those in the future market. Advocacy of future trading is also linked to reduction of risks, both for buyers and sellers by minimizing uncertainty when the price is pre-set, thus helping participants to know how much they will need to buy or sell. This helps reduce the ultimate cost to the retail buyer, because there is less of a chance that suppliers will jack up prices to make up for profit losses in the cash market. Similarly, producers (and sellers) can also ensure that prices will not fall further.[4] Future trading is also considered to allow risk-sharing among various market participants; for example, the farmers who can, in principle, sell by taking cover under future contracts to ensure remunerative prices. Similarly, the trader can buy in futures to hedge against volatile prices, which hedges the carrying risk to ensure smooth prices of the seasonal commodities round the year.

Arguments offered *against* unbridled trade in the future market of commodities rest at least on three claims which seem to include (a) the possibility of futures leading to rise in spot prices and inflation. Critics say that in case of some bad news about the future, the speculators start hoarding the commodities and hence artificially driving up the prices. However, as opposed to this, it can also be said in support of future trading, that with negative news about future, prices may

go up irrespective of whether futures market is there or not. (b) It is also pointed out that futures trading may drive up volatility in prices. (c) Finally, futures markets are not necessarily transparent or costless, and opportunities for trading are often monopolized by large traders/farmers, leaving little space for others in the market, an argument which applies to cross-border trade where developing countries turn out as insignificant players.

It can be seen that commodity prices boomed in the global market between 2002 and mid-2008. Thus, the International Monetary Fund (IMF) index of nominal prices for non-oil commodities quadrupled over the period. During this period, movements in commodity prices were often in *opposite* direction to the prices of financial assets in the equity markets, providing opportunities to diversify portfolios for those who operated across markets. The upward pace, however, was reversed with more than 35 per cent drop in commodity prices from their peak in April 2008. Also, since the severe downturn of global markets in the fall of 2008, the pattern changed with similar movements in prices across the equity and commodity markets. One also observes that the timing of these fluctuations in commodity prices indicates a close link to similar movements in real estate prices and the downslides in financial markets the world over. However, the drop recorded in commodity prices has been only one-seventh of the previous increases, thus recording a commodity price boom which has remained well above those in the first half of the decade (United Nations Conference on Trade and Development [UNCTAD] 2009: 53).

It has been pointed out that of late the future market in commodities witnessed large-scale entries of financial investors whose investment strategies are by and large driven by portfolio considerations, thus involving the financial market as well. As pointed out by the UNCTAD:

> ...a major new element in commodity trading over the past few years is the greater presence on commodity future exchanges of financial investors that treat commodities as an asset class. The fact that these market participants do not trade on the basis of fundamental supply and demand relationships and that they hold, on average, very large positions in commodity markets, implies that they can exert considerable influence on commodity price developments. (Ibid.: 54)

An evidence of 'carry-trade' across markets is visible in the simultaneous movements of prices, for commodities, equities, as well as for exchange rates in currency markets since 2008. One had witnessed a very different pattern with opposite movements in commodity and equity prices over 2002–5 (UNCTAD 2009: 67). The price-coordination across markets, as pointed out by UNCTAD, was related to the financial market boom which was recently followed by a crash (Ibid.: 54). As pointed out, 'financialization' also increases price volatility and 'hedging becomes more expensive and perhaps unaffordable for developing country users, as they [will] no longer be able to finance margin calls' (Ibid.: 74). The same argument probably also holds for intra-country future trade, where use of high margins can deter small traders. Thus, as held by the international think tank International Food Policy Research Institute (IFPRI), 'rising expectations, hoarding, and hysteria played a role in the increasing level and volatility of food prices, as did the flow of speculative capital from financial investors' (Robles et al. 2009: 2). A similar view was held by the Washington-based Institute of Agriculture and Trade Policy (Suppan 2008). The report points at the sharp rise in commodity prices between 2002 and mid-2008 which has been followed by a reversal.

The question, however, remains as to whether commodity futures have been effective in fulfilling their role in terms of 'price discovery' and 'risk transfers'. These claims can be fulfilled provided the market participants have access to information which is beyond public domain, including that 'derived from an intimate knowledge of specific events … and plans of (their) individual supply or demands in commodity markets' (UNCTAD 2011: 119). However, even when individual players in the commodity market can access information relating to the same market which is complete, information relating to other markets which are linked as aforementioned remains incomplete. This is because positions held by the financial investors who enter the commodity market as speculators remain one of the intractables in terms of access to information relating to the commodity futures. Thus, the risk-return considerations relating to future trade in commodities also remain heavily dependent on market situations in other asset markets as well as the overall economy (Ibid.). Often it generates 'herd behaviour' among investors, which explains the strong correlations between price movements in the commodity and

the equity markets in recent times. Thus, herd behaviour can generate 'noise trading' in the commodity market with changes in positions which are completely unrelated to market fundamentals. Such pseudo signals (UNCTAD 2011) only relate to the multiple markets where the financial investors operate.

With access to information as well as the underlying interest (commodities and/or financial portfolio) rather different among the participants, with some having a higher order of influence in the market as compared to others as price setters as well as their dominant mode of operation (as physical vs. financial investors), future trading in commodity markets fails to achieve much either in terms of price discovery (that is, future prices charting the path for spots) or in terms of risk transfers to those who are willing to assume risks in trading. Often it is the financial investor who manages these markets, not only by virtue of the large positions they usually are able to command but also by managing portfolios across multiple markets including equities and real estates. The situation often boils down to a typical case where information is either incomplete or unevenly accessible, which Keynes had described as one where 'we do not know'.

What, then, has been the evolving pattern in commodity markets under future trading? Can one relate the price movements in these markets to the hedge instincts of market participants who operate in the physical commodity market or to financial investors engaged in speculative activities, often having little or no link with commodities as physical entities?

Separating the commodities relating to the energy sector (oil in particular), one comes across the vast range of primary goods, and especially the food grains. The spiralling increases as well as the volatility in the food grain prices include aspects which can hardly be oversighted. The price rise has been accompanied by simultaneous expansion of future trading activities in global commodity markets, as can be observed in the rising outstanding value of equity-linked OTC derivatives as well as commodity derivatives (see Figure 11.1). The sudden spurt in the latter has been particularly noticeable during 2007 and 2008, which not only was tagging on to similar increases in equity-linked derivatives but even surpassed the latter. By 2009, there was a drop in the OTC derivatives relating to commodities, which was even more pronounced as compared to those driven by

equities, while since 2008–9 both are moving in the same direction.[5] Data relating to exchange-traded derivatives unfold a similar picture, at least in terms of parallel movements between the equity-linked and commodity-traded amounts.[6] Calculations by the UNCTAD report a pattern with high correlations between commodity and equity price indices over 1986–2011, which reflects the close links between the two markets and the operations of financial investors across markets (Figure 11.2). Prices in the commodity markets have thus been driven more by speculators and less by genuine traders active in the physical transactions of the commodities. *Trading in commodities thus remains*

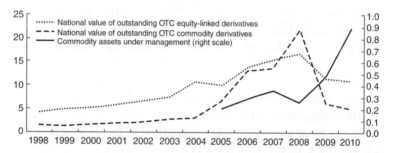

Figure 11.1   Financial Investment in Commodities and Equities as a Share of Global GDP (1998–2010)
Source: UNCTAD secretariat calculations, based on Bank for International Settlements (BIS), *Derivatives Statistics; Barclays Capital, The Commodity Inverstor, and UNCTADstat.*

Figure 11.2   Correlation between Commodity and Equity Indexes (1986–2011)
Source: UNCTAD secretariat calculations, based on Bloomberg.
Note: The data reflect one-year rolling correlations of returns on the respective indexes on a daily basis.

subject to the portfolio adjustments by financial investors for whom information relating to multiple markets turns out as more important than that relating to physical trading of commodities.

With limited or incomplete information, strategies calculated on the basis of estimated probabilities often do not work to the best advantages of the market participants. This brings us back to what we discussed earlier in this chapter on Keynes's notions regarding 'unknowns' in the sphere of probability calculations: the 'herd instincts' as well as 'animal spirits'. With financial markets getting drawn to the realm of commodities and their trading, formulating a package of relevant information becomes all the more difficult. And crisis faced in one market casts spell on the other, with the contagion spreading across markets. Thus, the collapse of the real estate market that led to large-scale financial bankruptcies in 2008 was also matched by sharp fall in commodity prices as well as in outstanding financial investments in commodities. Efforts to hedge and speculate on part of financial investors, which led to Ponzi situations in their balance sheet, had echo in their reduced positions in the commodity market, a situation which is well explained by the theoretical underpinnings of such events in the literature.

THE INDIAN SCENE: RISING FOOD GRAIN PRICES AND THE FUTURE MARKET—A SIMILAR PATTERN OF FINANCIALIZATION IN COMMODITY MARKETS?

We now look at country experiences, focusing on India, providing an instance of the functioning of future commodity markets in developing countries. Official policies in India on commodity future markets have been subject to frequent reversals, with the opening of future trading in specific commodities often followed by their de-listing and vice-versa. However, one can notice a consistent pattern in the official move to keep open these markets since the beginning of the major economic reforms in 1991.

Looking back, in 1996, a joint mission of UNCTAD and World Bank recommended the opening up of futures trading in India's commodity market and a minimization of government controls on such trade. Similar view was shared in the official National Agricultural Policy, announced in 2000. Following the suggestions, Nation-wide Multi-Commodity Exchanges (NMCE) have been set up since 2002,

using modern practices such as electronic trading and clearing, and the government has now allowed national commodity exchanges, similar to the stock exchanges, to come up and let them deal in commodity derivatives in an electronic trading environment. India's Forwards Market Commission (FMC) regulates these exchanges.

Of late, there has been an urgency of deliberating on the rising food prices in India, which have been subject to sharp increases despite the near stationary level of the overall wholesale price index (WPI) during recent years (see Figure 11.3). By 2006 it was reported in the media that future markets in commodities have been subject to speculative activities leading to large and unusual gaps between spot and future market prices.[7] Public concerns on these matters led to the appointment of a committee in 2008 on commodity future markets in the country. Contesting the claim that future trading has been beneficial for managing risks and discovering prices, the committee set limits in providing hedging facilities universally to all in the market, and especially to small traders. A genuine case for future trade, as suggested, should also rest in providing benefits to farmers who produce the traded commodities. However, in a supplementary note, the chairman of the committee drew attention to the rising international commodity prices as a major factor behind the rising spot market prices for agricultural products, thus dispelling the claim that future trade had been a factor behind such price increases (Sen 2008). Also, the statement cannot explain the continuing rise in food prices in India even when international prices start declining, as happened in the post-2008 months when prices in India continued to rise despite a drop in prices in the international market.

A singular aspect of future trading in commodities in India has been the concentration of trading in a few commodities.[8] This also indicates the presence of financiers holding large portfolios in the commodity market. Thus, as pointed out on the website of the Indian Multi Commodity Exchange (MCX) on 13 April 2008, 'MCX has enabled the Indian Corporate Sector, SMEs and MSMEs to hedge against commodity price volatility by providing more than 95% price correlation with global markets.'[9] However, the weight of agricultural commodities has been rather low in the WPI, with the combined weight of 87 agricultural goods in the WPI at less than 50 per cent, a fact which makes the WPI rather unrepresentative of the rising agricultural prices (data available at http://www.eaindustry.nic.in).

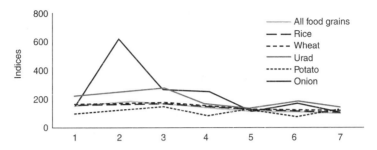

Figure 11.3   Wholesale Price Indices for India (2012–2006)
Source: http://www.eaindustry.nic.in/ (Last accessed on 7 May 2012).
Note: Serial numbers 1 to 7 respectively stand for 2012 to 2006; base year 2004–5.

Accordingly, comparing the all commodity index of the WPI may not reveal much about the impact of rising prices, especially on agricultural goods in general or for those under future trade.

Comparing the price movements for specific food items during 2006–12 to those for the WPI for all food items (Figure 11.4), one witnesses accelerated increases as well as volatility in spot prices of specific items like onion, potato, and urad (lentil), which were all under future trading till recent times. Thus, potato and urad show a much steeper price rise as compared to the all food index.

As pointed out earlier, the downturn in global stock markets since the second half of 2008 was matched by similar downslides in both global equity and commodity prices. However, the downslides were not reflected in the movements in food prices in India. The reasons may include continuing speculation in these items, matched by

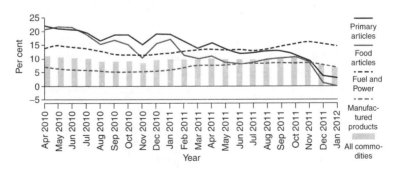

Figure 11.4   Year-on-Year Inflation for Major Groups in WPI
Source: Government of India (2011: 74).

hoarding, much of which may originate from portfolio considerations on part of the financial investors in commodity markets of India. Commenting on the current scenario, concerns have been in the uptrend regarding movements in commodity prices and the role of future trading.[10] This has led to measures which include the imposition of special margins at 10 per cent on all long (sell) contracts by the National Commodity and Derivative Exchange (NCDEX) for chana (chick peas) and mustard from 31 March 2008.[11]

On the whole, future trading in India in agricultural goods, and especially in food items, has resulted in neither price discovery nor reduction of volatility in food prices. Nor are there many effects in terms of farmers fetching higher prices in the market, as pointed out by the *Report of the Expert Committee to Study the Impact of Future Markets on Agricultural Commodity Prices 2008*. With the opening of cross-border trade, commodity prices in India have been guided by the upward movements in prices in international markets, which again are largely driven by financialized future trading. Future markets in India seem to have provided new avenues of speculation to traders as well as financiers, as has happened elsewhere.

* * *

With limited or incomplete information, strategies calculated on the basis of estimated probabilities often do not work to the best advantages of the market participants. This reflects what we pointed out earlier in this chapter on Keynes's notions regarding 'unknowns', the 'herd instincts', as well as 'animal spirits' in the sphere of probability calculations. With financialization getting drawn to the realm of commodities and their trading, formulating a package of *relevant* information on part of market participants remains one of the imponderables. As crises faced in one market spells cast on others, the contagion spreads across markets. A disaster as happened in 2008 with collapse of the real estate market leading to large-scale financial bankruptcies was also matched by sharp fall in commodity prices in global markets as well as in outstanding financial investments in commodities (see Figure 11.2). Efforts to hedge and speculate on part of financial investors, which led to Ponzi situations in their balance sheet in the equity market, had their cohort in their reduced positions in the commodity market, a situation which is well explained by the theoretical underpinnings of such events in the literature.

Concluding, we bring back here the need for regulation, both in the stock market as well as in future markets for commodities, to return some semblance of a coordination between financial and real activities. We also point at the need for state-level interventions, say, by building up a buffer stock in commodities at a national level that can take care of unwanted hikes and volatility in commodity prices.

NOTES

1. As it has been pointed out, 'Youthful Keynes (1921) of *Treatise on probability* still believed in reliable, rational people contemplating the "good" resulting from their actions and the degree they believed that it could occur. For mature Keynes (1931) faced people who are pursuing plethora of ends (good, bad, etc.) and using subjective degrees of belief regarding outcomes' (Bateman and Davis 1991).

2. For details, see Fantacci et al. (2010).

3. See, for excellent documentation and analysis, Fantacci et al. (2012).

4. We do not enter the debate on 'backwardation' of prices (when future prices are set by supplier below current spot price) and contango (when future prices are higher to cover costs of storage, etc.) which Keynes introduced in his writings on commodity future markets. See on this Fantacci et al. (2010). See also UNCTAD (2009: 56–7).

5. Commodity trading via the OTC route dropped from an outstanding amount of $3,101 million (June 2009) to $2,307 million (June 2010), followed by a rise, once again, to $2,585 million by June 2011. A parallel course can be observed in the value of aggregate equity contracts, changing from $6,504 million (June 2009) to $6,260 million (June 2010) and rising again to $6,841 million by June 2011 (http://www.bis.org/statistics/index.htm). This url was last accessed on 21 December 2011.

6. See http://www.bis.org/publ/qtrpdf/r_qa1203_anx23a.pdf. This url was last accessed on 21 December 2011.

7. Futures trading in commodities was expected to deepen the markets and ensure that farmers get better returns. But trends indicate that it has in fact led to speculative activities in the markets which are reflected in the large gap between the spot and futures market prices. According to futures market and the spot market data for the last settlement on National Commodity and Derivatives Exchange, the difference in the prices of nine agricultural commodities ranges between 4 per cent and over 18 per cent. Even the regulator is surprised at the trend—which, incidentally, is not a first time occurrence. 'The difference should be of the order of 1–2%, that's normal, but you can't have a situation where it's 15% or more. Wherever we have asked commodity exchanges to initiate corrective measures, the gap narrows and even vanishes,' said an official (*The Times of India* 2006).

8. As pointed out, in 2008, out of 43 items listed for future trading, 24 had a 98.7 per cent share of the market and 8 captured 84 per cent. Again, of the 21 goods which control 70 per cent of future trading, the weight in the WPI index was only 11.7 per cent (Government of India 2008).

9. See http://www.mcxindia.com/. This url was last accessed on 21 December 2011.

10. Between January and March 2012, mustard seed prices have risen by 101 per cent, chana 108 per cent, potato 170 per cent, mentha oil 172 per cent, soyabean 118 per cent, cardamom 185 per cent, and black pepper 122 per cent on the exchanges. Mustard seed, chana, potato, and soyabean are important contributors to the monthly food inflation index and impact consumer budgets. The FMC last week in February 2012 and in 2011 banned traders from taking fresh positions in the futures contracts of guar seed and guar gum on the National Commodity and Derivative Exchange (NCDEX) platform after speculative activities resulted in prices shooting up 500 per cent and 1,000 per cent, respectively, in the past year. 'Futures trade in seven commodities under government scanner due to 100 per cent price rise in 3 months' (ET Bureau, http://economictimes.com/ 30 March 2012, 01.46 AM IST).

11. 'Money Matters Posted' available at http://www.money-matters.in/Home/ Homepage.aspx Monday, 2 April 2012, 5:14 PM IST.

REFERENCES

Bateman, B.W. and J.B. Davis. 1991. *Keynes and Philosophy: Essays on the Origin of Keynes's Thought*. Aldershot: Edward Elgar.

Davidson, P. 1988. 'A Technical Definition of Uncertainty and the Long-run Non-neutrality of Money', *Cambridge Journal of Economics*, 12(3): 329–37.

———. 1991. 'Is Probability Theory Relevant for Uncertainty? A Post-Keynesian Perspective', *Journal of Economic Perspectives*, 5(1): 129–43.

Fantacci, L., M.C. Marcuzzo, A. Rosselli, and E. Sanfilippo. 2012. 'Speculation and Buffer Stocks: The Legacy of Keynes and Kahn', *European Journal for the History of Economic Thought*, 19(3), pp. 453–73.

Fantacci, Luca, Marcuzzo, Maria Cristina, and Eleonora Sanfilippo. 2010. 'Speculation In Commodities: Keynes' "Practical Acquaintance" With Futures Markets', *Journal of the History of Economic Thought*, 32(3): 397–418, September.

Government of India. 2008. *Report of the Expert Committee to Study the Impact of Future Trading on Agricultural Commodity Prices* (Abhijit Sen Committee Report). New Delhi: Ministry of Consumer Affairs, Food and Public Distribution, Government of India. Available at http://www.fmc.gov.in/docs/ Abhijit%20Sen%20Report.pdf. Last accessed on 7 May 2012.

———. 2011. *Economic Survey 2011–12*. New Delhi: Government of India.

Keynes, J.M. 1921. *Treatise on Probability*. London: Macmillan.

———. 1931. *Essays in Persuasion*. London: Macmillan.

Keynes, J.M. 1936. *The General Theory of Employment, Interest and Money*. London: Macmillan.

———. 1937. 'After the General Theory', *The Quarterly Journal of Economics*, p. 114, reprinted in D.E. Moggridge (ed.), *The Collected Writings of John Maynard Keynes* (CWK), D.E. Moggridge, Vol. XIV. London: Macmillan, pp. 109–23.

Minsky, H.P. 1986. *Stabilizing an Unstable Economy*. New Haven, CT: Yale University Press.

Moore, G.E. 1993 [1903]. *Principia Ethica*. Cambridge, UK: Cambridge University Press.

Pressman, S. 1996. 'What Do Capital Markets Really Do? And What Should We Do about Capital Markets?' *Economies et Sociétés*, 30(2–3), MP 10: 193–209.

Ramsey, F.P. 1931. 'Truth and Probability', in R.B. Braithwaite (ed.), *The Foundations of Mathematics and Other Logical Essays*. London: Routledge and Kegan Paul, pp. 156–98.

Robles M., M. Torero, and J. von Braun. 2009. 'When Speculation Matters', IFPRI Issue Brief 57, February, Washington, DC: International Food Policy Research Institute. Available at http://www.ifpri.org/sites/default/files/publications/ib57.pdf. Last accessed on 7 May 2012.

Sen, Abhijit. 2008. *Report of the Expert Committee to Study the Impact of Future Markets on Agricultural Commodity Prices*. Supplementary note, Chairman Abhijit Sen, ECFM. Available at http://www.fmc.gov.in/docs/Abhijit%20Sen%20Report.pdf

Sen, S. 2003. *Global Finance at Risk: On Real Stagnation and Instability*. London: Palgrave Macmillan.

———. 2011. 'Does the Current Crisis Remind Us of the Great Depression?' in O. Dejuán, E. Febrero, and M.C. Marcuzzo (eds), *The First Great Recession of the 21st Century: Competing Explanations*. Cheltenham, UK and Northampton, MA, USA: Edward Elgar, pp. 101–11.

Sen, Sunanda and Mahua Paul. 2010. 'Trading in India's Commodity Future Markets', ISID Working Paper, February. Available at www.http://isidev.nic.in/home.html

Shackle, G.L. 1974. *Keynesian Kaleidics: The Evolution of General Political Economy*. Edinburgh and Chicago: Edinburgh University Press.

Suppan, S. 2008. 'Commodities Market Speculation: The Rise to Food Security and Agriculture', 13 November, Minneapolis: Institute for Agriculture and Trade Policy. Available at http://www.iatp.org/files/451_2_104414.pdf. Last accessed on 7 May 2012.

The Times of India. 2006. 'Price Gap Widens in Spot, Futures Markets', *The Times of India*, 25 December. Available at http://timesofindia.indiatimes.com/business/india-business/Price-gap-widens-in-spot-futures-markets/articleshow/916142.cms?intenttarget=no#.T33Yu8kAAhw.email. Last accessed on 7 May 2012.

United Nations Conference on Trade and Development (UNCTAD). 2009. *Trade and Development Report 2009*. New York and Geneva: United Nations.

Available at http://unctad.org/en/docs/tdr2009_en.pdf. Last accessed on 7 May 2012.

United Nations Conference on Trade and Development (UNCTAD). 2011. *Trade and Development Report 2011.* New York and Geneva: United Nations. Available at http://unctad.org/en/docs/tdr2011_en.pdf. Last accessed on 7 May 2012.

12

Financial Keynesianism and Market Instability

L. RANDALL WRAY

Minsky liked to call his approach 'financial Keynesian', rather than 'Post Keynesian' because this better reflected his extensions of Keynes's *The General Theory*. All over the globe many are proclaiming the 'return of Keynes', but I think that Minsky would find many of the analyses invoking Keynes's name to be deficient. Yes, economists and policymakers have rediscovered Keynes's argument (Keynes 1936) that economies can be caught up in 'whirlwinds' of euphoric expectations. Thus, they have turned against 'efficient markets' beliefs that asset prices always reflect fundamentals. Many have called for some re-regulation of the financial sector. And most economists and policymakers have become 'Keynesian in the trenches', arguing for fiscal stimulus packages. Minsky would welcome these developments, but he would want more.

Minsky always insisted that there are two essential propositions of his 'financial instability hypothesis'. The first is that there are two financing 'regimes'—one that is consistent with stability and the other that subjects the economy to instability. The second proposition is that 'stability is destabilizing', so that endogenous processes will tend to move even a stable system towards fragility. While Minsky is best-known for his analysis of crises, he argued that the strongest force in a modern capitalist economy operates in the other direction—towards

an unconstrained speculative boom. The current crisis is a natural outcome of these processes—an unsustainable explosion of real estate prices, mortgage debt, and leveraged positions in collateralized securities and derivatives in conjunction with a similarly unsustainable explosion of commodities prices. Add to the mix an overly tight fiscal policy (so that growth required private sector deficits) and the crisis was not hard to see coming (Wray 2003).

Hence, the problem is the rise of what Minsky called money manager capitalism—the modern form of the previous stage of finance capitalism that self-destructed in the Great Depression of the 1930s. He characterized money manger capitalism as one dominated by highly leveraged funds seeking maximum returns in an environment that systematically under-prices risk. With little regulation or supervision of financial institutions, money managers concocted increasingly esoteric and opaque financial instruments that quickly spread around the world. Contrary to economic theory, markets generate perverse incentives for excess risk, pushing managers to take on ever more risk. Those playing along are rewarded with high returns because highly leveraged funding drives up prices for the underlying assets. We are now living with the aftermath as positions are de-levered, driving prices of the underlying collateral (homes, commodities, factories) down—the debt deflation.

Previous to Second World War, debt deflations operated quickly. As Minsky liked to point out, in the Great Depression asset prices fell by 85 per cent. However, in our post-war period, the Big Government (Treasury) and Big Bank (Central Bank) slow the self-reinforcing processes. As the experience of Japan has taught us, a debt deflation process can now unfold over a period of decades, rather than months. On the one hand, this allows us to avoid the worst consequences—in the US the official unemployment rate just barely breached 10 per cent (and has now come down below 8.5 per cent), not a 1930s-like 25 per cent. On the other hand, it can mean that the economy might stumble along for an entire generation. This fuels the belief—now common in the US—that the economy is already on the road to recovery. That, in turn, makes it much harder to undertake the fundamental reforms that are necessary.

Minsky would therefore recommend a more radical approach to dealing with the crisis. Some within the Obama administration have remarked several times that a crisis offers the opportunity for major

change—yet it has not yet taken any such action. I will provide some policy recommendations that I think are consistent with Minsky's policy proposals. Unfortunately, such radical reforms are not likely to be pursued until the financial system collapses again—perhaps a bigger crash than that witnessed in the summer and fall of 2008 will be needed. I do believe that such a scenario is still highly plausible, even with all the growing optimism that we survived the latest 'great crash'. Unlike the case of Japan—which could stumble along for decades, relying on its trading partners to inject needed demand—the US is the world's buyer of last resort. It will not get help from abroad, but rather will drag much of the world down should it crash again. Meanwhile, data from Euroland continues to worsen, and even China is slowing down. High energy prices in late spring 2012 are beginning to do their damage to the US. I do not believe we are out of the woods— collapse of a big euro nation (Italy or Spain) or collapse of a big US bank could still set off renewed crisis. That might lead to real reform.

Minsky (1986) argued that the Great Depression represented a failure of the small-government, laissez-faire economic model, while the New Deal promoted a Big Government/Big Bank highly success- ful model for capitalism. The current crisis just as convincingly rep- resents a failure of the Big Government/Neoconservative (or, outside the US, what is called neo-liberal) model that promotes deregulation, reduced supervision and oversight, privatization, and consolidation of market power. It replaced the New Deal reforms with self-super- vision of markets, with greater reliance on 'personal responsibility' as safety nets were shredded, and with monetary and fiscal policy that is biased against maintenance of full employment and adequate growth to generate rising living standards for most Americans (see Wray 2000, 2005).

Hence, we must use this opportunity to return to a more sensible model, with enhanced oversight of financial institutions and with a financial structure that promotes stability rather than speculation. We need policy that promotes rising wages for the bottom half so that bor- rowing is less necessary to achieve middle class living standards. And policy that promotes employment, rather than transfer payments—or worse, incarceration—for those left behind. Monetary policy must be turned away from using rate hikes to pre-empt inflation and towards a proper role: stabilizing interest rates, direct credit controls to prevent runaway speculation, and supervision. Fiscal policy will need to play a

bigger role in the future, providing a larger share of aggregate demand; only government can operate against the boom and bust trend that is natural for the private sector. This crisis has shown the folly of relying on monetary policy to 'fine-tune' the economy—something we understood quite well in the early post-war period. To be sure, it still could take another financial crisis to generate the conditions needed for real reform.

THE RISE OF MONEY MANAGERS

In the US (and in the developed world, more generally) there has been a long-term transition away from relatively tightly regulated banking towards 'market-based' financial institutions. Two decades ago there was a lot of discussion on the benefits of the 'universal banking' model adopted abroad (Germany, Japan), and there was some movement in the US in that direction. However, of far greater importance was the development of the 'originate to distribute' model best represented by securitization, and use of 'off-balance sheet' operations. Ironically, the push to increase safety and soundness through creation of international standards in the Basel agreements actually encouraged these developments—which, as we now know, greatly increased systemic risk. One of the most important results was the incentive to move assets off bank balance sheets in order to reduce capital requirements. If assets did not need to be counted, leverage ratios could rise tremendously.

Modern securitization of home mortgages began in the early 1980s. While securitization is usually presented as a technological innovation to diversify and spread risk, in reality—as Minsky (2008 [1987]) argued—it was a response to policy initiated by Federal Reserve (Fed) Chairman Volcker in 1979 (see also Kuttner 2007). This was the infamous experiment in monetarism, during which the Fed purportedly targeted money growth to fight inflation—pushing the Fed funds rate above 20 per cent (Wray 1994). If the Fed was willing to raise rates that much, no financial institution could afford to be stuck with long-term fixed rate mortgages. The long-term consequence was the recognition that the mortgage 'market' had to change—with banks and thrifts shifting assets off their books through securitization. Minsky (2008 [1987]) was one of the few commentators who understood the true potential of securitization. In principle,

most bank assets could be packaged into a variety of risk classes, with differential pricing to cover risk. Investors could choose the desired risk–return trade-off. Financial institutions would earn fee income for loan origination, for assessing risk, and for servicing loans. Wall Street banks would place the collateralized debt obligations (CDOs), slicing and dicing to suit the needs of money managers.

Minsky (2008 [1987]) argued that securitization reflected two additional developments. First, it contributed to the globalization of finance, as securitization creates assets freed from national boundaries. As Minsky argued, the post–Second World War depression-free expansion in the developed world (and even in much of the developing world) created a global pool of managed money seeking returns. While there were periodic recessions and financial crises, these were not sufficiently serious to wipe out portfolios through a debt deflation process. Packaged securities were appealing for global investors trying to achieve the desired proportion of assets denominated in the major currencies.

The second development is the relative decline of the importance of banks in favour of 'markets'. (The bank share of US financial assets fell from around 50 per cent in the 1950s to around 25 per cent in the 1990s.) This was encouraged by the experiment in monetarism, but it was also fuelled by continual erosion of the portion of the financial sphere that had been allocated by rules, regulations, and tradition to banks. The growth of competition on both sides of banking business— checkable deposits at non-bank financial institutions that could pay market interest rates; and rise of the commercial paper market that allowed firms to bypass commercial banks—squeezed the profitability of banking. Financial markets can operate with much lower spreads and much higher leverage ratios precisely because they are exempt from required reserve ratios, regulated capital requirements, and much of the costs of relationship banking. Since banks could not beat financial markets at this game, they had to join them. Hence, the constraints imposed by the Glass-Steagall Act were gradually eroded and then removed altogether in 1999.

Figure 12.1 shows the decline of banking and the relative increase of other portions of the financial system up to the crash in 2008. By far the most important change has been the rise of 'managed money' that includes pension funds, sovereign wealth funds, hedge funds, university endowments, mutual funds, and similar pools of managed money.

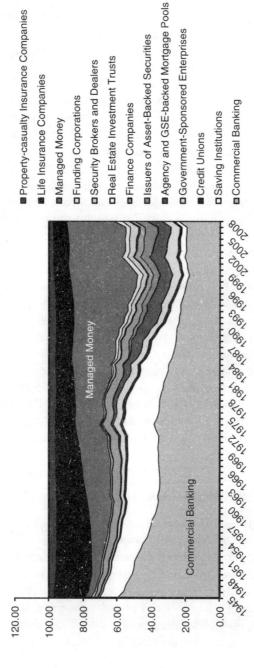

Figure 12.1   Share of Financial Institutions (Per Cent of Total Assets of the Financial Sector)
Source: Federal Reserve Flow-of-Funds Accounts.

The biggest losers were commercial banks and thrifts. To restore profitability, banks and thrifts would earn fee income for loan origination, but by moving the mortgages off their books they could escape reserve and capital requirements. As Minsky (2008 [1987]) argued, investment banks would pay ratings agencies to bless the securities, and hire economists to develop models to demonstrate that interest earnings would more than compensate for risks. They served as credit enhancers, certifying that prospective defaults on subprimes would be little different from those on conventional mortgages—so that the subprime-backed securities could receive the investment-grade rating required by pension funds. Later, other 'credit enhancements' were added, such as buy-back guarantees in the event of capital losses due to unexpectedly high delinquencies and foreclosures—the latter became important when the crisis hit because the risks came right back to banks due to the guarantees. One other credit enhancement played an essential role—insurance on the securities, sold by 'monoline' insurers. More importantly, credit default swaps (CDS) were sold as insurance, most disastrously by American International Group (AIG). This became little more than pure gambling, with institutions like Goldman Sachs packaging junk mortgages into junkier securities, then purchasing CDSs from AIG to bet that the securities would go bad. Goldman then pushed AIG into default by demanding payment on securities that the bank claimed were toxic. As the crisis unfolded, the monoline insurers were downgraded, which automatically led to downgrading of the securities they insured—which then forced CDS sellers to cover losses, forcing them to default—a nice vicious cycle that played to the advantage of Goldman and other investment banks.

PENSION FUNDS AND MANAGED MONEY

Not enough attention has been given to the role played by pension funds in fuelling the asset price boom and subsequent bust. In the immediate post-war period, private pensions held nearly 60 per cent of their assets in treasuries and almost all the rest in corporate and foreign bonds. However, treasuries were sold off and corporate bonds were replaced largely with equities over the course of the 1960s. In recent years, equities plus mutual funds (indirect ownership of equities) amounted for the vast majority of holdings. The total volumes

of pension funds grew rapidly over the post-war period and are now huge relative to the size of the economy (and relative to the size of financial assets). By the time of the dot-com crisis, private pension funds reached about half of US gross domestic product (GDP) while public (state and local government) pension funds were another quarter of GDP. Until the 2008 crisis, they were recovering towards their peak.

The crisis and recent decline of asset values both in absolute terms as well as relative to GDP have been historically large. Private plans lost about $1.79 trillion on their financial assets between 2007 and 2008, with their positions in equities and mutual fund shares losing $1.82 trillion. As a share of GDP, private pensions fell by nearly 14 percentage points between 2007 and 2008. The Millman 100 Pension Funding Index, which tracks the state of the nation's 100 largest defined benefit plans, reported a decline in the funding ratio from 99.6 per cent to 71.7 per cent. Public plans fell by about 9 percentage points of GDP. Individual Retirement Accounts (another form of tax-advantaged retirement savings) have lost another $1.1 trillion, bringing total losses of private retirement funds to about 2.9 trillion dollars (Nersisyan and Wray 2010).

Of course, it is not surprising to learn that pension funds suffer when financial markets crash. It is important to understand, however, that this is a two-way street: pension funds have become so large that they are capable of literally 'moving markets'. As they flow into a new class of assets, the sheer volume of funds under management will tend to cause prices to rise. Pension funds often follow an allocation strategy devoting a designated per cent of funds to a particular asset class. This takes the form of 'follow the leader' as the popularity of investing in a new asset class increases. This pushes up prices, rewarding the decision so that managers further increase the allocation to well-performing classes of assets. This adds fuel to a speculative bubble. Of course, trying to reverse flows—to move out of a class of assets—will cause prices to fall, rapidly as Fisher debt deflation dynamics are initiated.

A good example is the commodities boom and bust during the 2000s (which to some extent reversed into the recent boomlet that might be coming to an end by late spring 2012). As I explained in Wray (2008), the deregulation at the end of the 1990s allowed pension managers to go into commodities for the first time. Previously,

pensions could not buy commodities because these are purely speculative bets. There is no return to holding commodities unless their prices rise—indeed, holding them is costly. However, Goldman Sachs (which created one of the two largest indexes) and others promoted investment in commodities as a hedge, on the argument that commodities prices are uncorrelated with equities. In the aftermath of the dot-com collapse, that was appealing. In truth, when managed money flows into an asset class that had previously been uncorrelated with other assets, that asset will become correlated. For example, an equities boom that causes share prices to appear overvalued can generate a commodities boom as pensions diversify. Hence, by marketing commodities indexes as uncorrelated assets, a commodities bubble ensued that would collapse along with everything else. This is because when one asset class collapses—say, securitized mortgages—holders need to come up with cash and collateral to cover losses, which causes them to sell holdings in other asset classes. This is why silver and cattle became correlated when the Hunt Brothers' attempt to corner the silver market failed, as they had to sell cows to cover losses on silver.

I will not repeat my previous analysis (Wray 2008, which closely followed the work of Michael Masters [Masters and White 2008]—who exposed the role played by 'index speculators' in the commodities price boom), but in brief, most of the position taken was actually in commodities futures indexes as pension funds decided to allocate, say, 5 per cent of assets under management to commodities. However, there is a close link between index prices and spot prices—so the rising futures prices led to appreciating spot prices. While pensions only allocated a small proportion of portfolios to these indexes, this amounted to a huge volume relative to the size of commodities markets. For example, Masters showed that the allocation by pension funds (and other index speculators—with pensions accounting for about 85 per cent of all index speculation) to oil was equivalent to the total growth of Chinese demand for oil for the half decade after 2004. Index and spot prices literally exploded, in what was probably the biggest commodities price bubble ever experienced.

The bubble was also assisted by a policy change: as pension funds poured into commodities and commodity futures, driving up prices of energy, metals, and food, and as energy prices rose, the US Congress mandated biofuels' use—which added to pressures on food prices

that contributed to starvation around the globe. When pensions started to move out in the late summer and fall of 2008, prices collapsed (they moved about a third of their funds out; oil prices fell from about $150 a barrel to $40). Because other asset classes performed poorly through 2009, pensions eventually moved back in, and commodities prices regained some ground (oil prices doubled from the trough—but still barely exceeded half their peak price). While it is too early to tell, it looks like the boomlet may have come to an end—probably not because pensions have moved out yet, but rather because demand for the actual commodities remains sluggish in the face of the global downturn. The point is, however, that pension funds are big enough to destabilize asset prices. If they should turn tail and run out of commodities, prices would again collapse.

More generally, pension funds are part of what Minsky called managed money, and it could be argued that the global financial crisis really resulted from the way that managed money operates as huge flows of money under management have built up over the postwar period. These seek the highest total return, and in some cases (especially hedge funds) use high leverage ratios to increase return. Innovation plus leverage led to exceedingly risky positions in assets that finally collapsed, beginning in the market for securitized subprime loans. Pensions are just one component of managed money, of course, but they are government subsidized and protected: tax advantages are offered for retirement savings, and the government guarantees pensions (through a public corporation—the Pension Benefit Guarantee Corporation—that operates much like Federal Deposit Insurance Corporation [FDIC]—the insurer of bank deposits). In other words, pension funds are in an important sense a creature that owes its existence to government, and that competes with another creature of government, commercial banking. The competition between managed money on the one hand (including pensions) and banking on the other is what helped to produce the current crisis.

What is most important to see is that commercial banking was becoming increasingly irrelevant—as were other traditional lines of business such as thrifts and credit unions. Securitized products (agency and Government Sponsored Enterprise [GSE] pools included) plus managed money had taken over. Just before the current global crisis hit, pension funding was, on average, doing well—thanks to the speculative bubble. The crash caused the current underfunding.

To restore funding levels, pensions need a new bubble. Indeed, pensions are looking into placing bets on death through the so-called life settlements market (securitized life insurance policies that pay-off when people die early) (Auerback and Wray 2010). Ironically, this would be a sort of doubling down on death of retirees—since early death reduces the amount of time that pensions have to be paid, even as it increases pension fund assets.

To conclude, pension funds are so large that they will bubble-up any financial market they are allowed to enter—and what goes up must come down. The problem really is that managed money, taken as a whole, is simply too large to be supported by the nation's ability to produce output and income necessary to provide a foundation for the financial assets and debts that exist even in the aftermath of the financial crisis. Hence, returns cannot be obtained by making loans against production (or even income) but rather can be generated only by 'financialization'—or layering and leveraging existing levels of production and income. This is why the ratio of financial assets and debts grows continually—and why managed money has to continually innovate new kinds of assets in which to speculate.

FINANCIALIZATION AND DEBT

The other side of the asset management coin is the massive growth of private sector debt. The graph presented in Figure 12.2 is instructive, showing growth of debt that is much faster than growth of GDP.

There has been a long-term trend towards growing indebtedness. But what is striking is the very rapid growth of financial sector indebtedness over the past quarter century—from a fifth of GDP to 120 per cent of GDP. This represents a leveraging or layering of financial commitments on top of national income flows. The growth of securitization led to a tremendous increase of leverage ratios—typically at least 15-to-1 and often much greater—with the owners (for example, hedge funds) putting up very little of their own money while issuing potentially volatile commercial paper or other liabilities to fund positions in the securities. The relative economic stability of the post-war period encouraged financial innovations that 'stretched liquidity' in Minsky's terminology; this plus competition spurred financial institutions to increase leverage ratios, increasing credit availability. This is because for given expected losses, higher leverage raises return

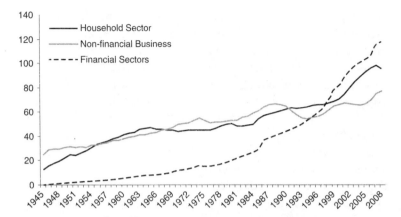

Figure 12.2   Credit Market Debt Outstanding (Per Cent of GDP)
Source: Flow-of-Funds Accounts.

on equity. With easy credit, asset prices could be bid up, and rising prices encouraged yet more innovation and competition to further increase leverage. Innovations expanded loan supply, fuelled home-buying, and drove up the value of real estate, which increased the size of loans required and justified rising leverage ratios (loan-to-value and loan-to-income) since homes could always be refinanced or sold later at higher prices if problems developed. The virtuous cycle ensured that the financial system would move through the structures that Minsky labelled hedge, speculative, and finally Ponzi—which requires asset price appreciation to validate it. Indeed, the virtuous cycle made Ponzi position-taking nearly inevitable. Many or most of the mortgages made in the 2000s were Ponzi from the beginning—incomes were overstated and it was often expected that the homes would be 'flipped' (sold at a profit) or that better financial terms would be negotiated later.

The Ponzi phase would end only if rates rose or prices stopped rising. Of course, both events were inevitable, indeed, were dynamically linked because Fed rate hikes would slow speculation, attenuating rising property values, and increasing risk spreads. When losses on subprimes began to exceed expectations based on historical experience, prices of securities began to fall. Problems spread to other markets, including money market mutual funds and commercial paper markets, and banks became reluctant to lend even for short periods.

With big leverage ratios, money managers faced huge losses greatly exceeding their capital, and began to de-leverage by selling, putting more downward pressure on prices.

As the subprime market unravelled, fears spread to other asset-backed securities, including commercial real estate loans, and to other bond markets such as that for municipal bonds. Markets recognized that there were systemic problems with the credit ratings assigned by the credit ratings agencies. Further, they realized that if mortgage-backed securities, other asset-backed securities, and municipal bonds are riskier than previously believed, then the insurers will have greater than expected losses. Ratings agencies downgraded the credit ratings of the insurers. As the financial position of insurers was questioned, the insurance that guaranteed the assets became worthless—so the ratings on bonds and securities were downgraded. In many cases, investment banks had a piece of this action, holding the worst of the securities, and they had promised to take back mortgages or had positions in the insurers that became insolvent.

Government was able to resolve the liquidity crisis, and propped up financial institutions by taking bad assets and guaranteeing others. Some estimates of total purchases, loans, and guarantees are above $20 trillion.[1] More importantly, government adopted 'forbearance'— allowing insolvent institutions to remain open, just as it did during the 1980s when the entire thrift industry was massively insolvent. As we discovered, during that period, the thrifts 'bet the bank' making extremely risky loans that greatly increased their insolvency, leading to a costly government bail-out. It is almost certain that banks today are making the same gamble. The biggest banks are announcing huge profits and are paying out nearly record bonuses (obviously the two phenomena are linked because if losses were recognized it would be harder to justify the bonuses). However, closer scrutiny shows that banks are not reporting significant profits on lending; rather, it is the trading business that is generating profits. The thrift fiasco showed how easy it is to manufacture fake profits: I sell you my bad assets at an inflated price, and you sell me yours. And since that produces 'market prices' that are high, we can each book higher prices for all the toxic waste assets that we are holding on our books.

Meanwhile, the true values of assets are plummeting because delinquency rates and default rates are exploding across all types of assets: residential real estate, commercial real estate, credit cards, auto loans

and leases, junk bonds (optimistically called high yield), home equity loans, and so on. Even some mainstream economists are beginning to argue that the situation of banks today is actually worse than it was in 2007. If so, another big crash is likely. Even if that does not occur, it is very difficult to see where recovery can come from. The US labour market is not expected to recover for years. Euroland looks poised for another financial crash—this one homegrown as Spain and possibly Italy appear close to default on government debt (following the example of Greece, and the likely upcoming default of Portugal; and as Ireland's crisis seems to have returned). Japan has slipped back into deep recession—and Toyota's problems with recalls will not help. While the 'BRICs' (Brazil, Russia, India, and China) still looked good at the end of 2011, I believe that only China is prepared to deal with the problems that will be created if both the US and Euroland collapse. Still, even Chinese growth has slowed.

FINANCIAL KEYNESIAN POLICIES TO PROMOTE STABILITY

In addition to destroying the 'efficient markets' myth, the global financial crisis also put to rest the belief that central banks can 'fine-tune' the economy. While most central bankers reacted to the crisis by lowering interest rates, there is no evidence that did anything. Japan's long experience with near-zero interest rates should already have disproved the New Monetary Consensus; however, economists always argued that for some reason Japan was a special case from which no lessons could be learned. (See Figure 12.3, which shows that the US followed in Japan's footsteps.) Further, Fed Reserve Chairman, Bernanke convinced markets that he would go further, with 'quantitative easing' (QE) that turned out to be little but a slogan. It never worked—it simply stuffed banks full of excess reserves. Even the NY Fed concluded that the first phase of QE lowered long-term interest rates by perhaps 50 basis points; extrapolating to QE2 the effect would be expected to total less than another 20 basis points. Only 70 basis points of reduction after nearly $2.4 trillion of asset purchases by the Fed. That is impotence on a grand scale.

In truth, interest rate cuts cannot do much, anyway, to restore economic growth, nor to quell financial market unrest. This does not mean that rate cuts are unwarranted, but they will not be effective.

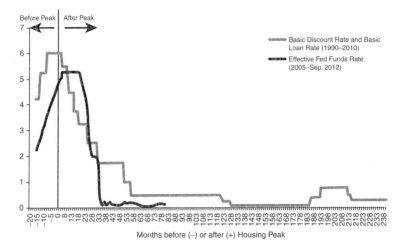

Figure 12.3   US Fed Funds Rate and Japan Overnight Call Rate before and after the Housing Peak
Source: Compiled by the author and Yeva Nersisyan.

And it must be remembered that lower rates mean lower interest income. That will become important as government debt grows relative to GDP. In the case of Japan, I had always argued that raising rates would actually increase the fiscal stimulus, by increasing earnings on government debt. Unfortunately, just as Japan had embarked on an experiment of raising rates, it was hit by the global financial crisis. Following the 'tried but failed' examples it had previously set, it again lowered rates.

While the US fiscal stimulus package (as well as packages adopted in much of the developed world) helped to put a floor on the downturn, it was simply too timid for the task at hand. And while it had some impact, it ran out of steam more than a year ago, and deficit fears as well as populist anger over the bail-out of Wall Street will prevent the president and Congress from enacting another one of significant size if the current weak recovery fails.

How big should it be? That is not the right way to go about answering this question. There is no magic number for government spending, no single deficit-to-GDP ratio that will ensure recovery. Indeed, as Japan's long experience indicates, large budget deficits can occur even with economic stagnation. (See Figure 12.4, which shows that the US

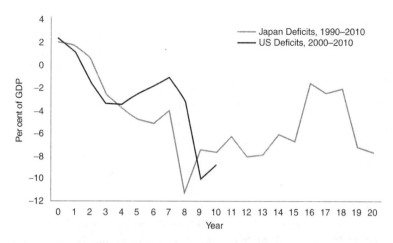

Figure 12.4   Deficit as a Per Cent of GDP: Japan (1990–2010) and US (2000–10)
Source: OECD and Federal Reserve Bank of St. Louis, Federal Reserve Economic Database.

is on track to follow Japan's example.) The reason is that deficits can be created in response to destruction of tax revenue by a recession or by proactive fiscal stimulus policies that will put the economy on a path to recovery. We can call the first of these the 'ugly way'; the second is the right way. Unfortunately, both the Japanese deficits as well as President Obama's deficits have mostly resulted the ugly way. And, unfortunately, politics usually dictates that policy will pursue the ugly strategy. Even during the Great Depression, policy was never stimulative enough to generate recovery; it was Second World War spending that finally turned things around. One can hope that we will not have to wait for either another great depression or another world war before policymakers will pursue deficits the 'right way' through a proactive fiscal stimulus of the appropriate size. We will know it when we see it because jobs will start to be created on a scale that will do some good—something like 300,000 per month on a sustained basis. Obviously, we are not likely to see that anytime soon—even though some weak job growth has returned, it is less than half the rate needed, and we do not yet know that it will be sustained.

I believe that continuing asset price deflation will wipe out several trillion more dollars of wealth in the US alone. House prices will likely continue to fall; some projections now show that half of all mortgages

will be underwater (mortgage greater than value of the house) before the real estate crisis ends. Millions of more households will lose or voluntarily give up their homes. A similar story is still unfolding throughout the consumer credit sector—credit cards, auto loans, student loans. The commercial real estate sector crisis continues to worsen in a serious manner. As should be clear from the earlier analysis, the answer is not just to deal with the asset price deflation, but also to prevent another asset price inflation. Managed money is exploring commodities, death settlements, 'peasant insurance' (firms take out life insurance policies on employees and hope for early death), and the cap-and-trade (in carbon) as possible avenues for speculative bubbles. The latest fad has been for hedge funds to buy up blocks of foreclosed homes at pennies on the dollar—speculating that prices will eventually bottom out—and even the Government Sponsored Enterprises (Fannie and Freddie) are moving into this market, buying homes and renting them back to former owners. Should they manage to produce another bubble, we can be sure that it will collapse sooner rather than later for the simple reason that with employment and income depressed, additional leverage and layering of financial assets on top of already burdened households and firms cannot be supported for long.

We will need debt relief for burdened homeowners and other indebted households. This is not the place for a detailed plan—many have been floated—but any real solution will require some combination of debt write-downs (meaning losses for financial institution owners), negotiation of better terms (rolling Adjustable Rate Mortgages [ARMs] into fixed low-rate mortgages), and government assumption of troubled mortgages and student loans. In addition, I would follow Minsky's proposal made in the wake of the Saving and Laons (S&L) fiasco to create an Reconstruction-Finance Corporation type institution to purchase and hold mortgages until the real estate sector recovers; Roosevelt's Homeowners Loan Corporation provides a model that can be followed. This is the way to support homeownership without bailing out owners of the private financial institutions that created the mess. The current approach—selling off the homes to hedge funds—will only concentrate wealth in the hands of the top few tenths of a per cent of the 'ownership society'.

While reforms have been proposed for Fannie Mae and Freddie Mac, both are saddled with a tremendous amount of bad debt while

they are required to appease markets that are uncertain government really stands behind them. Sallie Mae is in even worse shape. The best course of action would be to completely nationalize them and for the Treasury to explicitly guarantee their debts, to directly fund additional debt, and to increase oversight and supervision of activities to ensure they operate in the public interest. With leverage ratios as high as 65-to-1, the GSEs represent both a risk that more bail-outs will be needed as well as a risk to regulated for-profit financial institutions that are required to operate with lower leverage. Congress needs to rethink the role to be played by the GSEs in the home finance sector. It will be better for them to return to a role of supporting private lenders rather than competing with them.

This leaves us with the biggest policy challenge: what to do about what Minsky called money manager capitalism, characterized by vast accumulations of funds under management by pension funds, insurance funds, and hedge funds (Minsky 2008 [1987]). If a depression and worse debt deflation can be avoided, money managers are certain to create another asset price boom that will renew and extend all of the financial practices that caused the current crisis. Financial markets have a short memory that will allow the risky practices to come back even more virulently, spreading into new areas. The only way to prevent that is to re-regulate and to downsize. Memories will be improved if losses are huge, and if most of those now working in financial markets are never allowed to return to the financial sector.

To be sure, government has no legitimate interest in eliminating all risky practices. There is a place for managed money pursuing the highest returns even at the cost of high probability of catastrophic failure that wipes out private wealth. By the same token, there *is* a public interest in maintaining safety and soundness of at least a portion of the banking, student loan, and home mortgage sectors, as well as of pension and insurance funds. Given implicit and explicit government guarantees behind many of the liabilities of these regulated sectors, there is a justification for close regulation and supervision of activities. Insured banking deposits are explicit Treasury liabilities (FDIC 'insurance' is not sufficient, as we learned when the S&L crisis brought down Federal Saving and Loan Insurance Corporation), and uninsured bank liabilities have been treated as implicit Treasury liabilities in the case of banks considered 'too big to fail' (which today includes the issuers of most of the *volume* of liabilities). Only owner equity

is at risk—and often even that is not really at risk because the 'too big to fail' rescue usually comes down on the side of politics rather than economic considerations. Hence, it is legitimate to prohibit activities considered to be too risky or otherwise against the public interest. In recent years, much of the change made to bank regulations has been based on a flawed view of the proper role of banks—the goal has been to allow banks to become more 'market oriented'. For example, there has been a growing belief that bank assets should be 'marked to market', even on a daily basis. In a boom, this generates exceedingly risky behaviour as the market discounts default probabilities, permitting banks to participate in euphoric speculation that raises market value of risky assets. In a bust, banks see asset prices plummeting and are forced to recognize 'marked to market' losses, and even to sell into declining markets to push prices down further. Such behaviour is precisely the opposite of the behaviour that policy ought to encourage. While we cannot and should not go back to New Deal era practices, thorough reform is needed to make it more difficult for regulated and protected banks and thrifts to participate in the next speculative boom—or to contribute to the next collapse.

Perhaps the most important way banks helped fuel the latest booms was through off-balance-sheet-operations—liabilities that were hidden—including buy-back guarantees and 'special purpose vehicles'. These effectively committed the Treasury (through the FDIC and likely bail-outs as rescues became necessary) to unknown risks even as they allowed protected institutions to evade rules, regulations, and guidelines designed to maintain safety and soundness. There is little justification for such practice—except that it allowed these institutions to earn extra fee income in partial compensation for allowing relatively unregulated Wall Street banks to directly compete with them. Unfortunately, legislators were duped by Alan Greenspan's free market bias into repealing New Deal legislation that separated commercial and investment banking, not recognizing that market segmentation is required if some types of institutions are going to be more closely regulated. It may be too late to go back to such segmentation, in which case the only solution is to impose similar rules and supervision across all types of institutions that are allowed to operate in the same markets. Hence, any institution involved in originating, securitizing, distributing, and holding home mortgages ought to be subject to the same constraints: including

leverage limits and the requirement that *all* liabilities ought to show up on balance sheets.

With respect to commodities markets, price pressures can be relieved by dealing with the source: commodities futures purchases by managed money funds and oligopoly pricing by oil producers. The first is relatively easy to deal with: remove all tax advantages for funds that purchase commodities or indexes of commodities (both physical and 'paper' futures) and prohibit purchases of such assets by funds that benefit from government guarantees (such as the Pension Benefit Guarantee Corporation). In addition, the president could as necessary draw down the Strategic Petroleum Reserve to increase supply in spot markets (something Democrats had tried to force through Congress during the last boom although legislation was voted down by the House). If that is not sufficient to break the oligopolies' pricing, then the president must lean on allies including Saudi Arabia. A promise by the Obama administration that it will stop pursuing a cheap dollar Mercantilist policy would help to convince oil exporters to allow prices to fall, and would encourage other net exporters to stop reallocating portfolios away from the dollar. The US is much too large and much too rich to rely on export-led growth, as it has been trying to do in response to the crisis. In any event, the dollar's slide seems to have reversed, and US export growth has been hurt by the slumping global economy.

Some have argued that the best way to deal with the financial sector is to raise capital ratios—this is supposed to make banks less risky for two reasons: owners have more 'skin in the game' and equity is a cushion to absorb losses. I seriously doubt that higher capital ratios will do any good. There is always an incentive to increase leverage ratios or to increase risk to improve return on equity. Given that banks can finance their positions in earning assets by issuing government-guaranteed liabilities, at a capital ratio of 5 per cent for every $100 they gamble, only $5 are their own and $95 are effectively the government's (in the form of insured deposits). In the worst case, they lose $5 of their own money; but if their gamble wins, they keep all the profit. If subjected only to market forces, profit-seeking behaviour under such conditions would be subject to many, and frequently spectacular, bank failures. The odds are even more in the favour of speculators if government adopts a 'too big to fail' strategy—although exactly how government chooses to rescue institutions will determine

the value of that 'put' to the bank's owners. This is why guarantees without close supervision are bound to create problems—and raising capital ratios to 10 per cent or 20 per cent will not matter much: they are still gambling with $90 or $80 of government money.

Note that while the Basel agreements were supposed to increase capital requirements, the ratios were never high enough to make a real difference, and the institutions were allowed to assess the riskiness of their own assets for the purposes of calculating risk-adjusted capital ratios. If anything, the Basel agreements contributed to the financial fragility that resulted in the global collapse of the financial system. Effective capital requirements would have to be very much higher, and if they are risk-adjusted, the risk assessment must be done at arms-length by neutral parties. If we are not going to closely regulate and supervise financial institutions, capital requirements need to be very high—maybe 50 per cent—to avoid encouraging excessively risky behaviour. We used to have 'double indemnity': owners of banks were personally liable for twice as much as the bank lost. That, plus prison terms for management, would perhaps give the proper incentives. Failing that, the only solution is to carefully constrain bank practices—including types of assets and liabilities allowed.

Given the depressed state of the construction industry, this would be an ideal time for the federal government to rebuild and expand the nation's neglected infrastructure. Increasing such spending would be more stimulative than tax rebates, and would be targeted to a sector that is now suffering, while at the same time increasing America's productive capacity and living standards. As the estimated infrastructure needs amount to more than $2 trillion, this sector alone could generate a large portion of the jobs and consumer demand needed to keep the economy close to full employment for the next decade. A substantial portion of the infrastructure spending could be directed towards public transportation—thereby conserving petroleum use even as the new construction and manufacturing jobs would replace those lost in the automobile sector. The time is ripe for a major restructuring of American transportation.

Much of the planning and spending for public infrastructure needs to be done at the state and local levels, but it must be funded by the federal government—at least some in the form of block grants. This should be undertaken in conjunction with a New Deal–style programme that would provide training, jobs, and decent wages to

anyone willing to work—what Minsky and others call an employer of last resort programme. This is the only way to guarantee full employment without generating a wage and price spiral, and it will provide much of the labour needed to complete the projects. Just as the New Deal jobs programmes left a legacy of public buildings, dams, and trails, fruits of this programme would be enjoyed for decades.

As mentioned earlier, jobs and incomes are critically important. There are plenty of non-profitable, even though crucial, economic activities that require labour (not just the infrastructure programmes discussed earlier, but also social services). The Civilian Conservation Corps (CCC), Works Progress Administration (WPA), and other programmes of the New Deal employed millions of people, creating jobs very rapidly in extremely useful projects. In its first six years, the WPA spent $11 billion, three-quarters of that on construction and conservation projects and the remainder on community service programmes. During that time, WPA employed about 8 million workers. The CCC put approximately 2.75 million unemployed young men to work to reclaim government land and forests through irrigation, soil enrichment, pest control, tree planting, fire prevention, and other conservation projects. Workers earned a dollar a day, and had to send part of their wages home to their families. Through the National Youth Administration (NYA) the government made it possible for 1.5 million high school students and 600,000 college students to continue their education by providing them with part-time jobs to meet their expenses.

In addition to the job losses suffered during this crisis, the US has had a chronic shortage of jobs so that many potential workers (especially males with low educational attainment) have left the labour force. There are also many millions of workers who were forced to work part-time even before the crisis because they could not find a full time job. Currently, the number of people lacking a steady full-time job is about 26 million and this number is rising rapidly—in spite of some apparent improvement to official unemployment rates. Government employment programmes would resolve automatically these kinds of unemployment—providing jobs for those left behind in good economic times, and also for those who lose jobs in a downturn. In an upswing, the private sector would hire workers out of the government programme. This will also further strengthen the automatic stabilizer effect of government intervention since spending on the programme would be countercyclical.

The employment programmes would be permanent programmes rather than just available during a crisis (10–15 million people are left behind even in a boom). In addition, they could pay a living wage tied to productivity gains, which would help to restore the purchasing power of households that has been eroded by 35 years of stagnant real wages. This would put the growth process back on sound financial grounds—with consumption growing as real wages grow (in line with productivity to avoid fuelling inflation).

This is what Minsky recommended and would go some way towards reorienting the economy towards consumption, and towards consumption financed out of wage income. Minsky always argued that a high employment, high wage, high consumption economy is far more stable (Minsky 1986). Not only is greater equality good for the economy, he also argued that it supports democracy and security. Along these lines we will also need to strengthen the Social Security system for retirees so that they will not have to rely on money managers for their pensions.

In conclusion, appropriate fiscal stimulus—oriented towards job creation and restoration of public infrastructure, a rescue plan for homeowners, elimination of cheap dollar/Mercantilist policy, and removal of government-supported managed money from commodities markets—will provide an effective remedy for what ails the US economy. The 'Big Bank' Fed cannot do much more than it has already done; the rest is up to what Minsky called 'Big Government' policy operating in the public interest. The proper role for government has been neglected for too long. Hopefully, the 'hands-off' worship of the 'free markets' era has run its course and sensible policy formation will enjoy a resurgence.

NOTE

1. Work by my graduate students, James Felkerson and Nicola Matthews, shows that the cumulative sum of the Fed's lending and asset purchases reached $29 trillion. See Felkerson (2011).

REFERENCES

Auerback, M. and L.R. Wray. 2010. 'Toward True Health Care Reform: More Care, Less Insurance', Levy Economics Institute Public Policy Brief 110, Annandale-on-Hudson, NY: Levy Economics Institute of Bard College. Available at http://www.levyinstitute.org/pubs/ppb_110.pdf. Last accessed on 27 April 2012.

Felkerson, J.A. 2011. '$29,000,000,000,000: A Detailed Look at the Fed's Bailout by Funding Facility and Recipient', Levy Economics Institute Working Paper 698, Annandale-on-Hudson, NY: Levy Economics Institute of Bard College. Available at http://www.levyinstitute.org/pubs/wp_698.pdf. Last accessed on 27 April 2012.

Keynes, J.M. 1936. *The General Theory of Employment, Interest and Money.* London: Macmillan.

Kuttner, R. 2007. 'The Alarming Parallels between 1929 and 2007. Testimony of Robert Kuttner before the Committee on Financial Services', Rep. Barney Frank, Chairman, Washington, DC: U.S. House of Representatives, available online: http://www.truthout.org/docs_2006/100307H.shtml. Last accessed on 1 September 2009.

Masters, M.W. and A.K. White. 2008. 'The Accidental Hunt Brothers. How Institutional Investors are Driving up Foods and Energy Drivers', Special Report, 31 July. Available at http://www.loe.org/images/content/080919/Act1.pdf. Last accessed on 27 April 2012.

Minsky, H.P. 1986. *Stabilizing an Unstable Economy.* New Haven, CT: Yale University Press.

———. 2008 [1987]. 'Securitization', Levy Economics Policy Note 2008/2, Annandale-on-Hudson, NY: Levy Economics Institute of Bard College.

Nersisyan, Yeva and L. Randall Wray. 2010. 'The Trouble with Pensions' in Toward an Alternative Public Policy to Support Retirement, Public Policy Brief No. 109. Available at http://www.levyinstitute.org/pubs/ppb_109.pdf

Wray, L.R. 1994. 'The Political Economy of the Current US Financial Crisis', *International Papers in Political Economy*, 1(3): 1–51.

———. 2000. 'A New Economic Reality: Penal Keynesianism', *Challenge*, 43(5): 31–59.

———. 2003. 'The Perfect Fiscal Storm', *Challenge*, 46(1): 55–78.

———. 2005. 'The Ownership Society: Social Security Is Only the Beginning', Levy Economics Institute Public Policy Brief 82, Annandale-on-Hudson, NY: Levy Economics Institute of Bard College.

———. 2008. 'The Commodities Market Bubble: Money Manager Capitalism and the Financialization of Commodities', Levy Economics Institute Public Policy Brief 96, Annandale-on-Hudson, NY: Levy Economics Institute of Bard College.

13

Financial Globalization and the Future of the Fed

PERRY MEHRLING

The global financial crisis of 2007–9 provoked an unprecedented response by the Federal Reserve, which stepped in to catch collapsing markets on its own balance sheet—both money and capital markets, both domestic and international markets.[1] Take it as given that the Fed, a fundamentally conservative institution, embraced its new role only reluctantly and as a genuine last resort. Take it further as given that the Fed would prefer now to return as quickly as possible to the status quo ante. The argument of the present essay, however, is that no such return is possible. The world has changed, and the Fed must change with it; that is the main lesson of the crisis.

Before the collapse of Bear Stearns in March 2008, the Fed's principal weapon against the expanding crisis was the Fed Funds target, which it reduced from 5 per cent to 2 per cent. After Bear Stearns, the Fed began lender-of-last-resort operations in earnest, liquidating its holding of Treasury securities and lending the proceeds to banks and broker-dealers. And then, after the collapse of Lehman and American International Group (AIG) in September 2008, the Fed did even more, expanding both sides of its balance sheet at the same time, lending by creating new reserves from thin air. Today, the emergency loans have for the most part run off, but a trillion dollars of mortgage-backed securities have taken their place, and more than a trillion dollars of new reserves remain. The Fed's balance sheet is not back to normal,

and neither is the global financial system so narrowly rescued from collapse.

The title of the present chapter is meant to suggest the historic character of the times we are living in. In practice, Walter Bagehot's famous rule for central banks facing financial crisis—'lend freely but at a high interest rate'—proved insufficient for modern times, and the Fed found itself scrambling for additional weapons. In a previous work I have characterized this scramble as a shift from traditional lender-of-last-resort to 'dealer-of-last-resort', and from domestic lender-of-last-resort to international lender-of-last-resort (Grad et al. 2011). These were innovations in response to crisis, and they worked; what can we learn from them about the role of the Fed going forward?

Everyone now knows the broad outlines of what happened. Over the last 30 years, our familiar bank loan–based credit system was substantially replaced by a capital market–based credit system, some-times called the 'shadow banking system' (Financial Crisis Inquiry Commission [FCIC] 2011). The epicentre of the financial crisis of 2007–9 lay within that new system, which collapsed onto what remained of the traditional banking system, which then subsequently collapsed onto the balance sheet of the Fed and other public entities. Regulatory response to date—for example, Dodd-Frank and Basel III—has focused mainly on shoring up the traditional banking system, and so protecting the public purse from future encroachment. Regulatory treatment of the new shadow banking system was left for later.

But later is now upon us, and the question now confronts us: What is shadow banking, and how should it be regulated? The central thesis of this chapter is that shadow banking is nothing less than the latest institutional form taken by financial globalization, as it has grown up over the last 30 years.[2] It follows that the problem of regulating shadow banking is nothing less than the problem of regulating the global system of funding and risk transfer, as that system continues to evolve in the years to come.

THE THREE FACES OF SHADOW BANKING

Table 13.1 is a stylized picture of how the system worked, when it was working, in just six balance sheets. I give an abstract label to each of the balance sheets, rather than identifying them with specific financial

Table 13.1   Shadow Banking as (Jimmy Stewart) Banking

Securitization Trust		Investment Bank		Insurance Company	
Assets	Liabilities	Assets	Liabilities	Assets	Liabilities
RMBS	Hi tranche Mid tranche Lo tranche	Loans			Hi CDS

Shadow Bank		Pension Fund		Hedge Fund	
Assets	Liabilities	Assets	Liabilities	Assets	Liabilities
Hi tranche Hi CDS Liquidity Put	MM funding	Mid tranche	Pension liabilities	Lo tranche	Loans Capital

Notes: RMBS: Residential Mortgage Backed Securities; CDS: Credit Default Swap; and MM: Money Market.

firms, because often financial firms were involved in more than one of the pictured activities. I also leave out a lot of detail in order to emphasize that shadow banking must be understood as a system, not as the activity of any particular entity.[3]

In Table 13.1, the entity that I label as 'Shadow Bank' is so called because it most closely resembles the Jimmy Stewart bank that still serves as the analytical starting point for most of us. The Jimmy Stewart bank issued deposits and used the proceeds to fund mortgage loans. The Shadow Bank issued money market instruments and used the proceeds to fund mortgage-backed securities.

The analogy can be extended. Depositors in the Jimmy Stewart bank were protected from possible bank insolvency by a deposit insurance scheme (the FDIC) and from possible bank illiquidity by a lender of last resort facility (the Fed). Creditors of the Shadow Bank were protected similarly by a private asset insurance scheme—credit default swaps—and a private liquidity put to the traditional banking system.[4] But these were supposed to be ultimate backstops only. Just as the Jimmy Stewart bank held capital and liquidity buffers that kicked in before the government backstop, so too did the Shadow Bank. These buffers are what are most important to understand because they are what failed.

Unlike the case of Jimmy Stewart banking, the capital buffer of the Shadow Bank was not on its own balance sheet but rather in the rest of the system. Losses on the underlying mortgages were supposed to hit first the Lo Tranche, which I show as an asset held by a Hedge Fund.[5] Second losses would hit the Mid Tranche, which I show as an asset held by a Pension Fund. The capital of these two Funds was therefore in effect the capital buffer of the Shadow Bank. Only very severe losses would hit the Hi Tranche, and the credit default swap backstop was there to cover this presumably improbable event.

The liquidity buffer of the Shadow Bank was also in the rest of the system. By construction, the Hi Tranche assets of the Shadow Bank were collateral for short-term money market borrowing, such as term funding using Asset Backed Commercial Paper, which might, for example, be sold to an institutional Money Market Mutual Fund (MMMF). If that buffer dried up, there was always the general repo market where good collateral could be used to raise funding at shorter term. The liquidity buffer of the Shadow Bank was thus on the balance sheet of the MMMF and the repo dealer, not the Shadow Bank itself. Only very severe liquidity crunches would impair Shadow Bank liquidity, and to cover that presumably improbable event there was the liquidity put to the traditional banking system.[6]

From a Jimmy Stewart point of view, shadow banking thus looks like a way of doing more or less exactly what traditional banking does, but with more steps, less regulation, and no (direct) government backstop. For critics of shadow banking, it looks like a case of socially inefficient technology gaining a toehold because regulatory evasion makes it privately profitable. For enthusiasts, by contrast, it looks like a case of demonstrably superior technology gaining a toehold by finding ingenious ways to overcome inefficient and outmoded regulatory strictures. Instead of taking a position one way or the other in this ideologically fraught regulatory debate, I simply note the standoff and move on, because there are two other possible entry points for analysis, that have not been adequately explored in the literature, each of which casts the system in a somewhat different light.

The second way to understand the shadow banking system is as a mechanism to tap *global* dollar funding markets for *domestic* mortgage lending. Put simply, shadow banking can be understood as nothing more than an adaptation of existing mechanisms of global cross-border banking to the funding needs of dollar borrowers inside

the US. Dollar funding markets have long been the go-to source for those, such as the East Asian Tigers, looking to catch up, albeit at the risk of currency mismatch (Shin and Shin 2011). Shadow banking was just cross-border banking without the currency risk.[7]

On the supply of funds side, burgeoning demand for dollar deposits at global banks drove the search for new lending outlets. On the demand for funds side, promotion of mortgage borrowing had long been a staple of US government policy, and shadow banking was merely the next step. Well before the advent of shadow banking, Fannie Mae had introduced and promoted mortgage securitization as a way to reduce reliance on volatile bank lending by tapping deep capital markets for mortgage funding.[8] Shadow banking merely went one step further, tapping the global *money* market as well as the global *capital* market. Private label mortgage-backed securities could never hope to be as liquid as those supported by the market-making power of Fannie and Freddie. But by funding these illiquid securities in global money markets, their promoters were able to capture a liquidity premium as private profit.

From this perspective, the Jimmy Stewart frame of the regulatory debate seems largely beside the point. The point is not whether the regulation that shadow banking was escaping was good or bad; in a sense, shadow banking was not escaping anything, just tapping a new source of funds. Regulatory reform is presumably not going to shut down global dollar funding markets; it follows that it is not going to shut down shadow banking either.

This global perspective on shadow banking is, not incidentally, crucial for understanding the global character of the crisis. Why did incipient default on subprime mortgages, a relatively small fraction of the stock of outstanding mortgage debt, almost bring the whole system down? The Jimmy Stewart analogy does not help us to understand this at all; indeed that is why most economists missed the crisis. But when we understand that this small sub-set of outstanding mortgage debt was funded in global money markets, unlike most of the rest of mortgage debt, we see the channel for transmission to global cross-border banking, and to all of the other credits that cross-border banking supports. The crisis was global because the funding was global.

From this perspective, the story of shadow banking looks like a version of our familiar experience with global credit boom and bust,

which more usually involves the periphery of the global system rather than peripheral borrowers within the centre of the system. Notably, in response to the crisis, the International Monetary Fund (IMF) created its new Flexible Credit Line as a way of protecting its members from the consequences of global funding market disruption.[9] This time around, however, the disruption came from the centre, and that is why the Fed was pressed into service as international lender of last resort, both directly (Term Auction Facility) and indirectly (liquidity swaps), to the global cross-border banking system.

But even this second frame is too narrow, because it takes the funding source as given. The deeper question is why there was so much available funding. The literature focuses on several possible reasons: excess saving by China, dollar reserve accumulation in the aftermath of the Asian Financial Crisis, and expansionary US monetary policy. Probably each of these played some role in pumping up the global credit bubble, but for present purposes I would like to focus on a source that has received much less attention.

The third way to understand the shadow banking system is as the natural counterpart of the emerging system of global portfolio management, in effect a consequence of the revolution in modern finance.[10] In traditional asset management, if you want exposure to a certain risk class, then you buy risky assets that give you that exposure. In modern asset management, the same exposure can be (and in practice increasingly is) achieved by using derivatives of one kind or another, combined with holding a risk-free cash asset. This is a source of demand for cash assets that is simply not present in traditional asset management, much less in traditional monetary theory which focuses on transactions and precautionary demand. Shadow banking can be viewed as a new supply of cash assets, outside the existing deposit banking framework, which arose to meet that new demand for money.

In this regard, Table 13.2 is a stylized picture not so much of what shadow banking actually looked like, but rather of what it might look like in the future. Instead of all the complicated tranching of the actual shadow banking system, which served to strip risk out of the underlying mortgage loans, I am imagining a version of shadow banking in which all the risk-stripping is done using simple derivatives, in fact using the very same derivatives that the Asset Manager is using to achieve his desired risk exposure. The Shadow Bank is

Table 13.2 Shadow Banking as Financial Globalization

Shadow Bank		Global Funding		Asset Manager		Derivative Dealer	
Assets	Liabilities	Assets	Liabilities	Assets	Liabilities	Assets	Liabilities
RMBS	MM funding	MM funding	'deposits'	'deposits'	Client capital	CDS	CDS
CDS		Liquidity put			CDS	IRS	IRS
IRS					IRS	Liquidity put	

Notes: RMBS: Residential Mortgage Backed Securities; CDS: Credit Default Swap; IRS: Interest Rate Swap; and MM: Money Market.

thus the mirror image of the Asset Manager not only in terms of funding but also in terms of risk. Shadow Bank liabilities match Asset Manager assets, and Asset Manager liabilities (derivatives) match Shadow Bank assets.

From this point of view, two kinds of financial intermediary look to be crucial to the operation of the system (Mehrling 2012). First is global cross-border banking that takes care of the funding transfer; we have already discussed this dimension earlier as the second face of shadow banking. Second, and this dimension is new, is the derivative dealer that takes care of the risk transfer by intermediating between the Shadow Bank and the Asset Manager, serving as the derivative counterparty for both. Note that, for simplicity, I abstract from the position-taking of dealers, and show the balance sheet of the derivative dealer as so-called 'matched book'. Each short position (contingent liability) is matched with an equal and opposite long position (contingent asset).[11]

This way of thinking about the shadow banking system provides yet another perspective on the crisis. The actual shadow banking system, as pictured in Table 13.1, is clearly a lot more complicated than the idealized version in Table 13.2. From this point of view, we can understand the financial crisis as nothing more than the growing pains of an emerging adult shadow banking system. The problem was that the new shadow banking system had to grow on the foundation of what was already there. The fund transfer side of the system was very much ready but the risk transfer side was not, and is not.

In Table 13.1, the predominant mechanism for risk transfer is tranching; financial derivatives such as CDS enter only as the ultimate capital buffer once the first lines of defence (the Lo and Mid tranches) have been breached.[12] In Table 13.2, by contrast, tranching is gone, and derivatives are the predominant mechanism for risk transfer. Similarly, in Table 13.1, the predominant mechanism for liquidity backstop is reliance on MMMF and repo dealers (not shown) and an explicit liquidity put enters only as a last resort. In Table 13.2, by contrast, explicit liquidity puts are the predominant mechanism for liquidity backstop, both for the global funding system (funding liquidity) and for the derivative dealers (market liquidity).[13] My argument, in a nutshell, is that the financial crisis needs to be understood as part of a longer term evolution that is moving us in the direction of Table 13.2.[14]

THE FINANCIAL CRISIS AND FINANCIAL GLOBALIZATION

Take it as given that there was an excess supply of funds seeking risk-free deposit-like but deposit-alternative assets, and that the shadow banking system developed as an attempt to provide the assets those funds were seeking. The point to emphasize is that there was plenty of demand for the liabilities of the shadow banks but that, given the existing institutional organization of the system, *those liabilities were a joint product, and there was not necessarily plenty of demand for the other products.* Specifically, the literature is clear that placement of the Lo Tranche was a persistent bottleneck.

Table 13.1 shows the Lo Tranche being happily held by a credit hedge fund, which is funded by risk-loving client capital and an accommodating prime broker. Maybe that is the way the system started, but the demand for product quite soon overwhelmed the risk-bearing capacity of even the most risk-loving part of our financial system. The world wanted risk-free deposit alternatives, and there was a lot of money to be made by providing them, so hedge funds had to be persuaded to do their part. The way they were persuaded was by providing a way for them to hedge. The technology of credit default swaps, originally developed for hedging tail risk, was adapted for this additional purpose.

Table 13.3 shows one way that hedge funds were persuaded to play their assigned role.[15] It shows them holding the Lo Tranche but

hedging the risk by buying insurance on the Mid Tranche. And it also shows them buying that insurance from an investment bank which hedges its own exposure by buying insurance on the Hi Tranche.[16] In effect, the investment bank is acting as a derivative dealer, looking to achieve matched book notwithstanding the difference between assets and liabilities. The reason this works is that the fortunes of all three tranches depend ultimately on the performance of the same underlying mortgage assets, which means they are correlated. Correlation means you can use CDS on a higher tranche to hedge exposure to a lower tranche; the only hitch is that you have to get the hedge ratio right.

The crucial point is that such a hedge typically requires you (the investment bank) to buy insurance on a larger nominal quantity of the Hi Tranche asset than the nominal quantity of Mid Tranche assets you have insured. (A perfect hedge thus can easily appear, to an outsider who merely compares nominal exposure, as a directional bet.) In this way, the bottleneck in the placement of Lo Tranche gets transformed into a bottleneck in placement of Hi CDS, which was relieved by AIG (and other insurers).[17] Because of AIG, the key bottleneck for the expansion of the system was overcome for a while, but only for a while. When AIG pulled back, the days of remaining expansion were numbered.

But there was still money to be made, however, so the system did not immediately halt in its tracks. One temptation was simply to abandon the effort to achieve matched book, which was easy enough

Table 13.3 Risk Transfer Development, Stage One

Securitization Trust		Investment Bank		Insurance Company	
Assets	**Liabilities**	**Assets**	**Liabilities**	**Assets**	**Liabilities**
RMBS	Hi tranche	Loans			Hi CDS (SB)
	Mid tranche	Hi CDS	Mid CDS		Hi CDS (IB)
	Lo tranche				

Shadow Bank		Pension Fund		Hedge Fund	
Assets	**Liabilities**	**Assets**	**Liabilities**	**Assets**	**Liabilities**
Hi tranche	MM funding	Mid tranche	Pension	Lo tranche	Loans
Hi CDS			liabilities	Mid CDS	Capital
Liquidity Put					

to do since no one really knew what hedge ratio was necessary to provide a perfect hedge. Bullish investment banks were free to choose a low hedge ratio, while bearish investment banks were free to choose a high hedge ratio. If the bulls were right, they would make more money; if the bears were right, they would live to fight another day. One way to understand the crisis is that Bear Stearns and Lehman Brothers were bulls, while Goldman Sachs was a bear. But the bears could make money too, even after AIG pulled back, if only they could figure out a different way to hedge. Table 13.4 shows a stylized example of how this was done, using a synthetic Collateralized Debt Obligation (CDO).[18]

A synthetic CDO acquires risk exposure not by acquiring risky assets but rather by writing insurance on risky assets (shown here as a contingent liability) and then packaging that insurance with a portfolio of risk-free assets and selling the package in tranches. In this way, although the CDO writes the CDS, the ultimate risk exposure is passed through to the holder of the securities issued by the CDO. In Table 13.4, the Shadow Bank, now shown as an unhedged holder of the Hi Tranche, is bearing the risk that the Insurance Company was no longer willing to underwrite.

All of this explains why when the crisis came, the largest losses hit the issuers of the Hi CDS (AIG), the derivative dealers who got their hedge ratios wrong (Bear Stearns, Lehman), plus the shadow banks and those who wrote liquidity puts to them (UBS, Citibank). All of

Table 13.4 Risk Transfer Development, Stage Two

Synthetic CDO		Investment Bank		Insurance Company	
Assets	Liabilities	Assets	Liabilities	Assets	Liabilities
MM funding	Hi tranche Mid tranche Lo tranche Mid CDS	Loans			

Shadow Bank		Pension Fund		Hedge Fund	
Assets	Liabilities	Assets	Liabilities	Assets	Liabilities
Hi tranche Liquidity Put	MM funding	Mid tranche	Pension liabilities	Lo tranche Mid CDS	Loans Capital

these players mistakenly thought they were taking very little risk, and for a while the market thought so too, which allowed them to finance their positions in the global money market. When the reality of their risk exposure became clear, funding dried up and the resulting liquidity crunch caused a global financial crisis. Subsequently, the way the crisis played out was a consequence of the various backstops that the shadow banking system had in place directly within the traditional financial system, and indirectly with the government (Krieger 2011).

THE PAST AND FUTURE OF THE FED

On 23 September 2008, shortly after the failure of Lehman and AIG, I published a letter in the *Financial Times* urging the Treasury to step in as 'market maker of last resort in the index credit default swaps on the ABX'. (The Asset Backed Securities Index is a basket of mortgage-backed securities.) Given that the AIG anchor for the system was now gone, my idea was simply to have the government step in to provide that anchor instead. For pragmatic reasons, I urged this policy on the Treasury, not the Fed, but the issue in my mind was not so much solvency as it was liquidity; like most people, I was at the time blissfully unaware of the dubious quality of the underlying assets (i.e., the upward distortion of some prices), and hence mainly concerned to halt an incipient downward liquidity spiral.

My favoured policy was not adopted, although the subsequent Troubled Asset Relief Program (TARP) legislation provided explicit authorization for it (Section 102). Instead, the main actor was the Fed, which dramatically expanded its balance sheet on both sides, in effect substituting the impaired balance sheets of private money dealers, so putting a floor on the collapsing global money market. And then, starting in March 2009 as the emergency had begun to subside and funds were being repaid, the Fed entered as a bidder for mortgage-backed securities directly, in an operation that came to be called QE1 (for quantitative easing). Finally, as those mortgage-backed securities began to run off, the Fed entered again as bidder, this time for Treasury securities (QE2).

The Fed's balance sheet, as of July 2011, is shown in Table 13.5(a). Compare it with the balance sheet of July 2007, shown in Table 13.5(b).

Once upon a time, before the crisis hit, the Fed basically provided funding to the Treasury, by borrowing essentially at zero and lending

Table 13.5(a)   Federal Reserve (6 July 2011), in $ Trillion

Assets		Liabilities	
Treasury securities	1.6	1.0	Currency
Mortgage securities	1.0	1.6	Reserves
Other	0.2	0.2	Other
TOTAL	2.8		

Table 13.5(b)   Federal Reserve (4 July 2007), in $ Trillion

Assets		Liabilities	
Treasury securities	0.79	0.82	Currency
		0.01	Reserves
Other	0.12	0.08	Other
TOTAL	0.91		

Source: Federal Reserve Statistical Release H.4.1, 'Factors Affecting Reserve Balances', and author calculations.

at the Treasury rate (largely short-term bills and note). Today, in the aftermath of the crisis, the Fed's balance sheet is about three times bigger, and its composition is also very different. There is an entirely new category of mortgage securities (MBS plus Government Sponsored Enterprises [GSE] debt), and the Treasury securities are now almost all long-term. How should we understand this dramatic change?

Just as modern portfolio management allows asset managers to achieve risk exposures using derivatives, we could imagine the Fed doing the same. To see how the Fed could achieve the very same risk exposures using swaps, add short-term T-bills and long-term T-bonds to both sides of the balance sheet, and rearrange as shown in Table 13.6.

Table 13.6 Federal Reserve (6 July 2011), in $ Trillion, Restated

Assets		Liabilities	
Treasury bills	2.6	2.6	Currency/Reserves
Treasury bonds	2.6	2.6	Treasury Bills
Risky securities	1.0	1.0	Treasury bonds
Other	0.2	0.2	Other

Source: Federal Reserve Statistical Release H.4.1, 'Factors Affecting Reserve Balances', and author calculations.

Table 13.7   Federal Reserve (6 July 2011), in $ Trillion, Restated

Assets	Liabilities	
	2.6	notional liquidity put (global funding)
	3.6	notional liquidity put (derivative dealers)
Other 0.2	0.2	Other

Source: Federal Reserve Statistical Release H.4.1, 'Factors Affecting Reserve Balances', and author calculations.

Three fundamental risk exposures can be distinguished. The first line is a kind of overnight index swap, in which the Fed receives the three month T-bill rate and pays the overnight money rate. There is nothing new about that exposure; only the magnitude has changed since three years ago. The second line is a kind of interest rate swap, in which the Fed receives the long rate and pays the short rate. And the third line is a kind of credit default swap, with the Fed receiving the risky rate and paying the risk-free rate. The second and third lines are essentially new, and they are big.[19]

The point to emphasize here is the way the Fed's balance sheet has already begun to look like what we would expect if it were acting as liquidity backstop to the system of the future that we sketched in Table 13.2. In Table 13.2, the global funding system and the global derivative dealer system both are depicted as requiring some kind of liquidity put, but we did not specify who was on the other side of that put. Comparing the Fed's actual balance sheet with the idealized system of Table 13.2, it seems clear that in practice the Fed was on the other side of that put. On the one hand, it has provided backstop *funding liquidity* for the system, just as it did before the crisis (though now with triple the outstanding position). On the other hand, it has provided backstop *market liquidity* for the system by taking onto its own balance sheet risk exposures that the market was not willing to hold at prices that the Fed found acceptable. Table 13.7 makes this implicit backstop explicit by restating the risk exposures on the Fed's balance sheet as explicit derivative liabilities.

* * *

From a prudential standpoint, both microprudential and macroprudential, the task that lies before us is the constitution of a global funding and derivative dealer system that puts in place the liquidity and capital buffers for the market-based credit system. *These are*

not details to be added once we figure out what to do with traditional banks; the global funding banks and derivative dealers are the central financial intermediaries of our time, and must be the central concern of policy.

The technical challenge of constructing the new system is formidable, but as we confront that challenge it is important to appreciate that the political economic challenge is even more formidable. Simply put, the political economic equilibrium, established a century ago at the founding of the Fed, is no longer sustainable.

Three different bogeymen haunted the founders of the Fed: Big Government (Washington), Big Finance (Wall Street), and the Big World (foreign markets and nations). Against the first two, the founders' design relied on the language of the Real Bills Doctrine to ensure that credit would be directed preferentially to productive uses not speculation, and to private sector uses not government. As for the third, they did not explicitly rule out international lender-of-last-resort, but only because it never occurred to them to do so. They were operating in the context of an international gold standard and with no experience of central banking, and hence with no experience of the long tradition of central bank cooperation.

However, as soon as the system was born, it began to change and evolve in response to changing circumstances and challenges. World War, both I and II, was the biggest such challenge, and the consequence was a certain modus vivendi between the central bank and government, which is to say between the Fed and the Treasury. During wartime, the Fed acted as dealer-of-last-resort for the Treasury, insuring that the Treasury could always sell as many bonds as it needed by the simple stratagem of buying any that were left over. And then after the war the Fed maintained orderly markets in Treasury debt, so ensuring a privileged market position for that debt, and used the Treasury market to conduct its stabilization interventions. In this way, as the American people came to accept Big Government, so too did they come to accept their central bank as, in part, a government bank with legitimate responsibilities for government finance.

But the American people have yet to come to terms with Big Finance, much less with the Big World, both of which are at the very centre of the problem facing us today. During the crisis, the Fed used mechanisms of wartime *government* finance to support *private* banks and private markets, and not just domestic banks and markets but also *international* banks and markets. The Fed-Treasury Accord of

1951 marked a new comfort with the emerging relationship between the central bank and Big Government. The analogous Accords for Big Finance and the Big World are, as of yet, nowhere in sight.

NOTES

1. Although my own account of the crisis focuses on the Fed (Mehrling 2011), a rounded understanding of government response requires at a minimum also understanding the roles of the Treasury (Swagel 2009), the Federal Home Loan Bank (Ferguson and Johnson 2009), the Congress (Financial Crisis Inquiry Commission [FCIC] 2011; SIGTARP 2009), and even the global dollar funding system (McGuire and von Peter 2009). In academic circles, Brunnermeier (2009), Gorton (2010), and Krishnamurthy (2010) have become standard accounts. See also the invaluable 'Federal Reserve Policy Responses to the Financial Crisis', published as a special issue of the Federal Reserve Bank of New York's *Economic Policy Review*, May 2011.

2. To my knowledge, Minsky (2008 [1987]) was the first to suggest this connection as a link between securitization and globalization, but he lacked the background in finance to develop the point further.

3. For a more detailed account, see Pozsar et al. (2010).

4. Observe that I treat derivative contracts as (contingent) assets of the insured and (contingent) liabilities of the insurer.

5. Charles Morris (2008) famously emphasized the exposure of these hedge funds as the potential breaking point of the system as a whole, on account of their leverage; he was certainly prescient about the fragility of the system, but off target about how the system would break.

6. To avoid proliferation of balance sheets, Figure 13.1 does not show explicitly the Shadow Bank's source of funding (MMMF), or the issuer of the liquidity put (the traditional banking system).

7. The famous Union Bank of Switzerland Shareholder Report (2008) tells the tale of one such global Shadow Bank. Bank for International Settlements (2010) tells the tale of the disruption of the global funding system more generally.

8. Mortgage-backed securities were inherently less liquid than government and corporate bonds, which competed for investor funds. So Fannie and Freddie used their borrowing power, as Government Sponsored Entities, to make markets, backstopped by the Fed. This system broke down in the crisis. The Treasury took Fannie and Freddie into conservatorship, while the Fed took a trillion dollars of MBS onto its own balance sheet. Scharfstein and Sunderam (2011) survey the current state of play regarding reform of the GSEs.

9. See www.imf.org/external/np/exr/facts/fcl.htm. This url was last accessed on 29 October 2012.

10. Pozsar (2011) emphasizes the empirical importance of cash pools looking for the kind of cash assets produced by the shadow banking system. In what

follows, I focus on one particular, but rather generic, source of such demand. See also Caballero (2006).

11. For invaluable detail on the plumbing, see Singh and Aitken (2010) and Singh (2011).

12. Tett (2009) tells the story of the first CDS, used by J. P. Morgan originally to insure the tail risk for a portfolio of corporate loans.

13. The distinction between funding liquidity and market liquidity builds on Brunnermeier and Pedersen (2009).

14. What follows is essentially a further development of the contemporaneous account in Mehrling (2010). Gorton (2010) has a different story about CDS which emphasizes the role of the ABX index in pooling information that was formerly widely distributed, hence making public what had previously been private. In his telling of the story, this institutional innovation revealed the mispricing of the underlying mortgages.

15. My inspiration for this account is the story of Magnetar, told in Yves Smith (2010).

16. I remind you that my balance sheet headings are meant to be conceptual only. It often happened that an investment bank held the Lo Tranche itself in order to get the deal done, essentially a consolidation of the Investment Bank and Hedge Fund balance sheets.

17. My treatment of AIG is inspired by the account of SIGTARP (2009).

18. My inspiration for this account is the story of Abacus, laid out in the Securities Exchange Commission complaint (SEC 2010).

19. It should be pointed out that these numbers are low-end estimates of overall government exposure. Most of the implicit credit default exposure is on the balance sheet of the Treasury, not the Fed, as a consequence of its backstop of Fannie and Freddie.

REFERENCES

Bank for International Settlements (BIS). 2010. 'The Functioning and Resilience of Cross-Border Funding Markets', CFGS Paper 37, March. Committee on the Global Financial System, Basel.

Brunnermeier, M. 2009. 'Deciphering the Liquidity and Credit Crunch, 2007–2008', *Journal of Economic Perspectives*, 23(1): 77–100.

Brunnermeier, M. and L.H. Pedersen. 2009. 'Market Liquidity and Funding Liquidity', *Review of Financial Studies*, 22(6): 2201–33.

Caballero, R.J. 2006. 'On the Macroeconomics of Asset Shortages', in A. Beyer and L. Reichlin (eds), *The Role of Money: Money and Monetary Policy in the Twenty-First Century*. Frankfurt, Germany: European Central Bank, pp. 272–83.

Financial Crisis Inquiry Commission (FCIC). 2011. *The Financial Crisis Inquiry Report*, January. Washington, DC: Government Printing Office.

Federal Reserve Bank of New York. 2011. 'Federal Reserve Policy Responses to the Financial Crisis', *Economic Policy Review*, 17(1), special issue, May.

Ferguson, T. and R. Johnson. 2009. 'Too Big to Bail: The "Paulson Put", Presidential Politics, and the Global Financial Meltdown', Part I: 'From Shadow Banking System to Shadow Bailout', *International Journal of Political Economy*, 38(1): 3–34, and Part II: 'Fatal Reversal—Single Payer and Back', *International Journal of Political Economy*, 38(2): 5–45.

Gorton, G.B. 2010. *Slapped by the Invisible Hand: The Panic of 2007*, Financial Management Association Survey and Synthesis. New York: Oxford University Press.

Grad, D., P.G. Mehrling, and D. Neilson. 2011. 'The Evolution of Last-Resort Operations in the Global Credit Crisis', mimeo, 18 March.

Krieger, S.C. 2011. 'Reducing the Systemic Risk in Shadow Maturity Transformation', 8 March, Remarks at Global Association of Risk Professionals, New York City.

Krishnamurthy, A. 2010. 'How Debt Markets have Malfunctioned in the Crisis', *Journal of Economic Perspectives*, 24(1): 3–28.

McGuire, P. and G. von Peter. 2009. 'The U.S. Dollar Shortage in Global Banking', BIS *Quarterly Review*, March: 47–63.

Mehrling, P. 2010. 'Credit Default Swaps: The Key to Financial Reform', in S. Griffith-Jones, J.A. Ocampo, and J.E. Stiglitz (eds), *Time for a Visible Hand: Lessons from the 2008 Financial Crisis*. Oxford and New York: Oxford University Press, pp. 185–99.

———. 2011. *The New Lombard Street; How the Fed became the Dealer of Last Resort*. Princeton, NJ: Princeton University Press.

———. 2012. 'Three Principles for Market-based Credit Regulation', *American Economic Review Papers and Proceedings*, 102(3): 107–12.

Minsky, H.P. 2008 [1987]. 'Securitization', Levy Economics Institute Policy Note 2008/2, Annandale-on-Hudson, NY: Levy Economics Institute of Bard College.

Morris, C.R. 2008. *The Trillion Dollar Meltdown: Easy Money, High Rollers, and the Great Credit Crash*. New York: Public Affairs.

Pozsar, Z. 2011. 'Does the Secular Rise of Wholesale Cash Pools Necessitate Shadow Banking?' Unpublished mimeo.

Pozsar, Z., T. Adrian, A. Ashcraft, and H. Boskey. 2010. 'Shadow Banking', Federal Reserve Bank of New York Staff Reports 458. Federal Reserve Bank of New York, New York.

Scharfstein, David and Adi Sunderam. 2011. 'The Economics of Housing Finance Reform', Regulatory Policy Program Working Paper RPP-2011-07. Cambrige, MA: Mossavar-Rahmani Center for Business and Government, Harvard Kennedy School, Harvard University.

Securities Exchange Commission (SEC). 2010. 'SEC v. Goldman Sachs and Fabrice Tourre'. Available at http://www.sec.gov/litigation/complaints/2010/comp-pr2010-59.pdf. Last accessed on 27 April 2012.

Shin, H.S. and K. Shin. 2011. 'Procyclicality and Monetary Aggregates', NBER Working Paper 16836. National Bureau of Economic Research, Cambridge, MA.

SIGTARP (Office of the Special Inspector General for the Troubled Asset Relief Program). 2009. 'Factors Affecting Efforts to Limit Payments to AIG Counterparties'. Government Printing Office, Washington, DC.

Singh, M. 2011. 'Making OTC Derivatives Safe—A Fresh Look', IMF Working Paper 11/66. International Monetary Fund, Washington, DC.

Singh, M. and J. Aitken. 2010. 'The (Sizable) Role of Rehypothecation in the Shadow Banking System', IMF Working Paper 10/172, Washington, DC: International Monetary Fund.

Smith, Y. 2010. ECONned; How Unenlightened Self Interest Undermined Democracy and Corrupted Capitalism. New York: Palgrave Macmillan.

Swagel, P. 2009. 'The Financial Crisis: An Inside View', Brookings Papers on Economic Activity, 40(1): 1–78.

Tett, G. 2009. Fool's Gold: How the Bold Dream of a Small Tribe at J.P. Morgan was Corrupted by Wall Street Greed and Unleashed Catastrophe. New York: Free Press.

Union Bank of Switzerland. 2008. 'Shareholder Report on UBS's Write-Downs', Zurich: Union Bank of Switzerland. Available online: http://www.ubs.com/1/ShowMedia/investors/agm?contentId=140333&name=080418ShareholderReport.pdf. Last accessed on 27 April 2012.

14

Some Foreseeable Disasters of the Global Economy
The High Cost of Neglecting Keynes's Approach

ANNA M. CARABELLI AND MARIO A. CEDRINI

THE INTERNATIONAL 'NON-SYSTEM' IN HISTORICAL PERSPECTIVE

'In Washington Lord Halifax / Once whispered to Lord Keynes: / It's true *they* have the money bags / But *we* have all the brains' (Gardner 1980: xiii). This rhyme was written by Dennis Robertson during the Anglo-American negotiations of late 1945; as known, American money bags won against British brains. Its general meaning is that, if we are to adopt a power politics approach such as that used by historians like Skidelsky (2000), Keynes's revolutionary ideas about the post-war order could not compete with the rise of the US as a political and financial world power, destined to impose the weight of her money bags on the future international architecture. Undoubtedly the economist who did more than anybody else in his life, on both a theoretical and practical level, to reform the global order, Keynes was convinced that 'the ideas of economists and political philosophers, both when they are right and when they are wrong, are more powerful than is commonly understood. Indeed the world is ruled by little else' (CWK VII: 383). He believed that 'the power of vested interests

is vastly exaggerated compared with the gradual encroachment of ideas' (Ibid.). One might therefore easily associate his name to that 'defunct economist' today's 'practical men' should be 'slave of' (Ibid.), as predicted by the Keynes of *The General Theory*. But it would be wrong: or better, the moral to be drawn from how global economy behaved in recent decades is that today's practical men are not the slaves of Keynes himself.

For many decades, since the collapse of the Bretton Woods system and the anti-Keynesian counter-revolution, Post-Keynesian economists have been invoking a return to Keynes's plans for the post-war global order, in the attempt to show that an updated version of the Clearing Union proposal could help counteract the shortcomings of the international architecture. Yet the evolution of this latter from the 1980s to the current financial crises in the US and Europe provides a quite clear demonstration that Keynes had not been defeated on his specific global reform plans only. In truth, the last 30 years have witnessed the complete repudiation of the essence itself, and general philosophy, of Keynes's international economics. To see the point more clearly, it seems necessary to revisit the recent history of world economy from a particular perspective, which rests on the use of the concept of the international 'non-system'.

On writing, in 1983, on Keynes's contributions to the Bretton Woods regime, John Williamson defined the non-system which followed the 'Nixon shock' of 1971 (ending the Bretton Woods system itself) as the lack of 'a set of generally accepted rules and conventions regarding the proper way for countries to conduct those of their economic policies that have significant repercussions outside their own borders' (1983: 87). Now, the economic literature abounds in analyses of peculiar episodes—such as the East Asian crisis, or the historical saga of the Washington Consensus paradigm—of the post–Bretton Woods international order. Yet few economists have heretofore concentrated on such episodes by adopting a systemic view. The lack of legitimated international economic order has somewhat been taken as a general assumption and the 'normality' of the non-system has been given for granted, with the result of downplaying the role of the non-system as a particular kind of international economic order, albeit an unnatural and perverted one. On the contrary, the construction of a historical narrative of the current non-system (which evidently exceeds the limits of this article), shifting the focus exactly

on the lack of a true, legitimate, and rational global economic order, helps to understand the shortcomings of the current international architecture in a fresh way. Such shortcomings would first appear as the by-product of deliberate decision taken by policymakers of the world powers, although for purposes not necessarily connected with the resulting international non-system; a second and more focused glance would reveal the instrumental character of such defects, that is their being functional to constructing the international economic order which has developed in the last decades.

THE DISCIPLINARY ORDER OF THE WASHINGTON CONSENSUS

The story of the Washington Consensus provides a perfect illustration in this regard. As any developing region, Latin America had relied on external borrowing to finance its growth strategies in the post-war period. World recession in the 1970s, coupled with the sharp rise of oil prices, was responsible for a liquidity crunch which laid the seeds of the debt crisis in the early 1980s. Yet a decisive step towards the crisis burst was given by interest rate and exchange rate policies of the US, which then came to the rescue of Latin America by conceding financial assistance through the Brady plan. The term 'Washington Consensus' was introduced by John Williamson (1990) in the attempt to show that the neo-liberal reforms ('prudent macroeconomic policies, outward orientation, and free market capitalism', p. 18) endorsed by Latin American countries in the aftermath of the crisis were recognized as 'correct' by industrialized countries and justified requests for financial assistance. For a number of reasons—the post–Cold War world's 'urgent and widespread need for an alternative set of ideas on how to organize economic and political life' (Naím 2000: 88), but also the fact that the International Monetary Fund (IMF) and the World Bank perceived their task to be that of 'storming the citadel of statist development strategies' (Kanbur 1999: 2)—the reform package was soon adopted by the international financial institutions as policy prescription for development and 'correct' recipe to contrast financial crises of the 1990s. Only apparently a paradox, a relevant point which was *not* included in the list but had close ideological affinity to the 10 policy suggestions of the Consensus, namely capital movements liberalization, came to be seen as a basic precondition for

recovery: foreign capital should flow again into crisis-hit countries, in homage to the theory of financial market efficiency and to the benefit of creditors in industrial countries.

The Washington Consensus has been a fairly resounding failure, as demonstrated by the economic distress it produced in Latin America, which literally lost a decade—Argentina's collapse in 2001 being due to the adoption of an extreme version of the paradigm—but also by the negative performances it offered in the context of the Russian and particularly the East Asian crises. Stiglitz (2002) and Post-Keynesian economists have aptly stressed the anti-Keynesian philosophy of the Consensus programme. Capital market liberalization had pushed up the value of Asian currencies and produced unmanageable current account deficits. The IMF austerity solution was intended to restore market confidence, but its only result was to further depress the economies, which simply passed one's deficit to another; capital flights made the rest to delay the region's recovery. Remarkably, in the early 1990s, East Asian countries had been described as luminous examples of the results a country could obtain by following the Consensus. Stiglitz (2002: 213) correctly saw that

> together with the IMF, [the US Treasury] had told countries that followed the 'right policies'—the Washington Consensus policies—they would be assured of growth. The East Asian crisis cast doubt on this new worldview unless it could be shown that the problem was not with capitalism, but with the Asian countries and their bad policies. The IMF and the US Treasury had to argue that the problem was not with the reforms…but with the fact that the reforms had not been carried far enough. By focusing on the weaknesses of the crisis countries… they attempted to use the experience to push their agenda still further.

Much more was therefore at stake than declaring the end of the 'global apartheid which claimed that developing countries came from a different universe' (Williamson 2002: 2), and the end of development economics with it. As Rodrik (2000) argues, the US Treasury and international financial institutions used the Washington Consensus (in its various editions: the 'augmented' version of the late 1990s sought to remedy the early failures of the paradigm by focusing on institutions) as a means to promote an 'integrationist agenda' of hyperglobalization and (which amounts to the same thing) a safer world for capitals—liberalization of their flows being thus not a precondition of free-market economy but the veritable ultimate end

of the agenda. Worthy of careful attention is the theoretical framework used by Rodrik to illustrate this assertion. What he calls the world economy 'trilemma' compels to pick two and only two between (a) full integration of world markets, (b) democracy, and (c) national sovereignty, so as to obtain the mutually exclusive options of global federalism (a–b), the 'golden straitjacket' of the Consensus (a–c), and a new 'Bretton Woods compromise'. This helps to understand that today's non-system partly derives in truth from this failed attempt to construct an international economic order entirely based on market discipline.

KEYNES'S COMPLEXITY APPROACH TO INTERNATIONAL ECONOMIC RELATIONS

The current nostalgia for the 'embedded liberalism' (Ruggie 1982) of the Bretton Woods order—felt by Rodrik (2011) himself, Chang (2008), and United Nations Conference on Trade and Development (UNCTAD 2009) economists, among others—and its thin version of globalization seems therefore to rest on solid bases. Though substantially correct, references to the Keynesian character of the past order do not do justice to Keynes's contributions. For what Keynes teaches us is exactly that if the Consensus order could not work, this is not only because of the inefficacy of the austerity solution or of the damages capital movements liberalization may cause, but, more profoundly and more importantly, because an international economic order cannot rest upon the imposition of an orthodox model of capitalism against its actual and potential varieties, or even radical, fully heterodox alternatives to it (Cedrini 2008). What is at stake is not so much, to put it differently, the anti-Keynesian character of the Consensus orthodoxy—the IMF acted to impose the 'global conformity to an economic orthodoxy [that] Keynes had rejected', writes Newton (2006: 312)—but the fact itself that it has been imposed, and that it has been imposed as such, that is as an orthodoxy.

As a recent strand in the literature is suggesting (Carabelli and Cedrini 2010a; Vines 2003; see also Kirshner 2009), Keynes's international macroeconomics is the result of the development of an extremely powerful 'complexity approach' to international economic relations. This approach provides clear continuity with his general conception of economics as a moral rather than positivist science,

to be more properly identified with a way of reasoning about a complex economic material, made up of 'motives, expectations, psychological uncertainties' (CWK XIV: 400). Keynes's theory of economics is a framework to deal with a social world which is not explicable in terms of the individual behaviour of its separate parts; that is, in terms of micro-foundations and rational action theory. Consistently with the analysis of the fallacy of composition between particular and general interests he sketched out in *The End of Laissez-Faire*, Keynes conceived the international economic order as a complex object showing latent and actual conflicts, and had an 'extraordinarily clear understanding of how pieces of the global economy interact, driven by the policies of autonomous nations, in an only partly coherent manner' (Vines 2003: 339).

His international macroeconomics after the end of the pre-war gold standard led by Britain—which he wanted to reform along lines developed in *Indian Currency and Finance* (1913)—was the attempt to efficiently cope with the 'dilemma of the international system' (CWK VI: 272). In *A Treatise on Money*, having in mind the serious constraints posed on policy space by the renewed gold standard of the inter-war period, he identified such dilemmas with the clash between the needs prescribed by international discipline (as regards, in particular, exchange rates in terms of the international standard) and those inherent to the right to national autonomy (as concerns interest rates and foreign lending). Keynes devoted the 1920s and the 1930s to the search for a model of national behaviour consistent with the general interests of the system (Moggridge 1986). He finally found it, as the discussion of mercantilism from the point of view of the whole system makes evident in *The General Theory*, in the 'twice blessed' (CWK VII: 349) policies of regaining control over the interest rate, whereby countries could reach and maintain full employment and help their neighbours, at the same time, to achieve this same result. With the plan for an International Currency Union (ICU) in the 1940s, he offered a scheme of global architecture explicitly devised to defend and promote policy space in an overall expansionary environment, through a mix of truly international currency, symmetric adjustment, possibility of capital controls, and fully accommodating global monetary policy.

The ICU should provide, in other words, an international 'central control' (Ibid.: 379) of the kind of those justified by Keynes,

in *The General Theory*, as means to attain full employment while safeguarding the 'traditional advantages of individualism', that is 'personal liberty' and the 'variety of life' which emerges from such widened 'field for exercise of personal choice' (CWK VII: 380). Although the ICU plan is usually regarded as the effort to reduce the asymmetry of international adjustment, its final aim was exactly to safeguard each country's right to policy space and therefore to variety in defining its own version of national capitalism. The somewhat heretic proposal of an American gift, at the end of the Second World War, to an exhausted Britain—who had financed the Allies' war against Germany and incurred in enormous debts with both the US and the sterling area— provides a clear, both practical and symbolic illustration of the kind of international order desired by Keynes (see Carabelli and Cedrini 2010a). By granting a gift as a retrospective contribution to the financing of the war, he argued, the US would have offered Britain the freedom to actively contribute to 'the kind of [multilateral free-trade] post-war world' (CWK XXIV: 328) on which the Americans had 'set their hearts' (Ibid.: 280), the same that Britain herself was willing to implement by marching 'side by side' (Ibid.: 316) with the Americans. A world that the discipline and weight of a business loan, compelling Britain to accept what would have been regarded as the 'American conception' of the international economic system' (Ibid.: 61), would have conversely put at high risk. More in general, what Keynes had in mind was a system wherein creditors take the initiative to reduce global imbalances by granting debtor countries the freedom to choose their own path to development and growth, which in the end would accrue, as the experience of the Marshall plan suggests, to the benefit of creditors themselves.

Rodrik and other nostalgics of the Bretton Woods order are right in opposing 'the diversity of national policy' the system could not structurally interfere with, as Keynes himself observed (CWK XXIV: 608) in defending the agreement, to the 'outside dictation' (Keynes again, this time on the gold standard; CWK XXVI: 33) of the Washington Consensus. Still, though a complete reversal of the Bretton Woods philosophy, the Consensus has its ultimate roots in the disciplinary mandate Harry Dexter White's scheme assigned to the regime's institutions, whereas Keynes's plans, which assigned technical, not political mandate to the IMF and the World Bank, were explicitly conceived

in the awareness that 'distinct national circumstances implied that heterogeneity, not homogeneity was appropriate across various states' macroeconomic policies' (Kirshner 2009: 534). Freedom of capital movements, the main pillar (a little paradox, since Williamson had not included it in the list) of the Consensus, should have surrendered when clashing with each country's freedom to choose its own macroeconomic policies. Keynes directly, not generically the architects of Bretton Woods, is thence the economist we are not slave of.

THE UNREASONABLE SYSTEM OF 'BRETTON WOODS II' AND THE PROBLEM OF GLOBAL IMBALANCES

Despite its 'blocked' structure, the so-called 'Bretton Woods II' (BWII) system seems more respectful of policy space than the aborted Consensus order. This is not a paradox, since the fictitious spontaneity of BWII is in truth a direct legacy of the Consensus attempt to impose discipline as the main rule of the international order. According to the original (pre-crisis) BWII narrative (Dooley et al. 2003), Asian countries implement export-led growth strategies supported by undervalued exchange rates, capital and trade controls, and international reserves accumulation, with the aim of regaining a central position in the world system. Their mercantilism would result in happily sustaining the dollar's value and assisting the central country and world growth locomotive, the US, in financing its deficit. The view is highly controversial: a huge debate has developed centring on the true reasons lying behind the most salient aspect of BWII, that is, the unprecedented and costly accumulation of foreign exchange reserves by emerging markets. For sure, the strategy was taken 'in the context of the decision to adopt or reinforce the neo-liberal strategy of rapid financial liberalization, unrelated to the development of either deep financial markets or mature and effective regulatory structures' (Cruz and Walters 2008: 666–7). The moral developing nations have drawn from the Consensus saga is that it is safer, in a financially liberalized world, to rely on self-protection through increased liquidity rather than on external borrowing (Feldstein 1999).

The lack of shared views about the connections between global imbalances and the crisis burst (see Borio and Disyatat 2011; Serven and

Nguyen 2010; Obstfeld and Rogoff 2009) is not a reason for optimism.
In times of sustained world growth, supporters of the 'new economy
views' (Eichengreen 2006) about global imbalances welcomed the
emergence of a seemingly stable and performing international system,
one destined to endure in time despite the widening of disequilibria.
Dooley et al. (2009) were able to defend their own interpretation of the
post-1997 international scenario by claiming that 'Bretton Woods II
still defines the international monetary system': the 2008–9 crisis was
not driven by that dollar plunge (with a sudden stop of capital flows
from emerging countries to the US) which the so-called 'gloomy
views' about global imbalances believed to be the most likely outcome
of such huge current account disequilibria. Yet, on one side, while it
is a quite sure effect of the crisis that global imbalances as such have
reduced (Lane and Milesi-Ferretti 2011), uncoordinated responses
to the crisis (in the form of financial bailouts and impressive fiscal-
stimulus packages) have de facto brought about a sovereign debt
impasse in Europe, thereby seriously threatening the general stability
of BWII, and global imbalances remain a key issue of world economy
(Eichengreen 2011).

A central issue at stake in Dooley et al.'s (2003) interpretation
and in the whole debate on BWII is the rationality of the new order.
Apparently an indispensable, reasonable strategy of more or less
aggressive (that is, mercantilist) self-insurance voluntarily chosen
by individual countries in an open financial environment, reserves
hoarding as an outcome of the tacit coordination of the BWII regime
appears much less rational from the point of view of the whole
international system. The crisis has obviously directed attention to
Keynes's reform plans in the 1940s, but in truth, a lesser known part of
Keynes's work would be of great utility in forming reasoned opinions
about the sustainability of BWII. In elaborating a 'rational' (CWK
I: 71) reform of the gold standard regime in *Indian Currency and
Finance* (1913; see Carabelli and Cedrini 2010–11), Keynes argued
that a monetary system should combine 'cheapness with stability'
(CWK I: 91). His main concern was for the principal effects of what
he defined, with regards to India, as the 'original sin of mercantilism',
that is, the hoarding of gold, also (and mainly) in the form of reserves
accumulation. 'Wonderfully few... countries have yet learnt that gold
reserves, although no doubt they serve some purpose when they are
held for show only, exist to much better purpose if they are held for

use also' (CWK I: 125), he argued. On discussing the 1914 crisis, he added that:

> although many countries hold large quantities of gold, there are but few which pursue a rational policy in regard to it. At considerable cost they build up large reserves in quiet times presumably with a view to the next crisis; but when the crisis comes mistaken policy renders them as little able to use gold as if it were not there at all. (CWK XI: 247)

In truth, it appears that today's emerging countries did use international reserves, and effectively so, in the attempt to protect themselves from 'double drain' crisis scenarios with banking problems and capital flights (Obstfeld et al. 2009). Yet there have also been signs of reluctance to draw down reserves, for 'fear of losing international reserves, which may signal a deterioration in the credit worthiness of a country' (Aizenman 2009: 17). Keynes's 1913 words about the international economic system acquire the utmost importance and freshness once the specific perspective of the current non-system is adopted in making the parallel. Suffice it to reread page 71 of *Indian Currency and Finance*: we have never developed the ability—which Keynes invoked to justify his 'rational' reform—to cope with the spectacular effects of 'a change of ideas in Asia' (the passage to 'undervaluation-cum-intervention' strategies after the 1997 collapse). Asia has truly by now 'turned the tables on the West', but we have not learned yet how to control 'the most intimate adjustments' of our 'economic organism'. A direct legacy of Keynes's complexity approach to international economic relations is that in a structurally uncertain environment, systems and policies must rest on deliberate decisions taken on the basis of probable judgement (neither absolute rationality nor truth). They must be 'rational', that is to say, they must ground themselves on reasonable, neither arbitrary nor irrational, judgments, and they must not depend on the fulfilment of expectations, for mere luck does not turn foolish judgments into reasonable judgments. If the BWII regime, combining expensiveness with instability, is a by-product of the attempted Consensus order, the unintended evolution that has transformed global imbalances into an engine of global growth (under the tacit assumption of ever-growing American demand for foreign goods) neither makes them reasonable, nor justifies inactivity with regard to their persistence.

Here too, as Davidson (2009) among others shows, Keynes's ICU plan might prove of great utility. In commenting on the draft report of the 'Stiglitz Commission' (2009) of the United Nations for the reform of the international order, Kregel (2009) aptly observes that a new international reserve currency of the kind of the one invoked, with explicit reference to Keynes, by the governor of the People's Bank of China (Zhou 2009) and BRIC (2010) countries would not suffice, and should rather be coupled with a Keynes-inspired proviso of symmetric adjustment. But Keynes could not reasonably predict the abnormal patterns of today's global imbalances, with peripheral developing countries in a surplus position and the world superpower and growth locomotive, the US, acting as the system's deficit of last resort. Not only is a new international adjustment mechanism required, but also a mechanism which is 'also sufficiently compatible with global aggregate demand to provide full employment and support the national development strategies of developing countries' (Kregel 2009: 5). The desired mix of full employment and maintenance of the global standard's purchasing power is not the automatic result of the introduction of the ICU plan, but the product of coordinated symmetric adjustment policies, that is, of 'coordinated policy action taken mutually by members of the clearing union' (Ibid.: 2). As Davidson puts it, in the current 'interdependent global economy a substantial degree of economic cooperation among trading nations is essential' (2009: 136).

In truth, on two distant but similar occasions, that is, at the end of the two world conflicts, Keynes himself confronted himself with how to obtain coordinated international adjustments of this kind. On lines similar to those employed by Vines in the attempt to illustrate adjustment dynamics in the context of the Asian crisis, we have elsewhere (Carabelli and Cedrini 2010c) shown that the memorandum on post-war Britain written by Keynes in March 1945 for the negotiations of the American loan offers a useful guide to the highly complicated literature on global imbalances. Britain's economic destiny could follow three mutually exclusive paths, American financial assistance—and its precise nature—playing a fundamental role in orienting London's decision about her own future. While the lack of US contribution to alleviate Britain's debt burden would have compelled this latter to the isolationist choice of the 'starvation Corner', the option of an American loan ('Temptation')—which Britain finally

accepted—would have forced London to surrender to the 'American conception of the international economic system' and to adopt 'distasteful' second-best policies to redress her financial situation (CWK XXIV: 316). Keynes's solution ('Justice') rested on the 'psychological atmosphere of the free gift' (Ibid.: 340) he wished to obtain from the US, allowing Britain to approach the sterling area creditors with proposals of multilateral adjustment (in recognition of the shared responsibility for the war costs) and to participate in the construction of the new order.

Unilateral (Starvation Corner), bilateral (Temptation), and multilateral (Justice) adjustment are obviously also the alternatives for the unwinding of today's global imbalances. We therefore subdivided the global imbalances literature into three groups: first, 'made in' views, such as the twin deficits theory (requiring the US to attack its own deficits) and the 'global saving glut' hypothesis (blaming developing countries for the imbalances), both relying on an 'austerity solution'; second, the 'new economy' views, based on the aforementioned BWII interpretation, expressly suggesting the possibility of avoiding painful adjustments by the use of market mechanisms (the— pre-crisis!—attractiveness of US financial assets) supplemented by tacit intergovernmental agreement; and finally the 'shared responsibilities' views, calling for a multilateral approach to the imbalances. Keynes would have clearly favoured this latter approach. He would have likely followed UNCTAD (2004) in stressing, in positive, the fundamental role played by both the US and China in sustaining global demand (the latter is in fact the major engine of growth in Asia and outstandingly contributes to increased trade among developing countries) and, in negative, resounding failures on the part of other important surplus countries to take responsibility for world growth. He too would have argued, like Kregel (2006), that developed countries should grow through internal demand rather than by those policies which developing countries are (and should be) allowed to use in order to fill their gap with the former.

THE EUROPEAN DEBT IMPASSE IN THE LIGHT OF KEYNES'S *THE ECONOMIC CONSEQUENCES OF THE PEACE*

If Germany's enormous surplus, deriving from sluggish domestic growth, restrictive monetary and fiscal policies, and low-wages

strategies, has generally gone unobserved for a decade, it is only because in that same period, Europe—which obviously participated in the global-imbalances game, its firms being engaged in acquiring American assets and technology while keeping the value of their US subsidiaries' profits stable and protecting investment at home too (Kregel 2006)—has been in equilibrium with the rest of the world. The recent European debt impasse has quite naturally lifted the veil on Germany, and revealed that the European economic architecture shares many of the flaws which affect the international order, *in primis* the inability to cope with its imbalances and to restart growth through adequate countermeasures to the downturn. In truth, the European debt crisis has its origins exactly in the global financial collapse, which is responsible (via financial bailouts and fiscal stimulus packages) for the rise in public debts especially in Southern countries (Papadimitriou and Wray 2012). Yet yesterday's solution has become today's problem. Consider the letter sent by the President of the European Central Bank (ECB) Draghi and his predecessor, Trichet, to the Italian government in the summer of 2011:

Frankfurt/Rome, 5 August 2011.

Dear Prime Minister,

The Governing Council of the European Central Bank discussed on 4 August the situation in Italy's government bond markets. The Governing Council considers that pressing action by the Italian authorities is essential to *restore the confidence of investors.*

The Euro area Heads of State or Government summit of 21 July 2011 concluded that «all euro countries solemnly reaffirm their inflexible determination to honour fully their own individual sovereign signature and all their commitments to sustainable fiscal conditions and structural reforms». The Governing Council considers that Italy needs to urgently underpin the standing of its sovereign signature and its commitment to *fiscal sustainability and structural reforms.*

The Italian Government has decided to pursue a *balanced budget* in 2014 and, to this purpose, has recently introduced a fiscal package. These are important steps, but not sufficient.

At the current juncture, we consider the following measures as essential:

1. We see a need for significant measures to *enhance potential growth.* A few recent decisions taken by the Government move in this direction; other measures are under discussion with social partners. However,

more needs to be done and it is crucial to go forward decisively. Key challenges are to *increase competition, particularly in services to improve the quality of public services and to design regulatory and fiscal systems better suited to support firms' competitiveness and efficiency of the labour market.*

a) A comprehensive, far-reaching and credible reform strategy, including the *full liberalisation of local public services and of professional services is needed.* This should apply particularly to the provision of local services through *large scale privatizations.*

b) There is also a need to further *reform the collective wage bargaining system* allowing firm-level agreements to tailor wages and working conditions to firms' specific needs and increasing their relevance with respect to other layers of negotiations. The June 28 agreement between the main trade unions and the industrial businesses associations moves in this direction.

c) A thorough review of the rules regulating the hiring and dismissal of employees should be adopted in conjunction with the establishment of an unemployment insurance system and a set of active labour market policies capable of easing the reallocation of resources towards the more competitive firms and sectors.

2. The government needs to take immediate and bold measures to ensuring the *sustainability of public finances.*

a) Additional-corrective fiscal measures are needed. We consider essential for the Italian authorities to front-load the measures adopted in the July 2011 package by at least one year. The aim should be to achieve a better-than-planned fiscal deficit in 2011, a net borrowing of 1.0% in 2012 and a balanced budget in 2013, mainly via *expenditure cuts.* It is possible to *intervene further in the pension system*, making more stringent the eligibility criteria for seniority pensions and rapidly aligning the retirement age of women in the private sector to that established for public employees, thereby achieving savings already in 2012. In addition, the government should consider significantly *reducing the cost of public employees*, by strengthening turnover rules and, if necessary, by reducing wages.

b) An *automatic deficit reducing clause* should be introduced stating that any slippages from deficit targets will be automatically compensated through horizontal cuts on discretionary expenditures.

c) *Borrowing*, including commercial debt and expenditures of regional and local governments *should be placed under tight control*, in line with the principles of the ongoing reform of intergovernmental fiscal relations.

   In view of the severity of the current financial market situation, we regard as crucial that all actions listed in section 1 and 2 above be taken as soon as possible with decree-laws, followed by Parliamentary ratification by end September 2011. A *constitutional reform* tightening fiscal rules would also be appropriate.

3. We also encourage the government to immediately take measures to ensure a major overhaul of the public administration in order to improve administrative efficiency and business friendliness. In public entities the use of performance indicators should be systematic (especially in the health, education and judiciary systems). There is a need for a strong commitment to abolish or consolidate some intermediary administrative layers (such as the provinces). Actions aimed at exploiting economies of scale in local public services should be strengthened. We trust that the Government will take all the appropriate actions.

Mario Draghi, Jean-Claude Trichet[1] [emphasis added]

Now read again the parts in italics in the light of both the original list of the Consensus reforms and Rodrik's (2002) illustration of its 'augmented' version (Table 14.1).

The similarity of approach is evident. The ECB's 'austerity solution' for deficit countries like Italy is in truth a Bruxelles-version of the Washington Consensus recipe for *developed* countries. The country most severely hit by both the confidence crisis and the austerity solution is Greece, due to the astonishing volume of its public debt and the fact that the government had lied about its deficit when taking the decision to enter the euro area. This latter circumstance lies evidently at the basis of the 'Northern diagnosis', as De Grauwe (2011) calls the view whereby government profligacy is the true factor responsible

Table 14.1. Original Washington Consensus and Its Augmented Version

The Original Washington Consensus	The Augmented Washington Consensus (the original list plus)
Fiscal discipline	Legal/political reform
Reorientation of public expenditures	Regulatory institutions
Tax reform	Anti-corruption
Financial liberalization	Labour market flexibility
Unified and competitive exchange rates	WTO agreements
Trade liberalization	Financial codes and standards
Openness to DFI	'Prudent' capital-account opening
Privatization	Non-intermediate exchange rate regimes
Deregulation	Social safety nets
Secure property rights	Poverty reduction

Source: Rodrik (2002: 9).

for the crisis, and deterrent sanctions on today's deviants are required · to prevent future economic crimes.

There are now countless commentaries in economic newspapers (for example, Summers 2011; Krugman 2011) which make references to Keynes's *The Economic Consequences of the Peace* to highlight the impossibility for Greece to remedy her situation through austerity, and rightly so. Still, in general, there is little consideration for the imaginative work of practical economic diplomacy which Keynes made visible in the book. Here is a shining example of his complexity approach to international economic relations (see Carabelli and Cedrini 2010b). After describing the economic continent as a 'body' characterized by 'economic solidarity' between its parts, Keynes recognized that Germany's creditors were caught in an irresoluble 'dilemma' (CWK II: 58): due to the burden of Inter-Allied debts, they could not recede from asking Germany for impossible indemnities. By so doing, being so 'deeply and inextricably intertwined with their victims by hidden psychic and economic bonds' (Ibid.: 2), the Allies were in truth inviting not only Germany's destruction, but also their own. Keynes argued that Britain should have renounced her share of reparations in cash to the advantage of the Allies, and made an 'inevitable' (p. 92) appeal to 'the generosity of the United States' (Ibid.: 93). This latter was absolutely crucial:

> The financial problems which were about to exercise Europe could not be solved by greed. The possibility of *their* cure lay in magnanimity. Europe, if she is to survive her troubles, will need so much magnanimity from America, that she must herself practice it. It is useless for the Allies, hot from stripping Germany and one another, to turn for help to the United States to put the States of Europe, including Germany, on to their feet again. (Ibid.: 92)

Debts forgiveness was therefore conceived as a necessary precondition for Keynes's 'grand scheme for the rehabilitation of Europe' (CWK XVI: 428), a 'shared-responsibilities' plan of an international loan requiring the whole spectrum of countries involved to participate in the reconstruction. Keynes saw American assistance to the continent (including Germany's creditors) as the required ignition key allowing a spiral movement of magnanimity to spread along the chain of countries disposed to take part in the 'grand scheme'. Only a gift, acting as a 'strange attractor', could provide the starting engine

for this movement towards a more balanced international economy. Creditors should assume their responsibility.

Greece is now in the same position as Germany in 1919. The Northern diagnosis tells us that if borrowers are guilty of the impasse, they have to repay their debt; they have therefore to consume less and pay more taxes, with unchanged income. But the only possibility to realize savings on both the private and the public front without income reduction is offered by a trade surplus, and this requires cooperative trade partners, which Germany is not. The developing-country growth strategy adopted by Berlin throughout the decade is responsible for her lending policy to the rest of Europe, and Greece in particular. In Kregel's (2011: 9) fascinatingly clear words:

> Countries with undervalued currencies have higher rates of income growth than consumption growth, and as a result have higher savings rates.... But for every undervalued currency there must be an over-valued currency, suggesting that the 'behaviour' of the GIPS (Greece, Italy, Portugal, and Spain) is no more inherent in their culture than the fact that the EU GDP manages to grow at a positive rate, given German policies. And it is Germany's refusal to cooperate in a collective policy that imposes the opposite behaviour on its Eurozone trading partners.

Rodrik (2010) takes the same view: 'If others borrowed too much, doesn't it follow that Germans lent excessively?' And this is exactly the same argument used by Stiglitz (2003: 83) in treating the Asian crisis and the Washington Consensus: 'for every [Asian] borrower there is a lender [from developed countries], and the lender is as much to blame as the borrower.'

ON KEYNES'S LEGACY IN THE TIMES OF THE CRISIS

The illegitimate moralistic aspect of the Northern diagnosis has inter-esting implications for the historical parallel with Keynes's times, and for an assessment of Keynes's legacy in the times of the crisis. Let us first note that the 1945 memorandum on post-war Britain was but an updated version of the model of international adjustment outlined in *The Economic Consequences of the Peace*. Both result from Keynes's belief that 'interdependence required management, and that a "leader" was a great asset (if not an essential one) in doing this' (Markwell 1995: 209): hence the attempt to 'imbue the new hegemonic centre,

the United States, with the behaviour and ethics which pertain to the world creditor power' (Ferrari Bravo 1990: 407; our translation). This means that Germany has substantially failed as leader of the European continent: 'the solution to the Euro crisis is in Germany, not in Greece' (Kregel 2011: 8), but exactly as the Americans as Keynes saw them in 1919, Berlin seems to have a too 'strong desire to clear out of European responsibility (without even realising what this will mean to Europe)' (CWK XVI: 440).

But there is even more. If Keynes assigned so crucial importance, in his attempt to construct a 'sounder political economy between all nations' (CWK XXV: 43), to national 'freedom to choose', it is because in his ethical vision, economics is concerned with providing men the material preconditions for the enjoyment of a happy life and the possibility of individual choice of ends: freedom from economic pressures discloses 'the possibilities of personal life' (CWK IX: 125). It does not come as a surprise, therefore, that he could consider the 'sanctity of contract' (CWK XVIII: 384) as something radically different from 'an immutable law of nature'. In his vision, debt contracts cannot be preserved 'except by the reasonableness of the creditor':

> Debtors are only honourable in countries where creditors are reasonable. If creditors stand on the letter of the law, debtors can usually show them how little the law avails. Internationally, contract has nothing to support it except the self-respect and self-interest of the debtor. A loan, the claims of which are supported by neither, will not be paid for long. (Ibid.)

He even went so far as to define it a specific 'duty of the creditor not to frustrate payment': debtors cannot be asked to sacrifice their 'self-respect and self-interest' in favour of 'narrow calculations of financial self-interest' on the part of the creditor (Ibid.: 385). If Keynes were alive today, he would probably accuse Germany of being an unreasonable creditor and censure her 'anti-social' attitudes, as he did with France and the US in the inter-war gold standard.

Not even the European Union, with its promises of freedom, has succeeded in ensuring 'the proper liberty of each country over its own economic fortunes' (CWK XXV: 11). We are thus back to the main issue at stake at the beginning of the story of the neo-liberal non-system: like some uncelebrated antecedents such as the inter-war period gold standard, the unrestricted laissez-faire of its main

supporters has once again 'mistake[n] private licence for public liberty' (CWK XXIV: 622), and totally disregarded each member's right to national autonomy. A main lesson one can draw from revisiting the non-system in historical perspective is that we are definitely not slave of Keynes, but also that we are free to take inspiration from him, if our aim is to construct a radically different alternative to the current state of international affairs.

NOTE

1. Retrieved from: http://www.corriere.it/economia/11_settembre_29/trichet_draghi_inglese_304a5f1e-ea59-11e0-ae06-4da866778017.shtml?fr=correlati. Last accessed on 27 April 2012.

REFERENCES

Aizenman, J. 2009. 'On the Paradox of Prudential Regulations in the Globalized Economy. International Reserves and the Crisis: A Reassessment', NBER Working Paper 14779, March. National Bureau of Economic Research, Cambridge, MA.

BRIC. 2010. 'II BRIC Summit—Joint Statement', 16 April, available online: www.unaoc.org/docs/II-BRIC-Summit.pdf. Last accessed on 27 April 2012.

Borio, C. and P. Disyatat. 2011. 'Global Imbalances and the Financial Crisis: Link or No Link?' BIS Working Paper 346, May. Bank for International Settlements, Basel.

Carabelli, A.M. and M.A. Cedrini. 2010a. 'Global Imbalances, Monetary Disorder, and Shrinking Policy Space: Keynes's Legacy for Our Troubled World', Intervention. European Journal of Economics and Economic Policies, 7(2): 303–23.

———. 2010b. 'Keynes and the Complexity of International Economic Relations in the Aftermath of World War I', Journal of Economic Issues, 44(4): 1009–28.

———. 2010c. 'Current Global Imbalances: Might Keynes Be of Help?' in M.C. Marcuzzo, T. Hirai, and B.W. Bateman (eds), The Return to Keynes: Keynes and Keynesian Policies in the New Millennium. Cambridge, MA: Harvard University Press, pp. 257–74.

———. 2010–11. 'Indian Currency and Beyond. The Legacy of the Early Economics of Keynes in the Times of Bretton Woods II', Journal of Post Keynesian Economics, 33(2): 255–80.

Cedrini, M.A. 2008. 'Consensus Versus Freedom or Consensus Upon Freedom? From Washington Disorder to the Rediscovery of Keynes', Journal of Post Keynesian Economics, 30(4): 499–522.

Chang, H.-J. 2008. Bad Samaritans: The Myth of Free Trade and the Secret History of Capitalism. New York: Bloomsbury Press.

Cruz, M. and B. Walters. 2008. 'Is the Accumulation of International Reserves Good for Development?' *Cambridge Journal of Economics*, 32(5): 665–81.

Davidson, P. 2009. *The Keynes Solution: The Path to Global Economic Prosperity*. London and New York: Palgrave Macmillan.

De Grauwe, P. 2011. 'The Eurozone as a Morality Play', *Intereconomics*, 46(5), September–October: 230–1.

Dooley, M.P., D. Folkerts-Landau, and P. Garber. 2003. 'An Essay on the Revived Bretton Woods System', NBER Working Paper 9971, September. National Bureau of Economic Research, Cambridge, MA.

———. 2009. 'Bretton Woods II Still Defines the International Monetary System', *Pacific Economic Review*, 14(3): 297–311.

Eichengreen, B. 2006. 'Global Imbalances: The New Economy, the Dark Matter, the Savvy Investor, and the Standard Analysis', *The Journal of Policy Modeling*, 28(6): 645–52.

———. 2011. *Exorbitant Privilege. The Rise and Fall of the Dollar and the Future of the International Monetary System*. Oxford: Oxford University Press.

Feldstein, M.A. 1999. 'Self-Help Guide for Emerging Markets', *Foreign Affairs*, 78, March–April: 93–109.

Ferrari Bravo, G. 1990. *Keynes. Uno studio di diplomazia economica*. English translation, *Keynes. A Study of Economic Diplomacy*. Padova: Cedam.

Gardner, R.N. 1980. *Sterling-Dollar Diplomacy*. Oxford: Oxford University Press.

Kanbur, R. 1999. 'The Strange Case of the Washington Consensus. A Brief Note on John Williamson's "What Should the Bank Think About the Washington Consensus?"', Cornell University, 30 July. Available at www.people.cornell.edu/pages/sk145/papers/Washington%20Consensus.pdf. This url was last accessed on 27 April 2012.

Keynes, J.M. 1971–89. *The Collected Writings of John Maynard Keynes* (CWK), edited by D.E. Moggridge, 30 vols. London: Macmillan; volumes are identified as CWK followed by volume number in Roman numerals.

CWK I. 1971 [1913]. *Indian Currency and Finance*.

CWK II. 1971 [1919]. *The Economic Consequences of the Peace*.

CWK VI. 1971 [1930]. *A Treatise on Money: II. The Applied Theory of Money*.

CWK VII. 1973 [1936]. *The General Theory of Employment, Interest and Money*.

CWK IX. 1972 [1931]. *Essays in Persuasion*.

CWK XI. 1983. *Economic Articles and Correspondence: Academic*.

CWK XIV. 1973. *The General Theory and After: Part II. Defence and Development*.

CWK XVI. 1971. *Activities 1914–19: The Treasury and Versailles*.

CWK XVIII. 1978. *Activities 1922–32: The End of Reparations*.

CWK XXIV. 1979. *Activities 1944–1946: The Transition to Peace*.

CWK XXV. 1980. *Activities 1940–44: Shaping the Post-War World: The Clearing Union*.

CWK XXVI. 1980. *Activities 1941–46: Shaping the Post-War World: Bretton Woods and Reparations*.

Kirshner, J. 2009. 'Keynes, Legacies, and Inquiry', *Theory and Society*, 38(5): 527–41.

Kregel, J.A. 2006. 'Understanding Imbalances in a Globalised International Economic System', in J.J. Teunissen and A. Akkerman (eds), *Global Imbalances and the US Debt Problem. Should Developing Countries Support the US Dollar?* The Hague: Fondad, pp. 149–73.

———. 2009. 'Some Simple Observations on the Reform of the International Monetary System', Levy Economics Institute Policy Note 8. Levy Economics Institute of Bard College, Annandale-on-Hudson. NY.

———. 2011. 'Debtors' Crisis or Creditors' Crisis? Who Pays for the European Sovereign and Subprime Mortgage Losses?' Public Policy Brief 121. Levy Economics Institute of Bard College, Annandale-on-Hudson, NY.

Krugman, P. 2011. 'Depression and Democracy', *The New York Times*, 11 December, available online: http://www.nytimes.com/2011/12/12/opinion/krugman-depression-and-democracy.html?_r=1. Last accessed on 27 April 2012).

Lane, P.R. and G.M. Milesi-Ferretti. 2011. 'External Adjustment and the Global Crisis', IMF Working Paper 11/197, Washington, DC: International Monetary Fund.

Markwell, D.J. 1995. 'J. M. Keynes, Idealism, and the Economic Bases of Peace', in D. Long and P.C. Wilson (eds), *Thinkers of the Twenty Years' Crisis. Inter-war Idealism Reassessed.* Oxford: Clarendon Press, pp. 189–213.

Moggridge, D.E. 1986. 'Keynes and the International Monetary System 1909–46', in J.S. Cohen and G.C. Harcourt (eds), *International Monetary Problems and Supply-Side Economics: Essays in Honour of Lorie Tarshis.* London: Macmillan, pp. 56–83.

Naím, M. 2000. 'Washington Consensus or Washington Confusion?' *Foreign Policy*, Spring (118): 87–103.

Newton, S. 2006. 'J.M. Keynes and the Postwar International Economic Order', *History Compass*, 4(2): 308–13.

Obstfeld, M. and K. Rogoff. 2009. 'Global Imbalances and the Financial Crisis: Products of Common Causes', Federal Reserve Bank of San Francisco, Asia Economic Policy Conference, Santa Barbara, CA, 18–20 October.

Obstfeld, M., J.C. Shambaugh, and A.M. Taylor. 2009. 'Financial Instability, Reserves, and Central Bank Swap Lines in the Panic of 2008', *American Economic Review*, 99(2): 480–6.

Papadimitriou, D.B. and L.R. Wray. 2012. 'Fiddling In Euroland As The Global Meltdown Nears', Public Policy Brief 122. Levy Economics Institute of Bard College, Annandale-on-Hudson, NY.

Rodrik, D. 2000. 'How Far Will International Economic Integration Go?', *Journal of Economic Perspectives*, 14(1): 177–86.

———. 2002. 'After Neoliberalism, What?' Remarks delivered at a conference on Alternatives to Neoliberalism sponsored by the New Rules for Global Finance Coalition, Washington, DC, 23 May. This paper is included in a website called 'Policy Innovations. A Publication of the Carnegie Council'. Available at: http://www.policyinnovations.org/ideas/policy_library/data/01029/_res/id=sa_File1/ This url was last accessed on 27 April 2012.

Rodrik, D. 2010. 'Who Lost Europe?' *The International Economy*, Summer: 32–3. Retrieved from http://www.project-syndicate.org/commentary/who-lost-eur ope- Last accessed on 27 April 2012.

———. 2011. *The Globalization Paradox: Democracy and the Future of the World Economy*. New York: W.W. Norton & Co.

Ruggie, J.G. 1982. 'International Regimes, Transactions, and Change: Embedded Liberalism in the Postwar Economic Order', *International Organization*, 36(2): 379–415.

Serven, L. and H. Nguyen. 2010. 'Global Imbalances Before and After the Global Crisis', Policy Research Working Paper 5354, The World Bank, Washington, DC.

Skidelsky, R. 2000. *John Maynard Keynes*. Vol. 3: *Fighting for Britain, 1937–1946*. London: Macmillan.

Stiglitz, J.E. 2002. *Globalization and Its Discontents*. New York: W.W. Norton & Co.

———. 2003. 'Towards a New Paradigm of Development', in J.H. Dunning (ed.), *Making Globalization Good. The Moral Challenges of Global Capitalism*. Oxford: Oxford University Press, pp. 76–107.

Stiglitz Commission. 2009. 'Report of the Commission of Experts of the President of the UN General Assembly on Reforms of the International Monetary and Financial System', 21 September. Available at http://www. un.org/ga/econcrisissummit/docs/FinalReport_CoE.pdf. Last accessed on 27 April 2012.

Summers, L. 2011. 'How to Save the Eurozone', *Financial Times*, 18 July, available online: http://www.ft.com/intl/cms/s/2/324f9054-b0a7-11e0-a5a7-00144 feab49a.html#axzz1pJG7rYe3. Last accessed on 27 April 2012.

United Nations Conference on Trade and Development (UNCTAD). 2004. *Trade and Development Report. Policy Coherence, Development Strategies and Integration into the World Economy*. New York and Geneva: UNCTAD.

———. 2009. *Trade and Development Report: Responding to the Global Crisis. Climate Change Mitigation and Development*. New York and Geneva: UNCTAD.

Vines, D. 2003. 'John Maynard Keynes 1937–1946: The Creation of International Macroeconomics', *The Economic Journal*, 113(488): F338–61.

Williamson, J. 1983. 'Keynes and the International Economic Order', in D. Worswick and J. Trevithick (eds), *Keynes and the Modern World*. Cambridge, MA: Cambridge University Press, pp. 87–113.

———. (ed.). 1990. *Latin American Adjustment: How Much Has Happened?* New York: Institute for International Economics.

———. 2002. 'Did the Washington Consensus Fail?', Speech at the Center for Strategic & International Studies, Washington, DC, 6 November, Institute for International Economics. Available at www.iie.com/publications/papers/ paper.cfm?ResearchID=488. Last accessed on 27 April 2012.

Zhou, X. 2009. 'Reform the International Monetary System', 23 March. Available at http://www.bis.org/review/r090402c.pdf. Last accessed on 27 April 2012.

INDEX

About the Editors and Contributors

EDITORS

Toshiaki Hirai is Emeritus Professor, Sophia University, Tokyo, and co-founder and current President of the Keynes Society of Japan. He has worked on several aspects of Keynesian ideas in economics, philosophy, and policy, and has published several articles and books in this area. His most recent books include *Keynes's Theoretical Development—From the Tract to the General Theory* (2008) and *The Return to Keynes* (co-edited with B.W. Bateman and M.C. Marcuzzo, 2010). His current research interests are the study of globalization and capitalism from the point of view of both economic theory and social philosophy.

Maria Cristina Marcuzzo is Professor of Economics at the Sapienza University of Rome and past President of the European Society for the History of Economic Thought. She has worked on classical monetary theory (co-author of *Ricardo and the Gold Standard*, 1991, and co-editor of *Monetary Standards and Exchange Rates*, 1997) and the Cambridge School of Economics (co-editor of *The Economics of Joan Robinson*, 1996, and *Economists in Cambridge*, 2005). A collected volume of her essays, *Fighting Market Failure*, was published in 2011.

Perry Mehrling, Professor of Economics, joined the faculty of Barnard College, Columbia University, New York, in 1987, where he teaches courses on the economics of money and banking, the history of money and finance, and the financial dimensions of the US retirement, health, and education systems. He is also the Director of Education Programs, Institute for New Economic Thinking, New York. His most recent book is *The New Lombard Street: How the*

Fed Became the Dealer of Last Resort (2011). His best-known book *Fischer Black and the Revolutionary Idea of Finance* (2012) has just been released in a revised paperback edition. He posts biweekly at the Money View blog, ineteconomics.org/blog/money-view.

CONTRIBUTORS

Backhouse, Roger E. is Professor, University of Birmingham, UK.

Bateman, Bradley W. is Provost, Denison University, Granville, USA.

Carabelli, Anna M. is Professor of Economics, University of Eastern Piedmont, Vercelli, Italy.

Cardim de Carvalho, Fernando J. is Professor, Institute of Economics, Federal University of Rio de Janeiro, Brazil.

Cedrini, Mario A. is Assistant Professor, University of Turin, Italy.

Fantacci, Luca is Assistant Professor, Department of Policy Analysis and Public Management, Bocconi University, Milan, Italy.

Hirai, Toshiaki is Emeritus Professor of Economics, Sophia University, Tokyo, Japan.

Kregel, Jan is Senior Scholar and Program Director, Levy Economics Institute of Bard College, New York, USA.

López-Gallardo, Julio is Professor, Faculty of Economics, National Autonomous University of Mexico, Mexico.

Marcuzzo, Maria Cristina is Professor of Economics, Sapienza University of Rome, Italy.

Mehrling, Perry is Professor of Economics, Barnard College, Columbia University, New York, USA.

Noguchi, Asahi is Professor, School of Economics, Senshu University, Tokyo, Japan.

Rogers, Colin is Associate Professor, School of Economics, University of Adelaide, Australia.

Sen, Sunanda was Professor, Jawaharlal Nehru University, New Delhi and is currently Visiting Professor, Jamia Millia Islamia, Delhi, India.

Spahn, Peter is Professor, Institute of Economics, University of Hohenheim, Germany.

Wray, L. Randall is Professor, University of Missouri-Kansas City, USA.